EARLY FUR TRADE
ON THE NORTHERN PLAINS

Armorial bearings of the North West Company. Public Archives of Canada.

EARLY FUR TRADE ON THE NORTHERN PLAINS

Canadian Traders Among the Mandan and Hidatsa Indians, 1738-1818

THE NARRATIVES OF
John Macdonell, David Thompson,
François-Antoine Larocque, and Charles McKenzie

Edited and with an Introduction by
W. Raymond Wood and
Thomas D. Thiessen

UNIVERSITY OF OKLAHOMA PRESS : NORMAN

By W. R. Wood

An Interpretation of Mandan Prehistory (Washington, D.C., 1967)

Biesterfeldt: A Post-Contact Coalescent Site on the Northeastern Plains (Washington, D.C., 1971)

(editor, with R. B. McMillan) *Prehistoric Man and His Environments: A Case Study in the Ozark Highland* (New York, 1976)

(editor) *The Explorations of the La Vérendryes in the Northern Plains, 1738-43,* by G. H. Smith (Lincoln, 1980)

(editor, with M. Liberty) *Anthropology on the Great Plains* (Lincoln, 1981)

An Atlas of Early Maps of the American Midwest (Springfield, 1983)

Library of Congress Cataloging in Publication Data

Main entry under title:

Early fur trade on the Northern Plains.

(The American exploration and travel series; v. 68)
Bibliography: p. 333
Includes index.
1. Mandan Indians—History—Sources.   2. Hidatsa Indians—History—Sources.   3. Fur trade—Great Plains—History—Sources.   4. Indians of North America—Great Plains—History—Sources.   5. Great Plains—Discovery and exploration—Canadian.   I. Wood, W. Raymond. II. Thiessen, Thomas D. (Thomas David), 1947–
III. Series.

E99.M2E17   1985   978'.00497   85-1043
ISBN 0-8061-1899-7 (alk. paper)

The paper in this book meets the guidelines for permanence and durability of the Committee on Production Guidelines for Book Longevity of the Council on Library Resources, Inc.

To our parents

Contents

Illustrations

Maps

Tables

xiii

Preface

Writing in his memoirs of the year 1806, fur trader Charles McKenzie proudly boasted that he had been the first trader from Canada, or "North Trader," to return from the villages of the Mandan and Hidatsa Indians with "4 Packs of Beaver." While he may or may not have been the first Canadian trader to return from those Indians with a substantial quantity of beaver pelts—surviving evidence is not sufficient to judge the accuracy of his claim—he certainly was not the earliest North Trader to visit the Mandans and Hidatsas. Although contemporary records are incomplete, it is clear that many men—French, British, and Canadian—preceded him there.

The reader who expects to find in these pages a sweeping saga of one of the monumental episodes of the western Canadian fur trade will be disappointed. Rather, we have attempted to piece together the surviving fragments of one facet of that trade, one that involved, over the course of at least eighty years, French colonial authorities, the great Hudson's Bay and North West fur companies, lesser trading partnerships, and independent traders known as "freemen." We have tried to do this in two ways: first, by presenting a historical outline and description of the trade based on contemporary sources of information, and, second, through the actual words of some of the individuals who participated in the trade.

Our perspective on the subject focuses on details of the trade rather than its broad economic or political implications for the participating companies and nations. Authors such as Alwin and Jackson have described aspects of this trade pattern but usually have presented a partial picture based on only a portion of the available evidence. We have attempted to compile literal transcriptions of all the contemporary accounts of which we are aware and to distill from them details regarding the frequency and nature of the trade. We view the traders who traveled to and from these villages from posts in Canada not only as historical figures in their own right but also as agents of an alien culture who introduced new elements—economic, technological, and biological—which accelerated the process of culture change among the Mandans and Hidatsas and eventually resulted in an astonishing transformation of the Indians' culture and the virtual extinction of a centuries-old way of life in the Northern Plains. To this end we have compiled information relating to nearly seventy-five recorded trips between the Canadian posts and the villages on the Missouri River in central North Dakota.

This is not to denigrate the importance of the Spanish and American traders who ascended the Missouri River to the Mandan and Hidatsa villages beginning in the 1790s. We wish merely to point out that traders from Canada were essentially the only Euro-Americans with whom these native groups interacted for more than fifty years before the first recorded contact with Saint Louis–based traders and that consequently the North Traders were the first Euro-Americans to introduce aspects of European culture to the Mandans and Hidatsas. Beginning in the 1790s and continuing for nearly three decades, the North Traders and the traders from the south intermittently competed for and sometimes clashed over the trade with the Mandans and Hidatsas. Eventually that competition resulted in the withdrawal of the Canadian interests. Although records are incomplete, Canadian visits to these villages ended late in the first quarter of the nineteenth century, the last recorded Canadian trading expedition there occurring in 1818. Canadian visits surely could not have continued much beyond that date, because an almost continuous succession of American trading posts existed at and near the Knife River villages from 1822 on.

We acknowledge with gratitude the generous assistance of a host of individuals and institutions, both public and private, in two countries. Our research was supported in part by the Midwest Archeological Center, National Park Service, Lincoln, Nebraska, in conjunction with its ongoing research relating to the Knife River Indian Villages National Historic Site, North Dakota. We thank F. A. Calabrese, Chief of the Midwest Center, for his unfailing support, and his staff for assistance throughout the study. Marie Johnson and Sharon Rezac patiently endured the many revisions and editions and provided typing skills of the highest order. Much of the research was done while Wood was on sabbatical in 1980–81 at the University of Nebraska, and we thank Peter Bleed, Chair, Department of Anthropology, for his support, direct and indirect, during that time. Wood also thanks Richard N. Sheldon and other members of the National Historical Publications and Records Commission, National Archives and Records Service, for the opportunity to attend the Tenth Annual Institute for the Editing of Historical Documents ("Camp Edit") as an intern in the summer of 1981. That experience was invaluable, as was the advice and counsel provided generously on many occasions by our friend Gary E. Moulton, of the University of Nebraska.

Our work in the several archives housing the documents which we studied was made immeasurably simpler and more pleasant by the courteous, professional individuals with whom we have had the pleasure to work. We thank Denise Pelissier, Archivist, of the Archives Department, University of Montreal; Victor de Breyne, Manuscript Curator, and Elizabeth Lewis, Rare Book Librarian, Department of Rare Books and Special Collections, McGill University Libraries, Montreal; Brian Driscoll, Public Archives of Canada, Ottawa; D. F. McOuat, Archivist, Public Archives of Ontario, Toronto; and Shirlee Smith, Archivist, and G. Mark Walsh, Archivist, Hudson's Bay Company Archives, Winnipeg, Manitoba.

A host of other persons were instrumental in the research: Sister Roseline Lessard, of the Gray Nuns of Saint Hyacinthe, Quebec, provided us with information on the last years of François-Antoine Larocque, and the Reverend Jean-Roche Chonière, Chancellor, Diocese of Saint Hyacinthe, provided us with a copy of Larocque's burial record. Linda Ward-Williams provided the photograph of the mouth of Bighorn Canyon, Montana; Stuart W. Conner helped us trace Larocque's route from the mouth of Bighorn Canyon to the Yellowstone River with more confidence; and E. Leigh Syms provided Canadian source material. The InterNorth Art Foundation and the Joslyn Art Museum, through the courtesy of our colleague and friend Joseph Porter, provided excellent copies of Karl Bodmer paintings of Mandan and Hidatsa Indians. We are indebted to Stanley A. Ahler, University of North Dakota; John A. Alwin, Montana State University; Barry M. Gough, Wilfrid Laurier University; John C. Jackson, Portland, Oregon; and several anonymous referees for their valuable if sometimes disconcerting comments on earlier drafts of this study. These and many other courtesies have made the preparation of the work far less painful than we had anticipated.

We are especially grateful to the Hudson's Bay Company for permission to quote extensively from the Brandon House Post Journals and other company documents in the Hudson's Bay Company Archives, in Winnipeg.

W. Raymond Wood
Columbia, Missouri

Thomas D. Thiessen
Lincoln, Nebraska

Editorial Procedures

THE documents transcribed in Part Two rank among the most important of those produced in the Northern Plains in the years following the time of the Sieur de la Vérendrye and predating the American era. For this reason, and because earlier versions of them suffer from one or more major problems—the result of earlier standards of historical editing—our intent here is to make available new and more reliable editions of these manuscripts.

All spelling and grammar have been preserved. No words have been changed or modified in line with modern spelling or practices except to render the definite article with the letter *thorn* (*ye*) as *the*, or as otherwise explained in the introductory notes to individual transcriptions. All raised letters at the close of abbreviations or contractions are lowered to the line. All underscored words have been italicized, and passages which were scored out in the text appear in brackets in italics. Single words or brief phrases added by the editors to clarify the text are similarly enclosed, but in roman type, as are the spellings of ambiguous words following their appearance. A question mark enclosed in brackets means that the rendition of the preceding word is questionable. Words with missing letters, or misspelled words which are likely to require the reader to reread the entry to grasp the meaning, have the omitted letters in brackets, and misspelled words are followed by the correct spellings in brackets. Brackets also enclose such phrases as "three words illegible" or "blank in MS," as well as the page numbers of the original manuscripts. When only the right-hand pages of a manuscript are numbered, they have been denoted as, for example, page 1a, the reverse side of the sheet being numbered 1b. Other pagination peculiarities are described in the introductory notes to the individual transcriptions.

Punctuation and capitalization were the main problems. Punctuation is retained as in the original manuscript unless the editor's introduction to the document specifies otherwise. Capitalization follows that in the manuscript, but for some letters, such as *C* and *K*, the author's intent was not always clear. In such instances modern usage is followed. So that a particular entry can be located by date more easily, the month and year of the journal are uniformly centered on the page and have been added in brackets if they are not a part of the original text. Daily entries also have been made to begin new paragraphs when they did not originally do so.

Annotation has been confined to notes which are necessary to understand the content of the document. Only those persons and places that are relevant to our problems are emphasized. We have chosen to limit annotation to those elements having a direct bearing on the Mandan and Hidatsa trade.

Several documents in the Hudson's Bay Company Archives were especially helpful for our study. These records are cited in the format preferred by that office, for example, H.B.C.A., B.22/a/1, fo. 2d. In the example H.B.C.A. identifies the Hudson's Bay Company Archives as the document repository, and B.22/a/1, fo. 2d identifies section B of the holdings, which contains the records of Hudson's Bay Company establishments and administrative headquarters in North America; post no. 22, which designates Brandon House; document series a, post journals; volume 1, the individual journal for the 1793–94 trading season; and the reverse side (dorsum) of numbered folio 2.

These documents are valuable sources for fur trade studies in many different ways, and readers will find in them data relevant to many problems we have not emphasized. For the most part we have not been concerned with the routes taken by the explorers, except for that of François-Antoine Larocque in 1805. A new map of his route has been prepared for this book based on a careful reading of his journal, scholarly annotations of it in past editions, and our own retracing of his route, on the ground, in 1980.

PART ONE

EDITORS' INTRODUCTION

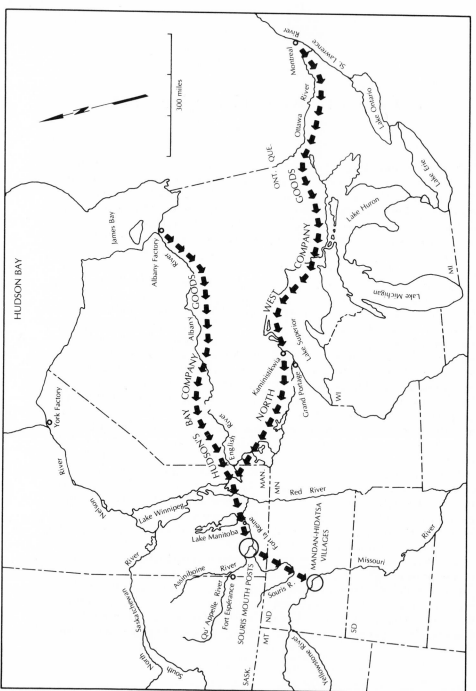

MAP 1. Sources and routes for Hudson's Bay Company and North West Company goods traded to the Mandans and Hidatsas.

The Canadian-Missouri River Fur Trade

THE fur trade of western North America consisted of two grand divisions, one Canadian and one American. The Canadian system, with its major depots and nerve centers in what is now the eastern part of that nation, was for a long time the province of competing French and British merchants operating out of Montreal and posts along Hudson Bay. This trade was along the north shores of the Great Lakes and the western shores of Hudson Bay and west across Canada by way of the Assiniboine, Saskatchewan, and other rivers and the many large and small lakes sprinkled across central Canada (map 1). The American system, on the other hand, was first dominated by the French, then by the Spaniards, and finally by the Americans, with its base in Saint Louis, near the mouth of the Missouri River. For the most part the latter trade exploited the basin of that river, although it also extended into the upper reaches of the Arkansas and other rivers in Colorado, Wyoming, and west. The two grand divisions of the North American fur trade thus met in what is now the western United States and Canada essentially along the modern boundary between these two nations.

The two systems overlapped in their interests in at least three areas: the upper Mississippi River basin in what is now Minnesota and Wisconsin, the Snake and Columbia river areas in the far west, and an area that came to be known as the Upper Missouri—specifically along the Missouri River at the villages of the Mandan and Hidatsa Indians in what is now west-central North Dakota.

The Mandans and Hidatsas lived just downstream from that part of the Missouri River known as the Big Bend, where the Missouri abruptly turns to the south, thus changing its previous easterly course a full eighty degrees. The two tribes lived where the Canadian– and the Saint Louis–based trade spheres overlapped, and until the boundary between the United States and Canada was established (and the Canadian trade was finally abandoned), the Mandan and Hidatsa trade was sought as eagerly by the Canadians as by the Saint Louis companies and free traders. Mandans and Hidatsas were important brokers in an intertribal trade network, a crucial one in the modification of American Indian culture on the Great Plains, for it was there that the expanding frontier of the horse met that of the gun. The Mandans and Hidatsas therefore found themselves in the enviable position of warehousing, as it were, horses and guns for distribution to tribes throughout much of the Northern Plains, often at a 100 percent markup from their original purchase price.[1]

The strength of the Mandan and Hidatsa villages as native trading centers was a major reason for their importance to Euro-American fur traders. With only a few exceptions, however, most studies of the fur trade on the Upper Missouri have treated the Mandan and Hidatsa trade only briefly, and then principally as a component of the Saint Louis–based trading system. But the Canadian connection was equally important for a very long time; furthermore, it led to international rivalry on the Upper Missouri at the end of the eighteenth century. Our purpose here is to offer a preliminary history of that trade, as well as new transcriptions of some of the basic documents for that history.

Many of the documents dealing with this trade have been published, but they were edited and printed long ago, and standards of historical editing have changed in the intervening years. In the preparation of part one it was found necessary to return to the original basic sources time and again to verify statements; accordingly, we decided to prepare and publish new transcriptions of some of the sources together with our

synopsis of the Canadian–Missouri River trade. The new transcriptions of five basic documents are given in part two; they cover events between 1797 and 1806.[2]

THE MANDANS AND HIDATSAS AND THEIR NEIGHBORS

In the prehistoric period, centuries before the arrival of Euro-Americans, Indians of the Great Plains were accomplished tradesmen in a wide-ranging trade network. Our knowledge of this prehistoric trade

---

[1]John C. Ewers, "The Indian Trade of the Upper Missouri before Lewis and Clark: An Interpretation," *Missouri Historical Society Bulletin* 10 (July, 1954):436–37, 439.

[2]In addition to these documents we also retranscribed the Mandan tour of Alexander Henry the Younger (Thiessen, "A New Transcription of Alexander Henry's Account of a Visit to the Mandan and Hidatsa Indians in 1806"), and the journal of John Macdonell at Fort Espérance for the years 1793 to 1795 (W. Raymond Wood, "Fur Trade Documents Bearing on the Mandan-Hidatsa Trade with Northwest Company Posts in Central Canada, 1793–1805: Four New Transcriptions" [Manuscript]. Because Alexander Henry's entire journal is now being prepared for republication by Barry M. Gough, it is not included here. John Macdonell's journal has recently been published elsewhere (W. Raymond Wood, ed., "Journal of John Macdonell, 1793–1795," in *Fort Espérance in 1793–1795: A North West Company Provisioning Post*, by Daniel J. Provo, pp. 81–139). In addition, relevant sections of the contents of the Brandon House Post Journals were also compiled (Thomas D. Thiessen, comp., "Excerpts from the Brandon House Post Journals Relating to Trade with the Mandan and Hidatsa Indians, 1793–1830"[manuscript]. The pagination of the manuscripts comprising the narratives in Part Two is explained in the prefatory remarks to each narrative, and manuscript pages are enclosed within brackets in the text (for example, [p. 6]). In footnotes throughout this book, manuscript pages are denoted by the prefatory abbreviation "ms."

is very thin, however, and must be reconstructed from those rare items in the archaeological record that have escaped the destructive passage of time. With the arrival of Euro-Americans on the scene we begin to detect in the ever-increasing documentary sources, as well as in the archaeological record, a complex native trading pattern. Indeed, as Wood has written elsewhere, "Aboriginal North America was blanketed by a network of trails and trading relationships linking, to a greater or lesser degree, every tribe to one or more of its neighbors."[3] On the eve of white contact in the Northern Plains the sedentary Mandans and Hidatsas were middlemen in a trading pattern in which nomadic Indian traders carried goods between the Spanish Southwest and the Assiniboine River valley near Lakes Winnipeg and Manitoba. The Crees and Assiniboins in this part of southern Canada exchanged goods with the Mandans and the Hidatsas, who in turn made further exchanges with the Crows, Cheyennes, and other High Plains tribes on the west and southwest.[4]

Consequently, when Euro-Americans began to expand their activities into the Northern Plains, objects of white origin were being exchanged along these and other native trade routes well in advance of actual contact with white traders. These alien goods began filtering into the villages of the Mandans and Hidatsas by way of their neighbors on the north and east, especially the Crees and the Assiniboins, in what has been termed the "indirect trade" zone.[5] By this means small numbers of trade goods found their way into Mandan and Hidatsa villages at a time when the real source of these goods—the whites at their posts along the shifting frontiers of the fur trade—had as yet heard only rumors of these faraway tribes, who were living at the very fringes of Euro-American commerce. Rumors of this kind, in fact, were the stimulus for the first visits by whites to the villages of the Mandans and Hidatsas on the Missouri River in 1738, when the French trader and explorer Sieur de la Vérendrye reached them from a post on the Assiniboine River.

For many decades the Siouan-speaking Mandans and Hidatsas participated in this indirect trade before the goods reaching them had any profound impact on their way of life. These two sedentary, horticultural, village-dwelling Indian tribes had lived for centuries along the banks of the Missouri River. Their ancestors had arrived in the area perhaps as early as the eleventh century A.D. They seem to have been consistently friendly with one another; at least they interacted to such a de-

[3]W. Raymond Wood, "Plains Trade in Prehistoric and Protohistoric Intertribal Relations," in *Anthropology on the Great Plains*, ed. W. Raymond Wood and Margot Liberty, p. 99.

[4]Ewers, "Indian Trade."

[5]Arthur J. Ray, *Indians in the Fur Trade: Their Role as Hunters, Trappers and Middlemen in the Lands Southwest of Hudson Bay, 1660-1870*; Arthur J. Ray and Donald B. Freeman, *"Give Us Good Measure"*: *An Economic Analysis of Relations Between the Indians and the Hudson's Bay Company Before 1763*.

gree that by the historic period their towns and customs were scarcely distinguishable to the casual visitor. Even today, archaeologists cannot be certain whether they are dealing with the village site of one or the other tribe without access to historic documentation. By the middle of the seventeenth century both groups were living in large, often fortified villages of earth lodges along the Missouri River in what is now west-central North Dakota. Some towns had populations approaching, if not exceeding, one thousand. The archaeological remains of both the Mandans and the Hidatsas of the late-prehistoric to early-historic periods (ending about the middle of the eighteenth century) are collectively known as the Heart River phase.[6]

One group of villages of the Heart River phase was clustered near the mouth of the Knife River and along the Missouri River for about thirty miles downstream. Most of these villages are identifiable as towns of the late-prehistoric to early-historic Hidatsas, for this was the traditional homeland of that group. A second group of villages was in the vicinity of the mouth of the Heart River, near modern Bismarck. This locality was traditionally the heartland of Mandan territory; the Heart River, indeed, took its name from the fact that it was considered the "heart" of the Mandan universe. The earliest towns of the Heart River phase lack evidence of Euro-American goods, but in the later villages trade goods began to displace some of the native technologies; for example, native stone arrow points became less common as those of metal were introduced. Major changes took place in both the Mandan and Hidatsa communities about the time of the devastating smallpox epidemic of 1780–81. There may have been earlier ones, perhaps as early as 1750, but little is known of them. The effects of the epidemic of 1780–81 were crushing: perhaps 68 percent of the villages' population of nearly 11,500 individuals perished.[7] The combined effects of population reduction and accompanying changes in material culture provide the justification for a final stage in Mandan and Hidatsa culture history, the Knife River phase.

This phase, which extended from about the middle of the eighteenth century to 1845, consisted principally of the Mandan and Hidatsa villages built at or near the mouth of the Knife River. After the epidemic of 1780–81 the Mandans left the mouth of the Heart River and moved north to live near the Hidatsa towns. The best documented of these villages are the five communities clustered at the mouth of the Knife River at the end of the eighteenth century (map 2). Two other villages, not as well documented, were farther upriver: Rock Village and Nightwalker's Butte were about thirty and forty-

[6]Donald J. Lehmer, *Introduction to Middle Missouri Archeology*, National Park Service Anthropological Papers, no. 1, pp. 131–72, 203–205.

[7]Donald J. Lehmer, "The Other Side of the Fur Trade," in *Selected Writings of Donald J. Lehmer*, ed. W. Raymond Wood, p. 107.

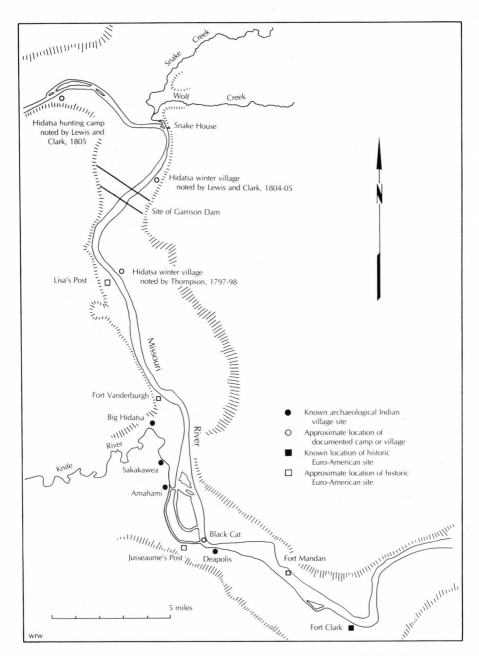

MAP 2. Mandan and Hidatsa villages near the mouth of the Knife River, and associated fur-trading posts.

five miles, respectively, above the Knife River. In many respects these towns were refugee camps, containing the remnants of devastated populations of many more villages—those which had amalgamated to offset the drastic reduction of their populations by disease in the late 1700s. Most of the towns were fortified by an enclosing palisade and ditch, for about the same time that smallpox was reducing their numbers so severely, hostile Sioux began attacking the villages. Many of them were destroyed. William Clark, for example, records that one Mandan village was "destroyed by the Soux and Small Pox."[8] The survivors of such towns, and those of other villages similarly reduced, found it necessary to live together in fewer communities for self-preservation. Small towns simply could not survive.

The rarity of Euro-American goods in Mandan and Hidatsa towns between about 1675 and 1780 indicates that most of these items were reaching them principally through indirect or intertribal trade, but during the Knife River phase direct trade became increasingly important, and their villages were flooded with alien goods. Native intertribal trade nevertheless continued into the full historic period, side by side with that of Euro-Americans. Intertribal trade was, however, appreciably diminished with the establishment of permanent white trading posts near the

Knife River, such as that of Fort Clark about 1831. By 1845, when most of the Mandans and Hidatsas moved to Like-a-Fishhook, a village about forty miles above the Knife River, intertribal trade was nearly extinguished.[9]

METHODS OF THE FUR TRADE

In the late eighteenth century and through the first two decades of the nineteenth, the Canadian fur trade was dominated by two large companies, the North West Company and the Hudson's Bay Company. The fur trade historian E. E. Rich has estimated that in 1795 these two concerns controlled 93 percent of the total Canadian fur trade, the North West Company accounting for roughly five and one-half times as much of the trade as the Hudson's Bay Company.[10] The rivalry between these two concerns ended only when they merged in 1821. Each company was supplied by different routes, reflecting in large part the history of their creation and growth. The history of these companies has been told many times in varying degrees of detail.[11]

[9]Occasional contacts for trading purposes, however, probably continued after the amalgamation of the Mandans, Hidatsas, and Arikaras into one community at Like-a-Fishhook village. John C. Ewers ("Indian Trade," p. 435) has stated that Assiniboin Indians were visiting the Mandans and Hidatsas as late as "the decade prior to the extermination of the buffalo" to trade for corn. This would probably have been around 1880.

[10]E. E. Rich, *The Fur Trade and the Northwest to 1857*, p. 188.

[11]Gordon Charles Davidson, *The North West Company*, University of California

[8]The Double Ditch Mandan site on the Clark-Maximilian map, sheet 17. Gary E. Moulton, ed., *The Journals of the Lewis and Clark Expedition*, atlas volume, map 28.

The following summary has been abstracted from these sources.

The North West Company was formed in the mid-1770s from a series of loose partnerships among several independent trading companies and individual traders. By 1779 it comprised eight separate parties holding among them a total of sixteen shares in the company.[12] Trading agreements between the partners expired every few years, and consequently the company was re-formed several times with different compositions of shareholders. Montreal was executive headquarters and marketing center for the company, while field operations were directed by an annual meeting of partners at Grand Portage or, after 1803, at Fort William, on the north shore of Lake Superior. The company took advantage of a long waterway supply route, developed and used extensively by the French before 1763, that stretched along the Saint Lawrence and Ottawa rivers and the Great Lakes and through the interconnected rivers and lakes of south central Canada (map 1). Goods and supplies flowed annually along these routes to the many trading posts west and north of the Great Lakes, and furs eastward to Grand Portage and, eventually, Montreal.

The Hudson's Bay Company, in contrast, was more than one hundred years older than the North West Company, having been granted a royal charter in 1670 following its founding in 1668. The company's activities were directed from London by a governor and an executive committee. For the first century of its existence the company confined its operations to several posts situated at the mouths of rivers draining into Hudson Bay. Indians were obliged to travel down these rivers to trade at the posts; little effort was made to carry the trade directly to the Indians in the interior of the continent as the North West Company traders did and the French before them. Beginning in the 1770s, the Hudson's Bay Company, under the pressure of increasingly effective competition for the furs of the interior regions of Canada, expanded its operations by penetrating the interior and there establishing posts in direct competition with the Nor'westers and other traders. Following that expansion there was a period of rapidly intensifying competition between the two major companies which ended only when the Hudson's Bay Company absorbed the North West Company in 1821.

Much of the history of antagonism and competition between these two great commercial concerns was centered on the valleys of the Red and Assiniboine rivers in southern Manitoba. This area was a separate administrative department for each company; the Assiniboine River valley was known to the Hudson's Bay

Publications in History, vol. 7; W. Stewart Wallace, ed., *Documents Relating to the North West Company*, Publications of the Champlain Society, vol. 22; E. E. Rich, *Hudson's Bay Company, 1670-1870*; Rich, *Fur Trade and the Northwest*; Harold A. Innis, *The Fur Trade in Canada: An Introduction to Canadian Economic History*; Marjorie Wilkins Campbell, *The North West Company*; Arthur S. Morton, *A History of the Canadian West to 1870-1871*; and others.

[12]Wallace, *Documents*, pp. 6–8.

Company as the Upper Red River District, while the North West Company called much the same area its Red River Department. In the 1780s and 1790s trading posts proliferated in that area. In early 1795, Robert Goodwin, the master of Brandon House, the Hudson's Bay Company's center of operations in the Assiniboine River valley, complained in a letter to another company official that "we have no less than 23 Canadian Houses in this River your Servants Occupy but three of these."[13] In their journals Nor'westers frequently referred to Hudson's Bay Company men as "the English," while they in turn were often called "the Canadians" or "the French" by the Honorable Company's employees. Although the North West Company began trading at the Mandan-Hidatsa villages earlier than did the Hudson's Bay Company, the competitive vigor of these companies was carried to the villages on the Missouri River from the mid-1790s on, when each company raced to send one or two trading expeditions there each year. John Macdonell's claim that the Mandan and Hidatsa trade had been "entirely neglected" after about 1797 is clearly contradicted by the large numbers of trading expeditions there in the next few years (Appendix, table 1).[14]

The date of the first trade at the Mandan and Hidatsa villages by the North West Company cannot be established. John Macdonell states that the company conducted trade with the Mandans and Hidatsas from the time that Pine Fort was established a few miles downriver from the mouth of the Souris River, which was 1785, according to another Nor'wester, Daniel Harmon. By 1793, when the Hudson's Bay Company extended its operations into the valley of the Assiniboine, the North West Company's trade with the Mandans and Hidatsas was well established. Pine Fort was abandoned in 1794, within a year of the establishment of Fort Souris, which was built in 1793 to be closer to opposition posts near the mouth of the Souris River. Fort Souris, which was also variously known as Rivière la Souris, Fort Assiniboine, and Macdonell's House and was rebuilt possibly twice in different locations, functioned as the base for the North West Company's trade with the Mandans and Hidatsas until at least 1817, except for a few years after 1807, when the former site of Pine Fort was reoccupied.[15]

[13]H.B.C.A., B.22/a/2, fo. 29.
[14]John Macdonell's "The Red River," ms. p. 11.

[15]Ibid., ms. p. 10. Morton *(Canadian West,* p. 269) gives 1768 as the date for establishment of Pine Fort, which is apparently based on a statement recorded in the Brandon House Post Journal by James Sutherland on September 11, 1796, to the effect that he had been told that Pine Fort "stood 28 years" until superceded by the establishment of Brandon House (H.B.C.A., B.22/a/14, fo. 11d). Since Pine Fort was abandoned in 1794 (Daniel Williams Harmon, *Sixteen Years in the Indian Country: The Journal of Daniel Williams Harmon, 1800-1816,* p. 90; Macdonell's "The Red River, ms. p. 8), this would place the date of the founding of Pine Fort as 1766, which seems improbably early in the absence of evidence for other Montreal-based fur trading activities in the Assiniboine River valley at that time.

Brandon House was the post from which the Hudson's Bay Company conducted its trade with the Mandans and Hidatsas. Built in 1793 as the headquarters for the company's Assiniboine River valley trade, Brandon House continued in operation, though rebuilt several times at different locations, until 1832 except for the years 1824–28, when the post was abandoned. The establishment was supplied annually from Albany Factory, on James Bay (map 1). At Albany the chief factor annually selected the man who would be master at Brandon House for each trading season. Each year, in late summer, the newly appointed master left Osnaburgh House, on Lake Saint Joseph in what is now west-central Ontario, with trade goods, supplies, and men to operate Brandon House over the winter and into the following spring.[16] After an arduous six-to-eight-week journey by boat through the Albany, English, Winnipeg, Red, and Assiniboine rivers and through Lakes Seul and Winnipeg, the brigade reached Brandon House in late September or early October. After a season of trading at Brandon House and several satellite posts, the fur returns were dispatched from Brandon House each spring, usually in April or May, along the same route back to Albany, where they were shipped to the fur markets of Europe. After 1810, Brandon House was supplied from York Factory, at the mouth of the Nelson River (map 1).

The official record of the Hudson's Bay Company trade with the Mandans and Hidatsas is contained in the unpublished Brandon House Post Journals preserved in the Hudson's Bay Company Archives in Winnipeg, Manitoba. In 1979, John Alwin published an excellent description of the company's trade with the Mandans and Hidatsas, for which he drew extensively on the Brandon House documents covering the period from 1795, when trade with the Mandans and Hidatsas was initiated from Brandon House, to the spring of 1812. Several annual Brandon House Post Journals for years after

Both Harmon's and Sutherland's statements regarding the founding date for Pine Fort are based on hearsay information. Wood, "Journal of John Macdonell" p. 86, entry for November 6, 1793; A. E. Brown, "The Fur Trade Posts of the Souris-Mouth Area," *Transactions of the Manitoba Historical Society*, 3d ser., nos. 17 and 18 (1960–62). For first-hand information on the reoccupation of Pine Fort, see François-Antoine Larocque's "Yellowstone Journal," ms. p. 48, and the Brandon House Post Journal entry for September 12, 1807 (H.B.C.A., B.22/a/15, fo. 3d). For convenience, we have chosen to refer to the North West Company forts that existed at various times near the mouth of the Souris River as Fort Souris, regardless of their several historical names. In the transcription, however, the historical names are preserved.

[16]H.B.C.A., B.22/a/1, fo. 8d. Brandon House was built near the mouth of the Souris River to compete with nearby posts of the North West Company and Peter Grant's independent company. David A. Stewart, *Early Assiniboine Trading Posts of the Souris-Mouth Group: 1785-1832*, Transactions of the Historical and Scientific Society of Manitoba, No. 5 (n.s.). Osnaburgh House is the point at which the Brandon House masters commenced maintenance of the annual journal describing the supply and operation of Brandon House for each trading season.

1812 were not used by Alwin but contain a few entries relevant to our synopsis of the Mandan-Hidatsa trade. Since the Brandon House masters kept a watchful eye on opposition traders and frequently recorded observations of their activities, the Brandon House Post Journals provide an invaluable supplement to the handful of surviving journals and memoirs left by North West Company traders who described the trade of that company with the Mandans and Hidatsas. These sources—Alwin's article, the Brandon House Post Journals, and the surviving North West Company documents—have been used to reconstruct the following pattern of trade for the Hudson's Bay Company at the Missouri River villages. The pattern of trade can be roughly considered to be about the same for the North West Company, although surviving documentation is not as extensive.[17] Table 1 in the Appendix is a calendar describing more than seventy round-trip visits between the Assiniboine River and the Mandan and Hidatsa villages made by white traders between 1738 and 1818.

Soon after arriving at the Assiniboine River posts in September or October of each year, the post master

sent small parties of men (usually two to eight) on horseback, or during the winter on foot with sleds drawn by dogs, to the Mandan and Hidatsa villages to trade for furs. This kind of trading is similar to that called by the traders·en dérouine, or the sending of men directly to Indian camps to collect furs in payment of goods taken on credit from the posts. The trading parties remained at the villages from several days to several weeks and occasionally for a period of months to barter for the furs of the natives and those of the resident free traders in the villages. Horses (or, in the winter, dogs) needed to haul the fur returns back to the establishments on the Assiniboine River were purchased from the Indians or free traders. After the return of the fall expedition, usually in December or January, a second party was sometimes sent to the villages with more goods to trade, depending on the time of year, the stock of trading goods on hand, and the willingness of the men to undertake the journey in spite of frequent rumors of hostile Indians along the route between the posts and the Missouri. Occasionally an individual with the fall expedition remained in the villages to continue trading over the winter and returned with the second party in the spring. On one occasion James Slater, who had left Brandon House with the fall party on October 9, 1801, remained in the villages and was stranded there when the Brandon House master could not persuade any of his men to make the spring trip. Slater was forced to return in April, 1802, with some "Canadians" (probably North West Com-

[17]John A. Alwin, "Pelts, Provisions & Perceptions: The Hudson's Bay Company Mandan Indian Trade, 1795-1812," *Montana: The Magazine of Western History* 29 (July, 1979): 16–27. A copy of one of the Brandon House Post Journals, similar to the one for 1810–11 in the Hudson's Bay Company Archives (B.22/a/18a), exists in the Selkirk Papers at the Public Archives of Canada (Manuscript Group 19, E1, vol. 62, microfilm roll C-16, pp. 16500–42).

pany men or indebted free traders) who were trading in the villages.[18] In the spring of each year, usually in April or May, the post master accompanied the shipment of the previous season's fur returns by canoe over the long water route to Albany Factory on Hudson Bay or, in the case of the North West Company, to Grand Portage, on Lake Superior.

The same men were often repeatedly sent to the villages, probably because of their familiarity with the route or the language of the Indians. For example, James Slater participated in the first nine Hudson's Bay Company expeditions to the villages. He remained at the Missouri after the departure of the ninth expedition from the villages and returned to Brandon House with the tenth company party. He also participated in two subsequent trips to the villages, the last in the winter of 1802–1803 (Appendix, table 1).

The trading season was the fall through the winter months and into the spring, when pelts were considered to be in prime condition. Summer pelts were not of as high quality, and consequently few visits to the Mandan and Hidatsa villages were made in the summer. There is no record of any summer trips to the villages by Hudson's Bay Company traders, and the only documented summer visits there by Nor'westers were those made in 1796, 1805 (one and possibly two visits), and 1806 (two visits). Summer trips were not always made for the primary pur-

pose of trading furs. Of the five North West Company summer expeditions to the villages (Appendix, table 1), one was probably sent there in that season to give Larocque optimal weather conditions for exploring toward the Rocky Mountains with the Crows, and one was made principally for the purpose of trading for horses. There are, however, records of resident free traders from the Missouri bringing furs to Brandon House to trade during the summer months (1799, 1804, 1806, and 1809; see Appendix, table 1).

At the Missouri the traders usually dispersed through several of the villages with a portion of the goods to trade. Part of the merchandise was used to pay for lodging and food, and some goods were given to prominent chiefs as a way of seeking favor and generosity in trade, a time-honored practice among Canadian fur traders. For an example of lodge price, see the entry of December 13, 1804, in Larocque's "Missouri Journal." The practice of gift giving is well illustrated in Larocque's "Yellowstone Journal." On June 19, 1805, Larocque gave a present of "¾ lb. Tobacco, one knife and 50 Rounds of amunition" to the Hidatsa chief Le Borgne for supporting his desire to travel to the Crow country. On June 27, 1805, Larocque also made a large gift of goods to visiting Crow chiefs at the Hidatsa villages as part of his request to travel with them.[19]

---

[18]H.B.C.A., B.22/a/9, fos. 8, 12d–13, 14d–15, 18d.

[19]See David Thompson's Journal, entry for December 30, 1797; Charles McKenzie's Narratives, third expedition account, ms. pp. 119–20, 129–30); François-Antoine La-

Victor Collot, the French former general who toured the United States in the mid-1790s, provides a description of this general trade pattern as it existed about 1796:

A few years since, the English merchants built small forts in several places on a river, called the Red River, which falls into that of the Asseniboines. The sources of this last river begin near the Missouri, towards the Mandanes country. They send their agents by land, either with horses in the autumn or spring, or with great dogs in the winter, which run with light and slender traineaux [sleds] on the snow, and traffic for bullocks' hides, wolf and fox skins, in exchange for powder, knives, glass beads, and vermillion. The passage from the Missouri to this river is reckoned by travellers who have made it several times, at a hundred of our common leagues.[20]

Although Collot did not travel far beyond Saint Louis, he met fur traders from the Upper Missouri country, including a man named Ménard from the Mandan villages, who undoubtedly told him much about the upriver trade. His description of the Canadian trade with the Mandans is remarkably accurate.

Trade in the villages must have been carried on vigorously by the traders of the competing companies, who frequently had men in the villages simultaneously. The journals often preserve complaints that the opposing company either had spoiled the trade with the Indians by giving them liberal prices for marginal furs or had managed to acquire most of the available furs from the Indians. For example, James Mackay, himself a former trader from Montreal among the Mandans and Hidatsas, wrote concerning the 1796-97 period when he was trading and exploring along the Lower Missouri River for the Spanish authorities in Saint Louis:

In the Course of the Year /93 & /94 the English Traders sent from their Post they have on the River Assiniboine, several of their hireling to the Mandaine Nation on the Missouri, but as these persons were sent by different Employers or Traders, and that in Consequence they found themselves on an opposition the one with the other, they paid Double the Value for their peltries they exchanged, which made the Indians think immediately, that Goods were not of that value which they had at first imagined; the immoderate desire that those unfit traders showed, to procure themselves pelteteries; convinced the Indians that it was not necessary to show so much friendship to the whites to entice them to return to them with goods, seeing that the only object that brought them was to procure pelteteries.[21]

John McKay, the Brandon House master for the 1804-1805 trading season, complained in his journal on February 27, 1805, that the North West Company had managed to obtain most of the Hidatsa furs that

---

rocque's "Missouri Journal," ms. p. 13; Larocque's "Yellowstone Journal," ms. pp. 5, 7.

[20]Victor Collot, *A Journey in North America*, vol. 1, p. 291.

[21]Abraham P. Nasatir, ed., *Before Lewis and Clark, Documents Illustrating the History of the Missouri, 1785-1804*, vol. 2, p. 493.

year: "the quantity of men and goods sent to the Mandals by Mr. Chaboillez is more than sufficient for these people, no less than three Clerks, [namely] Messrs. Henry la Rocque & McKenzie, besides 15 foremost Hands. I had only three men and could but barely spare them, when Henderson left the Big Bellies la Rocque had 900 Br. I had only 200 some odd."[22]

McKay is here referring to the North West Company party that traveled to the villages in the fall of 1804 under the leadership of François-Antoine Larocque, whose journal of the trip has survived (see Larocque's "Missouri Journal" in part two). McKay is mistaken, however, about some details of the North West Company's presence in the villages, since there is no evidence that Alexander Henry the Younger visited the Knife River villages before 1806, and the North West Company's parties to the villages at that time do not appear to have been large enough to have comprised "15 foremost Hands." It is interesting to note that a little over two weeks later, on March 15, 1805, the Hudson's Bay men returned to Brandon House with furs equaling 424 prime beaver pelts, making the value of the season's total fur returns from the Missouri equal to 768 such pelts, which should have ameliorated the severity of McKay's complaint.[23]

At the villages during the summer of 1806, Alexander Henry recorded in his journal on July 21 that

"were it not for the H.B. Co.'s servants, who come here to trade every winter, and have spoiled the natives by giving good prices for summer wolves . . . we might carry on a very advantageous trade with these people from our establishment on the Assiniboine, as the articles they require are of little real value to us."[24]

Occasionally during the later years of the trade at the Mandan and Hidatsa villages, the North West and the Hudson's Bay companies sent joint expeditions to the Missouri, usually for the purpose of presenting a stronger defense in case of attack by hostile Indians. Sometimes the returns were divided equally between the two companies. François-Antoine Larocque, who was in charge of Fort Souris for much of 1806 and 1807, mentions entering into some arrangements of this kind with Thomas Vincent, the master at Brandon House for the 1806–1807 trading season, but no records of any joint expeditions to the Missouri in that period have survived. The Brandon House Post Journals do, however, document two such joint expeditions to the Mandans and Hidatsas in the spring of 1812 and the fall of 1817.[25]

In addition to the North West and Hudson's Bay companies, other interests also concurrently competed for the Mandan and Hidatsa trade, although surviving documentation

---

[22]H.B.C.A., B.22/a/12, fos. 9d–10.
[23]H.B.C.A., B.22/a/12, fo. 10d.

[24]Alexander Henry, *New Light on the Early History of the Greater Northwest: The Manuscript Journals of Alexander Henry and of David Thompson, 1799-1814*, vol. 1, p. 356.
[25]Larocque's "Yellowstone Journal," ms. p. 48; H.B.C.A., B.22/a/18b, fos. 8, 12; H.B.C.A., B.22/a/20, fos. 21, 24–25.

is extremely scant. A man named Cardin traded in the villages in the spring of 1795 as an agent of Peter Grant's independent company, which maintained a trading establishment near the mouth of the Souris River in competition with the Nor'westers and the Hudson's Bay men. At the end of the 1794–95 trading season the Brandon House master noted in his journal that Peter Grant "had made out pretty well he having made some packs of Mandal Robes by sending Men across the Country to their villages."[26] Charles McKenzie remarked that "no less than five other Traders forming as many different Interests" had preceded him to the Missouri River villages in the fall of 1805.[27] One of these was the Hudson's Bay Company party which left Brandon House on October 22 accompanied by free traders Hugh Heney and Jean Baptiste La France (Appendix, table 1), but the identity of the other parties to which McKenzie refers is unknown.

Free traders often obtained goods on credit at the Assiniboine River posts with the promise that they would pay off the debt with furs traded from the Indians during the season. John Macdonell described this kind of trade in his "Red River" manuscript: "This trade was carried on by the men taking a certain number of skins as suits their circumstances at the prices of this Post [Pine Fort] upon

Credit & paying their Credits at their return."[28]

Available documents offer several examples of this. The seven French-Canadian free traders who accompanied David Thompson to the Missouri in 1797–98 had been outfitted by the North West Company to trade at the villages. Charles McKenzie was sent to the Mandan and Hidatsa villages in the summer of 1806 to meet a free trader who had been among the Arikaras trading goods obtained from the North West Company. Hugh Heney was equipped to trade in the Mandan villages by the Brandon House master in the fall of 1805. The same Brandon House master, John McKay, refused to outfit a free trader for the Missouri in the fall of 1809 because he considered the man a poor risk.[29]

Very little trade appears to have been conducted between traders from Canada and the Arikaras, who lived on the Missouri River near the mouth of the Grand River about 120 miles below the villages of the Mandans and Hidatsas.[30] At times the Arikaras

[26]H.B.C.A., B.22/a/2, fos. 19d, 20d–21; Wood, "Journal of John Macdonell," pp. 123–24, entries for January 25 and 27, 1795).

[27]McKenzie's Narratives, third expedition account, ms. p. 119.

[28]Macdonell's "The Red River," ms. pp. 10–11.

[29]David Thompson, *David Thompson's Narrative of His Explorations in Western America, 1784–1812*, Publications of the Champlain Society, vol. 12, pp. 209–10; McKenzie's Narratives, fourth expedition account, ms. pp. 1, 32; H.B.C.A., B.22/a/13, fo. 10; H.B.C.A., B.22/a/17, fo. 9.

[30]The Arikaras were, however, frequently visited by traders ascending the Missouri River from Saint Louis. See James Jesse Berry, "Arikara Middlemen: The Effects of Trade on an Upper Missouri Society" (Ph.D. diss., Indiana University, 1978), for a recent summary of trade with that group.

moved north for short periods and occupied villages within a few miles of the Mandan and Hidatsa towns. Two of La Vérendrye's sons visited an Arikara group, probably near the mouth of the Bad River near present-day Fort Pierre, South Dakota, during their travels in 1742–43. Surviving documents contain no suggestion of direct trade between the Arikaras and traders from the posts on the Assiniboine River, although one of the reasons for Charles McKenzie's trip to the Mandan and Hidatsa villages in 1806 was to meet the indebted free trader there who had been trading among the Arikaras lower on the Missouri.[31] The Caddoan-speaking Arikaras were closely related to the Pawnees living along the Platte River in what is now Nebraska and north-central Kansas. The Arikaras were often erroneously identified as Pawnees.

[31]Stephen A. Chomko, "The Ethnohistorical Setting of the Upper Knife-Heart Region," in *Papers in Northern Plains Prehistory and Ethnohistory*, South Dakota Archaeological Society, Special Publication, no. 10. ed. W. Raymond Wood; G. Hubert Smith, *The Explorations of the La Vérendryes in the Northern Plains, 1738-1743*, ed. W. Raymond Wood, pp. 112–13; Charles McKenzie's Narratives, fourth expedition account, ms. pp. 1, 32.

2

History of the Fur Trade

THE earliest direct trade between Euro-Americans and the Mandans may have begun soon after the Hudson's Bay Company established its first posts along the coast of Hudson Bay. Arthur J. Ray, following earlier interpretations by A. S. Morton, believes that the Mandans and Hidatsas visited Hudson Bay at least as early as the first and second decades of the eighteenth century.[1] Given the ambiguous nature of the documents being interpreted, identifying these Indians as members of these two horticultural tribes is perhaps an economical solution to the identity of the "Mountain Indians"; it is not, however, one which is supported by independent native or other testimony, and the identification poses more problems than it solves.

In 1714, James Knight became governor of the Hudson's Bay Company's interests in Canada and established himself at York Fort, at the mouth of the Nelson River. His deputy there was Henry Kelsey. Governor Knight successfully improved the trade of York Fort with Indian groups on the south and west by his efforts to eliminate warfare between different Indian bands and by gifts which he sent into the hinterland by prominent Indians. "Drawn by the offer of presents broadcasted inland, a mysterious people, the Mountain Indians, appeared upon the scene." Although these Indians told of mountains so high that their peaks could be seen only in good weather, they were also reputed to grow corn, a circumstance that prompted Morton to identify them as Mandans. Knight's name for them (Mountain Indians), Morton speculated, was probably an anglicized version of their name, Mai-tain-ai-thi-nish, as recorded by Kelsey in his journal on May 26, 1721.[2]

Thirty canoes of these Indians arrived at York Fort in 1715. Knight's comments on this deputation included the fact that they had come "the farthest" of the Indians trading there that year. It had taken them thirty-nine days to descend the Nel-

---

[1]Ray, *Indians in the Fur Trade; Their Role as Hunters, Trappers and Middlemen in the Lands Southwest of Hudson Bay, 1660-1870*; Morton, *A History of the Canadian West to 1870-1871.*

[2]Morton, *Canadian West*, pp. 127, 131, 134, 135; York Factory Journal, 1720-21, P.A.C., H.B.C., B.239/a/6, p. 19 (cited in Ray, *Indians in the Fur Trade*, p. 57 n. 13).

son River to the fort, and it required three months for them to return home. They did not leave a good impression on Knight: they "bordered on the worst sort of Indians in the country." This was not their first visit to the bay. One member of the party had been among a group who had visited Fort Albany sixteen years earlier, in 1699.[3]

The Mountain Indians returned to York Fort in 1716, this time accompanied by some Crow Indian slaves. Arthur Ray believed these Mountain Indians to have been Hidatsas, although at that time they were at war with the Crow Indians. Knight attempted to use some of the slaves to mend the rift between the two groups and so to open up trade with the Crows.[4] Although most of this group of Indians died of starvation on their return home in 1716, another group of Mountain Indians returned to the fort in twenty-two canoes on June 10, 1717.[5]

The last recorded visit of the Mountain Indians to York Fort took place in 1721, while Henry Kelsey was in charge. His journal documented their arrival on May 26.[6] No further mention of the Mountain Indians, or of the Crows, is to be found in Hudson's Bay Company journals for the period. The ambiguity of these accounts is not confined to the identity of these Indians. What would have induced the Mandans to travel such a distance over unfamiliar ground? They are not known to have traveled that far from home on any other occasion, although the Hidatsas were accustomed to raiding as far west as the Rocky Mountains. Were the guns the Mountain Indians obtained at York Fort sufficient to repay such a voyage, especially considering the fact that the Mandan staple of trade (corn) was a very heavy commodity to transport such distances in canoes—and that no mention of trade corn is made in the accounts? And can we really assume that the Mandans and Hidatsas actually descended the Nelson River in canoes, a means of transportation with which they were wholly unfamiliar? These and other queries lead us seriously to question this identification, while retaining it as a working hypothesis.[7]

Other problems attend the nature of the intertribal trade between the Mandans and their neighbors on the

[3]Morton, *Canadian West*, pp. 134–35; Ray, *Indians in the Fur Trade*, pp. 55, 57.

[4]Ray, *Indians in the Fur Trade*, p. 57; York Factory Journal, 1716–17, P.A.C., H.B.C., B.239/a/2, p. 58 (cited in Ray, *Indians in the Fur Trade*, p. 57 n. 11).

[5]Morton, *Canadian West*, p. 137; Ray, *Indians in the Fur Trade*, p. 60; York Factory Journal, 1716–17, P.A.C., H.B.C., B.239/a/3, p. 56 (cited in Ray, *Indians in the Fur Trade*, p. 60 n. 21).

[6]Ray, *Indians in the Fur Trade*, p. 57; York Factory Journal, 1720–21, P.A.C., H.B.C., B.239/a/6, p. 19 (cited in Ray, *Indians in the Fur Trade*, p. 57 n. 13).

[7]An earlier presumed contact with the Mandans, first suggested by Tyrrell, has not been accepted by later writers. In 1690, Henry Kelsey had traveled south from York Factory on Hudson Bay, and, somewhere on the plains of southern Canada, perhaps on the Assiniboine River, he had met some Indians he called the "Naywattame poets," a group which Tyrrell, following W. H. Holmes, believed to have been the Mandans (Samuel Hearne, *A Journey from Prince of Wale's Fort in Hudson's Bay to the Northern Ocean in the Years 1769, 1770, 1771, and 1772,*

north and east, the Assiniboins. There are two opposing hypotheses relating to the antiquity of the trade between them. Some sources, drawing on ethnohistorical documentation, believe that this trade was an old pattern, most likely predating Euro-American contacts, a view to which we subscribe. As early as the time of La Vérendrye there are accounts documenting that the Assiniboins were visiting the Mandan villages to trade on an annual, if not semiannual, schedule.[8]

Ray, on the other hand, believes that this trade was "largely a historic phenomenon," since it is "unclear just what the Assiniboine would have bartered to the Mandan before contacts with Europeans." On the contrary, he feels that the Assiniboin trade with the Mandans developed between 1670 and 1720, when he believes the Mandans were sending parties through Assiniboin territory

to trade along Hudson Bay. The Euro-American trade goods found archaeologically at village sites along the Missouri River dating to the late seventeenth century "were in all likelihood transported there by the Mandan themselves, and not the Assiniboine, as is commonly supposed."[9] The establishment of French posts along the middle Saskatchewan River in the 1750s, Ray and Freeman believe, severed the direct Mandan contacts with Hudson Bay posts, placing them in the indirect trade zone.[10] The Assiniboins would then have become the source for Mandan trade goods, the Mandans terminating their long-range sojourns to Hudson Bay.

Pottery from a number of sites in southern Manitoba and Saskatchewan is reputed to resemble Mandan or Hidatsa pottery. For example, a "Mandan" potsherd is reported from the Stott site on the Assiniboine River near present-day Brandon, Manitoba. Missouri Valley archaeologists and those Canadian specialists who have personally inspected pottery from Mandan and Hidatsa villages along the Missouri River agree that few of the Canadian finds of pottery in the "Mandan-Hidatsa tradition" actually originated in the Missouri Valley. It has nevertheless been suggested that the Stott site "Mandan" sherd was left by a Missouri Valley trading party en route to York Fort.[11]

---

ed. J. B. Tyrrell, Publications of the Champlain Society, vol. 6, p. 12; Henry Kelsey, *The Kelsey Papers*). Morton (*Canadian West*, pp. 112–13) and Ray (*Indians in the Fur Trade*, p. 25 n. 22) both believe, however, this group was part of the Assiniboin Indians.

[8]Pierre Gaultier de Varennes, Sieur de la Vérendrye, *Journals and Letters of Pierre Gaultier de Varennes de la Vérendrye and His Sons*, ed. Lawrence J. Burpee, Publications of the Champlain Society, vol. 16, pp. 253–54; John C. Ewers, "The Indian Trade of the Upper Missouri before Lewis and Clark: An Interpretation," *Missouri Historical Society Bulletin* 10 (July, 1954); G. Hubert Smith, *The Explorations of the La Vérendryes in the Northern Plains, 1738-43*, ed. W. Raymond Wood, pp. 39–53; and W. Raymond Wood, "Plains Trade in Prehistoric and Protohistoric Intertribal Relations," in *Anthropology on the Great Plains*, ed. W. Raymond Wood and Margot Liberty.

[9]Ray, *Indians in the Fur Trade*, p. 89.

[10]Arthur J. Ray and Donald B. Freeman, *"Give Us Good Measure": An Economic Analysis of Relations between the Indians and the Hudson's Bay Company before 1763*, p. 48.

[11]R. S. MacNeish, "The Stott Mound and Village Site near Brandon, Manitoba," *An-*

It seems unlikely, however, that Mandan trading parties traveling from the Missouri Valley to Hudson Bay—an airline distance of no less than eight hundred miles and an on-the-ground distance of no less than one thousand miles—would either carry with them pottery containers or travel accompanied by women, who traditionally made and used pottery in cooking. Male traveling parties, we believe, would be far more likely to carry parched corn and pemmican as supplies and to supplement those rations by hunting.

There is, of course, good evidence that the Mandans themselves did visit trading posts along the Assiniboine River, carrying goods to exchange with Euro-American traders there. This exchange appears to have been largely in Indian corn, which their women raised in great quantities. Peter Pond's map of 1785, in fact, documents that the "Maundiens" brought Indian corn for sale to Pine Fort (Fort Epinett). Earlier Jonathan Carver had noted that the Mandans ("Mahahs") carried Indian corn to Fort La Reine, probably in the 1760s.[12] Such exchanges would surely have been resented by the Assiniboins, since it would have threatened their role as middlemen between the Canadian traders and the Missouri Valley Indians. The degree to which this resentment may have

led to hostilities, however, is as poorly known as other details of this trade. For example, how much corn—and precisely what other goods—did the Mandans transport into southern Canada?

Relations between the Assiniboins (as well as the Crees) and the Mandans were not always amicable in the early historic period, and the Crees admitted that both they and the Assiniboins were almost constantly warring with the Mandans. There are, in fact, accounts in French documents of La Vérendrye's time describing Mandan Indians who were captured by either Crees or Assiniboins and sold as slaves. In 1733 several Mandan children, for example, were sold to Christophe Dufrost, Sieur de la Jémeraye, La Vérendrye's nephew, and taken to Montreal.[13]

In any event, whether the Assiniboin-Mandan trade is an old pattern or a historic one, from the standpoint of culture change in the Missouri Valley villages, the means by which alien goods were imported is less important than the changes they wrought in the native lifeways there. Mandans could have obtained Euro-American goods at any time after the establishment of the Hudson's Bay Company posts along the bay in the late 1600s. Whether those goods were reaching them by way of Assiniboin or other Indian middlemen, as we believe, or through direct Mandan contacts in the early years of the eighteenth century, as Ray and Freeman believe, only small amounts of such goods are recovered in archaeological contexts dating to the time before the initia-

nual Report of the National Museum of Canada for 1952-3, Bulletin 132 (1954): 36; E. Leigh Syms, personal communication to the authors, 1981; Ray, Indians in the Fur Trade, p. 89.

[12]Jonathan Carver, The Journals of Jonathan Carver and Related Documents, 1766-70, ed. John Parker, p. 137.

[13]La Vérendrye, Journals and Letters, p. 108.

tion of extensive direct trade in the years after 1780.

EURO-AMERICANS ARRIVE:
THE FRENCH REGIME

French expansion across what is now southern Canada followed rapidly after the appointment of La Vérendrye as commandant of the Posts of the North in 1727. At the time of his appointment the French posts were no farther west than the western extremity of Lake Superior. In the next decade La Vérendrye established a series of posts in western New France, including Fort La Reine on the north bank of the Assiniboine River, near what is now the town of Portage la Prairie, Manitoba. From that post in 1738, La Vérendrye and a small party, accompanied by a group of Assiniboin Indians, set out overland to visit the Mandan villages on the "River of the West"—the Missouri River. After spending ten days with the Mandans, he returned to Fort La Reine. A second trip to the villages was made by one of his sons, Pierre, in 1741. In 1742 two of his sons returned to the villages and then explored south and west of them, probably eventually reaching the Big Horn Mountains in modern Montana or Wyoming, returning to Fort La Reine in 1743.[14]

These explorations must have been disappointing to men seeking large numbers of beaver, for these animals were not as abundant on the plains as they were in the streams of western New France. In any event,

La Vérendrye was relieved of his command in 1744, and his western explorations were ended. Between 1738 and 1743 he and his sons had visited the Mandan and Hidatsa villages on three separate occasions. Precisely what goods may have changed hands during those visits is problematical, although we know that in 1738, on the way to their villages, La Vérendrye had given presents to the Assiniboins including powder, ball, tobacco, axes, knives, chisels, and awls; furthermore, he had provisioned his men for the trip with powder, ball, tobacco, and "various small goods such as awls, gun flints, gun screws, and firesteels—more for their own needs than anything else." He also carried a number of presents for the Mandans, including, again, powder and ball "and several small articles they valued highly because of their lack of them."[15] Two men whom he left at the villages on his departure in 1738 must also have had trade goods or gifts which they exhausted before they left, but they were never enumerated. Consequently, the number of items which reached the Mandans directly as a consequence of these three journeys could not have been very great. It is, of course, possible that independent contacts with them may also have been made about that time by others of their men, but if so, the records are silent on the matter.

La Vérendrye had discovered no Euro-Americans living in or near the Mandan villages in 1738, nor did his sons find any there a few years

---

[14]La Vérendrye, *Journals and Letters;* Smith, *Explorations of the La Vérendryes.*

[15]Smith, *Explorations of the La Vérendryes,* pp. 46–47, 63.

later. When the La Vérendrye brothers were on their way back to the Assiniboine River in 1743, however, they did hear of a French trader living on the Missouri River "three days' journey" from a locale which is believed to have been near the mouth of the Bad River, in central South Dakota; that is, the Frenchman was apparently living downstream somewhere in the vicinity of the Grand Detour.[16] Exactly when the next traders after the La Vérendryes reached the Mandans and Hidatsas is a matter for speculation.

What was the fate of Fort La Reine, built by La Vérendrye in October, 1738, as the springboard for visits to the Mandans? References to it are sparing and conflicting, but it seems to have been destroyed or left in ruins at least twice, once apparently at the hands of the Crees. Voorhis believes that a third fort was built about 1753 or 1754 and that it was abandoned "when the French garrison was drawn east," probably in 1763. The post was still standing, however, after Britain gained control of New France by the terms of the Treaty of Paris in 1763, at the end of the Seven Years' War. Until the cession Fort La Reine was apparently one of the principal French posts in western New France, probably because of its strategic location on the portage between the Assiniboine River and Lake Manitoba. An unnamed post is shown at or near its location on Peter Pond's map of 1785, but it is omitted from Pond's later maps. Voorhis says that the fort was probably occupied by the Hudson's Bay Company until they

built on or near its site in 1796. The new fort was called Assiniboine River Fort, and later Portage-la-Prairie, although it was also known as Fort des Prairies or Fort La Reine. On September 11, 1793, John Macdonell had referred to "the seite of an ancient Fort *de la Reine*," but he never later referred to it as active.[17]

References to French traders or missionaries from Fort La Reine (or from other posts on the Assiniboine River) making contact with the Missouri Valley tribes are equally vague. In 1805, while he was at Fort Souris, Daniel Harmon wrote that "it is now upwards of fifty years since a French Missionary left this, who had resided here a number of years to instruct the natives." This account would place the French in the vicinity of the mouth of the Souris River about 1755 or before, although the reference may not be to Fort La Reine itself. Louis Antoine de Bougainville's statement in 1757 that Fort La Reine "is the route to take for the upper Missouri" is from an account based on hearsay information. Although the accuracy of the statement is not questioned, the dates for which the comment holds true are uncertain.[18]

[16]Ibid., pp. 112–13, 123–27.

[17]Henry R. Wagner, *Peter Pond, Fur Trader and Explorer*, Yale University Library Western Historical Series no. 2, map 2. Ernest Voorhis, *Historic Forts and Trading Posts of the French Régime and of the English Fur Trading Companies*, pp. 100–101; Charles M. Gates, ed., *Five Fur Traders of the Northwest*, pp. 110-11, 111 n. 101; John Macdonell's "The Red River," ms. p. 9. See also L. A. Prud'homme, *Les Successeurs de la Vérendrye — Sous la Domination Française — 1743-1755*, Proceedings and Transactions of the Royal Society of Canada, 2nd Series, vol. 12.

[18]Daniel Williams Harmon, *Sixteen Years*

Among the documents that hint that Fort La Reine was in use by French traders who were traveling to the Missouri Valley is one that implies its use sometime before 1763. Peter Pond, whose trading career led him to the upper Mississippi River area between 1775 and 1778, composed a narrative of some of his activities in that area in which he noted that a former French soldier from the Illinois country had personally told him that he had

Desorted His Post & toock his Boat up the Miseeurea among the Indans and Spant Maney years among them. . . . He [eventually] Got among the Mondans [Mandans] whare he found Sum french traders who Belongd to the french facterey at fort Lorain on the Read River this facterey Belong to the french traders of Cannaday   those People toock Pinneshon to the facterey with them and the Concarn took him into thare Sarvis til the Hole Cuntrey Was Giveen up to the English and he then Came in to thare Sarvis.[19]

This Frenchman, whom Pond called simply "Old Pinneshon," may have been Pennesha Gegare, a French trader who was among the Sacs and Foxes in Wisconsin in 1753. He has also been called in print "Pennensha," "Penechon," and "Mons. Pinnisance." Gates credits Thwaites with identifying this man as "Pennesha George," a name for which we can

find no other source.[20] If Pond's "Old Pinneshon" and this man are one and the same, this allusion to French traders from Fort La Reine is probably referring to the decade between about 1744 (when La Vérendrye was relieved of his command in western New France) and 1753, at which time the trader was in Wisconsin.

BEGINNINGS OF TRADE UNDER THE BRITISH REGIME

Contradicting Jonathan Carver's published statement that the Mandans were trading at Fort La Reine in the 1760s is another observation which he penned in 1767 and is based on his travels the preceding year. Carver noted that the Crees and Assiniboins purchased Indian corn from the Mandans "for a few European trinkets as knives, hatchets, &c, [but that] the white people as yet have never opened a trade with them."[21]

One brief reference to an early visit to the Mandan villages from Canada concerns a trader named Mackintosh who "belonged to, or

[20]Augustin Grignon, "Seventy-two Years' Recollections of Wisconsin," *Third Annual Report and Collections of the State Historical Society of Wisconsin for the Year 1856* 3 (1857): 261–63. James Gorrell, "Lieut. James Gorrell's Journal," *First Annual Report of the State Historical Society of Wisconsin for the Year 1854* 1 (1855): 41; Lyman C. Draper, "Traditions and Recollections of Prairie du Chien," *Report and Collections of the State Historical Society of Wisconsin, for the Years 1880, 1881 and 1882* 9 (1882): 299; Jonathan Carver, *Travels Through the Interior Parts of North America in the Years 1766, 1767, and 1768,* pp. 43–45; Carver, *Jonathan Carver,* p. 83; and Gates, *Five Fur Traders,* p. 38 n. 28.

[21]Carver, *Travels,* p. 109; Carver, *Jonathan Carver,* pp. 20, 137.

in the Indian Country: The Journal of Daniel Williams Harmon, ed. W. Kaye Lamb, p. 90. Louis Antoine de Bougainville, "1757: Memoir of Bougainville," trans. and ed. Reuben Gold Thwaites, *Collections of the State Historical Society of Wisconsin* 18 (1908): 186.

[19]Gates, *Five Fur Traders,* pp. 38–39.

was in some way connected with the French Trading Company, as far back as 1772. According to his narration, he set out from Montreal, in the summer of 1773, crossed over the country to the Missouri River, and arrived at one of the Mandan villages on Christmas day."[22] No primary source survives of this visit, which cannot be confirmed in any other account. Mackintosh cannot be further identified, and his traveling companions, without whom such a trip would have been impossible, are unmentioned.

Another early visitor to the Knife River villages was Donald MacKay, who appears to have reached the Hidatsa villages in March or April, 1781. Later an energetic officer of the Hudson's Bay Company who founded Brandon House, an important center of the Honorable Company's trade with the Mandans and Hidatsas, MacKay was at this time employed by John Ross of the North West Company at a fort near the vicinity of Portage la Prairie in the Assiniboine River valley. Unfortunately, MacKay's account of this trip has not been published, and further details are not yet available.[23]

In 1785, Peter Pond produced a map which illustrates some of the information he had obtained during his trading career. On this map is a legend which says: "Here upon the Branches of the Missury live the Maundiens, who bring to our Factory at Fort Epinett [Pine Fort], on the Assinipoil River Indian Corn for sale. Our People go to them with loaded Horses in twelve Days." This reference, as we see later, is consistent with the time required for a trip as described between the Assiniboine River and the Missouri Valley. Pond's map shows a post on or near the site of Fort La Reine (though unlabeled) and Fort Epinett, or Pine Fort, as well as a third, unlabeled, post on the Assiniboine River between them. The map also carries labels for the "Maundiens," the "Bigg Belly's" (or Hidatsas, who are shown along the Assiniboine River), and the "Rapid Indians" (or the Algonquian-speaking relatives of the Arapahos, the Atsinas, who are often confused, even yet, with the Hidatsas). This map is the earliest documentary evidence to distinguish the Hidatsas as separate and distinct from the Mandans, and it implies detailed knowledge of their language and culture.[24]

Documentation improves significantly in 1787 with the arrival of James Mackay on the Assiniboine River. Mackay's "journal" of his experiences in the Northern Plains and of his later exploration up the Missouri River north from Saint Louis provides valuable, if somewhat chronologically confused, data on the Mandan and Hidatsa trade. Mackay's journal seems to be a compilation

[22]Henry R. Schoolcraft, ed., *Information Respecting the History, Condition and Prospects of the Indian Tribes of the United States*, vol. 3, p. 253.

[23]John C. Jackson, "Brandon House and the Mandan Connection," *North Dakota History* 49 (Winter, 1982): 12–14.

[24]Carl I. Wheat, *Mapping the Transmississippi West, 1540-1861*, vol. 1, p. 175 n. 8 and map 201; Wagner, *Peter Pond*, map 2; Thomas F. Kehoe and Alice B. Kehoe, "The Identification of the Fall or Rapid Indians," *Plains Anthropologist* 19 (August, 1974): 231–32.

of his experiences, probably made during the winter of 1803–1804, inasmuch as it was prepared for the edification of Lewis and Clark, whom he visited at their camp near Saint Louis. Some of the information may represent the situation in 1796–97 as much or more than that in 1787. Mackay is known to have made only one trip to their villages, in 1787.[25] Early in that year he traveled from the "River Catepoi," or Qu'Apelle River, to the Mandan villages, taking seventeen days to do so. He spent ten days with the Mandans, exchanging with them the "few Merchandizes" he had carried with him.

Mackay's journal of that expedition is the first eyewitness account of the Mandan and Hidatsa villages since the time of La Vérendrye, forty-nine years earlier. His comments on the Mandan-Canadian fur trade are especially illuminating. In a reference to Fort Espérance, which lay near the mouth of the Qu'Apelle River, about 230 airline miles due north of the Knife River villages, he says that it was "the furthermost wintering post of the English Traders from Canada." It was from that post that the "English Traders" left "to go and make their unlawful Trade on the Missouri with the Mandaines and other nations"—a trade that was unlawful, that is, from the standpoint of the Spanish government in

Saint Louis. From that post "the English Traders, during summer transport their Merchandizes and Peltries [to and from the Missouri River], on horses or mules, which they Buy or hire of the natives of the Country and in Winter they more often use Sledges drawn by one, two or more Dogs." This comment would, of course, have been more appropriate for the period when Mackay was an employee of the Spaniards (in 1795–97) than it would have been for him as an employee of the North West Company in 1787. Mackay's account goes on to comment that in 1793 and 1794 the English traders at their post on the Assiniboine River sent several of their men to the Missouri.[26]

The period from 1743 to 1785 is the least understood in the history of the Canadian–Missouri River fur trade. This trade, opened by La Vérendrye in the years 1738 to 1743, appears to have languished following his recall to eastern Canada. Once opened, however, the trade seems never to have been abandoned for very long. There are clues—unsatisfactory ones, to be sure—that traders from Fort La Reine continued to use that post as a base for visits to the Missouri River, as Bougainville's memoir of 1757 reveals. The passage of Pennesha Gegare from the lower Missouri River to the French traders at Fort La Reine through the Mandan villages seems to be good evidence of trade there before 1763, when Britain assumed control of Canada and the French regime ended. Curiously

[25]Abraham P. Nasatir, ed., *Before Lewis and Clark: Documents Illustrating the History of the Missouri, 1785–1804*, vol. 2, pp. 490–95. See also the introductory notes to the journal as it was published by Milo M. Quaife, ed., "Extracts from Capt. McKay's Journal—and Others," *State Historical Society of Wisconsin, Proceedings for 1915*, p. 187.

[26]Nasatir, *Before Lewis and Clark*, vol. 2, pp. 492, 493.

enough, however, four years later Jonathan Carver (who should have been in a position to know such things) tells us that whites had as yet "never opened a trade" with the Mandans. There is the possibility that Montreal-based traders reached their villages as early as 1773, as Mackintosh's poorly documented visit suggests. But, as we shall see, trade did not assume significant proportions until the founding in 1785 of Pine Fort by the North West Company on the Assiniboine River near the former site of Fort La Reine—a post which competed for a time with Fort Espérance farther upriver.

VISITORS FROM THE SOUTH: THE SPANISH PRESENCE

"Pinneshon's" early ascent of the Missouri River—if Pond's account of it is reliable—is not known to have been repeated until 1792. The next known visitor from the south by way of the Missouri (and the first visitor from Spanish Saint Louis) was another Frenchman, Jacques D'Église, who appears to have left and returned to Saint Louis in 1792, apparently spending only a brief time with the Mandans. When D'Église (known to the Spaniards as Santiago Leglise) arrived at the Mandans, however, he found that they were already in "constant communication" with Canadian traders. D'Église was not regarded as a reliable observer by his contemporaries, although his information on the Canadian traders we know was correct.[27]

On a later trip up the Missouri River in 1794–95 (but apparently not as far upstream as the Mandans),

D'Église brought back to Saint Louis with him two North West Company deserters, Juan Fotman (Jean Tremont) and Chrisostome Joncquard, whom he found living among the Arikaras. These two men corroborated his earlier information and provided many additional details. The Spanish commandant of Upper Louisiana, Zenon Trudeau, interviewed them on July 4, 1795, and recorded their declarations, which now provided the Saint Louis Spaniards with accurate firsthand accounts of North West Company activities at the Mandan and Hidatsa villages. Curiously enough, this testimony does not seem to have been augmented by that which could have been obtained from a man named Loison. In mid-1794 ("a few days" after March 29), this man—a bond servant of Joseph Garreau—had arrived at the Hidatsa villages from downriver and had returned to Saint Louis with Joncquard and D'Église.[28]

This information prompted the foundation of the Commercial Company for the Discovery of the Nations of the Upper Missouri (commonly called the Missouri Company), a coalition of Saint Louis Spanish merchants. This group sponsored an expedition by Jean Baptiste Truteau in 1794, with instructions to ascend the river to the Mandans. He is not known to have succeeded in this goal

[27]Bernard De Voto, *The Course of Empire*, p. 601 n. 13; Nasatir, *Before Lewis and Clark*, vol. 1, pp. 82, 160–61.

[28]Nasatir, *Before Lewis and Clark*, vol. 1, pp. 95, 330–35. De Voto (*Course of Empire*, p. 602 n. 18) erroneously comments that Loison had deserted from Garreau and made his way to Fort Espérance.

on his foray up the Missouri from 1794 to 1796, although he is documented as reaching the Arikaras.[29] The only other Spanish party known to have reached the Mandans and Hidatsas was that of John T. Evans, a Welshman in the employ of the Missouri Company. In 1795 he and James Mackay—who had by then moved to Saint Louis and was working for the Spaniards—led an expedition up the Missouri River and established Fort Charles (or Carlos) in what is now northeastern Nebraska. Evans and a small party of men from Fort Charles reached the Mandan villages on September 23, 1796. He spent the winter there, leaving on May 9, 1797, and returning to Saint Louis a little later. The Mackay-Evans expedition has been the subject of considerable study, inasmuch as it was the single most important expedition to ascend the Missouri River in the decade before that of Lewis and Clark.[30]

On his arrival at the mouth of the Knife River, Evans confiscated a post which some North West Company employees under the direction of René Jusseaume had built near the villages in 1794. It was probably unoccupied at the time; Evans's statement that he simply "took possession of the English forts" does not seem to imply dispossession of any occupants.[31] Evans and the Canadian traders who arrived a little later had several meetings, some of them hostile. Jusseaume, in fact, tried to kill Evans. In addition, Evans corresponded with Cuthbert Grant, John Macdonell, and James Sutherland, of both the North West and the Hudson's Bay companies, at their posts along the Assiniboine River. This correspondence and the part of Evans's journal which survives cast additional light on the Canadian–Missouri River trade of the period.

The Mackay-Evans expedition resulted in a substantial increase in geographical knowledge of the Upper Missouri River. A map made by Evans illustrating his route from Fort Charles to the Mandan villages was in fact an important guide for the Lewis and Clark Expedition. More important here, their expedition resulted in international rivalry for control of the fur trade on the Upper Missouri. From the Mandan villages Evans sent copies of a proclamation by Mackay to the Canadian posts along the Assiniboine—a proclamation which prohibited trade along the Missouri by British-Canadian interests. Several replies to this missive were made by Canadian traders.[32] The proclamation does not,

---

[29]Nasatir, *Before Lewis and Clark*, vol. 1, pp. 87–91.

[30]Abraham P. Nasatir, "Anglo-Spanish Rivalry on the Upper Missouri," *Mississippi Valley Historical Review* 16 (June, 1929–March, 1930); Nasatir, *Before Lewis and Clark*; David Williams, "John Evans' Strange Journey," *American Historical Review* 54 (January,

1949); Gwyn A. Williams, *Madoc: The Making of a Myth*; Gwyn A. Williams, *The Search for Beaulah Land*. See also Abraham P. Nasatir, *Borderland in Retreat: From Spanish Louisiana to the Far Southwest*, pp. 66–85.

[31]Nasatir, *Before Lewis and Clark*, vol. 2, p. 496.

[32]W. Raymond Wood, "The John Evans 1796–97 Map of the Missouri River," *Great Plains Quarterly* 1 (Winter, 1981): 39–53. Nasatir, *Before Lewis and Clark*, vol. 2, pp. 501–502.

however, seem to have seriously deterred the traders from Canada. An entry in the Brandon House Post Journal on November 12, 1797, records that John Macdonell sent one man with some Assiniboins to the Mandan villages "to learn if the Spaniard is there." The same entry also says that the men of a Hudson's Bay Company expedition, to be dispatched the following day, were to hide their trade goods one day's journey from the Mandans "until they see how affairs stands in the villages."[33]

The expedition also raised the question of who politically controlled the Upper Missouri. John McKay, the master at Brandon House for 1797–98, recorded in his journal on November 12, 1797, that "no one is sure whether that part of the Misoures where the Mandles are, belongs to the Spaniards. Mr. Evans last year acknowledged that the little Souris River was out of the line of the Spaniards." David Thompson's mission to the Mandan and Hidatsa villages in 1797–98 was stimulated by the controversy resulting from Evans's presence in the villages, for he left those villages only after "having made the necessary astronomical observations."[34]

The Spanish presence in the Mandan and Hidatsa villages was never significant, for only two Spanish expeditions are known to have reached them: those of D'Église in 1792 and of Evans in 1796. Since both of these

visits were the result more of exploration than of trading, it is unlikely that very much in the way of goods was introduced to the villages through them. There is no question but that the village trade was dominated by the "constant communication" between the Indians and the Canadian traders and augmented by occasional traders coming up the Missouri River from Spanish Saint Louis or from posts along the upper Mississippi River. The dominance of the Canadian presence was to continue until shortly after the Lewis and Clark Expedition.

THE NINETEENTH CENTURY

Following Evans's time, but before Lewis and Clark's arrival in 1804, a number of visits to the Mandans and Hidatsas from downriver took place. When, for instance, the two captains reached a point on the Missouri just north of the Cannonball River, they met two French traders named River and Grenier, who were on their way downriver, having been robbed a few days earlier by the Mandans near Square Buttes. These men had been in the employ of Joseph Graveline, who was trading at the Arikara villages near the mouth of the Grand River, in South Dakota.[35]

At least one and probably two ac-

[33]H.B.C.A., B.22/a/5, fo. 18.
[34]Ibid.; David Thompson, *David Thompson's Narrative of His Explorations in Western America, 1784–1812*, Publications of the Champlain Society, vol. 12, ed. J. B. Tyrrell.

[35]Meriwether Lewis and William Clark, *Original Journals of the Lewis and Clark Expedition, 1804–06*, ed. Reuben Gold Thwaites, vol. 1, pp. 198, 203. Clark recorded their names as "Reevey" and "Grienway" (ibid., vol. 5, p. 350). See also Pierre-Antoine Tabeau, *Tabeau's Narrative of Loisel's Expedition to the Upper Missouri*, ed. Annie Heloise Abel, p. 168 n. 22.

counts which purport to describe explorations west of the Mandan and Hidatsa villages before Lewis and Clark are fraudulent. Charles Le-Raye's "account" of his travels on the plains as a Sioux captive from 1801 to 1805, and first published in 1812, is regarded as a forgery by many scholars. This narrative is probably based in part on extant and reliable sources such as Patrick Gass's journals, although it seems likely that the forger may also have used as yet unknown, but authentic, travel accounts. A more obvious and universally recognized fraud is the "account" of a 1790 expedition by "Julius Rodman" from Saint Louis to the Rocky Mountains. The narrative, written by Edgar Allan Poe, is based on material from Washington Irving's *Astoria* and on the journals of Lewis and Clark and of Captain Benjamin L. E. de Bonneville.[36]

By the time of Lewis and Clark, traders had not penetrated much further up the Missouri River than the Mandan and Hidatsa towns. In 1805 the two captains named a creek (modern Indian or Skunk Creek) nearly 105 miles above the mouth of the Knife

River after Toussaint Charbonneau, who had earlier visited its vicinity in the company of an Indian hunting party. Two other Frenchmen had been only a few miles further upstream.[37] By this account the mouth of the Little Missouri marked the upstream limit of firsthand Euro-American visitation, although as we shall see later, a Frenchman named Ménard had become familiar with the Missouri as far west as the Yellowstone River before 1804.

The purchase of French Louisiana by the United States and the lure of beaver in the Rocky Mountains attracted a veritable flood of traders, trappers, and other travelers to the Upper Missouri country from Saint Louis. The opening of the Missouri River fur trade and the rush to the Rocky Mountain beaver country have often been told in detail.[38] Some of these men were bound for the Mandan and Hidatsa villages as a base for operations, while many more had other destinations above and below the Knife River villages. Because the increasing presence of Americans in the Mandan-Hidatsa villages eventually led to the abandonment of trade in that quarter by British and Canadian interests, the following discussion will focus primarily on those American travelers who actually reached the Mandan-Hidatsa villages and had an influence on

[36][Charles LeRaye], "The Journal of Charles LeRaye," *South Dakota Historical Collections* 4: 150–80. Scholars critical of its authenticity include De Voto (*Course of Empire*, pp. 613, 616); George E. Hyde (*Red Cloud's Folk*, p. 27 n. 4), and especially Clyde D. Dollar, "The Journal of Charles LeRaye: Authentic or Not?" *South Dakota Historical Collections* 41:67–191; Edgar Allan Poe, "The Journal of Julius Rodman," *Burton's Gentleman's Magazine* 6 (1840). See Charles L. Camp, "Edgar Allan Poe: 1840," in *Henry R. Wagner's The Plains and the Rockies . . . 1800–1865;* David Ketterer, *The Rationale of Deception in Poe*, pp. 141–45.

[37]Lewis and Clark, *Original Journals*, vol. 1, p. 308.
[38]See Richard E. Oglesby, *Manuel Lisa and the Opening of the Missouri Fur Trade;* Dale L. Morgan, *The West of William H. Ashley;* David Lavender, *The Fist in the Wilderness;* and David J. Wishart, *The Fur Trade of the American West, 1807–1840.*

British and Canadian activities there.

Among the several groups of travelers encountered by Lewis and Clark on their return journey down the Missouri in 1806 were Joseph Dixon and Forrest Hancock, who were bound for the Yellowstone River to trap. These two men may have been among the "obscure groups of traders" who ascended the Missouri in 1806–1807 and conducted trapping operations on the western side of the continental divide until 1810, according to Morgan.[39] However, several large, well-organized expeditions were soon making their way up the Missouri.

Manuel Lisa, representing the Missouri Fur Company, left Saint Louis for the upper Missouri in 1807, slightly ahead of the party headed by Nathaniel Pryor and Auguste Pierre Chouteau. The Pryor-Chouteau expedition was a joint military-trading venture with the objectives of returning the Mandan chief, Shahaka, or Big White, who had accompanied Lewis and Clark to Washington the previous winter, to his people and building a trading post near the Mandans. Neither objective was accomplished, for the party was fired on by the Arikaras near the Grand River and was forced to return to Saint Louis. René Jusseaume, who accompanied Big White as interpreter, was wounded in this attack. Lisa's party was more fortunate; it had reached and passed the Arikara vil-

lages before Pryor and Chouteau, and so went on to the mouth of the Big Horn River on the Yellowstone, where Fort Raymond was constructed.[40]

Lisa again ascended the Missouri River to the Mandan villages in the summer of 1809. This expedition, much larger than the earlier Pryor-Chouteau party, passed the Arikara villages without incident and successfully returned Big White to his people. The expedition went on to build a fort a short distance above the Hidatsa villages, the first of several American trading establishments near the mouth of the Knife River.[41] Henry M. Brackenridge, who accompanied a subsequent 1811 Lisa expedition, states that that post "is situated above all the villages, and sixteen hundred and forty miles from the mouth of the Missouri, and in latitude 47°.13′.N." He also described the fort as being "about six miles" from the nearest of the "villages below." However, this latitude description cannot be correct, since it would place the fort below the latitude of the later Fort Clark, which was several miles below the mouth of the Knife.[42] Another visitor to Lisa's Post in 1811, John Bradbury, has stated that the post was seven miles north of the third Hidatsa village, which

---

[39]Lewis and Clark, *Original Journals*, vol. 5, p. 329 ff.; see also Frank H. Dickson, "Hard on the Heel of Lewis and Clark," *Montana: The Magazine of Western History* 26 (January 1976): 14–25; Morgan, *William H. Ashley*, p. xxxi.

[40]Oglesby, *Opening of the Missouri Fur Trade*, pp. 54–62; Lavender, *Fist in the Wilderness*.

[41]Thomas James, *Three Years Among the Indians and Mexicans*.

[42]Reuben Gold Thwaites, ed., *Early Western Travels, 1748–1846*, vol. 6, pp. 138–41; Allen L. Truax, "Manuel Lisa and His North Dakota Trading Post," *North Dakota Historical Quarterly* 2 (July, 1928): 241.

would have been the Big Hidatsa site (see map 1).[43]

The Hudson's Bay Company continued to send trading parties to the Mandan-Hidatsa villages after Lewis and Clark had declared American sovereignty there, although there is no firm evidence that North West Company parties visited the villages between 1806 and 1812. The Brandon House Post Journals document the presence of three and possibly four Hudson's Bay Company trading parties in the villages during the years 1807 to 1809. In contrast, Charles McKenzie, in the opening remarks for his third and fourth expeditions to the villages, states that the North West Company department manager, Pierre Rochblave, only reluctantly sent men to trade in the villages in 1805 and 1806. The absence of any mention in the Brandon House Post Journals of North West Company parties being in the villages after 1806 and before 1812 suggests that the company may have abandoned the Mandan-Hidatsa trade during those years.[44]

Beginning in 1809, the Brandon House masters began to record in their journals occasional remarks about the presence of Americans in the Missouri River villages. In one instance, the reported presence of American trappers there led John McKay, the Brandon House master in 1809, to change his tactics and send men to the villages to trade with the Americans rather than the natives—a decision he later regretted. On September 30, 1809, McKay recorded that three Canadians and two Mandans had arrived at Brandon House, bringing news of Lisa's men at the Missouri: "the Canadians assures me that there is above 2 Hundred American Hunters gone up the Missi Sourie, I imagine they are gone with an intention to establish it."[45]

On October 9, 1809, McKay sent four men back to the villages with the two Mandans to conduct trade with the American trappers. The men returned to Brandon House on December 6, 1809, with a report of being coerced to trade for the poor-quality furs of the natives:

Arrived Wm. Yorstone and and men from the Mandanes and Big Bellies with better than 700 Wolves of the worst quality for which he gave the best of Goods. the Goods were intended for the free Americans but instead of finding Americans he found a Compound of Mallatoes, Negroes Creoles and Canadians from the Illinois under a Mr. Choteau who after selling his for [fur] at the Mandanes returned to the Illinois Wm. Yorstone and Men when finding how things went on, were for coming back immediately but they were stoped by the ~~Canadians~~ [lined out in original] Natives who told

[43]Thwaites, *Early Western Travels*, vol. 5, pp. 152-53, 165.

[44]John A. Alwin, "Pelts, Provisions & Perceptions: The Hudson's Bay Company Mandan Indian Trade, 1795–1812," *Montana: The Magazine of Western History* 29 (July, 1979): 16–27; Charles McKenzie's Narratives. In an 1831 statement based on hearsay evidence, Joshua Pilcher implied in a letter to Secretary of War Lewis Cass that the North West Company conducted an active trade with the Mandans and Hidatsas between 1809 and 1811 (microfilm roll 749, M234, Record Group 75, National Archives, Washington, D.C.).

[45]H.B.C.A., B.22/a/17, fo. 6d.

them that if they would not Trade their Goods for such furs as they had to give they would plunder them our Men were obliged to Comply. this will be a warning to me for the future how far I may believe the Reports of these Rascally Canadians.[46]

This is obviously a reference to the men at Lisa's Post near the mouth of the Knife River, whom Lisa had left there after he and Pierre Chouteau, Sr., one of Lisa's partners in the Missouri Fur Company, departed downriver for Saint Louis. A large part of Lisa's party was composed of American free trappers, whom Lisa had agreed to outfit for trapping operations in the Rocky Mountains; evidently few of these men remained at the fort when the Hudson's Bay Company party arrived there in the fall of 1809.[47] Thomas James, one of the American trappers accompanying Lisa, wrote in his memoir account of the expedition that "On our arrival at their village [that is, at a Hidatsa village], four or five agents of the Hudson's Bay Company were among them, but they immediately crossed the river with their goods and bore off to the northeast."[48]

Although it is clear from the Brandon House Post Journal for the 1809–10 season that no Hudson's Bay Company employees were in the Hidatsa villages at the time of the arrival of Lisa's expedition, James may be referring to the "3 Canadians and 2 Mandanes" who arrived at Brandon House from the "Missi Sourie" on September 30, 1809, bringing news of Lisa's arrival at the villages.[49]

The Hudson's Bay Company sent no expeditions to the Mandan-Hidatsa villages during 1810 and 1811. The reasons for this are not clear, but may include the death of the Brandon House master, John McKay, on July 5, 1810, or a mutiny in the early part of 1811 against Hugh Heney, who had replaced McKay as master.[50] Knowledge of Lisa's party on the Missouri may also have been a factor. Heney's successor at Brandon House, Alexander Kennedy, recorded the arrival of an American trapper at Brandon House on December 23, 1811, with news of the Missouri:

An American with an old Canadian arrived here from the Mandan Villages, they came on a visit, with tobacco to the Inds. a peace offering ~~The proper~~ *[lined out in original] they inform me that very few Americans are wintering on the Sourie and that the Indians there would trade with us if we would send there as they are discontented. with their present Traders. But as their peltries consist only of wolves & Foxes with some Buffalo robes— It would not be worth while in my opinion to* ~~make~~ *[lined out*

[46]H.B.C.A., B.22/a/17, fos. 7, 12–12d.
[47]See James, *Three Years*, pp. 27–33, for Thomas James's first-hand account of the friction between the American trappers and Lisa and his employees.
[48]James, *Three Years*, pp. 26–27. James's statement finds partial corroboration in a December 14, 1809, letter from Pierre Chouteau to the Secretary of War, in which Chouteau relates that before his arrival at the Mandans with the Lisa expedition he was told of three North West Company agents among the Mandans. A typescript of the letter is in the Missouri Historical Society, Chouteau Collection, Box 7, Pierre Chouteau Letterbook, pp. 146–47.

[49]H.B.C.A., B.22/a/17, fo. 6d.
[50]H.B.C.A., B.22/a/18a, fos. 3 and 11.

in original] carry them so far overland, which would be attended with a heavy expence as [lined out in original] at this time of Year horses can't travel so that we would be obliged to purchase horses there which would run away with all our profit. The American who had been a hunter towards the rocky mountains for this two years past, has upwards of 200 Br Skins but he will not part with them at a reasonable price— He says that the Americans will pay him 3 dollars pr # for them.[51]

In the January 2, 1812, entry, Kennedy stated that he was preparing to send Yorston and three men to the Mandan villages with the American trapper, who had promised to trade forty of his beaver skins "for a few articles which he is in want of." The same entry also states that the expedition will be undertaken jointly with a North West Company party provided by "my neighbor Mr Wills" and that "we shall trade jointly, each to supply a proportion of goods—and the returns to be equally divided between us—...."[52]

The expedition was delayed, however, because of a violent quarrel between Yorston and Kennedy on January 5, 1812, over Yorston's participation in the trip.[53] The joint Hudson's Bay–North West Company expedition departed on January 8, 1812, and returned to Brandon House on March 14, 1812: "At 3 PM our people from the Missesourie arrived with very poor returns they

say that the Natives at the Missesourie were prevented from trading with them by the Americans, who held out to them better encouragement than we could afford to give my people bro't about 60 beaver skins a few buffalo Robes 7 wolves and a bear Skin— & my neighbors people the same number They had some difficulty to get away from the Missesourie with the remains of the Goods they took there to trade."[54]

The Americans referred to in this entry were probably Lisa's men, who continued to occupy Lisa's Post, near the mouth of the Knife, which was probably abandoned shortly after Lisa's arrival in the Upper Missouri country from Saint Louis in the summer of 1812.[55]

There is little record of British

---

[51]H.B.C.A., B.22/a/18b, fo. 6d.
[52]H.B.C.A., B.22/a/18b, fo. 7.
[53]H.B.C.A., B.22/a/18b, fos. 7d–8; see also H.B.C.A., A.10/1, fos. 111Dd–111E.

[54]H.B.C.A., B.22/a/18b, fos. 8 and 12.
[55]A careful reading of John C. Luttig's journal written during Manuel Lisa's 1812–13 Upper Missouri expedition, particularly the entries for August 13 and 26, 1812, suggests that Lisa's post above the mouth of the Knife River was closed down in August, 1812. See John C. Luttig, *Journal of a Fur-trading Expedition on the Upper Missouri, 1812-1813*, ed. Stella M. Drumm, pp. 69 and 73. In a letter to the secretary of war dated December 1, 1831, the fur trader Joshua Pilcher stated that Lisa's post had been abandoned before the summer of 1811 because of "some difficulty with the Mandans and *Grosventres*, which may have been produced by the influence of the Northwest Company, which *at that time* had an intercourse with those Indians" (emphasis in original). Pilcher is almost certainly mistaken in his recollection, for the Brandon House Post Journal entry for March 14, 1812 (H.B.C.A., B.22/a/18b, fo. 12), indicates that Lisa's men were still active at the Mandan-Hidatsa villages at that date. Pilcher's letter is in microfilm roll 749, M234, Record Group 75, National Archives.

or Canadian fur trading activities at the Knife River villages during the War of 1812, despite the often-repeated assertion of historians that the British were fomenting anti-American sentiment among the Upper Missouri Indians at that time and were even agitating the natives to take military action against the Americans. Unfortunately, the Brandon House Post Journals for the 1812-13, 1813-14, and 1814-15 seasons—which could be expected to document the nature and extent of British political activities in the Upper Missouri during the War of 1812—are not known to exist.[56]

A Hudson's Bay Company expedition headed by Peter Fidler, then master at Brandon House, visited the Mandan villages in the spring of 1813. Although Fidler's journal for that period has been lost, Fidler referred to his 1813 trip in the March 7, 1818, entry in the Brandon House Post Journal (he was still master at that time). In relating information from some Indians who had recently come from the Mandan villages, Fidler states that "The very fat Tall Indian I saw when at the Mandan Villages Feby 1813, was kiled by his Country people 5 Days before the

Crees reached them—or about 12t last Month."[57]

The Fidler expedition of 1813 is also mentioned in several entries in the journal kept by Miles Macdonell, governor of Lord Selkirk's Red River Colony. On February 27, 1813, Macdonell recorded that "Mr. Fidler & Kiveny left there [that is, Brandon House] to go to the Missouri on 9th Inst. [that is, February 9, 1813] with 8 men & expect to be back by the 6th. March."[58] Fidler's return to Brandon House was nearly on schedule, for on March 18, 1813, Macdonell recorded that "Messrs. Fidler & Kivney reached Brand Ho. from the Mississaurie 8th. inst. [that is, March 8, 1813] & brot. Indian Corn, Beans, Pumpkins, & Tobacco for seed for the Colony."[59] No mention is made of the furs brought back by the expedition, but it is clear that the agricultural crop seed would have been sorely needed by the newly arrived settlers at the Red River Colony that spring.[60]

The War of 1812 disrupted American trading activities in the Upper Missouri. Lisa's Post near the Man-

[56]Luttig, *Journal of a Fur-trading Expedition*, p. 23; Oglesby, *Opening of the Missouri Fur Trade*, p. 133. Writing many years after the War of 1812, a former Lisa employee, Thomas James, recalled that the Hudson's Bay Company had "emissaries" among the Teton Dakota Indians at the mouth of the James River in 1809 (James, *Three Years*, p. 21). These "emissaries" are not documented in the Brandon House Post Journals, and if they were among the Tetons at all, they may have been from some other Hudson's Bay Company post.

[57]H.B.C.A., B.22/a/20, fo. 36d.
[58]P.A.C., MG 19, E1, vol. 62, microfilm roll C-16, pp. 16798-99.
[59]P.A.C., MG 19, E1, vol. 62, microfilm roll C-16, pp. 16807-808. The man identified as "Kiveny" and "Kivney" was probably Owen Keveny, who led Lord Selkirk's party of Irish and Scottish immigrants from Europe to the Red River Colony in 1812. He became a principal lieutenant of Miles Macdonell, the governor of the colony, and was murdered in 1816 by Charles Reinhard, an agent of the North West Company (Morton, *Canadian West*, pp. 549-82).
[60]Alexander Ross, *The Red River Settlement: Its Rise, Progress, and Present State*, pp. 23-24; Morton, *Canadian West*, pp. 550-53.

dans appears to have been abandoned in 1812, and he made an unsuccessful attempt to establish another post north of the Arikara villages above the Grand River in the winter of 1812–13. Following his failure, Lisa restricted his operations to the lower reaches of the Missouri River.[61] For several years thereafter, Americans considered building a series of military posts on the Upper Missouri, and an expedition was initiated for that purpose in 1818, but no American establishment was actually built near the Mandans and Hidatsas until late in 1822.

The next surviving Brandon House Post Journal following the gap in these records for the years during the War of 1812 relates to the 1815–16 trading season. In it, Peter Fidler records that a Hudson's Bay Company expedition to the Missouri was proposed for the spring of 1816 but was canceled by the governor of the Red River Colony for want of "a proper assortment of Goods to send there."[62]

During the winter of 1816–17, the North West Company sent two trading parties to the Mandans. The first party returned with news that the Mandans had "a considerable number of Beaver Skins," of which the Nor'westers were only able to trade for enough for two packs because of a shortage of trade goods. A second North West Company expedition attempted to reach the Mandans to trade for these skins but was forced to return by the Assiniboin or "Stone" Indians.[63]

The following November, Fidler made an agreement with his North West Company neighbor, John Haldane, to send a strong joint expedition to the villages. Fidler and Haldane agreed that each company should send "exactly the same kind & quantity of Goods" and that the returns would be divided equally between them, as "this is the general custom when we have formerly sent to that place." Fidler dispatched eight men for the villages on November 15, 1817, with a horse-drawn cart loaded with goods, and the North West Company sent a similar complement.[64] The joint expedition returned to the Assiniboine River forts one month later to the day, on December 15, 1817, with furs and horses worth over four times the value of the goods taken to the Mandan villages. While in the villages, the Hudson's Bay party lost three horses, and the Nor'westers two horses, to thieves. Fidler complained that replacement horses were traded from the Indians at a "very dear" cost, "near double the price we give for them in this Quarter." He also recorded that many of the furs brought back from the villages were marked and suggested that they had probably been plundered from American trappers, although he also reported that "our people could not learn from the natives of any Americans being higher up the Missouri than the Osage nation, where they Say they have a fort and garrison."[65] This is evidently a

[61]Luttig, *Journal of a Fur-trading Expedition*; Oglesby, *Opening of the Missouri Fur Trade*.

[62]H.B.C.A., B.22/a/19, fos. 15d–16d.

[63]H.B.C.A., B.22/a/20, fo. 21.

[64]H.B.C.A., B.22/a/20, fo. 21.

reference to Fort Osage, which was constructed on the lower Missouri River Under the direction of William Clark, in 1808 and garrisoned by the U.S. Army. The returns were divided equally between the two companies on the following day, and the hunter and interpreter engaged for the trip were paid in buffalo robes from the returns.

In 1818 the U.S. government initiated a joint military and scientific expedition to establish a series of military posts between the Yellowstone River and Fort Osage, the most westerly military establishment on the Missouri (located in modern Jackson County, Missouri, about twenty miles east of Kansas City). The expedition reached what is now Washington County, Nebraska, in the summer of 1819 and built a temporary cantonment, which was later moved to a blufftop location and named Fort Atkinson in honor of the expedition's leader, Colonel Henry Atkinson.[66] With funding cut by Congress, the expedition did not proceed past Fort Atkinson. However, it appears that word of the planned expedition may have reached Peter Fidler as early as March, 1818. In an entry dated March 7, 1818, Fidler recorded some information recently brought to him by a family of Cree Indians, just returned from a visit to the Mandans, who told him "that many of the Americans are low down the Missouri & that they learn they

are in the Spring coming up to make a Trading post at their Villages where Mesr Clark & Lewis wintered in 1804-5."[67]

Despite continued recommendations for a military fort at least as far upriver as the Mandan villages,[68] a post was not built near the mouth of the Knife River until 1822, and then it was a civilian commercial establishment, Fort Vanderburgh.

The last trading party sent to the Mandan villages by the Hudson's Bay Company for which we have documentary evidence was in the fall of 1818 and was a joint effort by Brandon House personnel and Red River Colony settlers. The expedition's primary purpose was to obtain horses for the Red River colonists, although two Brandon House employees went along to trade for furs. Accounts of the expedition survive in the 1818–19 Brandon House Post Journal kept by Peter Fidler and in a letter written by Archibald McDonald, the expedition's leader.[69]

On October 18, 1818, Fidler recorded in his journal that an Indian, recently arrived from the Mandans, brought an invitation from the villagers to send men there to trade for beaver skins. The Indian reported that they may have had as many as 200 beaver pelts. Word

[65]H.B.C.A., B.22/a/20, fos. 24–25.
[66]Morgan, *William H. Ashley*, p. xlviii; John Gale, *The Missouri Expedition, 1818-1820: The Journal of Surgeon John Gale, with Related Documents*, ed. Roger L. Nichols, pp. 77–88, 114–18.

[67]H.B.C.A., B.22/a/20, fo. 36d.
[68]Morgan, *William H. Ashley*, p. liii.
[69]The Brandon House Post Journal entries are found in H.B.C.A., B.22/a/21, fos. 34d, 37–38d, and 39d–40. McDonald's January 9, 1819, letter is in P.A.C., MG 19, E1, vol. 53, microfilm reel C-19, pp. 20520–27; see Jean M. Cole, *Exile in the Wilderness: The Biography of Chief Factor Archibald McDonald, 1790-1853*, pp. 85-86, for an abridged version.

reached Fidler on November 14 that the Red River colonists were mounting an expedition to the Mandan villages to trade for horses. Snowfall impeded the progress of this expedition, with the result that it halted about "2 Days walk" from Brandon House. When the party's leader, Archibald McDonald, and one other man, a Brandon House employee who had accompanied the group from the colony, arrived at Brandon House on November 28 to obtain dogs and sleds to replace their horse-drawn carts, Fidler decided to send another of his men along to trade for furs.[70]

When McDonald and his fellow travelers returned to the point where he had left his party, he found that all of the colonists had become alarmed at reports of nearby Indians and had returned to Red River, abandoning the goods. Fortunately, McDonald soon encountered an Indian family that had taken the expedition's goods into their care. Undeterred but angry at the cowardice of the colonists, McDonald proceeded to the Mandan villages with the goods and four companions, two of whom were Brandon House employees. The little group reached the Mandans on December 12 and spent six days among them trading for horses and furs. The men returned to Brandon House on December 26 with nearly 170 beaver skins and a few fox pelts. At Brandon House, Fidler recorded in his journal that the Mandans had informed his men that the Americans, who were presently "300 miles below," intended to settle at the Man-

dan villages the following spring. He also recorded that the "upper" village contained forty-four houses.[71]

After leaving the Brandon House men at their post, McDonald continued on to the Red River Colony with the nine horses that he had obtained at the Mandans. He later recorded that horses at the villages were "not so cheap or numerous as I had reason to expect at first."[72] Apparently the nine horses were not sufficient for the colony. Peter Fidler recorded in the Brandon House Post Journal on February 19, 1819, that McDonald was sending six men to the Saskatchewan River "to bring horses for the Settlement."[73] According to Fidler, the party expected to return with one hundred horses.

In April, 1819, Fidler made plans again to send men to trade with the Mandans. However, this time he intended to avoid any Americans who might be at the villages by asking the Indians to meet his people part way. His Brandon House Post Journal entry for April 6 reads:

Tyed up one fathom of Tobacco & sealed it & gave it to Blindy [probably a Cree or Assiniboin Indian], he with 4 others are going to the Mandan villages— this Tobacco is sent as a present to the Mandan chief— and also sent him word that at the Full Moon just after the Missouri freezes over which will be the Beginning of December next we will send men there with Trading Goods and

---

[70]H.B.C.A., B.22/a/21, fos. 34d, 37, 38.

[71]P.A.C., MG 19, E1, vol. 53, microfilm reel C-19, pp. 20525–26; Cole, *Exile*, p. 86; H.B.C.A., B.22/a/21, fo. 40.

[72]P.A.C., MG 19, E1, vol. 53, microfilm reel C-19, p. 20526; see also Cole, *Exile*, p. 86.

[73]H.B.C.A., B.22/a/21, fo. 44.

*for all those who have any furs to barter
to carry them to the upper village &
there meet us— and in case the Americans should go to settle there this summer as reported they intend to do— for
the Natives to meet us at the Dogs house
hill [probably Dog Den Butte, in northeastern McLean County, North Dakota]
which is nearly in the direct road from
this House to their villages.*[74]

Four days later, on April 10, Fidler regretfully recorded Blindy's unexpected return to Brandon House
without having delivered the message: "Blindy who went to the Mandans a few Days ago by which I send
a present of Tobacco & a Messuage
to the Chief returned— having been
only part of the way either fear or
laziness or both was the cause of
their sudden return I got the Tobacco
again."[75]

Brandon House continued in operation until 1824, but none of the
journals of the 1819–20 trading season to 1824 have been preserved.
Consequently, the last record we
have of Hudson's Bay Company
trade at the Mandan and Hidatsa
villages is McDonald's expedition
during the fall of 1818. Although it
is clear from later entries that at
least one more Hudson's Bay Company expedition was planned, there
is no evidence for any visits to the
Knife River villages by traders from
Canada after 1818.

The Americans, however, continued to be concerned about British
and Canadian trading activities on
the Upper Missouri. In 1820, General Henry Atkinson, commander of
the garrison at Fort Atkinson, the
most westerly American military establishment, twice wrote Secretary of
War John C. Calhoun to recommend
that troops be sent up the Missouri
at least as far as the Mandan villages
to counter the influence of British
traders there. William Clark, governor of Missouri Territory, was especially alarmed at rumors of British
traders in the Upper Missouri. On
January 16, 1823, and again on July
4, 1823, he wrote letters to Secretary
Calhoun reporting that the British
had erected trading posts near or on
the Missouri River in the vicinity
of the Mandans and Arikaras. However, as Morgan points out, Clark
was mistaken.[76] By the date of Clark's
letters, an American trading post
(Tilton's Post) was established and
operating at the Mandan village, but
no Canadian posts were closer than
the Assiniboine River.

Joshua Pilcher, a leading figure
in the Missouri Fur Company after
Manuel Lisa's death in 1820, stated
in 1824 to the Senate Committee on
Indian Affairs that he first visited
the Arikaras in September of 1822
while en route to the Mandans and
Hidatsas to build a trading post.
The fort which Pilcher erected during the fall of 1822, named Fort Vanderburgh after the man left in charge
of its operation, William Henry Vanderburgh, was ordered destroyed in
the spring or summer of 1823 after
the destruction of a company party
in the Blackfeet country and sustained competition from the so-called

---

[74]H.B.C.A., B.22/a/21, fo. 48d.
[75]H.B.C.A., B.22/a/21, fo. 49.

[76]Morgan, *William H. Ashley*, pp. liii, 20,
46, 239–40.

French Company headed by Bernard Pratte and his associates.[77]

Fort Vanderburgh was soon replaced by another post built by a different fur-trading company. James Kipp, representing the newly formed Columbia Fur Company, built a trading establishment near the Mandan village in May through November of 1823 which came to be called Tilton's Post after the nominal head of the company and actual manager of the post. That was the year when the Arikaras attacked and inflicted serious losses on William H. Ashley's party of trappers bound for the Rocky Mountains and when a punitive military expedition from Fort Atkinson shelled the Arikara villages in retaliation. Consequently, because of Arikara harassment after these incidents, culminating in the death of one of the company's employees, Kipp and Tilton both took up residence in the Mandan village, probably in 1824. During the summer of 1825, with the help of the Mandans, Kipp dismantled the abandoned Tilton's Post and used the salvaged timbers to enlarge and fortify his house near the Mandan village. In November, 1826, Kipp left the Knife River area to build and operate a post further up the Missouri at the mouth of the White Earth River, and it is unclear from published records whether or not the Mandan post continued in use after that time.[78]

In July, 1827, the Columbia Fur Company merged with the American Fur Company to form the Upper Missouri Outfit of the latter concern. The Upper Missouri Outfit constructed Fort Clark at the Mandan village about 1831, and that fort served as one of the company's major Missouri River posts for the next three decades.[79]

Many authorities, evidently beginning with Hiram Chittenden in his classic study of the American fur trade and continuing through Pilcher's biographer,[80] have placed Fort Vanderburgh several miles north of the mouth of the Knife River at a location near or identical with that occupied by the earlier post of Manuel Lisa. However, the most reliable information on this subject is provided by Prince Maximilian's travel narrative and a manuscript map of William Clark's, annotated by Maximilian. Maximilian passed by the site of Fort Vanderburgh on a steamboat about ten years after the fort's abandonment. In his narrative he describes the site as "about eleven miles from Fort Clark" (with respect to a downstream voyage) north of the "first Manitari summer village" (meaning the Big Hidatsa site), and as being "on the left bank, where the

[77]Ibid., pp. 24, 41, 157, 175; John E. Sunder, *Joshua Pilcher, Fur Trader and Indian Agent*, pp. 38–41, 54.

[78]Thwaites, *Early Western Travels*, vol. 23, pp. 223–28; Morgan, *William H. Ashley*, pp. 59–60. Maximilian is the best authority on Kipp's activities among the Mandans in the 1820s.

[79]Morgan, *William H. Ashley*, pp. 61, 246; John E. Sunder, *The Fur Trade on the Upper Missouri*, 1840–1865, p. 46.

[80]Hiram M. Chittenden, *The American Fur Trade of the Far West*, vol. 2, p. 957; Sunder, *Joshua Pilcher*, pp. 38–39; see also Thwaites, *Early Western Travels*, vol. 23, p. 364, and Ray H. Mattison, "Report on Historic Sites in the Garrison Reservoir Area, Missouri River," *North Dakota History* 22 (January–April, 1955): 24–25.

river is bounded by steep high hills." Maximilian also mentions that Pilcher "directed a trading post a little above the Manitari villages on the southern coast [that is, bank of the river]," which was abandoned in the spring of 1822 (Thwaites corrects Maximilian's date to 1823).[81] Maximilian carried with him during his Upper Missouri travels a copy of a manuscript map that William Clark had originally made during the Lewis and Clark expedition. Sheet 18 of this map has been published; it depicts a location approximately two miles north of the Big Hidatsa site which is labeled, in Maximilian's hand, as "Pilchers Post."[82]

Consequently, it is likely that Fort Vanderburgh was built only a short distance north of the Big Hidatsa site and not several miles farther to the north, on the former site of Lisa's Post, as is commonly believed (map 2).

During the time that Fort Vanderburgh and its successors were operating at the Mandans, there is no record of visits to the Mandan or Hidatsa villages by Canadian traders. In 1824, Joshua Pilcher offered testimony to the Senate Committee on Indian Affairs regarding the state of the fur trade along the Upper Missouri. In answer to the question, "What is the temper of the tribes which have an intercourse with British traders towards American citizens?" Pilcher responded:

It will be seen, from my answer to preceding questions, that the disposition of such tribes of Indians as have intercourse with British traders, particularly the Blackfeet, has been uniformly hostile towards American citizens, in so much that they have had no intercourse with any of those tribes, with the exception of the Mandans and Minatares. It has not been long since British traders had intercourse with these tribes; but they have been so reduced by war and pestilence, the quantity of furs obtained from them at present is so small, and the American trade having been introduced amongst them, that there has been no intercourse, to my knowledge, for the last two or three years.[83]

Pilcher's statement finds some confirmation in a letter dated November 23, 1825, in which Major General Jacob J. Brown, commander in chief of the U.S. Army, replied to yet another recommendation from Brigadier General Henry Atkinson that a military post be established among the Mandans:

With regard to the propriety of establishing a military post near the Mandans, as suggested by your communication of 21st July, it will be seen, by reference to the report of the commissioners, that no circumstances, either relating to the conduct of the British traders in a supposed intercourse with our Indians in that quarter, or as relates to the Indians themselves, would call for such a measure. The British traders, as stated in the re-

[81]Thwaites, *Early Western Travels*, vol. 23, p. 364; vol. 24, pp. 219, 223.

[82]W. Raymond Wood and Gary E. Moulton, "Prince Maximilian and New Maps of the Missouri and Yellowstone Rivers by William Clark," *Western Historical Quarterly* 12 (October, 1981): 376; Gary E. Moulton, ed., *The Journals of the Lewis and Clark Expedition*, map 29.

[83]*American State Papers*, Indian Affairs, vol. 2, p. 456.

port, never, of latter years, visit the Indians residing on the Missouri below the falls of that river, nor do those Indians visit the British establishments on Red River.[84]

It therefore appears that trading visits to the Mandan and Hidatsa villages by Canadian traders entirely ceased sometime between 1818, the date of the last documented expedition from Canada, and 1822, when the first of an almost continuous series of American trading posts was established among the villages at the mouth of the Knife River.

Documentation that the Mandans and Hidatsas were carrying goods north to exchange with the Canadian traders along the Assiniboine after 1818 is also sparse. In an undated reference to Mandan trade along the Assiniboine, the former Hudson's Bay Company employee Isaac Cowie remarked: "The Brandon House was resorted to by a number of different tribes, but principally depended upon the Assiniboines and Crees for its fur trade. To it also came the Mandans of the Missouri, bringing, besides the skins and meat of the buffalo, their Indian corn for sale." A much later reference to the same activities alludes to trade at Fort Ellice, which was at the mouth of the Qu'Apelle River: "The remnant of the Mandans came to it at peril of their lives, and it was resorted to by natives from a wide tract of country quite regardless of the international boundary, with no posts nearer than Portage la Prairie on the east, Fort Pelly on the north, and

Carlton House on the northwest, and none on British territory to the west."[85]

THE EARLIEST RESIDENT TRADERS

A number of free traders lived, either permanently or intermittently, in the Mandan and Hidatsa villages beginning about 1776. In the Brandon House Post Journals these men are called "residenters." Donald J. Lehmer called them "tenant traders."[86] The number of such men living in the Knife River villages may have been substantial, although only a few of them are named in the records available. Larocque, for instance, recorded on June 24, 1805, that "Lafrance, with the other white people from below, who reside at the Mandans," came to the Hidatsa villages to see a group of newly arrived Crow Indians.[87] Most of these men had native wives and children in the villages—families who lived and dressed much as did the other villagers, except that they would have had more ready access to trade goods than their neighbors. Save for Charbonneau's wife Sacagawea and her children, we know almost nothing of these families, although it is likely that many wives (like Sacagawea) had been slaves before they were purchased by their husbands.

Our records of such individuals are so incomplete that some resi-

[84]Ibid., vol. 2, p. 656.

[85]Isaac Cowie, *The Company of Adventurers . . .*, pp. 178, 180.

[86]Donald J. Lehmer, *Introduction to Middle Missouri Archeology*, National Park Service Anthropological Papers, no. 1, p. 169.

[87]François-Antoine Larocque's "Yellowstone Journal," ms. p. 7.

denters may have escaped mention in the surviving documents. In this context, it is worth keeping in mind that Toussaint Charbonneau — certainly one of the better-known and more long-lived residents — is nowhere mentioned in the Brandon House Post Journals, which is the longest and most continuous record of a single company's dealings at the villages. These free traders apparently at times took employment with the fur companies or conducted trade with them on a credit basis: that is, they traded in the villages goods obtained on credit from the companies with a promise to repay in furs obtained from the villagers. One reason that some individuals may be neglected in the fur company records is probably that they were never formally connected with the North West Company or the Hudson's Bay Company and are therefore not mentioned in the business records of those firms. Among the more prominent residenters were:

Cardin, — — —	La France, Jean Baptiste
Charbonneau, Toussaint	La Grave, François
"Chayé"	McCrachan, Hugh
Colter, John	Ménard, — — —
Garreau, Joseph	Morgan, — — —
Holmes, Samuel	"Roi"
Heney, Hughes (Hugh)	"Sooiee"
Jusseaume, René	Taylor, Robert

The earliest known Euro-American to become established as a resident in the Mandan and Hidatsa villages was a French Canadian named Ménard; his first name is lost to us.

Although he was one of the best known of the residents of those villages to contemporaries, his name is nevertheless spelled in their journals as differently as Mahnow, Manoah, Manor, Manore, Menire, Menor, Minor, and Minore. The date of his arrival at the villages and most other details of his life there are not at all clear. He appears to have lived in the village now known as the Sakakawea site (map 2). His wife was "a native woman, fair and graceful." David Thompson said that they had no children and that Ménard "was in every respect as a Native." Six contemporary sources, many of them by men who knew him personally or had corresponded with him — and who thus may have obtained firsthand information on the subject from Ménard himself — provide dates for his arrival between 1778 and 1783.[88]

[88]Two sources have suggested Ménard's first name, but neither has provided supporting documentation. In a footnote to the anonymously edited "Trudeau's Journal" (Jean Baptiste Truteau, "Trudeau's Journal," *South Dakota Historical Collections* 7: 404 n. 16), he is identified as "François Ménard, of Florisan." Ewers ("Indian Trade," p. 442) gives his name as Pierre Ménard. David Thompson, "David Thompson at the Mandan-Hidatsa Villages, 1797–1798: The Original Journals," ed. W. Raymond Wood, *Ethnohistory* 24 (Fall, 1977): 334; David Thompson, *David Thompson's Narrative of His Explorations*, pp. 226, 230. Following his expedition to the Mandans in 1792, D'Église, who had visited Ménard there, said that Ménard had "been with this nation for fourteen years," or since 1778 (Nasatir, *Before Lewis and Clark*, vol. 1, p. 161; DeVoto, *Course of Empire*, p. 601 n. 13). Three other references refer to Ménard's having lived with the Mandans for sixteen years. Juan Fotman (Tremont) testified in 1795 of his sixteen years' residence, but his testimony pertains

It may well have been Ménard's residence among the villagers that led Alexander Henry the Younger to state (in his journal entry for July 20, 1806) that it had been no more than thirty years (or since about 1776) since the Mandans "first saw any of us."[89]

Ménard was apparently a major source of information about the Upper Missouri, for no less than eleven contemporary sources mention him and information relative to the area: D'Église, Fotman (Tremont), Collot, Truteau, Larocque, McKenzie, Thompson, Tabeau, Clark, Henry, and the Brandon House Post Journals.[90] Five of these sources indicate that he had firsthand knowl-

edge of the Rocky Mountains and of the Missouri Valley above the Mandans, including the Yellowstone River.[91] He had been to visit the Crow Indians in what is now eastern Montana several times in the company of the Hidatsas—and once, on his own, he had been robbed by the Crows and had barely made it back to the Missouri River with his life. His visits to the Rocky Mountains, as well as his trip or trips to the Yellowstone River, are all at unspecified dates.[92] Charles McKenzie in 1806 noted that Ménard "had lately

---

to events that took place in 1794, so the year of his arrival could have been 1778 or 1779 (Nasatir, *Before Lewis and Clark*, vol. 1, p. 331). Victor Collot met Ménard in or near Saint Louis in 1796, commenting that he had lived *more than* sixteen years among the Mandans, placing his arrival in 1780 or before (Victor Collot, *A Journey in North America*, vol. 1, p. 292). Jean Baptiste Truteau, who had corresponded with Ménard during his 1794–95 expedition up the Missouri River, repeats the sixteen years' residence, implying his arrival in 1779 or 1780 (Nasatir, *Before Lewis and Clark*, vol. 2, p. 381). David Thompson, in his "fair journal" entry for January 5, 1798, alluded to Ménard as a "frenchman who is naturalized here by a residence of 15 years," or since 1782–83 (Thompson, "Mandan-Hidatsa Villages," p. 334, and David Thompson's Journal).

[89]Alexander Henry [the Younger], *New Light on the Early History of the Greater Northwest*, vol. 1, p. 341.

[90]For Jacques D'Église, see Nasatir, *Before Lewis and Clark*, vol. 1, p. 161. For Juan Fotman (Tremont), see ibid., p. 331. For Victor Collot, see Collot, *Journey in North America*, vol. 1, p. 292. For Jean Baptiste Truteau, see Nasatir, *Before Lewis and Clark*, vol. 2, pp. 376–82. For François-Antoine Larocque, see Larocque's "Yellowstone Jour-

nal," entry for June 15, 1805. For Charles McKenzie, see Charles McKenzie's Narratives, second expedition account, ms. p. 49. For David Thompson, see Thompson, *David Thompson's Narrative of His Explorations*, pp. 226–27, 230, 235; Thompson, "Mandan-Hidatsa Villages," p. 334; and Thompson's Journal, "fair journal," entry for January 5, 1798. For Pierre-Antoine Tabeau, see Tabeau, *Tabeau's Narrative*, p. 167. For William Clark, see Lewis and Clark, *Original Journals*, vol. 1, p. 205. For Alexander Henry, see Henry, *New Light*, vol. 1, pp. 311–12. For the Brandon House Post Journals, see the entries for April 26, 1798 (H.B.C.A., B.22/a/5, fos. 34d–35), September 29, 1798 (B.22/a/6, fo. 1), September 30, 1799 (B.22/a/7, fo. 1), October 2, 1799 (B.22/a/7, fo. 4), December 19, 1799 (B.22/a/7, fo. 10), March 30, 1804 (B.22/a/11, fo. 8), September 14, 1804 (B.22/a/12, fo. 5d), October 21, 1804 (B.22/a/12, fo. 7), October 22, 1804 (B.22/a/12, fo. 7), and February 27, 1805 (B.22/a/12, fos. 9d–10).

[91]For Fotman, see Nasatir, *Before Lewis and Clark*, vol. 1, pp. 332–33. For Truteau, see ibid., vol. 2, p. 381. For Collot, see Collot, *Journey in North America*, vol. 1, pp. 291–93. For Larocque, see Larocque's "Yellowstone Journal," entries for June 15 and 27, 1805. For McKenzie, see McKenzie's Narratives, second expedition account, ms. p. 49.

[92]Nasatir, *Before Lewis and Clark*, vol. 2, p. 381; and Larocque's "Yellowstone Journal," entry for June 15, 1805.

been rambling among the Rocky Mountains" and had reported that beavers were numerous there.[93] This information may well have provided the impetus for Larocque's assignment by Charles Chaboillez at Fort Montagne à la Bosse to visit the Crow Indians in the Rocky Mountains in 1805.

Surviving documents seldom afford us a glimpse into the personalities of the traders. However, John McKay, the master at Brandon House for the 1797–98 season, recorded in his journal an amusing incident which provides an insight into both his character and that of Ménard:

yesterday I heard the Canadians that went to the Mandles with several of the Natives from that place were expected in to Day, in consequence of which, last night after Dark, I sent James Sleter, Tom Tavill, Jno Lyons and Louis Jolly Caur, off to meet them. there is a Menor an old residenter amongst them who promised me his Furrs, provided I would send to meet him. this morning the men returned, and acquainted me that Menor had given all his Furrs to the Canadians [that is, to the North West Company] notwithstanding Menors Duplicity, he paid me a visit this Day, with some of the Mandles, he offered to sell me 3 fine Horses and a Slave Girl, to be paid next Fall, I told him to sell his Horses and Slaves where he sold his Furrs, that Birds of a Feather should all go to geather, the old Fellow pricked at what I said, says, Sir you are a stranger to me, but I perceive by what you say you mean to pass an affront on me and all my Country men. I told

him if all his Country men were like him, they Deserved to be affronted everywhere, and that if he Did not find the door quickly I would let him know what a man deserved that broke his word. he soon found the door, and I do not believe he will visit me in a hurry again.[94]

Ménard lived a quarter of a century at the Mandan and Hidatsa villages. He was murdered by Assiniboin Indians sometime between September 14, 1804, when he arrived at Brandon House in the company of Hugh Heney, and October 21, 1804, when word of his death reached Brandon House. He had been slain while returning to the Knife River villages from his visit to the Assiniboine River. His death, and the loss of his services as an interpreter in the villages, was lamented by John McKay, the master of Brandon House.[95]

Other tenant traders soon joined Ménard at the villages. René Jusseaume was to become one of the better known among them. He is known under a variety of spellings of his name, all of them save "Gissom" being readily recognizable. He apparently lived in the Mandan vil-

[93]McKenzie's Narratives, second expedition account, ms. p. 49.

[94]H.B.C.A., B.22/a/5, fos. 34d–35. John C. Jackson advises that "Tom Tavill" is actually Tom Favel (personal communication, October 12, 1982).

[95]H.B.C.A., B.22/a/12, fos. 5d, 9d–10; and B.22/a/12, fo. 7. Annie H. Abel says that he died about ten years earlier, but it is clear that her information pertains to another man. Tabeau simply mentions that Ménard "was massacred lately on returning from the English forts" (Tabeau, *Tabeau's Narrative*, pp. 167–68, note 21). Alexander Henry, in his journal entry for July 16, 1806, incorrectly gives 1803 as the year of his demise (Henry, *New Light*, vol. 1, pp. 311–12).

lage now known as the Deapolis site (map 2), where he had "a wife and family who dress and live like the natives."[96] Contemporary accounts of him are not especially flattering, one describing him as an "old sneaking cheat."[97] Two contemporary writers, both of whom knew him, provide statements on the length of his residence in the villages, which apparently began between 1789 and 1791.[98] The earliest mention of him is in John Macdonell's diary entry for April 13, 1794, in which he and a man named Cardin are reported to have arrived at Fort Espérance with a North West Company party returning from the Missouri.[99] He was apparently already a "residenter" at that early date.

Jusseaume led a North West Company expedition to the villages on October 17, 1794. While most of the men returned to Montagne à la Bosse on December 19, Jusseaume remained in the villages and did not return to the Assiniboine River until the following May 6. It was during this expedition that the company erected "a small fort and a hut" between the Mandan and Hidatsa villages under his leadership, which we refer to as Jusseaume's Post (map 2). Other documents describe his 1797 confrontation at the villages with the Spanish agent John Evans. Evans, who had seized and occupied the North West Company post Jusseaume had built, recorded that Jusseaume had tried to kill him but had been prevented from doing so by the Indians. Jusseaume later served as guide and interpreter for David Thompson's 1797-98 visit to the Missouri River. He was also engaged as an interpreter for the Lewis and Clark Expedition in 1804, and he accompanied the expedition to Washington two years later. A member of Nathaniel Pryor's party that attempted to return the Mandan chief Big White to the Knife River villages in 1807, Jusseaume was wounded when Pryor's party was attacked and forced back downriver by Arikara and Sioux Indians. He was not able to return to the villages until 1809, when Manuel Lisa's party ascended the Missouri River.[100]

The most famous of the white residents at the Knife River villages, however, is Toussaint Charbonneau, largely because of his marriage to

[96] Lewis and Clark, *Original Journals*, vol. 1, p. 209; Henry, *New Light*, vol. 1, p. 333.

[97] Henry, *New Light*, vol. 1, pp. 333, 401; see also McKenzie's Narratives, fourth expedition account.

[98] David Thompson, writing of the period 1797-98, says that Jusseaume "had resided eight years in their villages" (Thompson, *David Thompson's Narrative of His Explorations*, p. 209), which would place his arrival in 1789 or 1790. Alexander Henry recorded in his journal on July 20, 1806, that Jusseaume had lived on the Missouri "for upward of 15 years" (Henry, *New Light*, vol. 1, p. 333), or since 1791 or earlier. Toussaint Charbonneau, another free trader living in the villages, told Maximilian in 1833 or 1834 that he was "the only White man" in the Hidatsa villages when he first arrived there about 1796 or 1797 (Thwaites, *Early Western Travels*, vol. 23, p. 230), but this is contradicted by accounts which document Jusseaume and Ménard as living (at least intermittently) in the villages before Charbonneau said he arrived.

[99] W. Raymond Wood, ed., "Journal of John Macdonell, 1793-1795," p. 104.

[100] Ibid., pp. 119, 137; H.B.C.A., B. 22/a/2, fo. 19d; Nasatir, *Before Lewis and Clark*, vol. 1, p. 331; vol. 2, pp. 495-97; Thompson, *David Thompson's Narrative of His Explorations*, p. 209 ff; Thompson's Journal, "fair journal," ms. page 3a, Lewis and

the Shoshoni slave girl Sacagawea and their subsequent association with the Lewis and Clark Expedition. Born in or near Montreal about 1759, he is believed to have settled among the Hidatsas and Mandans in the period between 1796 and 1799.[101] Charbonneau continued to live in the Knife River villages until at least 1839 and possibly until his death sometime between 1839 and 1843, except for occasional periods of residence elsewhere resulting from temporary employment with various trading companies and the U.S. government. He is mentioned in nearly every major firsthand account of the Upper Missouri from the time of the Lewis and Clark Expedition through the late 1830s. It is therefore strange that he is nowhere mentioned in the Brandon House Post Journals, which often document dealings with his fellow residenters—probably a clue that he had no association with the Hudson's Bay Company and thus did not earn mention in the business records of that company. Before having settled in the Mandan-Hidatsa villages, he seems to have been an employee of the North West Company at Pine

Fort along the Assiniboine River.[102] In 1833, Prince Maximilian noted that Charbonneau lived in the middle village of the Hidatsas, now known as the Sakakawea site (map 2).[103]

Resident free traders probably traded furs, horses, food, slave women, and other material to fur company trading parties visiting the villages. They also appear to have been frequent visitors at the Assiniboine River posts, as numerous entries in the Brandon House Post Journals and in John Macdonell's diary at Fort Espérance reveal. The Brandon House Post Journals show that as early as December, 1793, "Two Canadians from the Missisurrie River arrived at the Canadian houses" with a great number of buffalo robes.[104] The amount of goods traded by such resident traders, however, was probably significantly less than the goods imported by parties from the Assiniboine River.

Clark, *Original Journals*, vol. 1, p. 209; Lavender, *Fist in the Wilderness*, pp. 95–118.

[101]Several biographical sketches of Charbonneau's life are available, including Stella M. Drumm, in Luttig's *Journal of a Fur-trading Expedition*; LeRoy R. Hafen, "Touissaint Charbonneau," in *The Mountain Men and the Fur Trade of the Far West*, vol. 9, ed. L. R. Hafen, pp. 53–62; and Dennis R. Ottoson, "Toussaint Charbonneau, a Most Durable Man," *South Dakota History* 6 (Spring, 1976): 152–85. See also Thwaites, *Early Western Travels*, vol. 22, p. 345; vol. 23, pp. 222, 229, 237; and Frank H. Stewart, "Mandan and Hidatsa Villages in the Eighteenth and Nineteenth Centuries," *Plains Anthropologist* 19 (November, 1974): 83–84.

[102]Macdonell's journal (Wood, "Journal of John Macdonell") carried eleven references to him in the period between 1793 and 1795.

[103]Thwaites, *Early Western Travels*, vol. 23, p. 357. Larocque's "Missouri Journal" (entry for November 24, 1804) mentions that the lower village of the Hidatsas was his usual place of residence, although the identification with the Sakakawea site in this case is not certain. We have used the spelling Sacagawea for references to the Indian woman because that is the spelling preferred by Lewis and Clark scholars. Because the spelling Sakakawea has been used by archaeologists in reference to the archaeological site of that name, this convention has been followed.

[104]L. R. Masson, *Les Bourgeois de la Compagnie du Nord-Ouest*, vol. 1, pp. 283–95, provides a much abbreviated version; for a full transcription, see Wood, "Journal of John Macdonell"; H.B.C.A., B.22/a/1, fo. 13d.

3

Some Aspects of the Village Trade

THE trip from the Assiniboine River posts to the Mandan and Hidatsa villages on the Missouri River was a distance of nearly two hundred miles, the actual distance depending, of course, on the post from which they departed, deviations from their course because of detours taken to avoid hostile Indians, and other variables. The time it took to make the journey also varied a great deal, depending not only on the above factors but also upon whether they used horses and on the weather. The route taken by David Thompson in 1797–98 (fig. 6) and by François-Antoine Larocque in 1805 (map 3) are representative of many others.

Peter Pond's 1785 map stated that it was a twelve-day one-way trip to the villages "with loaded horses," and in 1796 John Macdonell reckoned the journey as ten or twelve days' march in winter, giving the distance as one hundred leagues. As we have already seen, Mackay is reputed to have made the trip in seventeen days. In 1804, Larocque made the round trip in twenty days—a feat which Charles McKenzie said had been "almost incredibly expeditious." The following year, Larocque's time for the same trip was eighteen days, and Alexander Henry the Younger also took eighteen days to cover the same ground in 1806—six days to the villages, but twelve to return. The fifty-nine days it took David Thompson to make the round trip in 1797–98 were not typical; he was on foot, in the dead of winter with many delays because of blizzards, and with many days having thermometer readings well below zero.[1]

Although we have accumulated a list of more than seventy expeditions between the Assiniboine River and the Mandan villages (Appendix, table 1), many other journeys were undertaken but were not completed. Many expeditions were aborted for one reason or another, but usually because of hostile Indians. For example, on February 4, 1798, Hugh McCrachan and six men, including two Mandans, set out for the Missouri River with an "assortment of goods," but they were plundered by the Sioux. Two of the Canadians and a Mandan were killed, and the sur-

[1]John Macdonell's "The Red River," ms. p. 11; Charles McKenzie's Narratives, first expedition account, ms. p. 31; David Thompson's Journal.

vivors returned to Macdonell's House in a "sad worn out condition." So dangerous was the journey to the Missouri River at times that *engagés* at Brandon House sometimes refused orders to go to the Mandans; indeed, there was a mutiny at Brandon House in 1812 for precisely that reason.[2]

The residenters obviously lived in native earth lodges or in tipis together with their families, but the contemporary accounts are all but silent on the matter of dwelling arrangements of the traders who came to the villages to trade for only brief periods of time. In the absence of documentation that they built log cabins or other structures of familiar Euro-American form, it seems safe to assume that (like the residenters) they regularly lived with temporary hosts in native dwellings, paying their rent in trade goods. During Larocque's first expedition to the Missouri in the winter of 1804, he and his men moved into the earth lodges and tipis of a prominent family in one of the villages. In November, 1804, Larocque left William Morrison and another man "in the best Lodge we Could find." Charles McKenzie lived with Yellow Elk, a Hidatsa, in another village. Larocque himself alludes to the head of the Hidatsa family with whom he was staying, White Wolf, as "my landlord," and says they were living in a "leather tent." When some of the "wooden lodges" in his village were abandoned by their occupants that winter, however, he was quick to move into one of them.[3]

As far as the records show, the only structure actually built by the Canadian traders was "a small fort and a hut." A North West Company party headed by René Jusseaume built this post—which we call Jusseaume's Post—on the banks of the Missouri River between the Mandan and Hidatsa villages shortly after its arrival on the Missouri on October 27, 1794. The post was seized by John Evans for the Spaniards shortly after his arrival in the area in September, 1796. He named the establishment "Fort Makay" after his colleague and appears to have lived in it until his departure the following May. Edwin James alludes to the fort as being a "stockade trading post," although his testimony is hearsay. Jusseaume's Post was apparently on the right, or south, bank of the Missouri between the villages of the Mandans and Hidatsas "about a half league distant from the village of the Mandans" (map 2).[4] Its remains have never been located, but since the river does not seem to have significantly eroded its south bank in this area, the chances seem good that it may someday be discovered. Since it was occupied for

---

[2]David Thompson, *David Thompson's Narrative of His Explorations in Western America, 1784–1812,* Publications of the Champlain Society, vol. 12, ed. J. B. Tyrrell, p. 240; H.B.C.A., B.22/a/18b, fos. 7d–8.

[3]François-Antoine Larocque's "Missouri Journal."

[4]Edwin James, *Account of an Expedition from Pittsburgh to the Rocky Mountains,* vol. 1, p. 274; Abraham P. Nasatir, ed., *Before Lewis and Clark: Documents Illustrating the History of the Missouri, 1785–1805,* vol. 1, pp. 101–102, 331; vol. 2, pp. 389, 399, 462, 496. See also David Williams, "John Evans' Strange Journey," *American Historical Review* 54 (January, 1949): 517, 520–21.

at least two and one-half years (if it was indeed abandoned when Evans left it in the spring of 1797), there should be a reasonable amount of debris marking its location.

The Missouri River villages were, among other things, a place of refuge for men who wanted to escape their term of service with the fur companies, and many of them deserted to live there. Later, in the nineteenth century, the villages became a refuge for those who were seeking a means to avoid justice in Canada.

A number of early traders from western Canadian posts found their way south to Louisiana and Saint Louis. James Mackay, for instance, left Canada for reasons that are not recorded and moved to Saint Louis, where he began to work for the Spanish government. Others made their way south by making a trading trip to the Mandan villages, deserting the company, and descending the Missouri River. Mackay would therefore not have been without former Canadian companions in Saint Louis, and some of them probably accompanied him and John Evans on their expedition of 1795 to 1797 up the Missouri River. John Macdonell, in fact, wrote in 1797 that many of the company's employees deserted while they were on the Missouri River with the "intention of going to the Illinois and other places on the Mississippi."[5] Macdonell also chided John Evans in a letter of February 26, 1797, while Evans was living at Jusseaume's Post, that no "sensible person" would obtain a "grand idea of your Missouri

company [in] making use of such *Canaille* [riffraff] as I have reason to think many of your *Engagees* are by judging of the remainder by La Grave Garreau Chayé &c Such as are not run aways from here are Deserters from La prairie du Chien & other places in the Mississippi."[6]

Three North West Company men, for example, deserted in 1793 and 1795: Chrisosthomo Jonca (Chrisostome Joncquard), François La Grave, and Juan Fotman (Jean Tremont). Joncquard had traveled to the Missouri with a North West Company party on December 10, 1793. He and La Grave remained behind when the rest of the expedition returned to the Assiniboine River. Both men later deserted downriver to the Arikara and Cheyenne Indians. Fotman, on the other hand, first traveled to the Mandan villages with a North West Company party on October 6, 1794. He was one of the four men left in the villages when Jusseaume led the remainder of the party back to the Assiniboine, and he deserted down the Missouri River during Jusseaume's absence in the spring of 1795. Both Joncquard and Fotman went on to Saint Louis with D'Église on his return to that city from his second Missouri River expedition in 1795.[7] Another man, André Gou-

[5]Macdonell's "The Red River," ms. p. 11.

[6]Nasatir, *Before Lewis and Clark*, vol. 2, p. 503.

[7]Ibid., vol. 1, pp. 92, 95, 300–33; see also H.B.C.A., B.22/a/21, fo. 37. La Grave evidently maintained connections with the Mandans for many years, as he is reported to have had a wife and children at the villages as late as 1818, when he attempted to guide Archibald McDonald's party of Red River colonists to the Missouri (H.B.C.A.,

zeon, deserted the North West Company in 1800 and was later murdered by the Sioux in the company of five Mandans south of the Knife River.[8]

Nor was the Hudson's Bay Company immune to the same problem. Donald MacKay, in his entry in the Brandon House Post Journal for September 26, 1793, noted that "we keep a watch now as those Vagabonds of Canada who has abandoned themselves to live as the Indians may attempt to plunder, there is many of them now deserted & run away from their Masters & Employers." On October 2, 1793, he also commented that, on his arrival at Pine Fort, he found "John Miller and four Canadians at the Fort who said that the Canadians which we meet below was not good men that they run away from their Masters in the Missisippie River and took some Goods from their Masters & went to the Missisurrie River & lives now like Indians among them."[9] When men deserted the Canadian posts, they often carried with them goods stolen from the posts, as James Sutherland noted in the Brandon House Post Journal for April 7, 1797.[10]

In the fall of 1816, two of the men who were deeply involved in the Red River troubles of that year traveled to the Missouri villages, probably to prepare a place of refuge in the possible event of forced flight from Canada. During the years 1812 through 1816, animosity mounted between Lord Selkirk's settlers in the Red River Colony, who were allied with the Hudson's Bay Company traders in the Upper Red River District, and the North West Company men at posts along the Red and Assiniboine rivers. In June, 1816, this tension erupted into violent conflict, resulting in the massacre of the Red River Colony's Governor Semple and about twenty of the colonists as well as the forceful seizure and pillage of Brandon House. One of the North West Company's partners, Alexander Mc-Donell, was a primary instigator of the Brandon House sacking, and two members of a halfbreed family named Deschamps, François and his son Francis (or François), took part in the actual killing of Semple and his party.[11]

McDonell and one of the Deschamps men were at the Mandan villages during the fall following the Semple massacre. In a February 18, 1817, letter to the Earl of Selkirk, Michael McDonnell reported

B.22/a/21, fos. 37–38, and P.A.C., MG 19, E1, vol. 53, microfilm reel C-19, pp. 20520–27; see also Jean Murray Cole, *Exile in the Wilderness: The Biography of Chief Factor Archibald McDonald, 1790-1853, pp. 85–86).*

[8]Alexander Henry [the Younger], *New Light on the Early History of the Greater Northwest,* ed. Elliott Coues, vol. 1, p. 370.

[9]H.B.C.A., B.22/a/1, fo. 7.

[10]H.B.C.A., B.22/a/4, fo. 35.

[11]Arthur S. Morton, *A History of the Canadian West to 1870-1871,* 2nd ed., ed. Lewis G. Thomas, pp. 537–600. John Halkett, *Narratives of John Pritchard, Pierre Chrysologue Pambrum, and Frederick Damien Heurter, Respecting the Aggressions of the North-West Company Against the Earl of Selkirk's Settlement upon Red River.* The death of the elder Deschamps and the virtual extermination of his family at Fort Union in 1836 are described in the journal of Charles Larpenteur, *Forty Years a Fur Trader on the Upper Missouri: The Personal Narrative of Charles Larpenteur, 1832-1872,* ed. Elliott Coues, vol. 1, pp. 76–80, 87–101.

that a man named "Parezian" had arrived from the Red River and reported "that Mr. A McDonell & Deschamps had gone among the Mandans to raise them for war."[12] In 1817, a series of depositions by participants in or witnesses to the Red River troubles of the preceding year were recorded by Lord Selkirk and his agents. The deposition of Thomas Costello, dated July 26, 1817, at Red River, states: "In the month of October 1816, Mr. Alexander McDonell accompanied by a large Party of Half-breeds, a few Canadians and Deponent, Sweney, Hoy and Kennedy arrived at Qu'Appelle. A short time after their arrival at that place Mr. Alexander McDonell set off to the Mississiourie to make peace as Deponent was told by one François Ducharme a halfbreed, with the Mandal Indians in case Lord Selkirk should arrive in such force as to render it necessary for Alexander McDonell and his band of Assassins to seek a retreat in the United States."[13]

TRADE COMMODITIES AND RATES OF EXCHANGE

The traders' journals are not consistent in listing either the kinds of goods traded to the Indians or the furs and other materials the Indians exchanged in return. A listing of the documented Euro-American goods traded to the Mandans and Hidatsas, as compiled from the journals of Thompson, Larocque, McKenzie, and

Henry, is given in the Appendix, table 2. Many other items were of course traded, and still other personal possessions were given to the Indians as gifts or in payment. In fact, *any* item in the possession of the traders could have come into the Indians' custody, not only by the above means but also by the exchange of goods with other Indians who had stolen them from traders or by theft. An unusually large accumulation of goods came into the possession of the Hidatsas, for example, when a party of them killed and plundered a Euro-American group on the Saskatchewan River in about 1804. The inventory of the North West Company trading post, Fort Espérance, illustrating the goods inventoried by John Macdonell there on December 29, 1793 (Appendix, table 3), and the inventories of the Hudson's Bay Company's Brandon House for the years 1810–14 (Appendix, table 4) further define the range of goods available for the Mandan and Hidatsa trade. Archaeological investigations at several of the Mandan-Hidatsa villages of this period have recovered numerous examples of the more durable of these goods (figs. 1–3).[14]

The Mandan and Hidatsa villages held several attractions, both economic and personal, for the trad-

---

[12]P.A.C., MG 19, E1, vol. 8, microfilm roll C-3, pp. 3133–38.

[13]P.A.C., MG 19, E1, vol. 41, microfilm roll C-15, pp. 15879–86.

[14]François-Antoine Larocque's "Yellowstone Journal," ms. pp. 4–5 and n. 31; McKenzie's Narratives, second expedition account, ms. pp. 51–54 and n. 31; W. Raymond Wood, ed., "Journal of John Macdonell, 1793–1795," pp. 91–93 (entry for December 29, 1793); Donald J. Lehmer, W. Raymond Wood, and C. L. Dill, "The Knife River Phase" (manuscript), figs. 8.18–8.20.

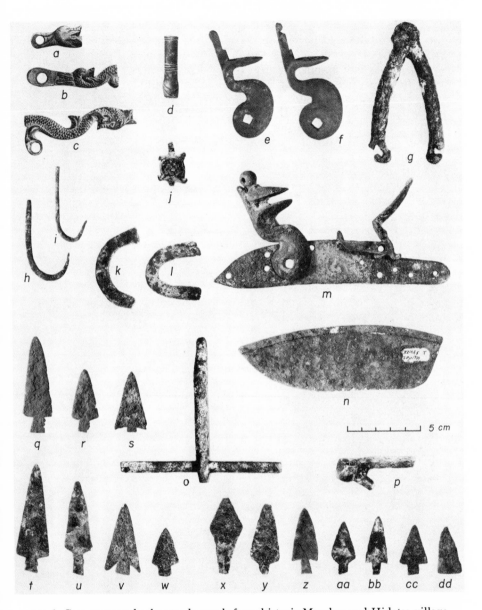

FIG. 1. Gun parts and other trade goods from historic Mandan and Hidatsa village sites: *a–c*, dragon gun side plates; *d*, ramrod ferrule; *e–f*, gun cocks; *g*, bridle part; *h–i*, metal fishhooks; *j*, lead turtle effigy made from a musket ball; *k–l*, firesteels; *m*, gun lock; *n*, metal hand-held "squash" knife; *o*, wrench; *p*, bullet-mold part; *q–dd*, metal arrowpoints. Provenance: *d–f, q–s*, Amahami site; *k, p, x–dd*, Rock Village; all others, Deapolis site. From Donald J. Lehmer et al., "The Knife River Phase" (manuscript), pl. 8.18.

FIG. 2. Axes and other metal trade goods from historic Mandan and Hidatsa village sites: *a-c*, axes; *d-e*, hand-held "squash" knives; *f-h*, mattocks: *i*, hatchet; *j*, bucket; *k*, blade for fleshing adze (?); *l*, bucket bail tab; *m-o*, butcher knives. Provenance: *l*, Amahami site; all others, Deapolis site. From Donald J. Lehmer et al., "The Knife River Phase" (manuscript), pl. 8.19.

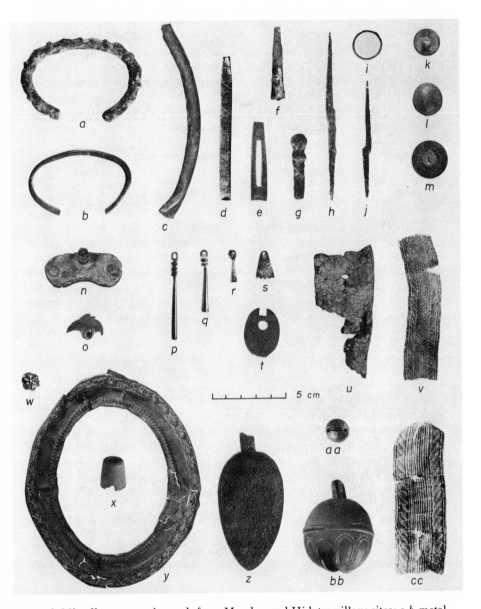

FIG. 3. Miscellaneous trade goods from Mandan and Hidatsa village sites: *a-b*, metal bracelets; *c*, brass tube; *d*, decorated brass strip; *e*, trigger plate; *f*, brass bangle; *g*, cock screw; *h*, *j*, double-pointed steel awls; *i*, finger ring; *k-m*, brass buttons; *n*, metal bucket bail tab; *o*, gunlock tumbler; *p-q*, brass pendants; *r-s*, ear bobs; *t*, flintlock topjaw; *u*, leather belt; *v*, *cc*, military braid; *w*, rosette; *x*, thimble; *y*, mirror (?) frame; *z*, steel spoon; *aa-bb*, brass bells. Provenance: *y*, Rock Village; *a-b*, *e*, *h*, *j*, *p-q*, *s*, *w*, *z*, *aa*, Deapolis; all others, Amahami site. From Donald J. Lehmer et al., "The Knife River Phase" (manuscript), pl. 8.20.

ers from Canada. Foremost among the economic attractions were, of course, the furs that could be obtained there. It is difficult to estimate accurately the numbers and kinds of furs being brought to the Canadian posts, because the traders tended to record only the gross value of fur returns in their day-to-day journals instead of complete lists of the kinds and quantities of the furs obtained and the goods given in exchange. Detailed accounting records of the trading transactions with Mandan and Hidatsa Indians have not survived. Nevertheless, a few clues are to be found in the traders' journals and memoirs. The lack of consistency in reference precludes any real notion of the quantity of goods which flowed between the villages and the Canadian posts. This is as true of the Indian goods which were traded to the Euro-Americans as its reverse. Indian goods (as also compiled from the journals of Thompson, Larocque, McKenzie, and Henry) consisted primarily of buffalo robes, wolf pelts, fox pelts, beaver pelts, otter pelts (rare), bear skins, horses, mules, dogs (for carrying provisions), Indian corn, bladders of fat, and slave women.

Wolf skins (probably including both coyote and wolf) and several kinds of fox skins (referred to as "foxes," "red foxes," and "kitts") are most frequently mentioned and probably constituted a large proportion of the Mandan-Hidatsa fur returns. Furs obtained in smaller quantities included beaver, buffalo, bear, and, in only one recorded instance, otter. Tabeau remarked that "A kind of little gray fox, the hare, and the

skunk" were among the furs traded from the Mandans by the North West and Hudson's Bay companies, but surviving records do not confirm trade in rabbit and skunk pelts.[15]

Beaver was, of course, the premium pelt of the trade, but relatively few of them seem to have been obtained from the Mandans and Hidatsas. Lewis and Clark, speaking of the Hidatsa Indians in their "Statistical View," state that "They have as yet furnished scarcely any beaver, although the country they hunt abounds with them; the lodges of these animals are to be seen within a mile of their villages."[16] Pierre-Antoine Tabeau, who traded with the Arikaras from 1803 to 1805 for Régis Loisel of Saint Louis, remarked that the abundance of beaver along the Upper Missouri to the Mandan country was not sufficient to justify the Canadian posts on the Assiniboine River: "I believe that it is not necessary to add that the beaver and the otter cannot become objects of trade with the hunters, the Sioux and the Ricaras, at least from the River Qui Court up to the Mandanes inclusively; for I understand that these could scarcely furnish them for the English companies."[17] Tabeau went on to suggest that trade with nomadic Indians living north of the Mandans was the primary reason that the Canadian posts were main-

[15]Pierre-Antoine Tabeau, *Tabeau's Narrative of Loisel's Expedition to the Upper Missouri*, ed. Annie Heloise Abel, p. 81.

[16]Meriwether Lewis and William Clark, *Original Journals of the Lewis and Clark Expedition, 1804–06*, vol. 6, p. 91.

[17]Tabeau, *Tabeau's Narrative*, p. 87. The River Qui Court is the Niobrara River.

tained, which is surely true, since the Brandon House records reveal that trade with Assiniboins, Crees, and Plains Chippewas constituted the bulk of that district's trade. The Hidatsa chief Le Borgne told Charles McKenzie in 1806 that "we have many good things but we have no Beaver" and asked McKenzie why white men valued beaver skins. Nevertheless, McKenzie, who left the villages with "6 horses well loaded," boasted that he was "the first North trader who crossed the Missurie with 4 Packs of Beaver."[18]

Although beaver skins were reported obtainable in small quantities from the Mandans and Hidatsas as early as 1795, surviving records show that beaver pelts were brought back from there by North West or Hudson's Bay traders only in 1804, 1806, 1812, 1817, and 1818.[19] Some of the beaver traded to the Canadians by the Mandans and Hidatsas may have been received by the latter groups in trade with other tribes or possibly as plunder taken from other whites. Peter Fidler reported a rather large quantity of beaver among the furs brought back from the Missouri in 1817 but speculated that they may have been taken from American trappers since "the greater part of them was marked with the Initials of 3 difft names & numbered."[20]

Most descriptions of fur returns from the Mandan and Hidatsa villages are given in the journals as total values expressed in terms of "made-beaver," the standard of value employed by the Canadian traders. One made-beaver equaled the value of one prime beaver skin.[21] Accordingly, the journals are replete with references to the total value of fur returns from the Missouri, expressed as quantities of made-beaver (indicated by the symbols MB, MBr, Br, and, occasionally, simply the word *beaver*), but seldom provide quantified statements regarding the fur composition of specific returns. Fortunately, however, a few such quantified descriptions do exist, which give some idea of what typical returns from the villages were like. In 1798, David Thompson recorded the following list of furs obtained from Jusseaume at the Mandan-Hidatsa villages:

60 bad Wolves
51 good do Mons. Jussomme for Journey
  as they are light
70 do to be left
  5 small foxes
  2 bad do
  2 Red Foxes
19 Buffalo Robes
12   do   do
17 Buffalo Robes for 51 Wolves[22]

In entries of the following dates in his "Missouri Journal," Larocque re-

---

[18]McKenzie's Narratives, fourth expedition account, ms. pp. 7, 33.

[19]H.B.C.A., B.22/a/2, fos. 20d–21; Larocque's "Missouri Journal," entries for December 9 and 20, 1804; McKenzie's Narratives, fourth expedition account, ms. p. 33; H.B.C.A., B.22/a/18b, fo. 12; H.B.C.A., B.22/a/20, fos. 24–25; and H.B.C.A., B.22/a/21, fo. 40.

[20]H.B.C.A., B.22/a/20, fos. 24–25.

[21]Arthur J. Ray and Donald B. Freeman, *"Give Us Good Measure": An Economic Analysis of Relations between the Indians and the Hudson's Bay Company before 1763*, p. 54.

[22]David Thompson's journal, entry for January 9, 1804.

corded the kinds and quantities of furs he acquired from the Mandans and Hidatsas:

December 9, 1804

40 Kitts
17 Wolves
8 Foxes
2 Beavers

December 20, 1804

545 Kitts
57 Wolves
4 Foxes
7 Beaver Skins[23]

The Brandon House Post Journals itemize the fur returns from the Missouri in only two entries:

March 14, 1812

about 60 beaver skins
a few buffalo Robes
7 wolves
a bear Skin

December 15, 1817

131 whole Beaver skins
26 Half Beaver
110 scrap Do.
3 large Bears
1 small Do-
13 Red foxes[24]

The 1812 trip to the Missouri was a joint undertaking between the Hudson's Bay and North West companies, and the March 14 entry recorded that the North West Company received "the same number" of skins as its share of the expedition's proceeds.

The fact that beaver skins are specifically mentioned in four of the five available itemized lists of Mandan-Hidatsa fur returns suggests that beaver pelts were brought back more often than is documented in the surviving journals.

Buffalo robes must surely have constituted a large proportion of the furs available to the Canadian traders at the Missouri River villages. However, they do not seem to have comprised a major part of the trade with the Mandans and Hidatsas until the development of efficient forms of watercraft transportation on the Missouri in the second quarter of the nineteenth century, when the Mandan-Hidatsa trade was left entirely to American interests based primarily in Saint Louis.[25]

The North West and Hudson's Bay traders seem to have held different ideas about the commercial value of buffalo robes. The North West Company appears to have actively sought buffalo robes and exported them to Montreal as a marketable commodity. In May of 1795, John Macdonell recorded that forty-six of ninety-one fur packs prepared for shipment eastward to Grand Portage, or slightly over one-half of the returns for the 1794–95 trading season, consisted of buffalo robes. In contrast, Robert Goodwin, the Brandon House master for the Hudson's Bay Company, recorded in his journal on November 9, 1795, that "Buf-

---

[23]Larocque's "Missouri Journal."
[24]H.B.C.A., B.22/a/18b, fo. 12; H.B.C.A., B.22/a/20, fos. 24–25.

[25]John E. Sunder, *Fur Trade on the Upper Missouri, 1840-1865*; David J. Wishart, *Fur Trade of the American West, 1807-1840.*

falo robes is a great part of the Trade [at the Mandan and Hidatsa villages] I do not know what Service they would be of to your Honors [the London Committee of the Hudson's Bay Company] The Canads [North West Company traders] have great use for them as they sell them at Montreal for the Cariols &c."[26] These records clearly show that buffalo robes were a major part of the North West Company's trade in the Red River Department at a time when the Hudson's Bay traders were wondering if they had any commercial value.

The North West Company probably obtained buffalo robes from the Mandans and Hidatsas throughout the period of their trade with the villagers. The earliest record of Mandan-Hidatsa buffalo robes being acquired by Nor'westers is in a December 22, 1793, entry in the Brandon House Post Journals which states that "two Canadians [probably free traders] from the Misisurrie River arrived at the Canadian houses [North West Company establishments] with great Quantity of Beaffaloe Robes."[27] John Macdonell recorded on April 14, 1794, that his men brought back two bales of buffalo robes from the Missouri. On July 1, 1796, Thomas Millar, the "summer master" at Brandon House, recorded that five North West Company men had just returned

from the Mandans with "6 Bundles of Buffalo robes." The French former general Victor Collot, writing of the year 1796, remarked that "English merchants" on the Assiniboine River sent men to the Missouri villages to "traffic for bullocks' hides" and other furs. Forty-eight buffalo robes were among the goods obtained from Jusseaume at the villages by David Thompson on January 9, 1798. Clark reported on October 26, 1804, that Hugh McCrachan was in the Mandan and Hidatsa villages "to trade for *horses & Buffalow* robes," although it is not clear whether McCrachan was acting as a free trader or a North West Company employee at the time. Although the quantity was probably not large, buffalo robes were among the goods divided between the North West and Hudson's Bay companies after their joint 1812 expedition to the villages.[28]

Buffalo robes seem never to have figured prominently in the fur returns of the Hudson's Bay Company from the Mandan and Hidatsa villages. A few robes were acquired by the company incidentally to the trade for other, higher-value furs, but they do not seem to have been commercially marketed by the company until many years later, after the Canadian trade with the Mandans and Hidatsas had ceased.[29]

[26]Wood, "Journal of John Macdonell," p. 135 (entries for May 9 and 11, 1795); H.B.C.A., B.22/a/3, fo. 8. "Cariols" refers to a form of small sleigh drawn by dogs or one horse, used by French-Canadians (Don H. Berkebile, *Carriage Terminology: An Historical Dictionary*, pp. 74–77).
[27]H.B.C.A., B.22/a/1, fo. 13d.

[28]Wood, "Journal of John Macdonell"; H.B.C.A., B.22/a/4, fo. 3; Victor Collot, *A Journey in North America*, vol. 1, p. 291; Thompson's Journal; Lewis and Clark, *Original Journals*, vol. 1, p. 206 (emphasis in original); H.B.C.A., B.22/a/18b, fo. 12.
[29]Arthur J. Ray, *Indians in the Fur Trade: Their Role as Hunters, Trappers and Middlemen in the Lands Southwest of Hudson Bay, 1660-1870*, p. 182.

59

The earliest masters at Brandon House did not recognize any commercial value to the buffalo robe trade other than the necessity to accept robes or risk losing the trade in other kinds of furs as well. The master for the first year of operation at Brandon House, Donald MacKay, recorded on March 20, 1794, that several Assiniboin Indians visiting the post had made him a present of "three foxes and Six Beafloe Robes," and MacKay "was obliged to take it, for if I refuse it they will go to the Canadians [the North West Company traders] with it and no Indians will come to me at all for they will bring both their furrs & Beafloe Robes to the house they go to." Five days later another group of visiting Indians presented MacKay with more buffalo robes: "I was presented with twenty six Beaffloe Robes for to get brandy, if I will not take it they will go to the Canadians who will pay the Value of Three Beaverskins each, I mean now to take them should I burn them for this year, and should the Company find fault with me, I cannot help it as no Indian will come to us if we do not take every thing the Canadians takes from them, I shall refer to the Chief [that is, the chief factor at Albany] what is to be done in this Case as it must be taken into Consideration for the future."[30]

MacKay's successor at Brandon House, Robert Goodwin, also wondered about the value of buffalo robes. He recorded in the post journal on May 17, 1795, the day that he departed Brandon House with the season's fur returns, that "I have sent down some of the [buffalo] Robes for samples to know if they would be of any consequence to Trade as it is easy to Send there [that is, to the Mandan-Hidatsa villages]."[31]

In the same entry, Goodwin also attributed the trading success of Peter Grant, an independent trader, to the fact that during the season he "made some packs of Mandal Robes by sending Men across the Country to their Villages."

During the following season, in the November 9, 1795, entry cited above, Goodwin still questioned the value of buffalo robes. Three days later, he dispatched the first Hudson's Bay Company trading party to the villages. The men returned on December 26, 1795, bringing "142 MB in Wolves Kitts & Robes." Although buffalo robes were among the very first group of furs that Hudson's Bay men brought back from the Mandan and Hidatsa villages, they do not seem to have been viewed as an exportable commodity. The Albany account book for that season shows that eleven buffalo robes, valued at twenty-two made-beaver, were given to company employees on credit, but does not indicate that any of the robes were shipped to England.[32]

[30]H.B.C.A., B.22/a/1, fos. 20d, 21d.

[31]H.B.C.A., B.22/a/2, fos. 20–21d. These "samples" may have been received at Albany, since the factory account book for the 1794–95 season indicates that the value of two hundred made-beaver was "Paid for Buffalo & Moose Skins detained at Albany" (H.B.C.A., B.3/d/104, fo. 59).

[32]H.B.C.A., B.22/a/3, fos. 8d, 10; H.B.C.A., B.3/d/106, fo. 61.

Several other remarks by Brandon House masters support the view that the Hudson's Bay Company did not consider buffalo robes a typical product of their trade in furs. James Sutherland, the master for the 1796–97 season, sent a letter on November 23, 1796, to John Evans, the Spanish agent who had seized the North West Company post at the Mandans, to inquire "if we may be permitted on any future ocasion to visit the Mandals and Trade Horses, Indian corn and Buffalo robes which articles we suppose to be unconnected with the Fur Trade." In his reply, received by Sutherland on January 16, 1797, Evans stated that the matter would have to be decided by another authority but that he believed that "the latter [that is, the trade in robes] will not be permitted as it is the staple Trade of this Countrie."[33] On departing Brandon House with the annual returns on May 23, 1798, John McKay recorded that he "left [behind] 40 Bags of Beat Meat and a great quantity of piece meat and Buffalo Robes."[34]

Several years later, on February 27, 1805, McKay recorded in the Brandon House Post Journal that the Assiniboin Indians foolishly trade valuable firearms to the Mandans and Hidatsas, but complained that they often cannot repay their debts at the Canadian posts because they "get nothing in return but Indian Corn and Buffalo Robes" from the Missouri River villagers.[35] On December 23, 1811, Alexander Kennedy recorded in the Brandon House Post Journal that the cost of transporting furs from the Mandan and Hidatsa villages would be excessively high, since the villagers' "peltries consist only of wolves & Foxes with some Buffalo robes."[36] Despite this essentially negative attitude on the part of the Brandon House masters toward buffalo robes, it is likely that robes frequently comprised a small portion of the Mandan-Hidatsa returns during most of the period that the Hudson's Bay Company traded at the villages. For example, on March 14, 1812, Kennedy recorded that his employees had returned from the Missouri, bringing "a few buffalo Robes" in addition to beaver, wolf, and bear skins.[37]

Despite the persistence of the early Brandon House masters, Donald MacKay and Robert Goodwin, in bringing buffalo robes to the attention of their superiors, it does not appear that the Hudson's Bay Company actively sought buffalo robes in the Upper Red River District trade, since no robes, with the two exceptions cited above, are reported in the Albany account books for Upper Red

---

[33]H.B.C.A., B.22/a/4, fos. 20–20d, 28–28d; see also Nasatir, *Before Lewis and Clark*, vol. 2, pp. 462, 463.

[34]H.B.C.A., B.22/a/14, fo. 15d. Piece meat refers to relatively fresh meat which was not treated to prevent spoilage before consumption, while "beat" meat refers to pemmican, which was meat that was pounded, mixed with tallow, and dried to retard spoilage. The latter was a major source of nourishment for fur trade brigades because of its portability and preserved qualities. See Charles M. Gates, ed., *Five Fur Traders of the Northwest*, p. 132 n. 8.

[35]H.B.C.A., B.22/a/12, fos. 9d–10.
[36]H.B.C.A., B.22/a/18b, fo. 6d.
[37]H.B.C.A., B.22/a/18b, fo. 12.

River, nor are they included in the standard of trade for any season. However, a few buffalo robes were traded in the district in the years following 1810, when administrative control of Brandon House had shifted to York Factory, but in such low numbers that they could not have constituted a significant part of the district's trade.[38]

The economic importance of the Mandan-Hidatsa furs to the Brandon House trade can be roughly gauged for certain trading seasons by comparing the Brandon House master's statements of the value of the villagers' furs with corresponding estimates of the value of the total fur returns sent to the factories on Hudson's Bay each year. This kind of estimate is not possible for the North West Company because company journals for the Red River Department are incomplete and there are no account books relating to the Mandan-Hidatsa trade.

While admittedly a minor component of the overall Brandon House trade, the total value of the Mandan-Hidatsa fur returns in comparison to the total value of the Upper Red River District returns can be roughly computed for a few years (Appendix, table 5). The figures in table 5 of the Appendix represent only a rough assessment of this trade, since the Brandon House Post Journals on which they are based do not necessarily report all furs brought back from the Missouri by company employees and free traders and because the journals provide no way of ac-

counting for overhead factors such as salaries and the cost of gifts given to Indians and horses purchased at the villages. The value of the Mandan-Hidatsa furs ranged from slightly over 6 percent (for the first year in which the Hudson's Bay Company conducted trade with the Mandans and Hidatsas, 1795–96) to slightly over 28 percent of the district returns. The average value for nine years is 14.5 percent. That the Mandan-Hidatsa fur returns were an important part of the Brandon House trade for at least some years is attested by a statement recorded in the post journal by Robert Goodwin on May 7, 1800, that "Brandon House is nearly the same as last year but would have been much less had it not been for sending twice to the Mandans during the winter."[39]

Horses were frequently purchased at the Mandan and Hidatsa villages to assist in transporting newly acquired furs back to the trading establishments on the Assiniboine River. Less frequently, mules and dogs also appear to have been purchased at the villages for the same purpose. The Canadian posts on the Assiniboine were regularly supplied by canoes and boats traveling long systems of largely interconnecting rivers and lakes. Since draft animals could not be practicably transported over long distances by such means, the traders turned to local Indian groups to fill their need for draft animals.

The Mandan and Hidatsa villages long served as an important hub of

---

[38]Ray, *Indians in the Fur Trade*, p. 210.

[39]H.B.C.A., B.22/a/7, fos. 28d–29.

intertribal trade, from prehistoric times until the latter part of the nineteenth century. In historic times, one of the most valuable commodities of intertribal exchange was the horse, which had diffused into the Northern Plains during the eighteenth century from southwestern tribes who had acquired horses from the Spanish. The Mandans and Hidatsas served as middlemen in a trading network between peoples living to the north and east and those to the south and west. As Ewers has pointed out, the sedentary village tribes of the Missouri River found themselves on the boundary between two expanding frontiers of trade, that of trading horses to the north and east and that of passing guns and other manufactured European items to the south and west.[40] Thus, the Mandans and Hidatsas, in the late eighteenth and early nineteenth centuries, were in a strategic position to capitalize on the barter of both types of trade commodities, including the sale of horses to Euro-American traders.

Traded from tribe to tribe in the Southwest, principally derived from stock stolen from the Spanish, horses reached the Northern Plains during the eighteenth century. Just when horses reached the Mandans and Hidatsas is a matter of speculation. Ewers has pointed out that the senior La Vérendrye reported no horses among the Mandans during his 1738–39 journey, though his son, Pierre, returned from the Mandans with two horses in 1741. Two more La Vérendrye sons, François and Louis-Joseph, in 1742–43 traveled to the Mandans and west from the Missouri toward the Rocky Mountains, but the account of their journey is silent on the matter of horses among the Mandans. However, the fact that they traveled back to Fort La Reine on the Assiniboine River in company with a large party of mounted Assiniboin Indians suggests that the Mandans may have had at least some horses by that time. Horses appear to have been common among the Mandans and Hidatsas by the early 1790s, when historic documentation becomes abundant.[41]

That the Mandan and Hidatsa villages were an important source of horses for the Canadian traders is attested by the May 17, 1795, entry in the Brandon House Post Journal which states, in part, that "it [that is, the Mandan-Hidatsa villages] is the very place the North West Company is supplied with all their Horses."[42] Usually, only enough horses—from one to eight but typically fewer than six—were bought at the villages to

---

[40]John C. Ewers, "The Indian Trade of the Upper Missouri before Lewis and Clark: An Interpretation," *Missouri Historical Society Bulletin* 10 (July, 1954); Donald J. Blakeslee, "The Plains Interband Trade System: An Ethnohistoric and Archeological Investigation (Ph.D. diss., University of Wisconsin, Milwaukee, 1975); W. Raymond Wood, "Plains Trade in Prehistoric and Protohistoric Intertribal Relations," in *Anthropology on the Great Plains*, ed. W. Raymond Wood and Margot Liberty, pp. 98–109; John C. Ewers, *The Horse in Blackfoot Indian Culture*, Bureau of American Ethnology Bulletin 159.

[41]Ewers, *The Horse*, pp. 4–5; G. Hubert Smith, *The Explorations of the La Vérendryes in the Northern Plains, 1738-43*, ed. W. Raymond Wood, pp. 104–14; Nasatir, *Before Lewis and Clark*, vol. 1, p. 161; H.B.C.A., B.22/a/2, 20d-21.

[42]H.B.C.A., B.22/a/2, fos. 20d-21.

transport furs back to the Assiniboine River posts, and occasionally individual horses were privately purchased by traders for their personal use. A few expeditions went to the Missouri River villages for the primary purpose of obtaining horses, drawn by the reputation of the Mandan and Hidatsa horses as superior animals. In 1793, David Monin traveled to the villages with several companions for the purpose of buying himself a "capital horse." Two partners of the North West Company, Alexander Henry and Charles Chaboillez, went there in 1806 to purchase horses for themselves. It is amusing to read Charles McKenzie's memoir of that period, which relates his frustrations in trying to procure a "famous runner" for each of the partners. In 1818, Lord Selkirk's Red River Colony sent men to the villages to purchase horses for the colonists. The expedition was successful in obtaining only nine horses for the colony, which had to seek elsewhere for larger numbers of them.[43]

Although traders frequently bought horses at the villages, available documents leave some question about the numbers of horses owned at any one time by the Mandan and Hidatsa Indians. For example, David Thompson stated that "in proportion to the population the Horses are few: the Chief with whom I lodged had only three," and that "for the sole purpose of hunting their Horses are too few."[44]

Thompson's remarks pertain to the winter of 1797-98. However, Charles McKenzie, writing of the year 1806, relates the difficulty that Alexander Henry and Charles Chaboillez had in selecting a suitable horse for each out of 1,500 at the villages.[45] Unsuccessful in buying a horse at the villages, McKenzie and the two partners traveled with a large group of Hidatsas to a Cheyenne camp, where they encountered equal difficulty in choosing from among 2,000 animals. Writing of the period 1833-34, Maximilian stated that the two Mandan villages together had over 300 horses and that the Hidatsas had only "250 or 300 horses in their three villages."[46] The latter figures agree well with Wolf Chief's estimate of 200 horses among the Hidatsas in early reservation times. McKenzie relates that the Hidatsas expected to receive 200 horses from the Cheyennes in exchange for an equal number of guns and a quantity of other goods in 1806. Larocque recorded that in 1805 the Hidatsa acquired 250 horses from the Crows.[47] It is likely that the number of horses among the Hidatsas and Mandans constituted stock on hand for trading and varied substantially as horses were bought and sold throughout the year.

Resident free traders from the Mandan-Hidatsa villages would some-

[43]Gates, *Five Fur Traders*, p. 112; Henry, *New Light*, vol. 1; McKenzie's Narratives, fourth expedition account; Cole, *Exile*, pp. 85-86.

[44]Thompson, *David Thompson's Narrative of His Explorations*, p. 230.

[45]McKenzie's Narratives, fourth expedition account.

[46]Reuben Gold Thwaites, ed., *Early Western Travels, 1748-1846*, vol. 23, pp. 272, 370.

[47]Gilbert L. Wilson, *The Horse and the Dog in Hidatsa Culture*, American Museum of Natural History Anthropological Papers, vol. 15, part 2, p. 174; McKenzie's Narratives, fourth expedition account, ms. pp. 26, 63.

times bring horses to sell at the posts on the Assiniboine River. Two "Canadians" from the Missouri offered two horses to Donald McKay, the Brandon House master, on December 22, 1793, and Ménard attempted unsuccessfully to sell three horses to John McKay at Brandon House on April 26, 1798. In addition to the two transactions with Jusseaume noted below, the Brandon House Post Journals also relate on April 3, 1800, that "Jessomme went to the Rapid River to sell his Horses."[48]

Horses from the Mandan-Hidatsa villages did not come cheaply. The Brandon House masters frequently complained about the high prices demanded for horses by the natives and the resident free traders at the villages. For example, Robert Goodwin recorded on April 3, 1796, that his men had bought two excellent horses at the villages but that the price was "very dear." Goodwin also remarked in the same entry that Thomas Millar, the man in charge of the trading party, made a deal to purchase a third horse from Jusseaume: "and he made an Agreement with Jessomme for another Horse, as I have not the Articles he wants for it, the payment will be referred till the fall, he would not sell His Horse unless he got the Watch also that Mr Millar had, which he was obliged to comply with altho the Watch belonged to myself that I lent him for the Journey."[49] Goodwin's successor at Brandon House for the next trading sea-son, James Sutherland, unexpectedly found himself obligated to pay Millar's debt to Jusseaume. On December 15, 1796, he recorded:

I had an unexpected Debt to pay this Day to Mr McDonell [John Macdonell, the master of a nearby North West Company post; possibly Jusseaume made the transaction with Millar on behalf of the North West Company], which was a Horse price contracted by Thos. Millar last winter at the Mandals and which was unpaid till now (Viz) 8 yd. of Callico in room of a gun which I had not to give, 4 yd. cloth 4# of Tobacco, 4# of Beads, 440 Ball, #18, 10# of Powder 1. 3pt Blanket, 1# of Vermillion—in all 45 Br and 4/15—

This extravagant price comes heavy on my small outfit and which should have been paid last year when there was more goods to have paid it with; the man, Millar bought this horse from took the advantage of him being in distress at the time as his Horses all died in going to the Mandals through the severity of the weather, and therefor could not bring back his furs without buying Horses one of which he was obliged to pay so dear for being on Trust—[50]

Several other examples of the price paid by Canadian traders for Mandan-Hidatsa horses have been preserved. In May, 1795, Goodwin paid Cardin, who had just arrived from the Mandans, the value of thirty made-beaver for a horse.[51] On October 10, 1799, Goodwin again reported a transaction with Jusseaume: "I had 30 Br. to pay Mr. Jessomme for a Horse he bro't here

[48]H.B.C.A., B.22/a/1, fo. 13d; H.B.C.A., B.22/a/5, fos. 34d–35; H.B.C.A., B.22/a/7, fo. 24d.
[49]H.B.C.A., B.22/a/3, fo. 15d.

[50]H.B.C.A., B.22/a/4, fo. 23.
[51]H.B.C.A., B.22/a/2, fo. 19d.

in summer in exchange for one I lent him last Spring."[52] On December 12, 1804, Larocque paid the following goods for a horse at the Mandan-Hidatsa villages:

1 fm [fathom] HB [Hudson's Bay] Red
    Stds. [strouds]
1 Chiefs Coat
1 large ax
100 Balls & powder
2 Knifes
2 doz Rings[53]

On January 6, 1805 Larocque again noted in his journal the price paid for another horse at the villages:

1 Blanket 3 Pt.
1 Pair Leggins
1 Hoe
1 Cassetete a Calumet
1 Lance
1 Eyed Dag
100 Balls & powder
1 Knife
a few Beads

In that same entry, Larocque also lists the goods given by his Indian landlord, White Wolf, for two horses:

1 gun
powder horn, & shot bag, with 100 Balls
    & powder
2 fms. HB Red Strouds
1 fm. Com. Blue
1 large but old Brass kettle
6 Killion quills
a pair of garnished Leggins[54]

In 1806, Alexander Henry paid the following goods, equaling one hundred made-beaver in value, for "a tolerbly good horse" at the Mandan-Hidatsa villages:

400 balls and powder
1 new gun
1 chief's scarlet coat
1 copper kettle
1 hand ax
1 iron lance three feet long
1 broad bead belt
2 wampum hair pipes
2 wampum shell pipes
½ pound blue beads
1 dozen brass rings
1 dozen hawk-bells
1 fathom red H.B. Co. strouds
½ dozen flints
½ dozen worms
½ dozen awls
2 large knives
1 mass B.C. beads
1 hornful of white powder[55]

Henry thought this a good price for the horse, although he considered high-quality horses difficult to obtain for a reasonable price at the Missouri River villages because of the reluctance of the natives to sell them: "They are extravagantly fond of their horses; many of them have from 20 to 30; yet it is impossible to purchase a common pack-horse for less than a new gun, a fathom of H.B. Co. red strouds, and 200 balls and powder. Their first-rate horses, such as are trained for war, or noted for running, can hardly be had for any quantity of goods."[56] It should be noted, however, that Charles Mc-

[52]H.B.C.A., B.22/a/7, fo. 4.
[53]Larocque's "Missouri Journal."
[54]Ibid.

[55]Henry, New Light, vol. 1, p. 355.
[56]Ibid., pp. 352–53.

Kenzie considered Henry a difficult customer to satisfy.[57]

Horses were sometimes purchased locally in the Assiniboine River valley more cheaply than they could be had at the Missouri. On September 27, 1796, James Sutherland, master at Brandon House, recorded in his journal that he had purchased a "fine young Mare which I got on reasonable terms much cheaper than they can be bought at the Mandans." In his journal entry dated December 15, 1817, Fidler complained that his men had purchased horses at the Mandans for "near double the price we give for them in this Quarter."[58]

In addition to horses, mules and dogs were at least occasionally purchased at the Mandan and Hidatsa villages by the Canadian traders. Mules were used as beasts of burden, while dogs were used to pull sleds carrying returns from the villages. On December 19, 1804, Larocque recorded the following price which he paid for a "stout mule" at the villages:

1 Gun
1 fm HB Red Stroud
300 Balls & powder
1 large ax
1 fm Tob
2 Knives
1 awl
2 flints
2 wormers
1 looking glass
3 Strings pipe Bead
a little vermillion[59]

Mules apparently commanded prices comparable to those of horses. A year and a half later, in 1806, Alexander Henry remarked that the Hidatsa chief, Le Borgne, had four mules with him on a trading visit to a Cheyenne camp. James Mackay also remarked that "horses or mules" were used by Canadian traders to transport furs from the Missouri River villages back to the Assiniboine River during the summer months.[60]

Only one example of the price paid for a dog at the villages has been preserved. On February 7, 1805, Larocque paid the following for a dog to use in transporting furs back from the villages:

20 Rds. amunition
1 knife
1 awl
13 China Beads
a little vermillion[61]

Surviving journals and memoirs document an infrequent trade in commodities other than furs and horses. Individual traders occasionally seem to have purchased female slaves, usually war captives, at the Mandan and Hidatsa villages. David Thompson's party returned from the villages in early 1798 with two women slaves "which the Mandanes had taken prisoners, and sold to the men, who, when arrived at the Trading House would sell them to some other Canadians."[62] John McKay, the master at Brandon

---

[57]McKenzie's Narratives, fourth expedition account.
[58]H.B.C.A., B.22/a/4, fo. 14; H.B.C.A., B.22/a/20, fos. 24–25.
[59]Larocque's "Missouri Journal."

[60]Henry, *New Light*, vol. 1, p. 394; Nasatir, *Before Lewis and Clark*, vol. 2, p. 492.
[61]Larocque's "Missouri Journal."
[62]Thompson, *David Thompson's Narrative of His Explorations*, p. 239.

House, noted the return of Thompson's party, including the two slave women, on February 3, 1798. Nearly three months later, on April 26, 1798, McKay recorded that Ménard offered to sell him "a Slave Girl" from the Missouri.[63] Female slaves, however, were not purchased as part of company transactions, but rather were privately obtained by individual traders.

In at least two recorded instances, the traders' returns from the villages included horticultural produce. In December, 1804, "5 Bags Corn" were listed among the proceeds traded by Larocque at the villages and probably sent back to the Canadian posts with Hugh Heney. Since corn, squash, and beans were raised in abundance by the Mandans and Hidatsas, and surpluses of these crops were a staple of the Mandan-Hidatsa trade with other tribes, it is likely that these commodities were at least occasionally brought back by traders who wished to vary their diet at the Assiniboine River posts. Peter Fidler's expedition to the villages in the spring of 1813 returned with "Indian Corn, Beans, Pumpkins, & Tobacco for seed" for Lord Selkirk's Red River Colony.[64] Since the Red River settlers experienced food shortages and other grave hardships during the first several years after the colony was founded in 1812, crop

seed must have been welcome there indeed.

On November 17, 1798, the Brandon House master recorded in his journal that two Mandans who were visiting the nearby Canadian establishment brought "one Kitt skin & 2 Bladders of fatt" to trade for liquor at Brandon House.[65] The fat was probably used as a dietary supplement at the posts or possibly to make tallow products. In this connection it is worth mentioning that none of the surviving journals document any instance in which traders transported liquor to the villages to trade to the natives, despite the fact that they are replete with references to liquor being frequently given or traded to Indians who visited the posts on the Assiniboine River. In 1819, a Catholic missionary, writing from Pembina, complained in a letter to his superior about traders inducing drunkenness among the Indians, but he observed that "The Mandan, who are eight days' journey from here, are exceptional in that they never drink rum."[66] Although his comments are based on observations made in the early 1830s, Maximilian noted that the Mandans did not trade for liquor from the American fur companies operating there at the time and that consequently "an intoxicated person is scarcely ever seen."[67]

Sexual access to Indian women undoubtedly played a considerable role in drawing traders to the Man-

---

[63]H.B.C.A., B.22/a/5, fo. 27; H.B.C.A., B.22/a/5, fos. 34d-35.

[64]Larocque's "Missouri Journal"; P.A.C., MG 19, E1, vol. 62, microfilm roll C-16, pp. 16798-99, 16807-808; D. W. Moodie and Barry Kaye, "The Northern Limit of Indian Agriculture in North America," *Geographical Review* 59 (October, 1969): 527.

[65]H.B.C.A., B.22/a/6, fo. 9d.

[66]Grace Lee Nute, *Documents Relating to Northwest Missions, 1815-1827*, p. 175.

[67]Thwaites, *Early Western Travels*, vol. 23, p. 277.

dan and Hidatsa villages. David Thompson traveled to the villages during the winter of 1797 in the company of several free traders who had obtained goods on credit from the North West Company. He remarked on one of the major motives of these men for making the trip: "The curse of the Mandanes is an almost total want of Chastity: this, the men with me know, and I found it was almost their sole motive for their journey hereto: The goods they brought, they sold at 50 to 60 pr cent above what they cost; and reserving enough to pay their debts, and buy some corn; [they] spent the rest on Women."[68]

Elsewhere in his memoirs Thompson asserts that "the white men who have hitherto visited these Villages have not been examples of chastity" and states that Jusseaume, McCrachan, and other men admitted to having often taken part in ceremonial sexual intercourse with Mandan women.[69] Alexander Henry remarked at length on the sexual proclivities of the Hidatsas, believing them to be "still more loose and licentious than the Mandanes." In this context note David Thompson's comment that the village women "do all they can to heighten the voluptiousness of Love." He noted that Hidatsa men "are always ready to supply a stranger with a bedfellow, if he has any property," and that they "are very complaisant in giving him [that is, a stranger] the choice of their women."[70]

Many visitors to the Mandan and Hidatsa villages have left descriptions of native ceremonies involving sexual intercourse in which white visitors were sometimes enticed to participate. Although the traders interpreted the sexual practices of the Mandans and Hidatsas from a narrowly ethnocentric and moralistic perspective, and condemned the behavior they witnessed, they failed to understand that sexual intercourse among Plains Indians often served as a medium for the transference of personal power from one man to another, or was performed in connection with fertility rituals relating to the abundance of buffalo and other needed food resources.[71] Nevertheless, the sexual opportunities stemming from these practices were considered a major attraction of the villages by traders of little conscience.

[68]Thompson, *David Thompson's Narrative of His Explorations*, p. 234.
[69]Ibid., p. 235.

[70]Thompson's Journal, entry for January 10, 1798; Henry, *New Light*, vol. 1, pp. 347–48.
[71]Thompson, *David Thompson's Narrative of His Explorations*, pp. 234–35; David Thompson, "David Thompson at the Mandan-Hidatsa Villages, 1797-1798: The Original Journals," *Ethnohistory* 24 (Fall, 1977): 335–36; Thompson's Journal, "fair journal," entry for January 9, 1798; Tabeau, *Tabeau's Narrative*, p. 197; Lewis and Clark, *Original Journals*, vol. 1, p. 245; Thwaites, *Early Western Travels*, vol. 23, p. 334; vol. 24, pp. 27–31, 39–43; Alice B. Kehoe, "The Function of Ceremonial Sexual Intercourse among the Northern Plains Indians," *Plains Anthropologist* 15 (May, 1970): 99–103; Katherine M. Weist, "Plains Indian Women: An Assessment," in *Anthropology on the Great Plains*, ed. W. Raymond Wood and Margot Liberty, pp. 255–71. See also Edward M. Bruner, "Mandan," in *Perspectives in American Indian Culture Change*, ed. Edward H. Spicer, pp. 216–17.

4

Epilogue to Part One

THE Canadian trade was respon-sible for introducing the first Euro-American goods to the Man-dans and Hidatsas. The French pe-riod, between the years just before La Vérendrye's arrival on the Mis-souri in 1738 and the cession of Can-ada in 1763, witnessed only a trickle of such goods to the Upper Missouri River tribes. For the same period we have only fragmentary and incon-sistent accounts of Euro-Americans reaching their villages from the south, via the Missouri River, or perhaps overland from the southeast, from Prairie du Chien on the Mississippi River. For most of the French period, therefore, the Mandans were only indirectly in touch with Euro-Ameri-cans, and the contacts they did have with such traders probably had little effect on their life-style.

Their appetite for the new goods, especially guns, metal kettles, and items such as steel awls—so patently superior to their own native bone counterparts—began to be met by the next wave of Canadian traders: British companies, especially Hud-son's Bay Company and the North West Company. These business co-alitions, operated by the English and manned by French and English em-ployees from Great Britain and east-ern Canada, were augmented by other traders, such as free traders who came to the villages from Saint Louis and from the Mississippi River. The Brit-ish period, between 1763 and about 1818, overlapped briefly with Span-ish expeditions to the Upper Mis-souri River between 1792 and 1797 and later with the Americans, be-ginning with Lewis and Clark and extending down to the reservation period in the late 1800s, when the fur trade was finally fully eclipsed. The British trade was most impor-tant between 1785, when Pine Fort was established on the Assiniboine River, and 1812. During that time the native desire for Euro-American goods crystallized into dependence on them, setting the scene for the establishment near their villages of permanent trading posts such as Fort Clark by the Saint Louis–based Amer-ican Fur Company about 1831. The establishment of these posts destroyed what little was left of the old inter-tribal trading system for the villagers by eliminating them as middlemen. A major source of their affluence was thereby dissolved; about all that re-mained to them were their crops, principally corn, and a few buffalo robes which they traded directly to the traders at the posts.

70

Between 1780 and 1837 the culture of the Mandans and Hidatsas all but collapsed under the dual effects of their loss of population through the arrival of diseases to which they had no natural immunity and changes in their material culture and social life brought about by new conditions. These changes, nearly all of them detrimental to their millennium-long way of life, were exacerbated by the hostility of the Dakota Sioux, a group that (together with disease) nearly destroyed them entirely.

Archaeologically, the most conspicuous harbinger of the Euro-American trade is the presence of ever-increasing volumes of white goods in the native village sites.[1] Edged tools rapidly replaced native stone and bone tools and quickly became necessities, for they reduced the expenditure of labor needed to produce and process foods and other goods, but such luxuries as mirrors, glass beads, and paint (or vermilion) were almost equally important. These commodities were augmented by a host of new elements, such as horse gear, gun accessories, and a multitude of other implements. By 1845, when the Mandans and Hidatsas left the mouth of the Knife River to found Like-a-Fishhook village further upstream, only remnants of their native technologies remained. The native pottery vessels remaining were essen-

tially heirloom pieces; tools formerly made of chipped and ground stone, except for hammers and whetstones, had all but vanished; and items made of bone were largely made for use in native games and ceremonies.[2] By that time, trade goods "no longer dribbled into the Northern Plains through tenant traders and Indian middlemen. . . . Instead, they came up the Missouri by the ton in keelboats and, later, in steamboats."[3]

Equally conspicuous in the archaeological record is the precipitous decline in the number of Mandan and Hidatsa towns. There appear to have been about twenty-four of their Heart River–phase villages before about 1780, some of them containing well over one hundred dwellings and with a total estimated population of about 11,500 individuals. Bowers, on the other hand, has estimated the pre-1780 Mandan and Hidatsa population at 9,000 individuals. Either of these estimates seems reasonable given the ambiguity in the nineteenth-century ethnohistorical data. Twenty-four years later there were only five Knife River–phase communities, with a total population of about 3,750 people.[4]

[1]See Dennis Toom, "The Middle Missouri Villages and the Early Fur Trade: Implications for Archaeological Interpretation" (M.A. thesis, University of Nebraska, Lincoln, 1979), for a discussion of significance of the relative amounts of trade goods in early postcontact villages in the Middle Missouri subarea.

[2]G. Hubert Smith, *Like-a-Fishhook Village and Fort Berthold, Garrison Reservoir, North Dakota*, National Park Service Anthropological Papers, no. 2, pp. 58–73. See also Donald J. Lehmer, "The Other Side of the Fur Trade," in *Selected Writings of Donald J. Lehmer*, ed. W. Raymond Wood, pp. 94–95.

[3]Lehmer, "Other Side," p. 101.

[4]Donald J. Lehmer, "Epidemics Among the Indians of the Upper Missouri," in *Selected Writings of Donald J. Lehmer*, ed. W. Raymond Wood, p. 107; Alfred W. Bowers, *Hidatsa Social and Ceremonial Organization*, Bureau of American Ethnology Bulletin

The introduction of acute crowd infections (measles, smallpox, influenza, cholera, whooping cough, and others), all of them diseases for which the Indians had no natural immunity, account for the massive depopulation of the Mandans and Hidatsas in the late eighteenth and early nineteenth centuries. From 1780 to 1838 the Mandans and Hidatsas endured several major epidemics, which can be grouped as follows:

1780-81. The first recorded smallpox epidemic was probably introduced from the Spanish Southwest by nomadic Indian traders coming to the villages.[5] Although hard evidence is lacking, it surely had been preceded by other epidemics of varying magnitude. Jean Baptiste Truteau, writing of observations made in 1795, noted that smallpox had struck the Arikaras, the first tribe downstream from the Mandans, at "three different times." There is a high probability that these epidemics would have been subsequently transmitted to the Mandans and Hidatsas (if they were not indeed the sources for the Arikara epidemics). This series of epidemics would include the 1780-81 outbreak (which was Plains-wide in scope) as well as earlier ones, since smallpox tended to erupt at about eighteen-to-twenty-year intervals.[6]

1806-12. During this time the Mandans and Hidatsas suffered a major epidemic,[7] although descriptions of it are so generalized that they can only be said to refer to acute respiratory infections. While not as devastating as the 1780-81 smallpox experience, this epidemic appears to have produced great hardship among the villagers.

1833. An epidemic of whooping cough occurred during that year at Fort Clark. Maximilian, while living at Fort Clark in November of this year, noted that a number of Mandans and Hidatsas had "died of the hooping-cough which was very prevalent."[8]

1837-38. The final major epidemic that these tribes endured was an outbreak of smallpox. Joshua Pilcher, an agent for the U.S. government on the Upper Missouri, said that these epidemics had turned the Upper Missouri "into one *great grave yard*," and by his estimate the Hidatsas had been reduced from one thousand to five hundred people, while only thirty-one Mandans remained of an

---

194, p. 486; Meriwether Lewis and William Clark, *Original Journals of the Lewis and Clark Expedition, 1804-06,* ed. Reuben Gold Thwaites, vol. 6, p. 89-91.

[5]Lehmer, "Other Side," p. 100; Marc Simmons, "New Mexico's Smallpox Epidemic of 1780-1781," *New Mexico Historical Review* 41 (October, 1966): 319-26; David Thompson, *David Thompson's Narrative of His Explorations in Western America, 1784-1812,* Publications of the Champlain Society, vol. 12, ed. J. B. Tyrrell, pp. 336-37.

[6]Abraham P. Nasatir, ed., *Before Lewis and Clark: Documents Illustrating the History of the Missouri, 1785-1804,* vol. 1, p. 299; Donald J. Lehmer, *Introduction to Middle Missouri Archeology,* National Park Service Anthropological Papers, no. 1, p. 174.

[7]Alexander Henry [the Younger], *New Light on the Early History of the Greater Northwest,* vol. 1, p. 343; Doane Robinson, "The Putrid Fever of 1812," *South Dakota Historical Collections* 12: 67-70.

[8]Reuben Gold Thwaites, *Early Western Travels, 1748-1846,* vol. 24, pp. 15, 18.

estimated population of sixteen hundred.[9]

As a consequence of the series of epidemics, the balance of power on the river changed radically, since the nomadic tribes suffered less than did the villagers. At one time the village Indians (including the Arikaras) had been about equal in power to the Sioux. Now they were reduced to a few towns which the Sioux were able to dominate and terrorize.[10]

The population decline led to the consolidation of the remnants of several different villages into a single one for survival. This amalgamation had a number of significant social consequences. To begin with, political authority, once wielded by power figures in each village, clashed when leaders from different villages tried to manipulate the policies of a single town. Losses of key individuals in political circles, as well as "in the ritual and ceremonial spheres must have seriously disrupted life" in these composite towns.[11] The list of such conflicts, losses, and disruptions can be expanded into every sphere of social life, and it was for this reason that Lehmer characterized the post-1780 populations as "disorganized," a term which seems mild considering that their culture had been shattered and that they lived in constant dread for their lives.

About 1780 or a little earlier, massive changes in the lives of both groups were also stimulated by the introduction of new technologies through the medium of the fur trade, as well as by the greatly reduced population. Indeed, these two factors served to reinforce one another. Both the Mandans and the Hidatsas had a number of craft specialists—that is, the men and women who made their pottery, arrows, and other "high-technology" elements of their material culture. Given a situation such as that of 1780–81, when perhaps two-thirds of a population containing such specialists was eliminated in one stroke, most of these specialists could also be expected to die, and their rights to fashion given forms would have disappeared. One of the most conspicuous changes in their material culture about 1780 was a massive shift in the way in which they made their handmade pottery. The elaborate decorative patterns and vessel forms of the old Heart River–phase pottery vanished and were replaced by designs and forms that are entirely new in composition. This change has been credited to the possibility that the potters who owned the proprietary rights to ceramic designs died during the massive population reduction accompanying that epidemic.[12] Whereas the old forms could not then be duplicated by the survivors, they could

[9]Francis A. Chardon, *Chardon's Journal at Fort Clark, 1834-1839*, ed. Annie Heloise Abel; Joshua Pilcher to William Clark, February 27, 1838 (microfilm roll 884, M234, Record Group 75, National Archives).

[10]The authors thank Michael K. Trimble for his assistance in compiling the record on Mandan and Hidatsa epidemics and population.

[11]Nasatir, *Before Lewis and Clark*, vol. 1, p. 299, documents these kinds of problems among the Arikaras; Lehmer, "Epidemics," p. 109.

[12]Donald J. Lehmer, W. Raymond Wood, and C. L. Dill, "Knife River Phase" (manuscript), pp. 183–85.

be replaced by new forms, or by trade goods. In this sense, the consequences of disease and the introduction of new goods may not be distinguishable. Their combined effects, in any case, produced the differences that set the Heart River phase apart from its successor, the Knife River phase.

Other major elements contributing to change were the disruptive effects of the arrival of the horse and of guns, the latter being traded in from Canada and the former coming to the villages largely by way of nomadic tribes from the Spanish Southwest. These two elements were clearly related to increased warfare between the Mandans and Hidatsas and their roaming neighbors, further stressing the villagers. Competition for furs and for Euro-American trade goods may also have fueled already existing animosities. Warfare was the principal factor that forced the Mandans and Hidatsas to live near each other for mutual protection, principally against the Sioux. The close proximity of the villages— bunched together at the mouth of the Knife River—led to rapid depletion of local resources, including timber as well as fur-bearing animals and game. This forced the villagers to go ever further afield in hunting, thus making them even more suscep-

tible to depredations by the Dakota Sioux. Meriwether Lewis, in an entry for April 11, 1805, remarked that the country from Fort Mandan to the mouth of the Little Missouri River "is so constantly hunted by the Minetaries [Hidatsas] that there is but little game" there.[13] The mouth of the Little Missouri River was about seventy river miles above Fort Mandan.

By 1845, the once powerful Mandans and Hidatsas were living in a single town, Like-a-Fishhook village. They had been reduced from two dozen villages to a single one and now had such a small population that their very culture was on the verge of extinction. A century earlier they, with their neighbors the Arikaras, had been the most influential and affluent peoples in the Northern Plains. Their towns had attracted Indian and white traders alike for hundreds of miles, and they were the culture climax in that part of the continent. The historical documents we have used here provide part of the story of their contact with Euro-Americans and their subsequent decline. When these data are combined with the results of archaeological research recently conducted in their villages, a fuller understanding of that history will be possible.

[13]Lewis and Clark, *Original Journals*, vol. 1, p. 296; see also p. 298.

PART TWO

THE NARRATIVES

1

John Macdonell's "The Red River"

THE first document we consider in this volume is a brief record of the geography, Indians, and Euro-American trade along the northeastern margin of the Northern Great Plains. The account, one of the first to describe in general terms the trade and trade routes of the Canadian West in the 1790s, provides a general background for the activities of the North West Company. It also provides the first description of the Mandans and their neighbors by visitors from Canada since the 1787 visit to those villages by James Mackay.[1]

The author of this account, John Macdonell, was born in Scotland on November 30, 1768. He migrated with his father to New York in 1773, then moved on to Canada a short time later. John's brother, Miles, later became the first governor of Lord Selkirk's Red River Colony. John signed his contract with the North West Company on May 10, 1793, and embarked at Lachine for the west fifteen days later, aboard a birchbark canoe bound for the fort of the River Qu'Appelle, where he

was to winter, arriving there on October 8, 1793. This part of his life is covered by a detailed diary which was published by Gates.[2] Macdonell's life for the next two years is contained in a second diary, published in part by L. R. Masson.[3] This second diary begins on October 11, 1793, and continues through June 7, 1795. The document published here is, in effect, a synopsis of certain parts of both documents, and postdates both of them.

In 1797, John became a partner in the North West Company, and he remained with them until 1815. For eight years he served the company in the general area of the River Qu'-Appelle, in 1804 he was in the Athabascan country, and in 1807 he returned to the River Qu'Appelle. He

---

[1] Mackay's journal for this expedition appears in Abraham P. Nasatir, *Before Lewis and Clark: Documents Illustrating the History of the Missouri, 1785-1804*, vol. 2, pp. 490-95.

[2] Charles M. Gates, ed., *Five Fur Traders of the Northwest*, pp. 63-119.

[3] L. R. Masson, ed., *Les Bourgeois de la Compagnie du Nord-Ouest: Recits de Voyages, Lettres et Rapports Inedits Relatifs au Nord-Ouest Canadien*, vol. 1, pp. 283-95. Louis Rodrique Masson, prominent Canadian politician and journeyman historian, edited and published numerous fur trade journals which had been collected shortly after the turn of the nineteenth century by Roderick McKenzie, a former partner in the North West Company.

was later stationed at Isle à la Crosse and at Lesser Slave Lake. During his stay in the west he took as his common-law wife Magdeline Poitras, the daughter of a trader on the Qu'-Appelle River, André Poitras, and his Indian wife.

In 1812 Macdonell returned east, serving briefly as a captain in the corps of Canadian voyageurs, but he was captured at the Battle of Saint Regis. By 1814 he was living at Point Fortune, on the Ottawa River. He ran a store there and ran boats to Montreal as well as serving as a judge. He died at the age of eighty-two on April 17, 1850, and was buried in the cemetery of Saint André (d'Argenteuil). His wife, Magdeline, survived him for twenty years. In 1853, a posthumous marriage legalized their union and eight children and made them his legal heirs.[4]

John Macdonell's manuscript, "The Red River," is in the Rare Books and Special Collections of McLennan Library, McGill University, Montreal, and is cataloged as CH 183.S164. It is written on handmade paper, 16.5 cm by 19.8 cm, bound in one signature of thirty-four pages. The paper is watermarked "GR" over "1794," beneath the seated figure of Britannia surmounted by a crown. The manuscript is entirely in brown ink and has been edited by another hand using a darker brown ink. A few minor changes in pencil, apparently by Masson, have been deleted from the present transcription. L. R. Masson's 1889–90 publication of this

journal was badly handled: grammar, capitalization, punctuation, and spelling were consistently modified to bring the language of the document into line with Masson's concept of modern usage.[5] Furthermore, beginning on manuscript page 24, substantial parts of sentences were deleted from many of the paragraphs. These were the circumstances that prompted the preparation of this new transcription; conventions followed in the transcription are given in the Editorial Procedures.

The version published here appears to be the copy sent to Roderick McKenzie, from which a second version was made, for opposite the first page is the note: "John McDonnell copied by order of Hon. R. McKenzie / in bound volume returned by Hist Society of Quebec / L R Masson Terrebonne." This second copy of the manuscript is also at McGill's McLennan Library, cataloged as CH 23.S59. Entitled "Some Account of the Red River," it is the sixth account in a bound volume measuring 20.3 cm by 33 cm, entitled "Some Account of the North West Company," by Roderick McKenzie. This second version is in one hand, in brown ink on hand made paper watermarked "1827." A number of words are underscored in pencil. This version appears to be the copy which Masson edited for publication in his *Les Bourgeois de la Compagnie du Nord-Ouest.*

The original manuscript apparently dates to about 1797, to judge from a reference on page 17 of the manuscript to the fact that Fort Es-

---

[4] Details of Macdonell's life are from Masson, *Les Bourgeois,* vol. 1, p. 267 n. 1; and from Gates, *Five Fur Traders,* pp. 63–65.

[5] Masson, *Les Bourgeois,* vol. 1, pp. 267–81.

pérance had been settled "these ten years past." Opposite the first page of the copy is noted, in Masson's hand and in black ink, the notation: "About 1797 viz., 10 years after Robert Grant established Fort Qu appelle which he called Fort Espérance." The title "The Red River" is deceptive to modern readers, for most of the text alludes to activities on the Assiniboine River. In Macdonell's time, however, the Assiniboine River was referred to as the "Upper Red River," while the modern Red River proper was alluded to as the "Lower Red River."[6]

THE RED RIVER
BY
JOHN MCDONNELL
OF THE NORTH-WEST COMPANY

[p. 1] After leaving the North-West Company's Fort at the bottom of the river *Ouinipique*,[7] we have near Eighteen leagues of the lake that goes by that name, to Coast along, before we come to the Entrance of the Red River.

This River enters Lake Ouinipique at its S.E. corner by three different channels; the middle channel is the deepest and most practicable; the others being choaked up by sand at their entrance into the Lake. It is encompassed with very tall Reeds; the wood being only discernible at a distance. This middle Branch is the Road of all Canoes, &c that enter the River. All the branches join a league above the entrance & two leagues higher the banks (tho' still very low) begin to be covered with wood.

Three leagues from the lake, the River *aux morts*[8] enters the R. River on the north side, here a large camp of Assiniboils, Krees and Saulteux[9] were massacred by the Sioux or [p. 2] Naudawesse, the most powerful nation in all the interior country. Ever since this

---

[6] Gates, *Five Fur Traders*, p. 97 n. 63.

[7] A contemporary spelling for the Winnipeg River.

[8] This river is now known as Netley Creek.

[9] That is, the Siouan-speaking Assiniboins and the Algonquian-speaking Crees and Chippewas.

slaughter the River has been Called with Proprity, *Riviére aux Morts.*

Two or three Leagues above R. aux Morts is a clear spot on which Mr. Joseph Frobisher is said to have pass'd a winter, which place we call *Fort a Mons. Frobisher.*

The first Rapid we come to is *Le Sault a la Biche* about three leagues above Mr. Frobisher's Fort and three more leagues long, at low water it is a great obstacle, but any other time the men push up the Canoes with setting-poles.

Near the head of *Sault a la Biche* the plains come to the very brink of the river but only in small openings of an acre & a half but the grass and other weeds are so tall owing to the moisness of the soil that it is very disagreeable walking. There is always plenty of water from the *Sault a la Biche* to the Forks,[10] reckonned six Leagues.

At the Forks the remains of several old Posts are still to be seen, some of which were built as far back as the time of the French [p. 3] Government. It as well as the Rivière aux Morts, is a favorite Indian Encampment. On these places we generally find some straggling Saulteux or Pilleurs from lake Rouge who generally have Provisions to Barter for liquor *en passant.*

Here we leave the Red & enter the Assiniboil River the smallest branch of the two, which is very shoal, full of sand banks, and one of the most crooked that fancy can conceive. A man on foot that marches straight thro' the plains in three Hours time can go as far as the Canoes can in a day.

The Red River properly so called takes its water near the head of the Mississipi and by it the southern Traders from La Prairie du Chien enter the Assiniboil, but is a long way about and very precarious as they are forced to come thro' the territories of the Sioux the most savage and barbarous of any nation of the plain Indians. This road is called passer par l'aile du Corbeau, after a portage of that name.

[p. 4] All along the bank of the Red River & a considerable distance from it on each side is very little frequented except by war parties, being a Road to war between the Saulteux and their Enemies the Sioux who are ever at variance.

From the Forks of the Assiniboil & Red River the plains are quite near the Banks, and so extensive that a man may travel from here to

---

[10] The term "the Forks" alludes to the junction of the Assiniboine River with the Red River, where the present city of Winnipeg now stands.

Fort des Prairies, Rocky Mountain, Missouri, Mississippi, and many other places without passing a wood a mile long. All the wood here, as in the rest of the plains, being only small tufts, here and there (called by the French, Flêts de bois) being surrounded by the plain the same as an Island is circumvented by water, and slips that grow on the richest lands, on low points near the river & on its banks.

Half a day's march for the Canoes [p. 5] higher than the Forks, is the passage so call'd from its being a good fording place & the first we come to of the Buffalo Fords. Here we often meet the first Buffalo being generally some straggling Bulls, and can get here in three days from the Entrance of the River into the Lake Ouinipique.

Besides the Buffalo we have another resource in the fish that abounds in this little River & take care to supply the canoes with fishing tackling on that account. The sturgeon of this River is reckoned the best in the North-West, but are only caught in small drawing nets of two fathoms long, chiefly in the spring of the year. The fish we catch with the lines are the Barbue or Cat-Fish, *Poisson* d'Oré, Pike, & *La Caiche,* a small species of white fish well known in the Saint Laurence about Montreal, and so common here, that I have seen them catch 30 or 40 one [per] man while smoking their pipes.[11]

[p. 6] All along the Assiniboil River may be seen the vestiges of many commercial settlements, many of which claim an ancient date. Blondishe's Fort is the first we come to, next is Fort la Reine, according to some, but others say Fort la Reine stood at the portage La Prairie.[12] After coming to Adhemar's Fort we get to the portage La Prairie in a day, (that is the canoe) by land the distance does not exceed six miles.

Portage la Prairie so called by the Indians time out of mind, is about eight days march by water for the Canoes from the Rivers mouth.

---

[11] Most of these fish can be identified readily, especially the lake sturgeon, *Acipenser fulvescens;* channel catfish, *Ictalurus punctatus;* and northern pike, *Esox lucius.* "La Caiche" is probably lake whitefish, *Coregonus clupeaformis.* Many fish in the Assiniboine have a golden hue; the goldfish *Carassius auratus* is an obvious candidate for the "Poisson d'Oré," but this species was introduced in the late 1800s in eastern Canada. The fish in question may be the golden shiner, *Notemigonus crysoleucas* (W. B. Scott and E. J. Crossman, *Freshwater Fishes of Canada*).

[12] La Vérendrye's Fort la Reine stood on the north bank of the Assiniboine River near the modern city of Portage la Prairie, named for the portage between the Assiniboine River and Lake Manitoba (Gates, *Five Fur Traders*, p. 111 n. 101). See Macdonell's comments on the portage following.

Across this portage which is about 12 miles over, the Fort Dauphin goods used to be carried under the French *commandants* to the lake Manitou-Ban & from thence to the River *Dauphine.*

At this place Mr. Wm. McKay in behalf [p. 7] of the North-West Company passed the winter of 1794/5 & had Mr. Réaume, Dejadon for LaViolette and Linklater for the Honble. H.B. Comp. to cope with, against a superior quantity of merchdise. & still made good returns.

Three leagues above the Portage La Prairie stood Le Fort des Trembles, or Poplar Fort;[13] in the year 1780 or 81 the Indians made an attempt to pillage the Traders, Messrs. Bruce & Boyer & in the scuffle that ensued two Frenchmen & seven Indians were kill'd upon the spot, owing to this affair the traders were obliged for fear of being cut off to reembark in their Canoes and return to winter at the Forks & the small Pox seizing the Natives & sweeping off three fourths of them, compelled them to lay aside their intentions of cutting off all the white men in the interior country as providence would have it.

Above the Fort des Trembles is a wood call'd La Grande Tremblière [p. 8] which stretches a considerable distance out into the plains, so that the common road of land passage is thro' the centre of it, this wood is about three leagues long but may be avoided by striking out thro' the plains at Portage La prairie. Above the Grande Trembliere the soil changes suddenly; the lower parts, from the River aux Morts to the extremity of the Grande Trembliere being generally a good soil very susceptible of culture & capable of bearing rich crops; whereas above it the soil has attained such a mixture of yellow sand that it is in some places covered with grass which seldom exceeds ancle height, covering the ground but very sparingly.

The Pine Fort[14] the lowest post the NW Co. had in the Assiniboine River we were obliged to abandoned in the year [17]94, as the Honble. H. B. Co. and other new comers had settled the year before

---

[13] Named for the quaking aspen, *Populus tremuloides.* Poplar Fort was also known as Fort des Prairies and Fort a la Corne; "it was one of the oldest and most continuously occupied of the establishments in the west" (Ernest Voorhis, *Historic Forts and Trading Posts of the French Régime and of the English Fur Trading Companies,* pp. 29–30).

[14] Pine Fort was a North West Company post on the north bank of the Assiniboine River eighteen miles below the junction of the Assiniboine and the Souris rivers; it was sometimes known as fort Des Epinettes, de Pins, and des Trembles (Voorhis, *Historic Forts and Trading Posts,* p. 138).

FIG. 4. The Assiniboine River near Portage la Prairie, Manitoba. Photograph by
W. R. Wood.

at River La Sourie about seven leagues by land [p. 9] higher up
the river & three days travelling for the craft by water; the posts
being too near each other as we had placed ourselves along-side of
the others at the above mentioned new station.

It is sometimes commanded the summer men to meet the Canoes
any place above the grande Trembliere with provisions on Horseback &c if such a step be necessary an express is hurried off over
land from any place above the Forks to give them warning. The
Bourgeois go always up by land from the place they first meet the
Horses, & generally from the River du Milieu horses or not. The
River du Milieu is ten Leagues below pine Fort.

The face of the Country from the Grande Trembliere to the
westernmost end of the Mountain du Diable is very poor & barren
& the soil mostly yellow sand all broken into little hillocks separated
from one another by as many little glens.

83

But at the Mountain du Diable which commences [p. 10] at the pine Fort & continues nearly two Leagues to its westward the country turns one great plain to the head of the Assiniboil River and even to Fort George and the Rocky Mountain.[15]

The Indians that trade at the River La Sourie are a mixture of all the Nations in the Assiniboil River; but the Krees are the most numerous; the others are roving *Saulteux* that are sometimes here sometimes at Fort Dauphin, sometimes at the lac du Manitou-*ban* and other places wherever fancy leads them, and Assiniboils the same as at Fort des Prairie but much more indolent than those to be met within the River du Pas.[16]

From the River La Sourie the trade with the Mandans and gros Ventres inhabitting both sides of the Missouri has been carried on since the pine Fort was thrown up.[17] This trade was carried on by the men taking a [p. 11] certain number of skins as suits their circumstances at the prices of this Post upon Credit & paying their Credits at their return. Many of the Cos. Servants deserting from the Mandan country with an intention of going to the Illinois & other places on the Mississipi the trade has since been entirely neglected.

The distance of the Mandan village upon the Missouri from our factory at River La Sourie is ten or 12 days march in winter. Supposed to be one Hundred leagues due South of this place. In going to the Mandan Country the people are sometimes obliged to sleep without any wood & in such cases experience has taught them to make fires of Buffalo Dung, dried in the sun, after the Indian manner; of which there is always plenty to be had; which shows the vast quantity of those animals that [p. 12] frequent the plains. There is so little snow at the Missouri that the Natives run down the Buffalo on horse back the whole winter thro'.

---

[15] Probably the North West Company fort on the North Saskatchewan River. Voorhis (*Historic Forts and Trading Posts,* p. 72) comments that it was the most westerly house in 1798.

[16] Fort Dauphin, also known as Dauphin Lake House, was built in 1775 and rebuilt twice later. During Macdonell's time it was on the Ochre River a few miles south of Dauphin Lake (Voorhis, *Historic Forts and Trading Posts,* p. 58). Fort des Prairies was the name applied to several posts along the Saskatchewan River, including Poplar Fort; see note 13 above.

[17] Voorhis, *Historic Forts and Trading Posts,* dates the construction of Pine Fort as 1784–85 and referred to it as the principal trading post for the Mandan trade until its abandonment in 1794. Apparently the post was later reoccupied and in operation, for in September, 1807, John McKay reported that a Mr. McKenzie was in charge at Pine Fort (H.B.C.A., B.22/a/15, fo. 3d).

These Indians live in settled villages fortified round about with Palisades which they seldom ever abandon & are the best husbandmen in the whole North-West, for they raise Indian Corn or (maize) Beans, Pumpkins, Squashes &c in considerable quantities; not only sufficient to supply their own wants with the help of the Buffalo, but also to sell & give away to all strangers that enter their villages. They are the mildest and most honest Savages upon the whole Continent & withal very fond of the white people.

They report that the Missouri from their settlements to the Rocky Mountains, is not obstructed with a [p. 13] single waterfall; and French Travellers from the Illinois and Pencourt affirm that it is one continued series of smooth Current till its junction with the Mississipi near the latter place.[18] The Missouri Indians say its only fall is down the eastern side of that Ridge of Hills call'd the Rocky Mountain which they describe as very high so much so that they cross the River under the sheet of water without its coming near them.[19] They suppose it takes its water near the summit of the Rocky Mountain. The Mandan village, on the Missouri by Mr. Evans Chart is 460 Leagues distant from the Illinois.[20]

But to return to the Assiniboil River, it is very shallow & full of rapids for a Day & a half's voyage for the Canoes to the Barriere, about five leagues over land from the Post at River la Sourie, but after that they go on well till they meet the [p. 14] sand banks after passing Mountain La Bosse.

Near a league above the Barriere on each side of the River, begins a ridge of hills about the distance of a mile on each side, & the summit of this ridge is only level with the rest of the plain Country above, forming a deep vale between them, at the bottom of which runs the assiniboil River which keeps a continual winding

---

[18] Pencourt, a corruption of the French word *paincourt* ("short of bread"), was a contemporary nickname for Saint Louis because of the occasional food shortages there (John Francis McDermott, *A Glossary of Mississippi Valley French, 1673-1850,* Washington University Studies, New Series, Language and Literature, no. 12, p. 110).

[19] This description of the Great Falls of the Missouri River, near the modern city of Great Falls, Montana, makes it obvious that they are relying on hearsay accounts of it.

[20] This reference to "Mr. Evans Chart" probably refers to Lewis Evans, a contemporary mapmaker and not to John T. Evans, who mapped the Missouri River from what is now northeastern Nebraska to the Mandan villages in 1796-97. W. Raymond Wood, "The John Evans 1796-97 Map of the Missouri River," *Great Plains Quarterly* 1 (Winter, 1981): 39-53.

from one side to the other of the hills called by the French *Grandes Côtes* in the valley below.

Those that go up the River by land owing to the continual windings of the River have plenty of time to Hunt Buffalo, Elk, Moose deer, Caberie [antelope] and Fowl of all kinds which abound in this country & nevertheless keep up with the Canoes. The country is so plentifull that the Canoes have always either fresh meat [p. 15] or Fowl for their Kettles.

The country here is as below, one large plain interspersed with small Islands of wood here & there, but the low points of land near the water are frequently shaded by groves of venerable oaks & Elms; the soil of the plains a mixture of Sand, Clay, Gravel & stones in many places, but the glen wherein the River Runs is a mixture of Clay and black mould.

The Mountain a la Bosse,[21] the nearest post to the NWest Compy's settlement at River La Sourie & distant from it 6 days voyage for the Canoes & two days for foot men thro' the Plains, has been frequently established & as often abandoned, owing to the Oppositions that Come into the quarter, as these Gentlemen when by themselves, establish as few posts as they conveniently can in Order to save property. On the Contrary, when incommoded by new comers they subdivide & divert the [p. 16] trade into as many little channels as they have men and clerks & men to occupy; well knowing that their opponents (who have but a few goods generally) cannot oppose them at every place.

This post turned out about sixty packs at an average for the NW Compy exclusive of Opposition Trade, but the returns from it are mostly Wolves and Buffalo robes.

Six days' march from Mountain a la Bosse the River qui appelle enters the Assiniboil River, and on it about two short days march in canoes farther up is Fort Esperance which has been settled these ten years past & was chiefly Mr. Robert Grants residence while he superintended the Red River affairs and has always been inhabited summer & winter ever since. It is at this post and Mountain a la Bosse that Most of the Red River provisions has been traded, being both Assiniboil Posts; for provisions [p. 17] are their chief returns.

River la Coquille is the nearest post to the River qui appelle &

---

[21] This is the post from which F.-A. Larocque left on his journey to the Yellowstone River in 1805; see François-Antoine Larocque's "Yellowstone Journal," n. 7.

distant from it about a days march over land, tho' in the fall it takes the Canoes four days by water; a trifling post as most of the Indians about it go to the River Tremblante & R. qui appelle; those that trade chiefly at this post are Saulteux.

River Tremblante is next to River La Coquille & distant from it little farther than it is from R. qui appelle this and the temporary posts established above it fournish most of the Beaver & Otters in the Red River returns. But this trade has been almost ruined since the H. B. Company enter'd the Assiniboil River by way of Swan River carrying their Merchandize from one River to the Other on horse back three days journey; who by that means & the short distance [p. 18] between Swan River & their factory at York Fort from whence they are Equiped can arrive at the Coude de l'homme in the Assiniboil River, a month sooner than we can return from the Grand Portage, & get All the fall trade and besides give Credits to all the Indians and send them a hunting before our arrival, so that we see but very few in that quarter upon our arrival. River Tremblante has ever been Mr. Cuthbert Grant's favorite residence since he came to the Red River.

Amongst the Saulteux in the Assiniboil River the same customs & superstitions prevail as in their native places, Lake La pluie and Lac Rouge.[22] When a relation or a friend of theirs dies, to testify their sorrow they pierce their arms and thighs in divers places with arrows, & in their Mournings daub [p. 19] their faces over with a mixture of earth & coal and frequently cut off their hair.

A Corps[e] is seldom taken out at the door of their Lodge, but the place opposite to where the deceased's head lays is raised up in order to make a passage for it. The body is gathered up with his knees in his belly to make him as short as possible & every thing he used about his person is interred with him viz, his arms & accoutrements, provisions for his journey, tobacco to smoke, a Dish & a wooden spoon, shoes & his best cloathing upon his back. Their favorite manner of disposing of their dead is upon scaffolds raised a mans height above ground, tho' they sometimes inter them in the ground.

After the funeral succeeds the funeral feast which is eaten sitting round the grave or scaffold where the deceased is deposited of which feast he is supposed to [p. 20] partake as well as of the Calumet

---

[22] Modern Rainy Lake and Red Lake.

of which the stem end is pointed towards him in order that he may smoke. A lock of his hair is cut off before the interment which is carefully wrapped up & carried about with them for the space of twelve months wrapped in a piece of the best Cloth to be had and garnished with porcupine Quills &c after their fancy.

Almost every great man or chief among the Indians is likewise a Juggler or doctor of Physic. Their medecines being simples they collect themselves, & when one teaches to another the virtue of an herb he knew not, their is scarce any bound to his liberallity in repaying his instructor; but since traders frequent these posts several Indians make use of European medecines.

Every Juggler pretends to have a familiar spirit who pays him [p. 21] frequent visits when his attendance is required & in emergencies directs by his answers which are generally as dark & ambiguous as those of the ancient Oracles among the heathens, and which may be interpreted many different ways. But this spirit never appears but in the *jonglerie* a small circular apartment raised a man's height, & inclosed with raw hides &c bound with thongs; into this place the Juggler is thrust sometimes tied neck & heels, & a few minutes after the Tabor & Chichiquoi begin beating & he kiks the Cords that bound him out of the Juggling place, tho' there could be no person seen within. The jonglerie is about three feet in diameter.

All the answers he gets from his familiar are during his stay in this juggling house. Most Indians put an implicit belief on what the person in the jonglerie says, for he speaks in two different voices to deceive his hearers.

[p. 22] The Krees were formerly a great & numerous nation; their language is spoken still by their descendants which is a Dialect of the Chippeway or Saulteux; they extended formerly from Lake Ouinipique (by some called Cristineaux or Killistinoe Lake) as far north as Athabasca and a considerable way into the Plains, by the River du Pas, Assiniboil River, and Swan River; covering several hundred leagues territory. But owing to their wars with their neighbours, the small Pox of 1780/81 and other misfortunes the third of the nation does not now remain.

Silver works and wampum are of no value in trading with them, & they never wear any of these articles as ornaments. They dress generally after the Assiniboil manner all in leather that is a shirt & Leggings, a Buffalo Robe or a Blanket by way of covering over the whole.

[p. 23] When an Indian swears, he takes the Master of life to witness, likewise the Earth, the fire & the water. They seldom pray to the Master of Life but when they are in imminent danger of Perishing.

At all other times their petitions are to Gog and Magog, or the evil spirit whom they very much dread; for they have such a sublime Idea of the Bounty of the master of life that they think it incompatible with him to afflict them.

But the evil spirit they say is always meditating some mischief or other to them and therefore they sacrifice to him to appease his anger and to divert him from his evil purposes.

Their only bloody sacrifice is to hang a Dog; all the other sacrifices they use consist of European merchandises, Country produce such as their own hunt &c, which they chiefly deposit upon scaffolds raised a certain height above the earth so as to be out of the reach of malicious beasts.

[p. 24] The Indians of the Red or assiniboil River in general have no ceremonies in their marriages or union of the sexes; a young man that has taken a wife for the first time is under great difficulties & out of modesty, bashfulness, or custom, appears but seldom in his father-in-law's Tent, or Lodge, in the day time. They always come to sleep with the bride after nightfall, & retire at day break.

They hunt the whole day to the emolument of their father-in-law, & in this servile condition they are obliged to remain the space of a year & sometimes longer if the bride does not bring forth a son or a daughter to deliver the young Indian from slavery; after that is done he [p. 25] is at liberty to choose for himself any residence he thinks proper; tho' he still remains in a manner tributary to his father-in-law & generally makes him some present according to his abilities as often as they meet or see each other in convenient situations.

And thus daughters are as much esteemed as sons by the Indians & indeed they bring them greater emoluments; for a young man as soon as he commences [as a] husband forsakes his father's tent, to which he seldom or ever returns as a residenton (for women have in general a great ascendant over their Indian Husbands & they always prefer living amongst those with whom they have been accustomed from their childhood) Tho' sons are much esteemed by them to make hunters & warriors, the two great business of all Indian's lives.

[p. 26] The Assiniboils are numerous in the Red River, and are divided into many tribes or families among themselves, such as *Les gens des Canots,* or the Canoe tribe; *Les Gens des Filles,* or the Girl's

Tribe; *Les Gens du Bois fort,* or the wood tribe, &c all speaking the same tongue with the Sioux, or Naudawesse; and originally a tribe of that numerous nation. Their dress consists like that of many of the Crees of a Buffalo Dressed skin, which they wear as the Saulteux or Augébois do the Blanket; under this Robe or covering in winter time, they wear a leather shirt, sometimes with the hair on, but Dressed in the same manner as their Robes, and having sleeves which are tied round their waists with leather thongs; on their legs they wear leggings made of Dressed leather without the hair and long enough to reach the middle of their Bodies & made of a convenient width, those for the young folks are made of Wolf, Caberie, & other skins of a finer quality which they dress as white & pliable as chamois. Their shoes as well as those of the Crees are always made of Buffalo leather the hair turned inwards which serves them as socks. On their Heads their caps are of Foxes and Fishers' skins with the hair outwards as well as to the head, it generally being only a Cavell skin the belly of which is not ripped open &c the head and tail of the beast tied so that [p. 28] the head of the wearer is encompassed by it all round & the tail hangs down below their two shoulders leaving the top or crown of the head without any covering but the hair nature supplied it with.

As for their hair they generally allow it to grow as long as they can & to every tress of any length they find to it [word illegible] of strings (& gun worms of which this part of their hair is full) till they find it of sufficient length (that is from three feet till it reaches their knees, that is on one side of the head; and they take as much pains to keep it short on the other side as they do to lengthen it on this; least this lock which hangs down on one side over their shoulder should come to meet any violence [p. 29] when they intend to get intoxicated, they tie up or coil it like a cable on the top of their head in the form of a mitre which gives them an uncouth aspect. It is generally so entangled having never been combed if once ridded they would lose the half of it. This ridiculous custom is not peculiar to the Assiniboils, or Assiniboit, as the Crees call them but the latter are as fond of it & follow it as much as they do.

These people generally winter together in large Camps, & make what the French call *Parcs,* an enclosure of wood in the form of a fence & circular, into which they drive whole herds of Buffalos. [p. 30] This seems to be an antient custom amongst all Indians inhabiting the plains being a method that all travellers thro' these parts speak of & which they want neither powder or Ball to execute.

The night previous to their sending for the Buffalo two, or more young men are prevailed upon to make themselves ready by a harangue the chief makes (for Indians know no command) to go & fetch the Buffaloes. Two & sometimes one is sufficient to bring them to the ranks, where tufts of Bushes and other obstacles are stuck up in the snow or ground to hide a person behind it from the Buffaloes, & thus every man, woman & child in the Camp have their stations.

A good runner frequently goes before the band with the hair of his robe outwards & half bent so as to represent a Buffalo & by that means decoys them into the park which has a small door behind to make him a passage.[23]

[p. 32] After the whole band is entered the women stand upon the door which has an easy ascent about upon the outside but is quite steep within and the paramount of the camp lights a pipe & offers the end to the Buffaloes or to some old Bull amongst them whom he takes for the father or chief of the Band whom he harangues sometimes to that effect. After thanking the master of life for sending them food for themselves and their children, "My grandfather we are glad to see you, & happy to find that you are not come in a shameful manner for you have brought plenty of your young men with you; be not angry at us; tho' we are obliged to destroy you to make ourselves live."

After the harangue is over they smoke their pipes sitting around the *Parc* & then they shoot all the herd down with their arrows; for fire arms are prohibited upon this occasion. The slaughter being finished the chief of the Park distributes a little [p. 33] swansdown coloured in Vermilion upon each Buffaloe's head, & leaves every person at liberty to take what he thinks proper. But so superstitious are these creatures that the chief of the Park thinks that if he was to eat any of this meat thus killed, it would be out of his power to make the buffaloes enter his Park ever after; and so he must have meat kill'd in the open Fields for his own use.

They testify their sorrow for their deceased much in the same manner that the Crees and Saulteux do by piercing their thighs & arms with arrows, Cutting their Hair & covering their heads with

---

[23] Manuscript page 31 is a pencil sketch of the bison pound being described. The sketch is not reproduced here because it is too faint to reproduce well; generally, however, it closely resembles the sketch of an Assiniboin bison pound illustrated by Lowie (*Indians of the Plains,* fig. 3, p. 15).

patches of earth and their women cut their hair & scarify their legs.

Their men as well as those of the Crees have no dancing but the women of both nations dance by themselves by moving all at the same time from right to left and then back again without giving themselves any other [p. 34] motion than shifting their toes & heels alternately & without breaking their order in the least, having all their faces the same way, & being drawn up in one or two lines according to their number or as the ground permits.

The Assiniboils of the Red River are in general a very lazy, indolent, perfidious set; & I believe the worst hunters of any Indians in the NW who have traders amongst them. Their whole hunt consists of Wolves, Foxes, Kitts, & Buffaloe Robes. As for Beavers, otters & other good furs they seldom take any. They are likewise great thieves & will steal from a rusty iron nail to a horse or any thing else they get an opportunity of taking. Stealing horses is quite a necessary trade amongst them, & they steal them from the Tents in their country, as well as from the Mandans & Groventres of the Missouri. The assiniboils &c of Fort des prairies & amongst themselves & their neighbors the Krees.

Most of the Red River Indians go to war during the absence of the Canoes at the grand Portage upon the Rocky Mountain Snake Indians or any of the nations at some distance from their own country upon which they first fall. In these excursions they take 40 days, or two months, sometimes travelling night and day especially on their return, if they have been successful for fear of a pursuit & they mostly return by different routes; leaving the wounded to shift for themselves if they cannot follow them.

2

David Thompson's Journal

D AVID THOMPSON, one of the giant figures of Canadian exploration, was born in London on April 30, 1770, of Welsh parentage. His father died two years after his birth, and in 1777 young David entered Grey Coat School, Westminster, one "devoted to the education of poor boys." There he was trained in mathematics in preparation for entering the navy, but he was instead articled by the school to the Hudson's Bay Company when peace with France resulted in a curtailment of naval recruitment. In the fall of 1784, as a young man of fourteen years, he landed at Fort Churchill, on Hudson Bay, as an apprentice clerk for the company. For the next twenty-eight years he lived in what was to become western Canada, trading with the Indians and traveling some fifty-five thousand miles in his explorations.[1]

With the expiration of his term of service, Thompson left the services of the Hudson's Bay Company and became an employee of the North West Company on May 23, 1797. Six months later he made his one and only visit to the Mandans and Hidatsas on the Missouri River—the topic of this second selection. Thompson's purpose in making this expedition was not to trade, but to determine the latitude and longitude of the Mandans—and to try to induce the Mandans to establish "a regular trade with the North-West Company." Thompson later went on to explore much of western Canada; he also crossed the Rocky Mountains and explored the Columbia River to its mouth, living for some years in Oregon. He left the fur trade in 1812 and went to live in Montreal, although he returned to the West in 1817 to 1826 when he was involved in the survey of the United States–Canadian boun-

---

[1] David Thompson's life is related in detail by himself in *David Thompson's Narrative of His Explorations in Western America, 1784-1812*, Publications of the Champlain Society, vol. 12, ed. J.B. Tyrrell, pp. xxiii–xcvii. See also *David Thompson's Narrative, 1784-1812*, Publications of the Champlain Society, vol. 40, ed. Richard Glover, pp. xi–cii; and David Thompson, *Travels in Western North America, 1784-1812*, ed. Victor G. Hopwood, pp. 1–38, 326–31. Thompson probably traveled 55,000 miles in the period 1784–1812; by the time he had completed the Canadian-American border survey in 1826, the figure was over 80,000 miles (Thompson, *Travels*, pp. 3–4).

dary from Quebec to Lake of the Woods. He eventually settled at Longueuil, opposite the city of Montreal, where he died in poverty on February 10, 1857, at the age of eighty-seven years. He is buried in Mount Royal Cemetery, Montreal.[2]

Thompson left to history a massive legacy of documents. Their very bulk and detail has to date discouraged full publication. Elliott Coues used Thompson's journals extensively when he was editing and annotating the manuscript journal of Alexander Henry the Younger for publication in 1897, but the sheer size of Thompson's journals deterred him from considering publishing them as such.[3] Thompson's journals were, however, condensed into memoir form by Thompson himself between 1846 and 1850, a task he undertook at the age of seventy-six years. Relying heavily on his field notes, but augmenting them significantly with his recollections, Thompson composed a manuscript which was published by J. B. Tyrrell in 1916 as "David Thompson's Narrative of His Explorations in Western America, 1784–1812." This narrative was reedited and reprinted by Richard Glover in 1962 and reprinted in condensed and modernized form by Hopwood in 1971.[4]

The originals of the manuscript journals of David Thompson are the property of the government of Ontario and are deposited in its archive at 77 Grenville Street, Toronto. These journals are very extensive, and only a small part of them is transcribed below—that is, the entries for his journey from John Macdonell's House, on the Assiniboine River, to the Mandan-Hidatsa villages on the Missouri River, and his return to Macdonell's House between November 26, 1797, and February 6, 1798. That period is contained in chapters 13 through 15 in his "Narrative."[5] The entries for part of that period (December 30, 1797, to January 10, 1798, plus the entry for January 12, 1798) were published by one of the editors of this volume in slightly different form in the journal *Ethnohistory* in 1977.[6]

There are two separate copies of his journal: (1) what appears to be the original copy of his field notes and is in Volume 5, Book 9, pages 36–48 (Thompson's Book 8); and (2) a later copy, a "fair journal," which is in Volume 4, Book 7, pages 4–23 (Thompson's Book 7). The original journals are in a bound volume of handmade paper, the pages measuring 19.8 cm by 31.8 cm; the "fair journal" is in a volume with pages measuring 20.3 cm by 24.7 cm.

Microfilm copies of both versions of Thompson's notes are available

[2]Thompson, *David Thompson's Narrative of His Explorations;* pp. lxxiv; see also pp. xli, lvi.

[3]Alexander Henry [the Younger], *New Light on the Early History of the Greater Northwest,* vol. 1, pp. xx–xxi.

[4]Thompson, *David Thompson's Narrative of His Explorations;* Thompson, *David Thompson's Narrative, 1784–1812,* Thompson, *Travels in Western North America.*

[5]Thompson, *David Thompson's Narrative of His Explorations,* pp. 209–42; and Thompson, *David Thompson's Narrative, 1784-1812,* pp. 160–81.

[6]David Thompson, "David Thompson at the Mandan-Hidatsa Villages, 1797–1798: The Original Journals," *Ethnohistory* 24 (Fall, 1977): 329–42.

from the archives, as is a typed transcript prepared largely by Miss E. I. Gilby, beginning in 1913. The present version was prepared using photocopies of the transcript as well as microfilms of the originals. This version was then checked against the originals during a visit to Toronto in June, 1979. Save for a few typographical errors, the typewritten transcript was quite accurate. The microfilm copy of the "fair journal," however, is so faint that most of it is impossible to read.

Both versions of the journal are given here: the entries for the same day follow one another for ease in comparison, with the original given first and the "fair" copy second. Thompson's symbol for sun (a dot enclosed in a circle) has been transcribed as "sun" (in square brackets) to simplify typesetting; other conventions followed in transcription are given in the Editorial Procedures.

Several differences may be noted between the text of the "Narrative" and the present transcription, notably in the temperatures recorded for some days, in the hours given for certain events, and whether an event took place in the morning or afternoon. The reasons for these discrepancies are not clear, but the original journals were inspected carefully, and the transcription given here is the best reading of each figure.

The originals of both versions are in brown ink, with a few editorial emendations in pencil which have been deleted herein. There are also a few changes by Thompson himself. These latter changes have not been indicated, since they add nothing to the content, consisting simply of duplicated words and deleted word choices. Much of the first part of the original journal is quite faint, and in places some of the words are not legible. Many of the faint passages, especially those on manuscript pages 39 and 40, have been traced over in a darker brown ink, perhaps by Thompson himself.

Each page of the original journal is numbered. These numbers are enclosed in brackets. However, in the "fair journal" only every other page is numbered. The unnumbered intermediate pages are noted as "half pages"; that is, unnumbered manuscript page 2b follows numbered page 2a.

A variety of observations in other volumes of his notes relating to this expedition are not included here. Among those observations are astronomical ones, as well as brief notes on the courses and directions Thompson took on this expedition. These may be found in Volume 5, Book 8, pages 12–22 and 44–50; in Volume 5, Book 10, pages 261–63; and in Volume 16, Book 41. Two of the pages in Book 10 also contain brief comments on the distance from the Mandan villages to the Rocky Mountains and on the source of the Missouri River.

The document following differs from the published "Narrative" in several ways. Chapter 13 of the "Narrative," "Journey to Mandane Villages," begins with an introduction to that journey based on his recollections and on scattered information in the journals. Most of the chapter, however, consists essentially of expanded transcriptions of his raw field notes for the period from November 29 and December 30 on the way to

95

the Missouri. Chapter 14, "The Mandanes and Their Customs," consists almost entirely of recollections, although it contains scattered data — mostly on village population — from his journal entries for the period from December 31 to January 10 while he was actually at the Mandan villages. Chapter 15, "Return Journey to McDonells House on Mouse River," is a blend of his field notes and his memory of the trip. Consequently, the field notes offered here provided the basic information and chronology for his reminiscences in his "Narrative" — basic data which are not available in published form elsewhere.

Two maps illustrate this expedition. Although Thompson produced a map of his visit to the Mandans, no such map is now among his effects. A copy of a map believed to have been made by Thompson, probably copied by Meriwether Lewis, however, is in the Lewis and Clark manuscript maps collection in the Library of Congress. That map is shown as fig. 7. In 1843, Thompson sent the final draft of his large map of his surveys to London. That part of the map showing the route from Ash House to the Knife River is shown as fig. 6.[7]

This overland trip was undertaken in the dead of winter, and the temperature on many days was nearly forty degrees below zero (Fahrenheit). Thompson, on three separate days on this trip (December 8, 10, and 19 and January 22) was called on to observe that each of these days was "the worst day I ever saw in my Life." The temperature was only part of the problem, for the lack of food on January 22 meant that his "days allowance" was "the Marrow Bone of a Buffaloe which had been pretty well Knawed by a Wolf." Little wonder his diary records "Thank God" on his return to Macdonell's House.

[DAVID THOMPSON'S JOURNAL]

[November 1797]

[p. 36][8] Novr. 26, 1797 — Sunday. A cloudy snowy Day. Ther. −4. My Men looking for the Horses all Day but could not find them.

[p. 2b] November 26th Sunday. A cloudy snowy day — a Man all day looking for the Horses, but could not find them.

---

[7] See, for example, John Logan Allen, *Passage Through the Garden: Lewis and Clark and the Image of the American Northwest*, pp. 87, 90; and Thompson, *Travels in Western North America*, p. 329.

[8] On the page of the journal opposite the first entry transcribed here are the names of the nine men who accompanied Thompson on his expedition: "Rene Jus-

Novr. 27th, Monday. A cloudy snowy Day, Ther 0—lookt for the Horses till 4 P.M. before they were found—got all ready to sett off the Morrow Morn.

November 27th Monday. A cloudy snowy day. Searching the Fields for the Horses 'till 4 PM when they were found, and we got ready to set off the morrow morning.

Novr. 28th Tuesday. A fine clear Day—at 9½ AM set off Co [course] 75W 1M at the Ho [Macdonell's House] crossed the Red [Assiniboine] River.[9] S60W 7M to a pt of woods all Plain. S50W 6M. This Co the woods from the Moose Head Hill (which at begg. of Co lay abt NWbW 6M from us) forms a line close on our right. Two low Hills lie—one SE of us abt 2M long. The other SSE 3M long—each abt 9M distant—abt 4M on this Side [of] the Hills the River la Sourie runs (or the Mouse River) & discharges itself into the Red River below the House a distance. Very cold Day. Wind WSW a smll Gale—froze a little of my nose—at 2¾ PM put up— at 9 PM Ther −20.

November 28th Tuesday. A fine claar Day. At 9½ AM set off crossed the River and Co S75W 1M. S60W 7M—all Plains to a Point of woods S50W 6M, this Co the woods from the Moose Head Hill. A WSW Gale arose with very cold bad weather, we put up at 2¾ PM—at 9 P.M. Ther −20.

Novr. 29th Wednesday. A very cold Day with a Westerly wind & Rain at 7 AM. Ther −27 at 9 AM −22—lay by—by far too cold to proceed.

November 29th Wednesday. A very cold day with a westerly wind and Rime—too cold to proceed with the Horses—at 7 AM Ther −27 at 9 P.M. −22.

Novr. 30th Thursday. A very cold Day & Westerly Gale. Ther at 7 AM −32 at 9 PM −32. A most terrible cold Day. The men killed 2 Cows.

---

somme, Joseph Boisseau, Hugh McCracken, Alexis Vivier, Pierre Gilbert, Fras. Perrault, Tousst. Vaudril, Ls. JBt. Houl, and Jbte. Minie." Jusseaume was the guide and interpreter, and Boisseau was Thompson's "servant." Note that on his entry for Monday, January 22, 1798, Thompson says that sixteen people returned from the villages with him: presumably the ten men on the expedition plus two captive Sioux women who had been sold to the men, two young Mandan men, and two others.

[9] Thompson left John Macdonell's House (sometimes called Fort Assiniboine), on the north bank of the Assiniboine River about twenty airline miles southeast of the modern city of Brandon.

November 30th Thursday. A very cold day and westerly Gale. Ther at 7 AM −32 at 9 PM −32 most dreadfully cold−as much as we can do to keep ourselves warm, with a large fire before us. We killed 2 Cow Buffaloe, but such was the force of the cold that it was with difficulty we could stand to cut up about 100 lbs of Meat from each.

[December 1797]

Dec. 1st Friday. A very cold Day. Wind WSW a smll Gale. Ther at 7 AM −37° at 8 PM. −32. Vivier killed a Cow.

[p. 3a] December 1st Friday. A very cold Day. Wind WSW a small Gale. Ther at 7 AM −37 at 8 PM −32. Killed a Cow Buffaloe.

Dec. 2nd Saturday. A very cold Night−at 8 AM Ther −36−at 8 PM Ther −15 a terrible cold Day−but moderated towards Evening. Wind WSW a Gale. Vivier killed a Cow. Tent very Smoky.

December 2nd Saturday. A very cold Night. Wind WSW a Gale at 7 AM Ther −36 at 9 PM −15−a terrible cold Day, but towards evening moderated.

Dec. 3rd Sunday. A blowy snowy Day. Wind WNW. Ther at 7 AM −3. We could travel this Day were it not for the high Drifts which prevent us from seeing a ¼ M before us−& we have a very large Plain to cross. These several Days worked a few Observations. Tent smoky. At 8 AM Ther −2.

December 3rd Sunday. A snowy Day. Wind WNW a Gale−at 7 AM Ther −3 at 8 PM −2. We could have travelled this day had we not a very large Plain to cross, and the Drift is so high that we could not see a quarter of a Mile before us.

Decr. 4th Monday. At 7 AM Ther 4. Wind WbS a strong Gale all Day, part Clear & part Cloudy at 9 AM sett off Co by the [sun]. SWbS 10½ M to the Mouse River. Went down the Bank to the Tents of Stone [Assiniboin] Indians. Stopd abt ¼ H−then went off WSW ½ M up the River at end of Co crossed it then Co WbS 6M put up below the Bank close to the River 1M short of Co crossd a Brook−at begg. of Co the River comes from the NWd 2M of Co gone the River distt. abt 1½M then approaches nearer to end of Co. The River is abt 14 yds × [wide]. Banks moderate. No Woods but a little along the River & those of Oak Ash &c−put up at 3¾ PM. Windy Day.

December 4th Monday. Wind WbS a Gale all Day, partly Clear, partly Cloudy. At 9 AM we at last set off and crossed to the Mouse

River. Co by the Sun SWbW 10 ½M went down the Bank to 5 Tents of Stone Indians, stopped about ¼ Hour—then went WSW ½M and crossed it—then SWbS 6M put up below the Banks, close to the Rivulet at 3¾ PM—all is one vast Plain except a few straggling Ash Oak and Elm &c along the margin of the Stream.

Decr. 5th Tuesday. A fine Morn. Ther at 7 AM—13 at 7¾ AM set off Co abt South 4M to a smll Hammock of Aspins along side the Brook we crossed yesterday—& which we recrossed at end of Co. Co So 5½M crossd and recrossd the Brook which comes from the Turtle Mountain.[10] SbW 7M 1½ PM. The Turtle Mountain not appearing & the Weather seeming likely to change we struck off for the Woods of the Mouse River & went abt [p. 37] WNW 6M NWbW 7M all Plain without the least Woods—at 6½ PM we most providentially came to a fine Hammock of Oak & Ash close to the Stream of the River & put up—a stormy Day. Wind South—at 5¼ AM the wind changed to a Gale at WNW with Drift and by 7 PM it increased to a Storm. Cloudy.

December 5th Tuesday. A fine morning. Our Guide Mons. Jussomme telling us we had a very large Plain to cross before we could see any woods—at 7¾ AM we set off to cross to the Turtle Hill. Co abt South 4 Miles + 5½M SbW 7M to 1½ PM—here coming on elevated Ground, the Weather clear, we expected to have before now sighted the Turtle Hill—but no sign of woods appearing anywhere, we began to dispute the capacity of our Guide, and seeing the weather threatening a storm we struck off for the woods of the [p. 3b] Mouse River, from whence we had come this morning—WNW 6M, NWbW 7M all vast Plain, without even the sign of woods but the Spot we direct our course to—at length the Night came on quite dark, several of the men were for putting up on the open Plain, rather than wander all Night, but a few of us determined to hold on, and they not choosing to be left behind unwillingly followed us 'till 6½ PM when we fortunately stumbled on a hammock of woods, almost perished with Thirst. We struck a Fire, and quickly melted some Snow and quenched our Thirst ere we thought of anything else, some took a mouthful, others quite overcome with Fatigue threw themselves down on the Snow and slept out the Night. The Snow had been very slippery all day, with a hard Gale ahead since Noon, so that we could hardly advance.

[10] This is modern Turtle Mountain, which Thompson also calls Turtle Hill, on the present North Dakota-Manitoba boundary. Thompson later refers to another "Turtle Hill" in present-day North Dakota, but the latter is the present day Killdeer Mountains (see footnote 25 below).

Decr. 6th Wednesday. A heavy Gale from WNW with cloudy warm Weather, the Snow thawing. We were obliged to lay by not only for the Weather but to hunt Provisions & refresh the Dogs & Horses—abt 2 PM 2 Stone Indian Men paid us a Visit of abt 10 Minutes and then went off to their Tents which are at a Distance from us. We find ourselves abt 3M below the old House—where People resided 2 years ago.[11] Vaudril killed 2 Bulls. Worked an Obsn.

December 6th Wednesday. A heavy Gale from the WNW with cloudy warm weather, the Snow thawed. We were obliged to lay by all day to refresh ourselves, the Horses and Dogs—and to hunt for Provisions. We killed 2 Bull Buffaloe. Two Stone Indian Men paid us a visit of about 10 minutes and then went away to their Tents.

Decr. 7th Thursday. A cloudy warm Day. At 7½ AM set off Co up along the River SW 2½M SWbS 2M to the [Ash] House—at which we put up at 9¾ AM as we had not Time enough to cross to the Turtle Hill. My yellow Horse quite Lame & too poor to continue the Journey. Ther at 7 AM +25. Steped the River la Sourie in 19 Steps—say 17 Yards—several small Hammocks of Aspin abt us but mostly all Oak & Ash. An Indian paid us a Visit & then went away. No Success in Hunting. Snow with a westerly Gale. Horses that have white Feet have the Hair soon come off with the Snow especially if it be hard, while those who have black Hair on their Legs etc. care little for the Snow, even when it is hard. Monsr. Jusomme has a fine Mare with us. One of her Feet is white & the other is black. The white Foot has the hair off it & a small hole in the Flesh while the other Leg tho' equally exposed has not a single Hair injured. My yellow Horse has unfortunately all his four Feet white, which is at present the cause of his lameness.

December 7th Thursday. A cloudy warm day. At 7½ AM set off Co up along the Mouse River SW 2½M. SWbS 2M to the old Ash House settled 2 years ago, and abandoned in the following Spring, here we put up with the advice of our Guide Monsr. Jussemme, as we had not Time enough before us to cross the great Plain to the Turtle Hill. The Mouse River is here about 17 yards wide.[12]

[11] Ash House, built in 1795 and abandoned in 1796, was near the present town of Hartney, Manitoba (Ernest Voorhis, *Historic Forts and Trading Posts of the French Regime and of the English Fur Trading Companies*, p. 32).

[12] G. A. McMorran, in his "Souris River Posts in the Hartney District," *Papers Read before the Historical and Scientific Society of Manitoba*, 3d ser., no. 5, pp. 50–55, reconstructs Thompson's route from Macdonell's House to Ash House in an effort to pinpoint the location of the latter post.

Decr. 8th Friday. A fine clear sharp Day. Would have set off but I wished to give my yellow Horse in Care to the Indians to take in to the House. At 10 AM an old Man came to whom I gave the Horse in Care with a note to Mr. McDonnel—Obsd for Latde & Longde & [sun] & [sun] Do NLs—at Night Jupiter 86°.43½'—No Success in Hunting. Our Provisions all done. Ther −18.

[p. 4a] December 8th Friday. A fine clear sharp Day. We wished to set off but questioning our Guide, we found his Ideas of the Country so confused that we could not venture to follow him. We therefore expecting to see some Indians, with whom we hoped to prevail to guide us, passed the day. At 10 AM our old Man came, who informed us we should find a few Tents of Stone Indians a few Miles higher up the River. One of my Horses knocking up I gave him in charge of the old Man to be taken to the Mouse River Settlement.

Decr. 9th Saturday. A fine Sharp Day at 7 AM Ther −26. At 8½ AM set off Co West 2M crossed the River—at end of Co close to the River. Co WSW 3M. Co SW 2½M to 8 Tents of Stone Indians. This last Co small Hills of Sand—put up at ll AM. Met several of the Stone Indians going to the House with Provisions & Wolf Skins. The old man had my Horse with him—took 10 Pieces of Meat from them. Hired a young Stone Indian to accompany us to the Mandin Village—gave him a Pistol, 30 Rods of Ammunition—2 knives & a Fathom of Tobacco. The Men are to give him on his return to the House a 10 Skin Keg of Liquor. [p. 38] A fine high Sand Knowl, Bank of the River close to us. Viewed the River a part of it lies abt SSW 3M from us, it then winds to the Westward. Set the Turtle Hill S30E by the Compass—Mr. Thorburn's. Sharp Night. We are on the right side of the River. No woods but a little along the River, and on the Turtle Hill.

December 9th Saturday. A fine sharp Day. Ther −26. At 8½ AM set off Co west 2M—crossed the River. Co WSW 3M. SW 2½M to 8 Tents of Stone Indians, with whom we put up at ll AM—here we engaged a young man to accompany our Guide to the villages of the Manden Indians on the Missesourie River. The Price a Pistol, 30 rounds of Ammunition, 2 large Knives, 1 fathom of Tobacco and 2 Gallons of Grog.

Decr. 10th Sunday. A fine sharp clear Morn. Ther −20−bW 8 AM when the Wind arose a Gale from the Sod. & by 9 AM increased to a perfect Storm with such heavy Drift as obscured the Hemisphere—it was little better than Night as we could not see 100 yards abt us. At 7½ AM set off Co S 30° Ed.—by the Compass Distance 22M. The Storm prevented us reaching a few Shrubs of Oak 'till 5¾ PM when we put up—several of us much frozen. As bad a Day as ever I saw in my Life. Poor Hool at 10¼ AM lost his Dog & Train & with them all his Venture—at 7 PM Showers of Rain, Hail, Sleet & Snow—which with the Storm contd. all Night.

December 10th Sunday. A fine sharp clear Morning. Ther −20. About 2 PM this Morning, the young Man we had engaged as our Guide came and delivered back all the Goods, saying his Friends had dissuaded him from such an hazardous Journey—as they all well knew the Sueix Indians were on the Road to cut off any Party that would dare to attempt to go to the Manden Villages. There was no Remedy—early this Morning from a Knowl, they pointed out to me a small patch of woods on the Turtle Hill, to which we had to cross and at 7½ AM we set off—our Course S30E 22M. At 8AM a heavy South Gale arose, which soon increased to a dreadful Storm. The wind roared like distant Thunder—with [p. 4b] such terrible Drift that the Earth & Skies seemed confounded together, it was almost as dark as Night, we could actually not see more than 100 yards around us, hoping from its extreme violence, it was only a temporary Storm of an Hour. We continued on, all of the Men following me close—about 10 AM one of the Men missed his Dogs and Sled with all his venture worth about 150 skins value. We stopped a few minutes to give him Time to look for them—he attempted to quit us, but found himself unable to do it, as in all probability he cound not have found us again, and would have been lost. We held on thro' the stormy gloom 'till Night came down on us in the wide Plain, here the Men began to despair of surviving the Night, as we were without Shelter, and almost exhausted. After encouraging them with the assurance that we could not be far from the woods, and that I was guiding them in the right Course thereto, we continued, scarcely moving half a mile in an Hour. At length one of the men fell quite exhausted. We lifted him up, but no purpose, he could not stand; perishing as we were ourselves, we could not assist him, and recommending him to Providence, held on about half an Hour more I found myself entangled among some Shrubs and stopping there, the rest of the men came, when one Man remaining as a Centre, we extended [*dispatched*] ourselves a little, feeling with our Hands, for wood large enough to make a Fire, which we luckily found among some small sapling Oaks. We kindled a Fire, and made [p. 5a] a barricade against the wind; having quenched our Thirst with some melted Snow; we began to cast about the relief of the poor fellow who had fallen behind — but none of us durst undertake to find him: indeed it was impossible in such a dark storm to trace one foot of our Road back again. At length we thought we heard the voice of a Man, we agreed to extend ourselves from the Fire within call of each other towards the Sound. The farthest of us by this means soon heard him call distinctly. We found the poor wretch crawling on his Hands and Knees almost delirious with weakness. Tho' a stout hearty Man of 27 Years of Age, we hauled him along, tho' scarcely able to stand ourselves, having taken a mouthful, we lay down under the Lee of a hammock of Saplings, which Kept the Wind pretty well from us, thankful to Providence that we had escaped with our Lives.

Decr. 11th Monday. A cloudy Day & southerly Gale with Showers of Snow — the Snow thawing. At 8 AM set off & went abt 200 yards to a Hammock of Oak, Ash & Aspin, where we put [up] — a bad snowy Day. No Success in Hunting.

December 11th Monday. A cloudy, southerly Gale with Showers of Snow. Almost all the Men are much frost bit in the face. We were so much fatigued that we could hardly move, at 8 AM we removed our Tent about 200 yards to a Hammock of Aspin, which the darkness of the Night prevented us from seeing — here we lay by all day, to refresh ourselves. Short of Provisions, and no success in hunting.

Decr. 12th Tuesday. A mild snowy cloudy Day. SSW Gale small Hool set off for the House but thick weather coming on he turned abt & followed us. We are each to give him 2 Beaver's worth of Goods to make him some amends for his Loss. At 9 AM set off Co along the W Side of the Hill. S10°E 2M. S2°W 6M — at 3 PM put up. These courses are corrected. Stoped abt 1 Hour for 2 men who were hunting but they havg. no Success I took my Mare. Ran & killed a tolerable good Bull — took 4 sled Loads of him. A Stormy Evening with Snow.

December 12th Tuesday. A mild snowy cloudy day. SSW Gale with dark foggy weather. At 9 AM we set off to go along the Hill [p. 5b] to the last Willows, then to camp ready to cross the great Plain to the Mouse River. Co S10E 2M. S2W 6M at 3 PM put up — having no Provisions, two of us approached a Herd of Bulls, and after firing about 15 Rounds without effect, they retired. Seeing this I mounted my Horse and ran down a Bull, he cost me 3 shots before I could kill him, as he gave Battle.

Decr. 13th Wednesday. A very stormy Night & Day with very high Drift. Wind North, clear Sky. Could not proceed. Obsd for Longde & Latde [sun] CDs NLs & [sun].

December 13th Wednesday. A very stormy Night and Day, with high Drift, wind North. Could not proceed. Observed for Latde. and Longitude.[13]

[p. 39] Decr. 15 Thursday. Breeze Ther −20. At 8¼ AM set off Co along the Hill So 2M SE by S 6M. SE 2½M. SE by S 2M. A Brook to [get] the Tent Poles[14] we then went down along another bold Brook of 4 Yds. Co S by E 2½M. So by E 2M. Put up at 3¾ P.M.

December 14th Thursday. A cold misty day, northerly Breeze—not daring in this foggy weather to cross the great Plain, we set off and held on along the Hill. So 2M SEbS 6M. SE 2½M. SEbS 2M to a brook—then passed on to another bold Brook of 4 yds cross—down along which we went SbE 2½M. SSE 2M—advancing out to the Plain, to a clump of small willows, which we cut down for fire wood. We put up at 3¾ PM.

Decr. 15th Friday. Cold Day. Wind NW could not proceed as we have a large Plain to cross—did not find the Horses till 4 PM. Vaudril killed an old Bull & I wounded [a line of the text is illegible].

December 15th Friday. A very cold day. Wind NW a small Breeze—having no Provisions we hunted and one of the Men Killed an old Bull. Buffaloe are very scarce here—no Cows whatever to be seen. The weather cleared, and we saw the woods of the Mouse River.

Decr. 16th Saturday. A NW Gale weather very thick & Drift. The People unwilling to set off, but as I had seen the Mouse River yesterday I told them to get ready & at 8.20 AM we set off. Co S5W 19M put up at 3½ PM at the Sand Knowl near the Mouse River abt 2M short of Co crossed the Rivière du Saule or Willow River 4 yds × [wide].[15] Walked hard without once stopping. The Snow very hard & from being often thawed & froze is in many Places actually covered with Ice. The River Mouse runs here abt East 4M with 3

[13] This observation point was on the west edge of Turtle Mountain near the present international boundary (see fig. 6).

[14] According to Thompson's memoir, they cut dry "Aspin" (*Populus tremuloides*) here to use as tent poles (*David Thompson's Narrative of His Explorations,* p. 218).

[15] Willow Creek, still called by that name, enters the Souris River about five miles east of the modern town of Upham, McHenry County, North Dakota.

pts. The Willow River comes from SE & falls into the Mouse River abt 6M below where we crossed it. Hool killed 2 Good Cows. Thank God for they are [two words illegible]. Near this Spot 15 Tents of Stone Indians were killed by the Sieux or Nadowessies 2 Years ago. Abt 1M a most terrible Gale of wind with excessive high Drift arose from the North & continued.

December 16th Saturday. A NW Gale, with Drift and thick hazy weather. The men exceedingly unwilling to undertake to cross the large Plain, in this weather, from having already suffered so much— but as we had an aft wind, I got them to follow me at 8.20 AM. We crossed SbW 19M to the Mouse woods—to the [p. 6a] Sand Knowls— where we camped. One of the Men Killed 2 good Cows—a Blessing, as we have not tasted a bit of good Meat this long time—here last year 15 Tents of Stone Indians were cut off by the Sieux Indians, only 4 young Men escaping. My men are sometimes much downcast as they expect to see some of those Indians waiting to cut us off on our Road to the Missesourie. In the evening a very heavy Gale of Wind arose from the NWd with very high Drift, had we not fortunately crossed the Plain today, and got under the shelter of the woods, we must have perished.

Decr. 17th Sunday. A cold clear sharp Day. Wind North a heavy Gale with high Drift—lay by. At 8 AM Ther −22. Obs for Latde [sun] [word illegible]—at 9 PM Ther −23. Black Night with terrible wind & Drift. Workd Obs.

December 17th Sunday. A cold clear sharp Day, with a heavy Gale from NWd. Observed for Latitude—at 7 AM Ther −22 at 9 PM −23. A clear cold Night with terrible wind and Drift.

Decr. 18 Monday. A fine but too cold Morn'g. Ther −32. At 8½ AM a Gale from SSW sprang up. At 2 PM Ther. −7. I went a hunting killed 2 good Cows & 1 Bull wounded 2 other Bulls—could not proceed to Day for the Wind—at 5 PM a most terrible Storm from WbN arose with High Drift & contd. all Night from WNW. Woods of Aspin, Oak & Ash all along the River.

December 18th Monday. A fine morning, but too cold to tye up our things &c. At 7 AM Ther −32. 2 PM minus 7—in the afternoon I went a hunting and about a mile from the Tent Killed 3 Cow Buffaloe. We returned with Dogs and Sleds to bring home the meat but before we were half finished a terrible Storm from the NWWd arose and drove us home, had it been a head wind, altho' the distance was no more than a Mile we could never have reached the Tent.

Decr. 19th Tuesday. A most terrible Storm with exceeding high Drifts and bold all day from NNW. At 8 AM Ther −17. The very Heavens obscured I never saw a worse Day in all my life. The roar of the wind resembled the noise of the waves of the Ocean when dashed on the Rocks by continuous Storm—[two words illegible]. Mended my Snow Shoes which I broke yesterday. Ther. at 9 PM −27. Storm moderating.

December 19th Tuesday. A most terrible Storm with exceeding high Drift. The very Heavens are obscured and resemble Night. The roaring of the wind is just like the noise of the waves of the Sea when furiously dashed on the Rocks. At 8 AM Ther −17. 9 PM −24. Storm moderating.

Decr. 20th Wednesday. A very sharp clear morng. At 7 AM Ther −41—had the large Ther been here it would have showed −51— Wind NNW a small Breese—did not find the Horses till 9½ PM. At 10 AM set off. Co over Sand Hills close to the Mouse River SSE 4M. S by E 2M. So 3M. S by W 2M. SSW 2M put up at 3½ PM close to the Stream. A few Herds of Buffalo. Woods along the River all Oak. A few Hammocks of Oak & Aspin from 1 to 2M from the River. These Co by the Sun. Snow abt 1 foot deep. My Man got a little lamed by the hard icy surface of the Snow. All Day [several words illegible]. Hool killed an old Bull whose meat [several words illegible].

[p. 6b] December 20th Wednesday. A very clear Morning, and uncommonly cold. At 7 AM Ther −41. Wind NNW a small Breeze— at 9½ AM set off Co up along the Mouse River. SSE 4M. SbE 2M. So 3M. SbW 2M. SSW 2M put up at 3½ PM close to the Stream— saw a few Herds of Buffalo, but distant—a small ledge of Woods run along the River here of Oak, Ash, Elm, Aspins &c—from about 10 to 40 yds deep all the rest on both sides is boundless Meadow.

[p. 40] Decr. 21st Thursday. A stormy snowy Morn. At 8 AM it cleared with fine Sharp weather for the rest of the Day—could not proceed as Hugh McCraghen is very ill. Vaudril killed a good young Bull but we did not go for any of it as it was too dist—the People in the morng killed an old Bull for the Dogs. No Cows at all abt us. At 7 PM Ther −26.

December 21st Thursday. A stormy snowy Morn—at 11 AM it cleared and fine sharp weather for the rest of the Day. We could not proceed as Hugh McCraghen is very ill. Killed a Bull for the Dogs, he was too old and poor to be eaten by us. 7 PM Ther. −26.

Decr. 22nd Friday. A very Sharp clear Day. Wind a light Breeze South at 7 PM. Ther −32. At 8 2/3 H AM set off Cos along the River SSW 6M abt at end of Co, a range of Sand Hills with Patches of small wood extendg from the River WNW 7M. Co SSW 4M. A range of low Sand Hills by NEbE in dist. from the River 3M. Also on the Wd Side a range running off to the first Co SSW 4M—end of Co opposite the Sand Hill abt WNW 4M from me—it is in the first range which is the Main Range. Co SW by S 1M. Co SW 2M. Co SWbW 2M at 3½ PM put up walked a gentle Pace without stopping. Parts of the River have no woods—at best but a mere Ledge mostly all Oak. Cold clear Night—could not Observe as the woods were too Shady. Fighting. Cos by the Sun.

December 22nd Friday. A very sharp clear Day. Wind a light Breese from the southward—at 7 AM Ther −32—at 11 1/3 AM set off. Co along the River SSW 6M + 4M. SWbS 1M. SW 2M. SWbW 2M—at 3½ PM put up—narrow Ledges of wood today, and frequently none at all along the River side.

Decr. 23rd Saturday. A cloudy cold snowy Day 'till noon when it cleared & became fine. At 8½ AM set off. 3 men went ahead to hunt they killed 4 Bulls. No Cows at all abt us. Co S50W 9M end of Co high Banks walked on along below the Heights. Co S60W 3M uneven Ground the latter part. Abt 3 PM we put up at the Stream where they usually strike off for the Mississourie.[16] The Woods mostly all Oak—No Aspins more of the Oaks abt 3 fath rod good—bled Hugh McCraghen who is very ill. Obs for Latde. Jupiter 90° 2′—good—& for Longde Aritis & [word illegible].[17] Ther. −2 to be put to Obs.

December 23rd Saturday. A cloudy cold snowy Day 'till Noon when it cleared, and became fine—At 8½ AM set off sent 3 Men ahead to hunt they Killed 4 Bulls—no Cow Buffaloe to be seen. Co S40W 9M. S60W 3M—at end of Co put up at the Bight of the Mouse River, where we generally take the great Plains to the Missesourie— here are Patches of very fine woods below the Heights of the River, of Oak, Elm, Ash, Birch &c &c, some of the Oaks I measured 3 fathems girth, and very fine—bled poor Hugh McCraghen, an hon-

---

[16]This mention refers to the southwest extent of the large meander of the Souris River near the modern town of Velva in McHenry County, North Dakota. See François-Antoine Larocque's "Yellowstone Journal," note 20.

[17]A monument to David Thompson's explorations has been placed near this site (fig. 5), near the now-abandoned town of Verendrye, North Dakota.

est Irishman, he is of the greatest Service to me, as by his Information only I guide myself and conduct the March, a few of the Men have seen the Road, but like Mons. Jussemme cannot be relied on.

Decr. 24th Sunday. A fine mild Morn & Day. Wind Southerly at 2 PM a small Gale from WSW arose. The Drift pouring down the Hills resembled a Fall. All Night a Storm. At 8½ AM we set off for the Wd end of the Dog Tent Hill.[18] Co to the top of the Heights ESE ½M then S48W 19M to a Gully of the Hill—the foremost reached it at 4½ PM we did not get to it till 5 PM walked tolerably Hard. At 1½ PM the very Elbow of the Mouse River or its SW extremity bore NW by W 1½M from us—hilly Ground deep Snow. The River Mouse then comes from WNWd.

[p. 7a] December 24th Sunday. A fine mild Morn & Day. Wind South. At 2 PM a strong Gale arose, and the Drift pouring down the Hills, over the sheet of Ice resembled the Water of a heavy high Fall. At night the Wind increased to a Storm. At 8½ AM we set off for the west End of the Dog Tent Hill. Co on the top of the Heights of the Mouse River ESE ½M—then left the River and went across the Plains S48W 19M to a Gully of the Hill, with a small spring of water and a little wood, the first of us got there at 4½ PM, but the others did not come up 'till 5 PM. The Country is full of Knowls and waving Ridges of meadow Land, wholly without woods, but in some chance hidden Ravine, that has a small Spring of Water. We are not in the usual Route, but to the westward of it—for fear of the Sieux, who are said to be in wait for us.

Decr. 25th Monday. A clear stormy Day from NWbW obliged to lay by. No success in Huntg—froze the tips of my Fingers with my Gun. Obsd for Latde [sun]. The Mouse River above the Elbow as viewed from the top of the Hill comes from the WNWd 10 yds ✕— fine large Oak abt it but no Aspins, Poplars &c. The usual Road bore S13°W from where we started yesterday. We leave it for fear of the Pawnees [Arikaras]. The Dog Tent Hill lies [p. 41]ENE & WSW 4M long it is not very high—perhaps abt the Height of the Banks of the Red River at Mr. Grants above the level of the Plain & is very unequal Ground in its north Front. There are several

---

[18]Now known as Dog Den Butte, this feature is shown on Thompson's maps (figs. 6 and 7) north of Long Lake. This lake still goes by the same name. Both features are in northern McLean County, North Dakota.

FIG. 5. A monument to David Thompson at now-abandoned Verendrye, North Dakota. Photograph by W. R. Wood.

Gullys say abt 9 or 10 which have patches of Oak Ash & Aspins with Springs of good Water. Wind Calming. Ther −15.

December 25th Monday. A clear stormy Day from NWbW— could not proceed. Obsd for Latitude—in the evining the wind calming. Ther −15.

Decr. 26 Tuesday. At 7 AM Ther −16. At 7½ AM a most terrible Storm arose from SSW & continued the whole Day & Even the roaring of the Wind resembled the Noise of the Waves of the Ocean when dashed by the Tempest on a sloping Shore. Hool went a Hunting he killed a good Cow & a good Bull but it being distant he could only bring a load of it. The wolves got the rest. Made 2 Pair of Shoes. At Noon Ther −2 at 8 PM Ther +2.

December 26th Tuesday. At 7 AM Ther −16. At 7½ AM a most terrible Storm arose from SSW and continued the whole day and evening — excessive bad weather. The wind roared among the Hills like distant Thunder. One of the Men Killed 2 Buffaloe, but could only take a small Load on his Back and abandoned the rest to the Wolves, tho' we are next to starving, and our Dogs ready to eat us for want of Food. We wish very much to avoid our Enemies by not taking the usual Route, yet the fear of crossing the wide Plain that extends without the least Shelter from hence quite to the Missesourie, and will take us 2 good days to [p. 7b] cross it, seems to most of us worse than a Battle.

Decr. 27th Wednesday. A clear Day with a Storm from WSW all Day — took wood for a pair of Snow Shoes. No Sucess. Wounded a Bull. At 7 AM Ther +5 at noon +20 at 9 PM +25. My Gun quite useless.

December 27th Wednesday. A clear day with a Storm from WSW. At 7 AM Ther +5 at Noon +20 at 9 PM +25. After much reasoning about the line of our future march, I determined to attempt the great Plain, as we might probably cross that, whereas we are sure to be outnumbered by perhaps 10 to one by our Enemies — and should we even gain the day, the care of the wounded &c would prevent our penetration any further into the country. We accordingly cut wood &c to haul with us to make a fire with.

Decr. 28th Thursday. A very fine warm clear Day. Thank God. At 7 AM Ther +20. At 7.40 AM set off to cross the great Plain that lies between the Rivers Mouse & Missesourie — took Firewood & Tent Poles with us. Co abt S40W 22M — hilly Road & deep Snow. At 4½ PM put up on the Plain. At the Time we put up I viewed the Land. The little Lake lay abt SSE of me 8M a pt of woods seemingly the Missesourie S6W 15M extending in Gullys to the SW 18 or 20M then ended. Saw very few Buffalo. At 3½ PM saw abt 10 or 12 Men on Horseback about 4M beyond the little Lake. They were going for the river. They were not the Convoy of the English who this Day left the Manden Village on their return. The Lake must have been the Grand Lake & not the little Lake as Mr. Jussomme said.

December 28th Thursday. A very fine warm clear Day at 7½ AM set off to cross the great Plain. Our Course was S40W 22M — hilly Road and deep Snow — bad walking. At 3 PM about 2M to the left of us saw a Line of Horsemen bending their Course towards the Missesourie also, but much lower down than our Course. We supposed them the Sieux, who tired of waiting for us, were proceeding home. We now kept always in the Vallies, taking care not to show ourselves. At 4½ PM we put up—and at dark Kindled a small fire to warm ourselves and dry our things &c.

Decr. 29th Friday. A very fine warm Day. At 7.20 AM set off Co at S25W 15M to the Missesourie below the Heights of which close to the Stream we put up at 3½M— very Hilly Ground. Saw many Buffalo to Day. We stopped much viewing the Country & waiting for the Dogs who were running off after the Cattle. Abt 2M from the River 2 Fall Indian Men came to us & soon after another. One of them went off & killed a good Bull for us. They slept with us all Night. Pierre killed an old Bull. The River here is abt 280 yd wide with high steep Banks suppose 15 Fath. This is the Elbow of the Missesourie or its Northern Extremity.[19] Woods of Oak Ash & Aspin with Elms.

December 29th Friday. A very fine warm day. At 7¼ AM set off Co S25W 15M to the Missesourie River, below the Heights of which, close to the Stream we put up at 3¼ PM, here the Stream is 290 yds wide in one single Channel. The Banks of the Stream are about 18 ft high. Above these are the great Banks, or Heights of the River, which rise about 500 ft above [p. 8a] the level of the River, are sloping, full of inequalities, with Patches of various woods, along the Stream mostly Ash, Poplar, Aspin &c. Three of the Willow [Hidatsa Indians] commonly called the flying Fall Indians came to us, happy to find we had brought them a good supply of Arms and Ammunition to enable them to continue the war with the Sieux. One of them ran down a good young Bull—very acceptable of us.

Decr. 30th Saturday. In the Night a northerly Gale arose with very cloudy Weather. At 7.40 AM set off down the Missesourie. Walked below the Heights of the River & on the River. Co SbE abt 6M to the upper Fall Indian Village.[20] Co SSE 4M. SEbS 3M to

[19] The "elbow" of the Missouri River, or the "Big Bend of the North," is the point where the course of the river changes from easterly to southerly, near the present-day Garrison Dam.

[20] An unnamed Hidatsa winter village on the east bank of the Missouri River a few miles below Garrison Dam. See map 2 for the names and locations of the Hidatsa villages identified in the following four notes.

opposite the greater Village of the Fall Indians.[21] Co SE 1½M to opposite the middle Village[22]—then Co So 1M SSE 1¼M to the 4th Village[23] then Co SEbE ¾M to the principal Village of the Mandens.[24] At 3 PM Menie, Hool, Vivier & Murray staid at the upper Village [p. 42] Vaudril with Mahnow [that is, Ménard], the rest at the principal Village of the Mandens—expended abt 3 feet of Tobacco.

December 30th Saturday. At 7.40 AM set off down the Missesourie River. We walked all the way on the Ice, except at places where the River was open for about ½ Mile. Co SbE 6M to the upper village of the Willow Indians—SSE 4M SEbS 3M to the greater village of the Willow Indians—SE 1½M to the middle village. Co So 1M. SSE 1¼M to the 4th village, mostly all Manden Indians, SEbE ¾M to the principal and last village, part Manden & part Willow Indians at 3 PM here myself, the Interpreter and 2 men put up with myself, the others staid at the especial request of the Indians, at the village we passed. They all appeared not only friendly, but even troublesome with their civilities.

Decr. 31st Sunday. A very cloudy Day with Snow from the Etd. Turned 2 pair of Galley Snow Shoes. Assembled the principal Men of the Village and after a short Speech presented the principal Man with a laced Coat—he gave it to another &c &c—expenses 3 ft of Tobacco & 1 Coat.

December 31st Sunday. A very cloudy day with Snow from the eastward. Assembled the principal Men and smoked with them about 2 Hours. Their conversation chiefly turned on their inveterate Enemies the Sieux and Pawnees [that is, the Yanktonai Dakotas and the Arikaras], and in the extreme difficulty of their ever being able to open out a passage to our Settlements for the purposes of Trade, to which I much pressed them.

[January 1798]

Janry 1st 1798, Monday. A very cloudy Day. Went to the Fall Indian Village—took with me 1 fath of Tobacco & the other laced Coat. Passed thro' the Village of Mahnow & exchanged my Gun with

[21] Big Hidatsa, 32ME12.
[22] Sakakawea Village, 32ME11.
[23] Black Cat, 32ML5.
[24] Deapolis, 32ME5.

him. Gave with it 1 3-lb Carat of Tobacco, 50 rods of Ammunition, 1 Dog, 1 piece of Soap, 1 Bottle of Peppermint & a lump of Sugar — promised him 40 rods of Ammunition. Then went to the principal Fall Indian Village where the Coat went off with as little Ceremony as a Person tired sits down to rest himself. Co from the great Fall Indian Village to the lesser N15W 5½M across Land to the River & then an Island & then main Channel. Arrived at 3 PM. Staid all Night. Hospitable. A river from the Turtle Mountain[25] runs close by the great Village of the Fall Indians. Counted 82 Huts. Expences 1 Coat & 4 ft of Tobacco.

[p. 8b] January 1st Monday. A very cloudy day. Went to the great village of the Willow Indians, here the Chiefs again assembled, our conversation was the same as that of yesterday but carried on in a more spirited manner. The feelings of these People seem to be more lively, but far less reflection as the argument they advanced one minute they abandoned the next — elated with their success of last Summer, they have forgot their many defeats, and of course no hopes could be entertained of their ever coming to our Settlements to Trade — indeed they seem to have but little that is valuable to us. I then went off to the upper village, where I was more hospitably received, and where contending factions had less sway. These seemed fully sensible of the advantages of a regular supply of their wants. They said they had often attempted it, but were always plundered by the Stone [Assiniboin] Indians, who were jealous, that if once they had free access to our trading Houses, they would become too powerful; &c &c — passed the Night; very cloudy.

Janry 2nd Tuesday. A very fine clear Day. After a tolerable good Breakfast at 9 AM Mr. Hugh McCraghen, Vivier & me set off for the greater Village of the Fall Indians, arrived there at 10.35 AM. Walked a good Pace in a hard Path Co S15E 5½M. The Village is situated on the Banks of the little River 30 yds wide on the north Side — it comes from the Turtle Mountain to the Westward. Staid abt an Hour then took Horse & set off Co to the lesser Village of the Mandens which is also situated on the Turtle Mountain River. S20E 1¼M. Abt ½M below this Village in a SEbS Co the little River falls into the Missesourie. Then Co S30E 3M to the Manden Village — exd. & ad-

---

[25] That is, the Knife River, also referred to below (in the entry for January 2) as the "Turtle Mountain River," since the Killdeer Mountains, which Thompson called "Turtle Hill" (see fig. 7), are on the upper reaches of Knife River.

justed my Sextant. Expns. of the Day, 2 ft of Tobacco for smoking, 1 oz of Vermillion for Bread.

January 2nd Tuesday. A very fine clear Day. At 9 AM set off returned to the greater village of the Willow Indians. After staying about an Hour, I returned to my Quarters at the lower village, examined and adjusted my Sextant.

Janry 3rd Wednesday. A clear Day. Traded a quantity of Beans, Corn &c — and abt 16 fath of Line. Obsd for Latde [sun].

January 3rd Wednesday. A clear day. Observed for Latitude and Longitude.

Janry 4th Thursday. A cloudy Day. Working with my Snow Shoes. Obsd for Longde [sun].

January 4th Thursday. Cloudy weather, making a Pair of Snow Shoes to carry me back to the Mouse River, as the snow is increasing fast.

Janry 5th Friday. A cloudy snowy Day. Went to the Village of Mahnow and got him to call in 2 of the Rock Mountain [Crow] Indians Natives [p. 43] of the head of the Missesourie & from them the following account. From the Village looking to the Head of the Yellow Stone River the Sun now sets abt 20M to the right Hand of it & from the head of the Yellow River to the head of the Missesourie is 8 Days Journey NbW of very bad Mountainous Road. At the Scource of the Missesourie [is] a high Fall & many Springs. The Mountain [is] very high there & another River not so large goes off on the other Side Strikes SbW. Its Scource they cannot find. There are also 3 Ridges to the Mountain 2 of them lie beyond the West River. The River of large Corn [is] abt 4 Days South of the Yellow River & runs east & north to the Yellow Stone River. The Yellow Stone River after receiving it forms one great Bight to its Junction with the Missesourie. The Shell River [is] abt 3½ Days Journey south of the Missesourie; to its Junction with the Missesourie 12 Days. The Yellow Stone River from its Head to its Junction 22 Days. The little Missesourie to its Junction [is] 26 Days from the Mountain, & the Knife River which passes the Turtle Mountain of the West & joins the Missesourie at this Village 29 Days Journey good walking — as per Drawing[26] & Account. At the Scources of all the River[s], especially of the Missesourie numberless Brooks

[26] See fig. 7.

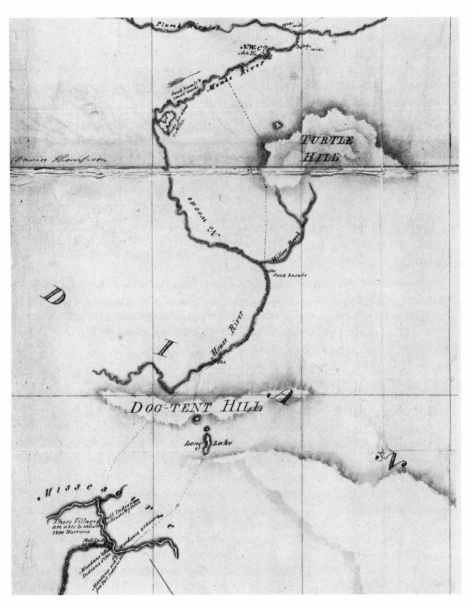

FIG. 6. Detail from David Thompson's map of 1843, illustrating his route to and from the Mandan and Hidatsa villages. Public Record Office, London.

are pouring in on all Sides from the Mountain. There is no Snow on the Mountain at the Missesourie in the Summer altho' it is higher than the other neighbouring Parts. The little Missesourie comes from Lakes & Swamps with Springs abt 16 Days Journey from hence—drew my Drafts before the Natives who exd. & corrected them. 1 Bottle of Tenae for Mahnow & 40 Rods of Amm.

[p. 9a] January 5th Friday. A cloudy, snowy Day. Went to the village of Manore, a frenchman who is naturalized here by a residence of 15 years. Some of the Natives of the Rocky Mountains southward of the Head of the Missesourie being here I got him to call them, and spent the Day in conversing with them, drawing Maps of their Country &c &c. They appeared to be very intelligent, as almost all the Natives of the Mountains are—[they] fully comprehended with a little explanation the drift of all my Questions, and answered direct to them. When done I gave them a little Tobacco—for which they were thankful. I then returned to my Quarters.

Janry 6th Saturday. A cloudy Day with very much Snow. Netting my Snow Shoes.

January 6th Saturday. A cloudy Day with a heavy fall of Snow—netting my Snow Shoes, as nobody else knows how to do it.

Janry 7 Sunday. A cloudy bad Day—finished my Snow Shoes.

January 7th Sunday. A cloudy bad day.

Janry 8 Monday. A stormy Day. In the Evening it became clear & I obsd the whole Night for Latde & Longde.

January 8th Monday. A stormy Day—in the evening it became Clear, and I passed the whole Night in observing for Latde, Longde, etc. etc.

Janry 9 Tuesday. A storm with warm Weather from the West. Obs for Longde [sun] CD. Could not observe at Noon. Stormy—getting all ready to set off. Traded 4 Dogs. Account of Monsr. Jussome's Furrs

 60 bad Wolves
 51 good do Mons. Jussomme for Journey as they are light
 70 do to be left
 5 small Foxes
 2 bad do
 2 Red Foxes
 19 Buffalo Robes
 12 do do
 [p. 44] 17 Buffalo Robes for 51 Wolves

The 19 Buffalo Robes were all that was at our arrival. The other 12 he collected from the Indians & the 17 for the 51 Wolves. The Rascal of an Indian who had the Furrs in Charge traded 24 Wolves with the English 15 for a Gun 4 for a Hatchet & 3 for Powder—he also gave 12 Robes away in the Summer.

January 9th Tuesday. A stormy day with mild weather from the westward. Obsd for Longitude—getting all ready to set off on our return having now fully accomplished the Object for which I came. My time has been spent in noticing their Manners and conversing about their Policy, Wars, Country, Traditions, &c &c[27] in the Evenings I attended their Amusements of Dancing Singing &c. which were always conducted with the highest order and Decorum [p. 9b] after their Idea of thinking; but to me, a stranger, notwithstanding all their arguments, I could not help thinking them the most uxorious Race I have seen and one of the old Priests of Venus would quickly have got them to build a Temple to that becsse [because] one thing in their Favor is, they have a handsome cleanly race of women, who do all they can to heighten the voluptiousness of Love, and as they have little else to do, they seem to have succeeded— as much as they could wish—especially the Dancing Women.

The upper village 31 Houses—7 Tents of Willow Indians

2nd	do	82	do	—	of	do
3rd	do	52	do	mostly all Manden Indians		
4th	do	40	do	do	do	
5th	do	113	do	2/3 Mandens—1/3 Willow Ind		

318 Houses and 7 Tents

Janry 10th Wednesday. A very fine Day. Obsd for Longde Reg— ulus. At 8½ AM we set off from the Manden Village on our return. Co on the River downwards ENE 2M then turned abt NW 1M up the Banks to the top of the Heights which may be abt 500 ft. At the top of the Bank set the Village S32W 2½M by the Compass. The Missesourie runs to the Northd of Et 7M more then turns SEd when past the Pawnee Village.[28] At the top of the Heights 10¼ AM—

[27] Thompson appears to have made no notes on these observations at the time, but they seem to have provided the major part of the information he gives on the Mandans in chapter 14 of his *Narrative*.

[28] This is a reference to the Arikara village on the Missouri River near the modern town of Washburn. The village is believed to be identifiable as the Greenshield site, 320L17 (Stephen A. Chomko, "The Ethnohistorical Setting of the Upper Knife-Heart Region," in *Papers in Northern Plains Prehistory and Ethnohistory,* ed. W. Raymond Wood, South Dakota Archaeological Society, Special Publication, no. 10).

obliged to leave a Dog. Co in the Plains abt NE 13M at 5 PM we put up in the Plain without either Wood or Water. The Dogs being too heavy loaded to proceed farther. The old Manden Man & Woman who were coming with us returned as they were not able to keep up with us. A fine warm Day. In the Night the White Man[29] came to us. 6 Indians in Co.

January 10th Wednesday. A very fine day. Obsd for Longitude. After all my Exertions to get some of these People to visit our Settlements I had the pleasure of seeing 4 young Men agree to follow us. At 8½ AM set off to go by the usual Route, as our apprenension of the Sieux being in our way is dissipated. Co down the Missesourie ENE 2M — then turned up the Banks of the River to the top of the Heights — NW 1M. Co in the Plain NE 13M. The snow thawing and being deep, the Sleds heavy loaded made us move heavily on. At 5 PM we put up in the open Plain. We were extremely thirsty — having no wood could not make a Fire to thaw the Snow.

Janry 11 Thursday. A fine Day. At 7¾ AM set off. Co NE 3M to the little Lake at 9 AM — put up as we are not able to gain the Woods of the Long Lake today. Hool killed a Bull. I went a huntg. but my Gun continually snapt expd. 8 Balls. Pierre Gilbert with an Indian went for the flesh of the Bull & returning it being Night they wandered out of the way & Slept in the Plain all Night.

January 11th Thursday. A fine day. At 7¾ AM set off. Co NE 3M to the little Lake or Pond with a few large scattered Oaks — [p. 10a] At 9 AM it being too late to cross the next large Plain, we camped here for the day. One of the men went a hunting and Killed a Bull. A man with him went for the Meat, but missed the Road and wandered about all Night.

Janry 12 Friday. A fine clear warm Morng but stormy Night. Pierre [Gilbert] & the Indian returned at 8½ AM — but they said it was too late to set off for the Long Lake. Vivier killed an old Bull close to us for [the] Dogs. At 11½ AM the Weather became cloudy.

Remarks

The upper Village Fall Indians 31 Houses 7 Tents
2nd   do   do   82 do

---

[29]The "White Man" was a Mandan or Hidatsa "Chief in the prime of life" (Thompson, *David Thompson's Narrative of His Explorations*, p. 239).

3rd Mahnow of Mandens &
      a few Fall Indians   52*
4th across the River   40
5. lower Village   113
                                _____
                                318 & 7 Tents

    * 37 Mandanes
      15 Fall Indians
         Fall Indians 1336.
         In tents to make the number
         220 to 2500 souls.[30]

The White Man returned to the Village. In the Eveng. Snow.

January 12th Friday. A fine clear warm Morning— by 8½ AM the men of yesterday came to us, but they were too much fatigued to be able to walk all day. We were therefore obliged to pass the day again here.

Janry 13 Saturday. All Night a Gale from the West which contd all Day—blows too hard to proceed. The Pawnee [Arikara] Village abt SE 12M from us. Miserable Times in an open Hut—exposed to the inclemencies of the Weather. Hool killed 2 Cows. Thank God. But we only got a good Meal out of the whole.

January 13th Saturday. A heavy Gale from the westward. One of the Men killed 2 Cows, but we could only get a good Meal out of the whole. Weather too stormy to proceed.

[p. 45] Janry 14th. A close Morng & bad stormy Afternoon with much Snow—lay by.

January 14th Sunday. Foggy Morning, and bad stormy snowy Afternoon.

Janry 15 Monday. A close warm Morng. At 2 PM smll Rain—at 3 PM wind changed to a Storm at NbW with thick weather.

January 15th Monday. A close warm Morning. At 2 PM small Rain. At 3 PM wind changed to a Storm at NbW with thick weather.

Janry 16 Tuesday. At 5 AM a most terrible Storm with Snow & excessive high Drift broke out & contd all Day. At 5 PM the Snow

[30]The entry denoted by the asterisk is written in what appears to be Thompson's hand, but in a crabbed style such as might be made by an old person with an unsteady hand—and Thompson was more than seventy years of age at the time he wrote his "Narrative" using these notes. "Fall Indians" refers to the Hidatsa Indians.

ceased but the Drift contd shifted our Lodge. Living most miserable in an open Hut—only Corn to eat.

January 16th Tuesday. At 5 AM a most terrible Storm came on and continued all day. At 5 PM the Snow ceased, but the Drift continued, and as we are quite without shelter we were almost suffocated—passing our Time sitting in the Snow under an Oak with a Blanket wrapped round us.

Janry 17 Wednesday. The Weather more moderate but still bad & cold. No Success in Huntg. A very fine Evng. An Indian Returned to the Village.

January 17th Wednesday. The weather more moderate, but still bad and cold—no success in hunting—fine Evening.

Janry 18 Thursday. In the Night a parcel of Bulls came to us— the young Men killed one of them—which this Morng the Dogs eat up at one Meal (31 Dogs) & picked his Bones. A very fine Morn & day. I wanted the People to set off but Mr. Jussomme would not go. Vivier & Hool also. To remember Jussomme to Mr. Thorburn & the Agents for it. Yesterday I got a close [?] Jacket of Buffalo made for me & today a pair of Shoes of do from Hugh.

January 18th Thursday. A fine Day. I wanted the people to set off, but their things was so full of Snow, wet and froze that it required all day nearly to get them to rights.

Janry 19 Friday. A fine Morng. At 7.30 AM set off. Co the Head of the Long Lake. N13°E by the Compass 16M. 5½ Hours sharp Walking 1H PM Co on the Lake winding. N8°E 2½M at 2.20 PM put up. For the 1st—1½M the Lake ¼M to ½M wide then quite narrow for ¼M then widens to ¼M—3 small patches of wood at end of Co— good Woods with Tent Poles on the east Side; put up on the W Side—good large Woods but no Poles. A Spring of Water close to us. At 8½ AM a Storm with high Drifts broke out at SW it lasted 2H— then a good moderate Gale & fine. Eating Corn. Snow & Drift with a Gale at Night.

[p. 10b] January 19th Friday. A fine morning. At 7.30 AM set off. Co over the Plain to the south end of the Long Lake N13E 16M. Co in the Lake N8E 2½M here we found woods to make a good Fire and put up at 2.20 PM—a fine spring of water close to us. Snow and Drift with a heavy Gale all Night.

Janry 20 Saturday. A fine Day wind Westerly a moderate Gale. At 7¾ AM set off. Co on the Long Lake No 1M N10W 2M end the Long Lake. 2 patches of Wood near the End—then Co in a Gully to close to another smll Lake with a patch of wood N15W 1M we then went up the Bank on the left & sighted another smll Lake with a spot of good Woods by the Compass N35W 3½M to the Lake—it is ¼M by ¼M. Co over hilly Ground. N40W 1M. N20W 2M. N10W 2M—put up at the Gully I formerly set from the Mouse River at 4 PM. Vivier killed a Bull thank God. The Dog Hill abt 3M to the Eastd of us—set the Mouse River. The Elbow N8W. The Place we are to make N2E—only Co this Day by the Compass. In the Eveng high Drifts.

January 20th Saturday. A fine day. Wind westerly a moderate Gale. At 7¾ AM set off Co the Lake North 1M N10W 2M then to a Pond of water N14W 1M. Co over hilly Ground N40W 1M. N20W 2M. N10W 2M to the north side of the Dog Tent Hill—put up in the Bottom of a deep Gully with a spring of water and a few Oaks and small Aspins, in the evening high Drift.

Janry 21st Sunday. In the Night a Northerly Storm with Snow & high Drift & exceeding close Weather broke out & contd all Day—lay by.

January 21st Sunday. In the Night a heavy Storm broke out at North with Snow and very high Drift—could not proceed.

[p. 46] Janry 22nd Monday. A most terrible Storm at West all Night & this Day with thick Snow and excessive high Drifts. The poor Fellows who are living in the Hut could not light their Fire & were obliged to crowd in with us 16 in all. This is beyond all Doubt the worst Day I ever saw in all my Life it is absolutely impossible to see 10 yards before you. Those who bring wood to the Tent Strike it with the wood ere they see it. The Tent is drifting full altho' we are full 80 Feet below the level of the Plain in a narrow Gully whose bottom is only 20 yards. Those in the Hut were near perishing. A little Meat and Corn.

January 22nd Monday. A most terrible Storm at west with thick snow and excessive high Drift. The poor fellows who have made a Hut were nearly suffocated in it—and were obliged to come into the Tent which however small is obliged to contain us all 16 in number. All their things are so buried under the snow that they cannot get them. The Dogs are drifted over with Snow that we walk on them without seeing them, such is the effects of the Storm and Drift, that it is almost as dark as Night, and we cannot actually see distinct 10 yards before us, and altho' we are in the bottom of a Gully full 50 feet beneath the level of the Plain—yet it is as much as we can Keep from being buried under the Snow, it is without

121

Doubt the worst day I ever saw [p. lla] in my Life. We have no Meat, fortunately yesterday I picked up the Marrow Bone of a Buffaloe which had been pretty well Knawed by a Wolf—and this my day's allowance.

Janry 23rd Tuesday. A very strong Storm of Wind at West with high Drift but clear Sky. Two of us attempted to hunt but we were not able to resist the Wind. Eating Corn.

January 23rd Tuesday. All day a very heavy Storm from West, with low Drift and clear weather. Hunger obliged two of us to hunt— my Companion soon returned—seeing some Buffaloe about ½ mile to windward of me I strove to reach them, but the wind tossed me down so often that I was glad to shelter myself in the Gully with the rest.

Janry 24th Wednesday. A fine cloudy warm Day. Northerly Breeze. At 7.20 AM set off Co N2°E 9½M. Hool killed 2 Cows. Co to the River 2½M then Co down the River NE 2M put up at 4 PM. The last 2M bad Road with deep Snow. Plenty of good Meat. Thank God. Fell in with the Track of the English at the River. This morng 2 of the Manden young Men returned to their Village 2 still in Co. Louis—Vivier—Minies staid behind waiting on Monsr. Jussomme.

January 24th Wednesday. A fine cloudy warm Day northerly Breeze. At 7.20 AM set off N2E 9½M. One of the Men Killed 2 Cows of the Meat of which we loaded on Sleds, we were very much in want. Co to the Mouse River + 2½M. Co down along the River NE 2M at 4 PM put up, as we have much bad road with deep Snow—part of the Men remained behind to dry their Things &c that were buried under the Snow. This morning two of our Manden Indians returned to their village—two of them yet remain with us.

Janry 25th Thursday. A hard Gale at NE with Snow in the Morng & thick weather all Day. At 7.40 AM set off Co abt NE 3M—1¼M gone pass the Place we put up as we went then Co abt N35E 9M to where we put up as we went. At 1½ PM a very bad Day & stormy Eveng. No Cattle abt the River.

Janry 25th Thursday. A hard Gale at NE with Snow in the morning. At 7.40 AM set off Co NE 3M. N35E 9M—put up to wait the People behind. No cattle about the River.

Janry 26 Friday. A hard Gale of Easterly Wind with cloudy Weather all Day—lay by waiting for the People behind. They came up to us at Noon & put up abt 1M beyond us. Hool killed 2 Bulls.

Workd Obs All yesterday from the old Tent Place. The woods all on the West Side of the River.

January 26th Friday. A hard Gale of easterly wind with cloudy weather—lay by all Day—waiting the People. They joined us at Noon. One of the Men Killed 2 Bull Buffaloe.

Janry 27 Saturday. A tolerable Day. Wind a small Gale Easterly & Varble. with at Times thick Weather. At 7½ AM set off Cos by the Compass N12°E 4M. N8°E 9M. North 2M to the Place where we put up as we went—then Co North 3M—put up at a Pt of Woods at the River. The River tolerable Straight today. The Sand Knowls as formerly. A bold Line of woods lying NW & SE on our right. The NWd end opposite to us, now 1M dist.

[p. llb] January 27th Saturday. A tolerable Day. A small Gale Easterly, with thick weather at times. At 6½ AM set off Co N12E 4M. N8E 9M. North 2M North 3M put up.

Janry 28 Sunday. A southerly Breese with very thick warm Weather. Hool went a huntg—he killed a young Bull & at 10 AM we set off & went along the River N5W 4½M N20°W 4M to opposite the Place we put up at the Sand knowl. We kept it abt ½M Et of us then Co NW 1½M [p. 47] to a point of River wood to close by where I killed 2 Cows—put up at 3 PM.

January 28th Sunday. A southerly Breeze, with warm and very thick weather. We have so many Dogs hauling Sleds that they always keep us short of Provisions. One of Men went a hunting and Killed a young Bull. At 10 AM we set off, and held still down along the River N5W 4½M. N20W 4M. NW 1½M put up at 3 PM ready to cross the great Plain with the first clear weather.

Janry 29th Monday. A very thick rimy Day. Light Airs Variable— lay by. Vivier killed a good Bull. Hool & Vaudril killed another far off. Workd Obs.

January 29th Monday. A very thick rimy day, with variable light airs. The Men did not care to cross the Plain, and I wished the Men and Dogs to be all fresh for that purpose—spent the day in hunting, as we do not expect to see any more Buffaloe.

Janry 30th Tuesday. A very Close thick Day—it was almost as dark as Night the whole Day—without once clearing. At 7 AM set off for the Turtle Mountain. Co N10°W by the Compass 24M to the Woods. We put up at 4½ PM abt 3M ENE of the Place where we took Tent Poles. Thank God—as we made the Woods which we did not

Missesourie

Missesourie

Missesourie

Lepin

Turtle

Hill

River

These Villages are able
to raise about 1200 Warriors

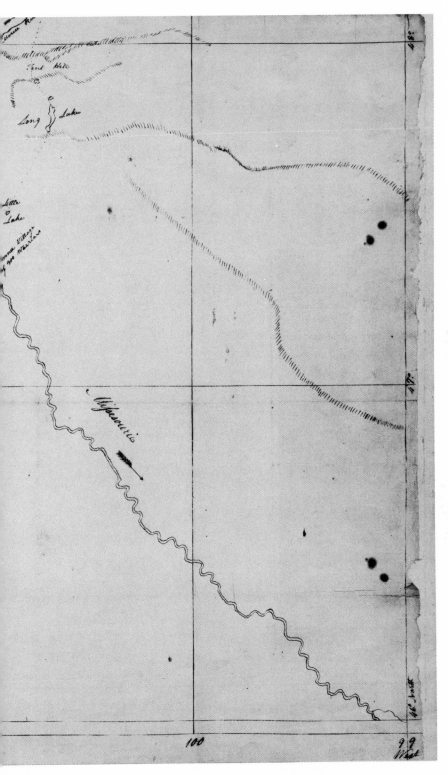

FIG. 7. Detail from David Thompson's map of 1798, showing the location of the Mandan and Hidatsa villages. Library of Congress.

see 'till we were within ½M of them. The Weather cleared. Wind Easterly. Saw on the Hill 21 male Deer. No Cattle except a very few Bulls.

January 30th Tuesday. A very close calm thick foggy Day—it was almost as dark as Night—as the weather was calm I determined to cross the Plain, part of the Men could not be brought to venture, but on seeing us about to set off without them they begged hard to wait them half an Hour; we then at 7 AM set off Co N10W 24M to the woods of the Turtle Hill. At 4½ PM—we have walked more than this distce. but cannot bring the inequalities of the Ground into the account. The Day kept so very thick that I was several times obliged to stop and count the Men, Sleds, &c. and all the afternoon part of the Men behind thinking themselves wandering in the Plain without hope of seeing woods, and fearing a storm, Kept cursing my folly and rashness in setting [p. 12a] off to cross such a large Plain in such weather, when they reached the intended Spit and found themselves safe, they all agreed that I had done well, and could not help confessing that had the Irishman with old Boisseau consented they would have lain down in the Plain and waited clear weather.

Janry 31st Wednesday. A very fine Warm Day—light Airs from SWd. At 7 A, set off Co N52W 2M. N30W 4½M. The Place where we put up when we killed the Bull & where I obsd is now N30°E ½M dist. Co N7°W 7½M. The weather so warm that we can hardly walk—put up at 2½ PM. The Place where we put up when we crossed from the Mouse River as we went—is now abt North 1¼M beyond us. Set the Woods—a bold Body of abt 3M bears Wt 24M. There also seems to be Woods among sand Knowls WNW 21M distt. The woods we have to make bears N44W & extends to N20°W, The Woods of NW seem to be 2 or 3M nearer than the last Co—all these Cos by the Compass. The Sun set S50W to Night—tolerable good Horizon.

January 31st Wednesday. A very fine warm Day. At 7 AM set off and went along the Hill N52W 2M. N30W 4½M. N7W 7½M at 2½ PM put up—ready to cross the last great Plain.

[February 1798]

Febry 1st Thursday. A very fine Day. Wind a southerly Breese. At 6.10 AM we set off from the Hill to the Mouse River Co N40°W 19M to the Isle of Woods Wtd of where we left the Indians at the Sand Knowls. Co N6E 3M to the Sand Knowls where we again found the Same Indians in the same Place near end of Co crossed the

Mouse River. Went beyond the Indians to put up NE ½M—put up at 3½ PM. We made the Isle of Woods at 1 PM walked sharply— then found a pitching Track & stopped to make a drink of Water. 6 or 7 Tents of Stone Indians. They behaved kindly to the Manden young Men.

February 1st Thursday. A very fine day with southerly Breeze at 6.10 AM set off Co to the Mouse River N40W 19M. Co down along the River NbE 3M. NE ½M—put up at 3½ PM. We have now the great Road of the Stone Indians to walk in, which is so well beat down that we do not require Snow Shoes.

Feby 2nd Friday. A fine day. At 6¾ AM set off Co N30E 6M to opposite & close to the old House where I obsd then Co abt N30°E 4½M to the high Knowl close to the River. Co abt N35°E 9M to the Plumb River—it is 13 yds wide & comes from behind the Boss Hill. Went abt ¼M beyond it to a Gully close to the River & put up at 3½ PM. Walked fast on a good hard Track without Snow Shoes. All this Day we have kept the Mouse River tolerable close on our right—it has very little Woods. Met at our up putting Place— several Stone Indians—suppose 5 Tents. The Mouse River is here abt 30 yds wide & open in several Places. All Plain to the Etd—we still see the Turtle Hill bending to the Etd—but little Woods to the Wtd. The English passed here only 8 Days ago.[31]

February 2nd Friday. A fine Day. At 6¾ AM set off Co N30E 6M + 4½M. N35E 9M to the Plumb River, which comes from the NWd & falls into the Mouse River—put up at 3¼ PM.

[p. 48] Febry 3rd Saturday. At 1 AM got up—& at 1.50 AM we set off for the House of Mr. McDonnel at the Red River. Co abt NE by the Compass 8M—across the Plain to the Woods of the Moose Head then Co NE 6M to the last Woods & close to the high Knowl of the Moose Head. Sandy Ground then Co N75°E 7½M to the House at 10½ AM. Thank God—the last Co all Plain. A fine Moon light Night & southerly Gale. A very fine Day.

February 3rd Saturday. A very fine day. At 1.50 AM set off. Co NE 8M across a Plain to the woods of the Moose Head NE 6M. N75E 7¼M to the Settlement of the NW Coy. Mr. John McDonald. Thank God.

---

[31] The "English" referred to are probably the three members of the Hudson's Bay Company party which Thompson noted left the villages on December 28 bound for the Assiniboine River. See Thompson's entry for December 28 and table 1.

Febry 4th Sunday. A very fine Day—drawing a horizontal Dial. Hugh McCraghen, Minier, Murray & 2 other Men set off for the Missesourie. Obsd for Latde.

Febry 5th Monday. A very fine Day. Westerly Gale of Wind—set the Dial—writing my Journal &c—& getting ready to set off tomorrow for the Calling River—got a pair of Blue Molten Trowsers from Mr. McDonnel—& got a pair of Jumping Deer Skin Trowsers also made—2 pair of good Shoes & 2 pair of Socks.

Febry 6th Tuesday. In the Night a NbW Gale of Wind arose with Snow. At 6 AM the Snow ceased—& light thin Clouds—with a strong Gale. The Men thought it blew too hard & cold to proceed. Upon considering the long Time it would take I gave over my Journey to the Calling River—& shall begin drawing off the Journies I have made. From this time to the Commencement of my Journey down the Stone Indian River [on 26 February 1798] I employed myself wholly in Calculations & Drawing.

February 4th Sunday to February 25 Sunday. This Time Spent in writing up my Journals, arranging and working my Observations, drawing off the Countries I have passed over and Observing for the Latde Longde &c of this Place &c &c, and getting ready to survey the rest of this, the Stone Indian River and then the Red River—to the Mississippe—by the River St. Louis to Lake Superior, and along the south Side of that Lake to the Falls of St. Maries. The Gentlemen laugh at this Scheme as a piece of Quixotism, how far I shall succeed, Heaven Knows.

3

François-Antoine Larocque's "Missouri Journal"

FRANÇOIS-ANTOINE LAROCQUE was born on August 19, 1784, at L'Assomption, Quebec. He studied for a short time at the College de Montreal, but shortly after his father's death in October, 1792, "he was sent to the United States to learn English. He was to prefer expressing himself in that language for the rest of his life."[1] Two of Larocque's journals, both of them in English, are still extant. The first journal details his first and second trips to the Missouri River and the Mandan-Hidatsa villages: it is usually called the "Missouri Journal," and it is the subject of this chapter. His third and final trip was his visit to the Missouri River and beyond, to the Bighorn Mountains in what is now Montana and Wyoming; this account is called the "Yellowstone Journal," and it is the topic of the next chapter of this book.

When François-Antoine was seventeen years of age, he joined the North West Company's short-lived competitor, the XY Company, as a clerk; he left eastern Canada for the west on April 26, 1801. Arriving at

Grand Portage in June, he spent some time at Fort Charlotte, several miles west of Grand Portage, but was later sent to winter on the English River (modern Churchill River), later moving down to the Assiniboine River. Sometime between 1802 and the fall of 1804, Larocque left the employ of the XY Company and entered the service of the North West Company. November 11, 1804, found him on his way from Fort Assiniboine to the Mandan and Hidatsa villages on the Missouri River. Shortly after his arrival, he met and visited with Captains Lewis and Clark several times and, in fact, offered to accompany them on their way west from Fort Mandan, but they declined his offer.

On February 12, 1805, Larocque returned to the Assiniboine River, where he learned that the XY Company had merged with the North West Company. After an eight-day stay at the fort, Larocque returned to the Missouri River for the new company with additional trading supplies for the men there. The "Missouri Journal" ends abruptly on February 28, two days following his return. He left us no record for his activities for the next three and one-

[1] *Dictionary of Canadian Biography,* vol. 9, s.v. "François-Antoine Larocque," p. 455.

half months. During that time, however, he returned to the Assiniboine River, for when his next account commences, it is June 2, 1805, and he is on his way to the Missouri River for a third and final time. On this last trip, however, he was under orders from Charles Chaboillez to visit the Rocky Mountains and to discover how abundant beavers were there; the account of that mission is presented in his "Yellowstone Journal."

At the age of twenty-one, and accompanied by only two companions, Larocque preceded William Clark to the middle reaches of the Yellowstone River, which Clark descended in the summer of 1806. Larocque returned to Canada with a richly detailed account of his journey, together with reminiscences of the Crow Indians which are still basic references. This expedition consumed four and one-half months and concluded with his return to Fort Assiniboine on September 18, 1805.

Larocque left the West for Montreal in 1806, never to return. He first founded a business, which failed. In the War of 1812 he fought as a captain of the Chasseurs Canadiens, and he was taken captive and imprisoned at Cincinnati for six months. Several years after the war, in 1818, he married Marie-Catherine-Emilie Cotte. He was one of the founders of the Bank of Montreal in 1819, and he remained active in business until his retirement in 1841 at the age of fifty-seven. In 1853 he traveled for over a year on visits to many of the major cities of the United States, including Cincinnati. In 1855 he entered the Hotel Dieu of Saint Hyacinthe, Quebec, where he spent the

rest of his life, fourteen years, in meditation and prayer. He died peacefully on May 1, 1869, at the age of eighty-four, and he was interred in the basement, or burial vault, of the church of the Hotel Dieu in Saint Hyacinthe (fig. 8).[2] He was well regarded by the Gray Nuns of Saint Hyacinthe, according to documents in their archives, and by his friends and business associates. The bishop of Saint Hyacinthe conducted his funeral service, and at least one member of Parliament was among the pallbearers. The graves in the burial vault of the church were disinterred between October 27 and November 27, 1897, and were reburied in the cemetery of the Gray Nuns of Saint Hyacinthe, Quebec. A gravestone bearing the inscription "Antoine Larocque, 1869" is still to be found there on the same stone that also bears the names of a number of other persons.[3]

Larocque kept a daily account of his activities on his first and second expeditions to the Missouri River in 1804 and 1805. The original of that document has been lost, but what ap-

[2] The burial record of Larocque is in the Bishop's Residence of the Cathedral of St. Hyacinthe, Quebec Province, Canada, on leaf 3 of vol. 4 of the *Registre des Baptêmes, Mariages, Sépultures.* Fig. 8 was obtained from Father Jean-Roche Choinière, Chancellor, Diocese of Saint. Hyacinthe, who also gave permission to publish it.

[3] Information on Larocque's last years, and on his burial and reburial, is contained in uncataloged archives of the Gray Nuns of Saint Hyacinthe. Photocopies of documents relating to these events were provided the authors through the courtesy of Sister Roseline Lessard of that institution. Sister Lessard also photographed Larocque's present grave site for us.

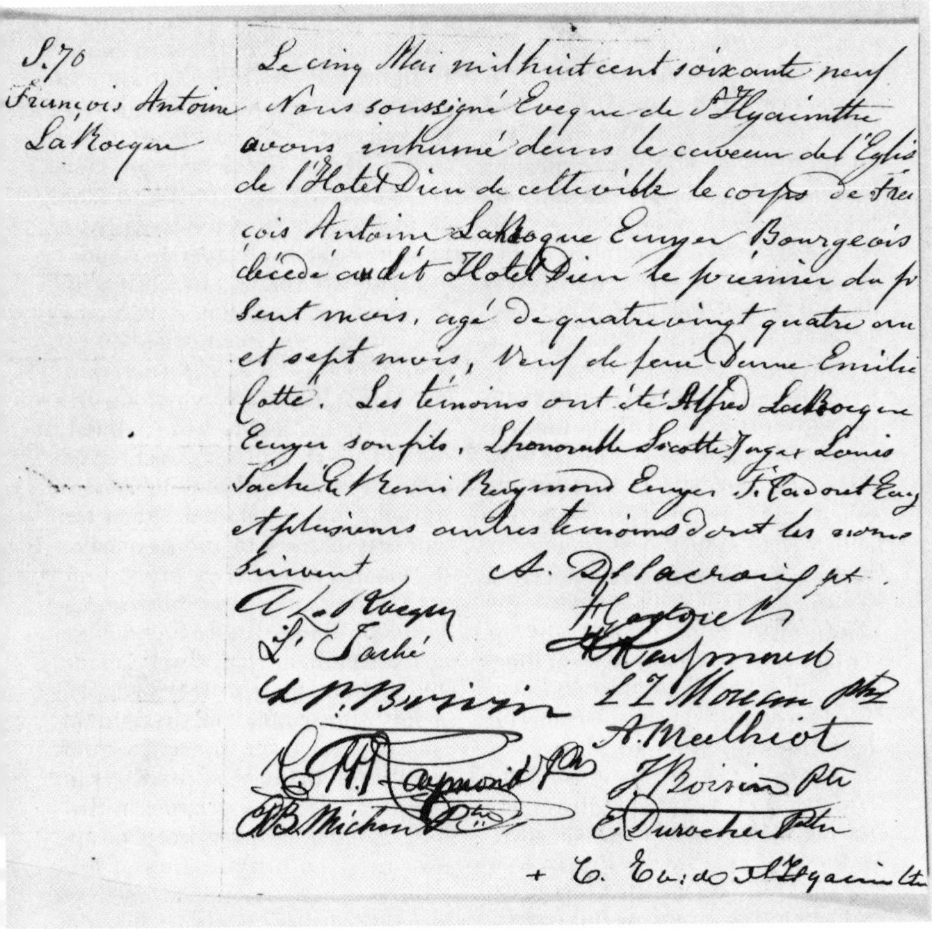

FIG. 8. Burial record of François-Antoine Larocque. Diocese of Saint Hyacinthe, Quebec, Canada.

pears to be a careful copy of it was apparently sent to Roderick McKenzie, and that copy eventually found its way into the hands of L. R. Masson. It is now in the National Archives of Canada, Wellington Street, Ottawa, cataloged as M.G. 19, C1, in Vol. 3. The journal, in English, consists of twenty-three pages of text in a loosely bound notebook of handmade paper measuring 30 by 32 cm. The paper is watermarked "1803." The manuscript is a copy of the original or of another copy and is written in brown ink, apparently in a single hand.

L. R. Masson edited and published part of this journal in his *Les*

Bourgeois de la Compagnie du Nord-Ouest: Recits de voyages, lettres et rapports inedits relatifs au Nord-Ouest Canadien, in 1889-90. That edition, however, is incomplete. Masson's version contains many ellipses, indicating that the journal was significantly abbreviated, and numerous other deletions were made silently. Larocque failed to make entries for only twelve days of the period from November 11, 1804, to February 28, 1805. Masson's edition, however, contains entries for only thirty-seven days (38 percent of Larocque's original entries), but none of the entries for those thirty-seven days are complete. In other words, about seventy per cent of Larocque's journal was deleted in Masson's edition. Furthermore, every sentence has been altered by Masson in one way or another—by updating some of Larocque's spellings to modern usage, such as substituting "creek" for "Crick"; by changing Larocque's admittedly arbitrary capitalizations of many letters; by many punctuation changes; and by spelling out most symbols and abbreviations. Some of the abbreviations were expanded without justification. For example, Larocque's "Mr. McK." became "Mr. [Charles] McKenzie," when when it could equally refer to Alexis McKay, who also accompanied Larocque and McKenzie to the Missouri River.

Although Masson retained the bare bones and highlights of the expedition, he deleted the admittedly sometimes mundane, day-to-day activities of the traders and removed information of great significance. He deleted, for instance, the numbers and kinds of pelts exchanged with the local Indians as well as a table listing various skins and trade goods and their values. All of this is indispensable information indeed for understanding the economics of the fur trade. Furthermore, the deleted sections preclude a reconstruction of Larocque's itinerary, which in turn permits us to identify more precisely the villages in which he and his partners were trading. Masson's changes therefore necessitated a new and verbatim transcript of this important document.

The present version was first transcribed from a photocopy provided by the National Archives of Canada. This transcript was then verified against the original on a visit to Ottawa in June, 1979. Every effort has been made to assure a precise transcription, although several standardizations have been imposed on the text, as given in the Editorial Procedures. One deviation from those standards is the substitution, in this version, of periods in place of dashes. Commas which were obviously intended as periods have been rendered as such, and periods are added at the end of sentences which ended at the ends of paragraphs and at the ends of lines on the page.

[p. 4]

MISSOURI JOURNAL
WINTER 1804–1805

November 1804

[p. 5] Sunday 11th. Sett off from Fort assiniboine,[4] at 2 oClock P.M. for the Missouri with a trading Equipment. We had 9 horses, 5 of which were loaded with the Co/ [Company's] property. Our Company Consisted of Charles McKenzie, Bte. Lafrance, Wm. Morrison, Joseph azure, Bte. Turenne & alexis McKay, & Myself. Encamped about 3 Miles from the Fort, Close to a Small pond of Stagnated water, In order to wait for Morrison, who had Remain'd behind, with one horse & load. He arrived an hour after. Sent McKay to the Fort to fetch Provisions for himself which he had forgot. Messers. Chaboillez & Heney[5] Came to See us. They remain'd with us a few hours, Bade us farewell & departed.

Monday 12th. Sett off at break of day. Cross'd the River aux prunes[6] at half after 9 & Stopp'd at 11 oClock on the Side of a Brook to Rest our horses & take our dinner. Remain'd there 3 quarters of an hour & proceeded. Encamped after Sun Sett at Some Sandy Hills upon River la Souris.[7]

Tuesday 13th. Departed Early in the Morning, did not Stop at all till half past 3 P.M. when we Stopp'd to pass the Night, on the Side of the 1st little River of the Elk Head, which is a piece of high Ground upon the South Side of the River la Souris, opposite which on the North Side 2 Small Rivers, discharge themselves, their Course nearly from West to East, that of R. l. S. at this place S. to North.

---

[4] Fort Assiniboine was on the south bank of the Assiniboine River at the mouth of Souris River in 1805 (Ernest Voorhis, *Historic Forts and Trading Posts of the French Régime and of the English Fur Trading Companies*, p. 33).

[5] Charles Chaboillez and Hugh Heney.

[6] Modern Plum Creek. See Larocque's "Yellowstone Journal," n. 11.

[7] Larocque is not explicit enough in this journal to permit us to trace his route in other than very general terms. The "Yellowstone Journal" is more precise and allows us to follow the route.

Our Course Since leaving the Fort has been with little variation, west of South.

Wednesday 14th. Sett off in a S.S.W. direction but the plains being burnt, Made us Change our Course to N.W. by W. In order to find food for our horses having been Informed that the plains were not burnt in that direction. Encamp'd at Sun Sett at the last woods upon the 2nd River of the Elk Head having Cross'd the lst River, Nearly at its Source in the plains. Mr. McK. broke his gun. Saw 2 Buffalo Bulls & while we were making the Campment 2 men went & Kill'd them. They brought part of the Flesh of the best of them.

Thursday 15th. Removed our Situation to about 7 miles higher up the Same River, there being better food for our horses, & from whence the traverse of the plains is Shorter to River la Souris, as It was Impossible to get to that River, from where we Slept last night, by day, & there is not a Stick of wood In the Intermediate Space. Kill'd a fat young Bull. Very Cold weather, Strong N.W. wind.

Friday 16th. Sett off Early in the morning the wind blowing from the Same Quarter as yesterday, & very Cold. [p. 6] Did not Stop at all in the Course of the day. Perceived the woods upon the Souris at Sun Sett & arrived at them, before dark, when we Encamp'd on the Banks of the River. Course today was S.S.W. at 10 oClock, A.M. Cross'd a Crick in the plains that had little or no Current & Call'd by the Indians Deep River, from its being very deep in Some places, where the water gathers, & forms into Lakes. Saw a great plenty of Buffalo. The plains were burnt in a great many places.

Saturday 17th. Proceeded & followd the Course of the River, at 2 oClock arrived at the End of the Woods. Not knowing at what distance the next woods were, & being loth to Encamp without Fire, Stopp'd here for the night. The men kill'd 2 Old Bulls & 2 ducks. Course South.

Sunday 18th. Sett off ½ hour before daylight. Walked hard till 12 oClock when, we arrived at the Woods. Stopp'd one hour to Refresh ourselves & horses. Resum'd our Course, still following the River, & Encamped on it, at Sun Sett. Course South till 12, & S.S.E. the Remainder of the day.

Monday 19th. Departed, Still following the River Course as Yesterday. Saw 2 very large Band of Buffalo Cows, upon which we fir'd. Kill'd one. Stopp'd at 12 oClock to Cook some of the Flesh, after one hours Rest Sett off again, ascended the Hills of the River, & proceeded direct South, the River la Souris, makes a Bend here & turns Easterly.

The plains being on fire to the South West, & the Wind blowing from that Quarter, brought such volumes of smoke, as prevented us from seeing 100 Yds before us, so that we were fain to stop at a Crick which lay in our way (& which disembogues in the Souris) & there pass the night. Azure Kill'd a Red Deer.[8]

Tuesday 20th. Went down the Crick & Came to the River, which we followed for an hour & a half. We again ascended the hills. The wind having shifted South, the weather was Clear for about 2 hours, when it again veered to the S. West, & we were Involved in Smoke but not so thick as yesterday. At 10 A.M. we stopp'd On a Hill to look at a dark Spot which appeared moving. By the help of a Spy glass, found it to be Buffalo. As we were moving off, heard a number of people, hooping & hallooing, as Indians generally do when at War. Some Hills prevented us from seeing, who they proceeded from. We immediately unsheathed our guns for defense, as we were Certain that [p. 7] if they were numerous Enough, they would Endeavor to pillage us of our Goods, it being their fix'd determination, to prevent as much as they Can, any Communication, between their traders & the Missouri Indians; as they wish to Engross that trade themselves. However, they Immediately appeared to the number of Eight, & behaved very peaceably, they asked for a little Tob[acco], which I gave them, 4 Inches to Each & 20 R'ds amunition among them all. As we were going off, one of them went before the Horses, & Endeavored to prevent them from passing, being I suppose displeased at not getting more. He let fall his Robe, & put an arrow to his Bow, as if to let fly at the horses, however we soon Caused him to give way & went on. One of them followed us for about 1 mile & being question'd said he wanted more Tob. I Refus'd giving him any, being very sorry, they had got any at all.

They Informed us that they were Coming from the Missouri Villages, where a great number of their Nation that is Assiniboines had been & were on their way back, with whom they said we would probably meet, likewise with a band of the Knisteneaux [Crees], who had also been there, trading Corn & horses. Continued our Journey & Encamp'd at Sun Sett on the side of a Crick. The plains all Burnt, excepting the spot, on which we Encamped. When it was dark we tied our horses, with long Cords to pickets fix'd in the ground, In order that they might not go at a distance from us during the

---

[8] Elk or wapiti, *Cervus canadensis.*

night. Kept watch over them all night by turns, being apprehensive that some of those vagabonds had follow'd us, to steal them.

Wednesday 21st. Departed from thence, our Course as Yesterday, South. Encamp'd at the Grand Coulé, at 3 P.M. being the last woods, this side of the Missouri. Plains all burnt, except some spots along the Coulé, upon which our horses fed.

Thursday 22nd. Prepared to sett off, But two horses belonging to Lafrance & to Azure were missing. Remaind here the whole day searching [for] them but to no Effect. Kill'd a Bull; at sun sett Removed a little higher upon the Coulé, to a better place for the feeding of our horses, where we kept them tied to pickets all night.

Friday 23rd. Sett off at break of day taking the loads of the horses that were missing on Mr. McKenzies horse & my own. Found the Assiniboin Road leading to the Missouri at 9 oClock A.M. At Mid day passed one of their [p. 8] Encampments, Counted 75 fireplaces, passed two more Encampments in the Evening & stopp'd for the night, by the side of a small Lake—Round which there was grass for our horses, & no where Else. We saw Hills that are on the side of the Missouri River at 3 P.M. Mr. McK. kill'd a Bull, Running, with a pistol.

Saturday 24th. Sett off at sun rise, 2 hours after met with two of the Big Belly [Hidatsa] Indians,[9] who were going a hunting, they appeared to be well pleased to see us. Smoked a pipe with them & proceeded. At mid day Saw the smoke of one of the big B. Villages, to the South of which we passed, at 2 arrived at another of their villages, where I Enquired for Charbonneax (it being his usual place of Residence)[10] & was Informed by an HB [Hudson's Bay] man who is there for the purpose of trade, that he was with some Americans, below the Mandan villages to whom he was Engaged.[11] Being

---

[9] The Hidatsas were commonly called the Gros Ventres, hence the name "Big Bellies" for them. See the "Yellowstone Journal," note 9.

[10] Toussaint Charbonneau's usual place of residence was the middle Hidatsa village, now known as the Sakakawea site (map 2), named for the Shoshoni woman now known as Sacagawea.

[11] William Clark did not record the arrival of the Larocque party until November 27, 1804, when he noted that Lafrance had "took upon himself to speak unfavourably of our intentions &c. The principal Mr. La Rock (& Mr. McKensey) was informed of the Conduct of their interpreter & the Consequences if they did not put a Stop to unfavourable & ill founded assursions &c &c." (Meriwether Lewis and William Clark, *Original Journals of the Lewis and Clark Expedition, 1804-06*, ed. Reuben Gold Thwaites, vol. 1, p. 227). Their "interpreter" was Touissaint Charbonneau, Sacagawea's husband.

unwilling to leave the HB here alone to get the whole trade of this village, I got the Horses unloaded & made a small Equipt. of goods, which I gave in Charge to Mr. McKenzie.

Sunday 25th. Left Morrison with Mr. McK. in the best Lodge we Could find & proceeded to the Mandan villages, with the Remainder of the goods (Excepting an Equipt. destined for the upper village of the B. Bellys). On the Road thither, met with Captain Lewis, Chief of the American party (with Jusseaum & Charbonneaux), had about a quarter of an hour Conversation with him, during which he Invited me to his house & appeared very friendly.[12]

Arrived at the Mandan village at 3 P.M. Entered in the Lodge of the Black Cat the Chief of that village. Sent for the Grand, the Chief of the other Mandan village.[13] Gave them both a Chiefs Cloathing, & Explained to them the motive of my coming &c &c. Gave a pipe of Tob. to all the grown men as usual. Sent Azure & McKay, with the Grand, on the other side of the River, with an Equipt. of goods in Charge of Azure.

Monday 26th. Lafrance traded 350 skins in wolves [and] in kitts, from the Indians of this village, he being the person, to whom I gave this outfit in Charge. The Indians appeared to be of a very thievish disposition.

Tuesday 27th. Went over to see Azure & what trade he had which was about 250 plues.[14] Returned to the Blk. Cats. Cap't. Lewis [p. 9] Return'd from above & stopp'd at the Lodge. Spoke to Charbonneau about helping, as Interpreter in the trade to the big Bellies, he told me that being Engaged to the Americans, he Could not Come without leave from Capt. Lewis & desired me to speak to him—which I did. Capt. Lewis told me that as he had no business for Charbonneau, but at times during the winter, he had no objection to his helping me, upon Certain Conditions, which agreeing to, Charbonneau promised me, that he would Come next morning.

Wednesday 28th. The Blk. Cat went to dine with the Americans, with 2 other Chiefs upon an Invitation from Capt. Lewis, who had

[12] Fort Mandan was subsequently swept into the Missouri River; see map 2 for its location with respect to the villages.

[13] Black Cat was the chief of the village that now bears his name; the Grand was the chief of the Mandan village now known as the Deapolis site (map 2).

[14] A large beaver pelt, *plus,* a standard against which other pelts were measured (John Francis McDermott, *A Glossary of Mississippi Valley French, 1673–1850,* Washington University Studies, n.s., Language and Literature, no. 12, p. 122).

also Invited me, but expecting Charbonneau, I declined going. Exceeding bad weather, wind N.E. & snowing very hard.

Thursday 29th. Still very bad weather which as I thought prevented Charbonneaux from Coming. In the Evening the weather cleared, went to see what was the Reason he did not come, was very politely Received, by Capts. Lewis & Clarke & pass'd the night with them. Just as I arrived, they were dispatching a man for me, having heard that I Intended giving Flags & medals to the Indians which they forbid me from giving in the name of the United States, saying that Government, look'd upon those things, as the Sacred Emblem of the attachment of the Indians to their Country. But as I had neither Flags, nor medals, I Ran no Risk of disobeying those orders, of which I assured them.

They next Called Charbonneau, & gave him leave to Come with me, but strictly enjoined him not to utter a word, which might any way be to the prejudice of the United States or of any of its Citizens, to the Indians, although I should order him to so to do, which (say they), turning to me, we are very far from thinking you would.[15]

Their party Consists of 40 odd men besides themselves, & are sent by Government for the purpose of Exploring the N.W. Countries, to the Pacific Ocean so as to settle the Boundary Line between, the British & the American territories. Likewise to make it known to the Indians, on the Missouri, & the adjacent Countries that they are under, the Government of the big Knives, who will protect them & supply them with all their wants, as long as they shall behave as dutifull Children to their Great Father the President of the United States &c (which has been the [p. 10] Continued subject of their Harangues to the Indians, throughout the Winter).

They showed me their passports & Letters of Recommendation from the french, Spanish & British Ministers at the City of Washington, which say the object of their voyage is purely scientific & Literary, & no ways Concerning, trade, desiring all persons under their Respective Governments, to aid & assist, that party as much as in their power lies, in Case they should be in want of any thing in the Course of their Voyage. They have likewise Letters of Credit from the American Government for the payment of any draughts, they should draw upon it.

[15]Clark also comments on this conversation in his entry for November 29, 1804 (Lewis and Clark, *Original Journals,* vol. 1, pp. 228–29).

FIG. 9. Aerial view of the Knife River villages. Big Hidatsa is in the left center; the power plant at the top left is built on the Deapolis site. The view is southeast. North Dakota State Highway Department.

They left Philadelphia in the spring 1803. Came down the Ohio & pass'd the winter at the mouth of the Missouri at St. Lewis in the Illinois Country. It took them the whole summer to Come to the Mandans, at which place they arrived in October last. They made treaties of peace with all the Indian Nations they saw on their Road, excepting the Sioux's, with whom they were very near Coming to an Engagement. They made presents of a Flag, Medal, Chiefs Cloathing, tobacco, knives, Beads & other trinkets, to Every Chief of the Indian nations, which they saw, but have not given a single shot of amunition.

They told me that it was not the policy of the United States to Restrain Commerce & fetter it, as was the Case when Louisiana belonged to the Spanish, that we & all persons who should Come on their territories, for trade or for any other purpose, will never be molested by an American Officer or Commandant, unless his behaviour was such as would subject an American Citizen himself to punishment. Nor will any trader be obliged to pay for permission to trade, as was formerly the Case under the Spanish, as no Exclusive privilege will be granted. Every one shall be free to trade after his own manner. One thing that Government may do, as it has already done, about Detroit & other places, where opposition in trade Ran high, is to have a public store, well assorted of all kind of Indian goods, which store, is to be open'd to the Indians, only when the traders, in opposition Run to too Excessive lengths; for the purpose of under selling them, & by that means, keep them quiet. No Derouines to take place, no Liquor to be sold (that is, of a Spirituous kind) &c &c.[16] In short, during the time I was there, a very Grand Plan was schemed, but its taking place is more than I can tell [p. 11] although the Captains say they are well assured it will.

Friday 30th. Returned to the Mandans. Charbonneau got Ready to Come with me, but just as he Was setting off, he Received orders to follow Capt. Clarke who was going, with 25 men, to join a party of Mandans, & Repulse a some Siouxs, who kill'd a Mandan yesterday & were supposed to be in the neighbourhood. Went to see Azure, & give him directions how to make the packs as I intend to send to the Fort very soon, having wherewith to load the Co/ horses.

December [1804]

Saturday 1st. Capt. Clarkes Expedition did not succeed, & Charbonneau joined me here this morning, prepared to sett off with him to settle, the upper village of the B. B's. when Mr. McKenzie & an HB man arrived. We all sett off together & slept at the little village in Mr. McK' Lodge.

Sunday 2nd. Left this village in the morning, with Charbonneau & Turenne with the upper village outfit, at which place we arrived

---

[16] The term *en dérouine* meant "to go trade with the Indians on their own grounds away from the trading post" (McDermott, *Glossary,* p. 66; see also Alexander Henry [the Younger], *New Light on the Early History of the Greater Northwest,* vol. 1, p. 166 n. 37). Larocque is here describing the American system of government-run trading posts, or "factories," which were located in the Indian country to control the trade with the Indians and prohibit traffic in liquor. Founded in 1796, the system was not successful, and it was abandoned in 1822. The nearest factory to the Mandans and Hidatsas was Fort Osage on the lower Missouri River a few miles east of present-day Kansas City (see Hiram Martin Chittenden, *The American Fur Trade of the Far West,* vol. 1, pp. 12–16).

at midday. Entered in the Lodge of the White Wolf, a great Chief, & a well disposed Indian towards the Whites. Clothed him as a Chief & Harangued him &c—he got a good Bed made for us & we fix'd our goods & gave him 30 R'ds Amt, 3 Knives, 1 awl, vermillion & a few Beads.

Monday 3rd. Sent the Co/ horses down to the Lower village, there being no food for them here, plains being all burnt. The Indians of this village are all out a hunting, they have been out about a month, & are expected daily.

Tuesday 4th. Mr. McK. having no Gun bought one for him for which I gave a Battle ax.[17] Traded 2 kitts for 1 doz' Rings. The HB people have traded at this place, since their arrival, 140 skins, & 10 do at the lower village. None of them have been at the Mandans.

Wednesday 5th. Snowing very hard, wind N.W. In the Evening my man went to see the HB trader, & found him Ready to sett of with an Indian, having Each a small bundle on their backs. He came & told me of it, upon which I ordered him & Charbonneau to get Ready. [p. 12] Made a small Equipt. of goods into two parcels, got an Indian to guide them & sent them in pursuit of the HB, who not finding the Indians where they expected returned. My people who were going met them, so they all Returned together & arrived at the village at 11 oClock at night.

Thursday 6th. Charbonneau having obtained leave of absence but for 6 days & this being the last day, he Returned. Wrote to Captains Lewis & Clarke, thanking them for their kindness in sending Charb. with me & Requesting more of his time, now & then If he Can be Spared.

Friday 7th. A Band of Buffalo appearing in sight all the Indians went in pursuit of them & Returned, in the Evening with their horses loaded.[18] Mr. Mck. arrived here Remained a few hours & departed.

Saturday 8th. An HB Man arrived who told me that our people below were preparing for their departure to the Fort. The HB tying their Furrs to send a man, & 2 horses loaded, to the Fort with our people. About 24 Indians arrived from their Fall Hunt, but brought no great quantity of skins.

---

[17] He had broken his gun on the way to the villages on June 14; he had been without one for twenty-one days.

[18] This hunt is described in much greater detail by Clark (Lewis and Clark, *Original Journals*, vol. 1, pp. 234–35).

Sunday 9th. Traded last night & today

40 Kitts	20		1 fm HB Red Stds	12
17 Wolves	17	for	1 do 'Bleu	10
8 Foxes	8		2 Capots	6
2 Beavers	2		amunition	15
	47		trinkets	4
				47

Monday 10th. The people arrived from below on their way home. Charbonneau Came with them and brought me, 7 wolves, 1 otter & 18 kitts.

Tuesday 11th. The people looking for their horses all day but Could not find them. Traded a few skins. Exceeding Cold weather.

Wednesday 12th. Still seeking the Horses, but to no Effect, in the Evening 6 were found, but there is still 3 wanting. Bought a horse for which I paid

1 fm HB Red Stds.	100 Balls & powder
1 Chiefs Coat	2 Knifes
1 large ax	2 doz Rings
	Vermillion & a few Beads

Paid Charbonneau for the skins he brought me on the 10th & gave him 1 Cotton shirt, 1 pair Corduroy trowsers, 1 fm Tob.

Thursday 13th. Despairing of finding the horses. Got an old man to make an Harangue, offering 30 Balls & powder, 1 knife & a bit of Tobacco to him who would find the horses & bring them to me. [p. 13] Gave my Landlord, the White Wolf—50 Balls & powder, 2 knives, 2 awls, ½ fm Tob, 2 flints, 2 Wormers & a little vermillion. Intending to sett off to morrow morning for the Fort. Harangued him &c. Spoke to Charbonneau about his debt telling him that as he had two horses, he might send one in part payment &c. He consented, & Early in the morning I sent Morrison to Fort Mandan for the horse. Wrote a few lines to Capt. Lewis & to Mr. McK.

Friday 14th. Morrison arrived with Charbonneaus horse, brought a note from Capt. Lewis. Sent Indians to seek the horses, which have not been found as yet. Offered 40 Rds, 1 looking glass, 1 knife & a bit of Tob. Heard that the horses had been found & left at the little village below. Sett off with Morrison to go & fetch them. Returned after dark & found Mr. Heney who was just arrived from the Fort Assiniboine with two Inds. He brought a letter from Mr. Chaboillez, which altered my plan as to going to the Fort, so that I will now pass the Winter here.

Saturday 15th. Sett off with Mr. Heney to go to the Americans. Slept at Mr. McKenzies.

Sunday 16th. Arrived at Fort Mandan[19] being the name the Americans give to their Fort, which is Constructed in a triangular form. Ranges of houses making two sides, & a Range of amazing large pickets [in] the front. The whole is made so strong as to be almost, Cannon Ball proof. The two Range of houses, do not join one another, but are join'd by a piece of fortification made in the form of a demi Circle, that Can defend two sides of the Fort, on the top of which they keep a sentry all night, & the lower part of that building serves as a store. A Centinel is likewise kept all day, walking in the Fort.

Monday 17th. We Remain'd here all day. The Captain Enquired a great deal of Mr. Heney, Concerning the Sioux Nation, & Local Circumstances of that Country & lower part of the Missouri, of which they took notes.[20] Settled with Jusseaume for some skins he had, which he delivered to me to the amount of 36 plues in Beaver.

Tuesday 18th. Returned home[21] taking the skins I had from Jusseaume on a sled, that Mr. Heney got from the Americans. Slept at Mr. McKenzies. Heard that 16 horses had been stolen at the upper village by the Assiniboines.

[p. 14] Wednesday 19th. Arrived at my Lodge. The Report of so many horses being stolen was confirmed, among which was 2 belonging to the Co/ and 2 to Lafrance. People buying horses. Bought a stout mule for which I paid

1 Gun	1 large ax	1 awl	1 looking glass
1 fm HB Red Stroud	1 fm Tob	2 flints	3 Strings pipe Bead
300 Balls & powder	2 Knives	2 wormers	a little vermillion

---

[19] On the sixteenth William Clark noted that Larocque was accompanied to the fort by Hugh Heney; the latter was carrying a letter from Charles Chaboillez (Lewis and Clark, *Original Journals,* vol. 1, pp. 237–38). The only other useful description of Fort Mandan is in Patrick Gass, *A Journal of the Voyages and Travels . . . to the Pacific Ocean,* pp. 71–72.

[20] Lewis and Clark "found Mr. Henny a Verry intelligent Man from whome we obtained Some Scetches of the Countrey between the Mississippi & Missouri, and Some Sketches from him, which he had obtained from the Indins. to the *West* of this place . . ." (Lewis and Clark, *Original Journals,* vol.1, p. 238).

[21] Clark notes that Heney and Larocque left on this date (ibid.).

About 60 warriors sett off to Revenge upon the Assiniboines for stealing their horses. Took an Inventory of the Remaining goods here.

Thursday 20th. Sold an old gun to Turenne to help him buy a horse, wrote to Mr. Chaboillez, & the people sett off for the Assiniboine River. Sent 6 partons [?] of Furrs Containing

545 Kitts	7 Beaver skins
57 Wolves	5 Bags Corn
4 Foxes	1 horse

I kept two of the Co/ horses here, being so poor & sore backed, that they were not able to go to the Fort. Made Morrison Remain to take Care of them.

Friday 21st. 3 Indian Lodges arrived but brought no skins. 8 warriors Returned without having seen an Enemy.

Saturday 22nd. Three more Lodges arrived, traded 24 skins, in wolves & kitts with them, which was all they had. Gave the man of the Lodge 5 Balls & powder.

Monday 24th. Snowed a little in the morning, traded 2 kitts for 12 hawk Bells. Could not find the horses, this Evening although we saw them twice today.

Tuesday 25th. This village being situated on the most northern Bend of the Missouri,[22] Consequently nearest to the Assiniboines, who steal horses every day, & the plains being burnt all Round about, The Indians have determined upon leaving it some to go up the River, & others down where Mr. McK. is. 3 Lodges sett off today the others are shortly to follow. Budge the HB trader[23] went down to the lower village, found the horses about [sun] sett & Immediately, went after him to see what he was about, took down the horses, to leave them there, as there is less danger of their being stolen, & better food. Slept at Mr. McKenzies.

[p. 15] Wednesday 26th. Hearing that there was a band of Indians hunting 2 days march off, sent Morrison to the American Fort to

[22] This village is now beneath the waters of Lake Sakakawea (map 2).

[23] George Budge was a Hudson's Bay Company employee who made several trips from the Assiniboine River to the Mandans between 1800 and 1806. He left Brandon House on October 19, 1804, accompanied by George Henderson and Tom Anderson. His activities at the Mandan villages are referred to by both Larocque and by William Clark. Budge and Anderson returned to Brandon House on March 15, 1805 (H.B.C.A., B.22/a/12, fo. 6d; and B.22/a/12, fo. 10d). He is mentioned in the Lewis and Clark journals on December 16, 1804, as George *Bunch* (Lewis and Clark, *Original Journals*, vol. 1, p. 238).

fetch Charbonneau, in order to go to them, as I hardly get a skin when the HB trader is with me, for he understands & talks their Language Well, & is known by all the Indians. My getting skins at the Big Bellys since my arrival was owing to my having such goods as pleased the Indians, i.e. Strouds, Capotries, Iron Works, &c, which my opponents had not, but at present, that my trading goods are such as he has likewise, he gets nearly the whole trade. In the Evening an Indian told me that some Hunters were to arrive tomorrow, at the summer village of the Big Bellies. Made out a small Equipt. of goods at night & prepared to go to them.

Thursday 27th. Sett off at break of day with Mr. McKenzie, whose landlord the Yellow Elk, came with us also. Arrived at the village at 10 oClock A.M. The Indians were not yet arrived from hunting, went through all the Inhabited Lodges & gathered, 1 Beaver, 12 wolves & 4 kitts. At 2 P.M. Budge arrived, & a little after the Indian hunters. Charbonneau & Morrison also arrived here, traded, in all 24 wolves, 10 kitts & 2 Beavers.

Friday 28th. At break of day—Mr. McK. & Charbonneau went to the Soulier Village, they took some trading articles, & brought back 3 Wolves & 4 kitts. Charbonneau Returned to the American Fort, with promise of Coming back on the 2nd of January, to go to the Borgnes Camp, for I could not get him to go now, it being so near to New Years day. Saddled & loaded our horses & departed. The HB trade there was 24 skins in wolves & kitts. Arrived at Mr. McK's. at midday, left Morrison there to take Care of the horses & proceeded alone to the upper village, arrived at my Lodge at sun sett.

Saturday 29th. A great many Indians sett off to go to the little village & a hunting. The White Wolf desired me to send for my horses, to take down my things, as he too is going to Remove. Wrote a note to Mr. McKenzie, to that Effect, by a woman that was going down. 2 Assiniboines arrived last night, & were well Received by these Indians. They brought back two of the horses that were stolen some time ago. [p. 16] Mem[orandum]. that on the 25th I took down to Mr. McK. the following articles, of which I knew he was short, as I then Expected we would have to go to the Indians, viz, 1 doz' awls, 2/3 lb vermillion, 134 branches blue Beads & 6 knives. Morrison arrived in the Evening with two of the Co/ horses & mine to take down the goods & Furrs.

Sunday 30th. All the Indians going down. Took all the Co/ property down upon 3 horses, excepting 2 Bundles, which the White

Wolf put on his own horses. Left those goods to the Care of Mr. McKenzie & sett off at night with Morrison to go & Enquire news of those Assiniboines. They said they were 18 Lodges, at 3 days march, that they had some skins & wanted me to go with them, having little goods, no horses fit to go & the opposition to watch withal (whom I Expected would sett off every day for the Borgnes Camp), prevented my going. Pass'd the Remainder of the night in the Lodge of the Collier de Loup's Son.

Monday 31st. Gave a pipe of Tob. to those Assiniboines & sett off to Return to the lower village. On going down perceived some Indians who were Coming down the Hills on the opposite side of the River. Went to see who they were, & found them to be the Petit Vieux an Assbn. Chief & 6 other men of his band. Returned with them to the Camp I had just left, where I gave the Chief 1½ feet Tob. & to Each of the others, 4 Inches. There are 30 Lodges of them & say they have plenty of Furrs, especially Beaver, they slept two nights to Come here. Went down to the L. village at night vexed to the soul that it was out of my power to go to them, but determin'd that if Charbonneau kept his word as to Coming on the 2nd Jan[uar]y, to send him & Mr. McK. to the Borgnes Camp & I & Morrison, to go to the Assiniboines some way or other, if the Petit Vieux would be here yet.

[p. 17] January 1805

Tuesday 1st. Fix'd my goods & self in the White Wolfs Lodge, with whom I have liv'd till now, & with whom I Intend to pass the winter although in the same village with Mr. McKenzie, & in a Leather Tent as Mr. McK[enzie]s Lodge is too small & thronged to admit of two more people. The Furrs that were brought from above, laying on the ground in McKs. Lodge & being fearfull, that the mice would damage them, tried to find some other Lodge, where they might be hung, but the arrival of so many Indians from above who had no Leather tents of their own has so thronged the wooden Lodges of this village that I could find none.

Wednesday 2nd. Tried again to find a Lodge for the skins, but to no purpose. My Landlord, gave me 2 wolves, 1 Fox & 7 kitts which he got from other Indians. I paid him with amunition, 58 Rounds.

Thursday 3rd. Charbonneau arrived at dark, with a man Engaged to the Americans, desired Mr. McK. to get Ready to go to the

Borgnes Camp with Charbonneau, next morning & gave the American 1 knife for his voyage he having none.

Friday 4th. The HB having heard that I Intended to send to the Borgnes, got their horses in, at night, to be Ready to follow us, but I put them out soon after, & in the Morning—Mr. McKenzie, Charbonneau & the other man were gone 5 hours, before they were Ready to follow them. It being now in my power to go to the Assiniboines, sett off with Morrison to go to the Elbow of the River, & see if there were any more of them there, but they had been gone two days. Could not prevail upon any person to guide us to the Assiniboine Camp, they being too much afraid of them. Returned to my Lodge & arrived after sun sett.

Saturday 5th. There fell 4 Inches of snow in the night & the wind blew very strong all day from the N.W., snow & sand drifting Most Violently. A Mandan brought me 20 kitts for trade, which I Refused being out of season & not half stretched, he Carried them to the HB, & got [p. 18] Amunition for them.

Sunday 6th. Last night some young men arrived, with 4 horses, which they stole from the Assiniboines (& which had been stolen from them, by the Assbn. on the 18th last month) among which was one of the Co/ but now, by Indian Law, belongs to him, that Risked his Life in the Stealing of him. They offered him to me for something less than another would have Cost me, being in want of horses I took him at the following price—

1 Blanket 3 Pt.	1 Cassetete a Calumet	100 Balls & powder
1 Pair Leggins	1 Lance	1 Knive
1 Hoe	1 Eyed Dag	a few Beads

The White Wolf (my Landlord) also purchased two of his own Horses back again from the same young men, & gave 1 gun, powder horn, & shot bag, with 100 Balls & powder, 2 fms. HB Red Strouds, 1 fm. Com. Blue, 1 large but old Brass kettle & 6 Killion quills, & a pair of garnished Leggins. Very Cold Weather, strong wind.

Monday 7th. We are in a Continual state of alarm for our horses. The plains being burnt except in a few places Compels us to keep them where they are most liable to be thieved. At 10 oClock at night, we were alarmed by the Report of Some Assbn. being seen who were taking away Horses. This news put the whole village in an uproar. Everyone went to seek his horses. Sent Morrison to look for ours, one way, & I & an Indian, went another. We all Returned unsuccessfull, having been unable to find them.

Tuesday 8th. Sent Morrison, Early in the morning to seek the horses which he found in the woods. 9 of the Indians horses were gone. At 2 oClock P.M. the HB arrived from the Indian tents, with about 80 plues in wolves & kitts. At night being anxious to know what was become of Mr. McKenzie, who was gone to the same tents, & had sett off, before him, went to see him, when to my great surprise he told me that he had seen them only when he pass'd them. Enquired as well as I could from the Indians Concerning them & was told that the Indian who was to guide them, did not sett off with them, they waited for him a long while on the other side of the Missouri, when seeing the HB passing, they Endeavor'd to follow, but were delayed by their Horses being gone from them. [p. 19] However they sat off, but the wind blowing hard & the snow drifting, they Could not see, nor follow the tracks of the HB & to all probability have lost their Road.

Wednesday 9th. A Number of Indians sett off to go a hunting. Exceeding Cold weather, & blowing very hard. Wind N. West.

Thursday 10th. More Indians sett off some to Remain at their summer villages & the others going a hunting. The HB took 2 horse Loads of their skins &c to the summer village. Their Landlord going to hunt likewise. The Departure of so many Indians, Caused some wooden Lodges to be Empty. The White Wolf took possession of the largest being the Rats Lodge, into which we Removed ourselves, from our leather tent. Took the skins out of Mr. McKenzies Lodge, where they lay upon the ground & hung them up in this one, luckily the mice did not hurt them. Suspecting that the HB had a notion to go in the plains with the hunters, prepared an Equipment of goods with which I Intend to send Morrison to the Indians, where he will Remain, untill they Come back.

Friday 11th. Sent Morrison off in the morning with an Indian to guide him to the Rats Lodge, with whom he is to Remain. Gave him one of the Co/ horses, to take his things with him & kept the other two here, & am to take Care of them myself. The HB sett off with the Remainder of their property to the summer village, so that I am the only white man in this place. I told Morrison to go with the Indians whether the HB went or not, to show them how to make traps, & Encourage them to kill wolves. It is so very Cold in these Lodges, that the Ink freezes in my pen while writing, although I sit as close to the fire as I can without burning my Legs.

Saturday 12th. Went down to the little village to see if the HB had left that place, & If I could get any news of Mr. McKenzie. Met

Budge who was Coming to Enquire, after a Bundle of his property that had been stolen from him by the Indians. Remain'd there a Couple of Hours & Returned home, heard that Mr. McK. had been seen at the Tents & that he was Coming. Morrison did not stop there yesterday, but went on.

[p. 20] Sunday 13th. Very Cold weather, more Indians going off. The young men of this Lodge went out a hunting but kill'd nothing. They returned in the Evening.

Monday 14th. Mr. McKenzie arrived in the Morning. Charbonneau & Pied ferme, left him in the morning, the day before, to go to the Americans Fort. They arrived at the tents 3 days after the HB had left them, of Course they had but little trade, he brought 12 large wolves & 3 kitts with about 28 kitts belonging to Charbonneau.

Tuesday 15th. The White Wolf went out a hunting. Very mild weather.

Wednesday 16th. Mr. McK. & I made a general washing of our Linen. My Landlord, arrived at night he kill'd nothing, & visited the Americans on his way home.

Friday 18th. Went down to Fort Mandan,[24] in the morning, to Return a Book I had borrow'd, & to see if there was any particular news. Arrived there at 3 P.M. & Remain'd the whole day.

Saturday 19th. Breakfasted, with these Gentlemen & sett off at 10 oClock to Return home. Went into the Blk. Cats Lodge, at the Mandans En passant. Arrived at my Lodge after sun sett.

Sunday 20th. There has been no trade going on this long while, but it is Impossible to Refrain making some small daily Expenses, which though it appears Nothing, or next to nothing, Runs away with more goods than is Expected. Thinking on this today, & being anxious to know how I stood in my accounts, desired Mr. McK. to take a General Inventory of his Returns & Remaining Goods, Intending to do the same myself tomorrow, as the tending of the horses, prevented my doing it today. Captain Clarke upon being Informed that I had to take Care of the horses myself, & that they were in danger of being thieved, desired I would send them down, & that he would have them taken Care of with his own.

My Landlord went down to the Americans to get his Gun Mended. They have a very Expert smith, who is always Employed in making

---

[24]According to Clark (Lewis and Clark, *Original Journals*, vol. 1, p. 250), he was accompanied by McKenzie.

dift. things & working for the Indians, who are grown very fond of them although they disliked them at first.

[p. 21] Monday 21st. Took the Inventory, the Results of which is a Balance of Eighty Four skins, on the side of the Book it ought to be notwithstanding which the profits must be very little, for the skins are far from being of the good kind. Two of the horses have been stolen, & the others Runs the greatest danger of being so too. My Landlord arrived from Fort Mandan with his gun well mended.

Tuesday 22nd. Some Indians went out a hunting, but Returned unsuccessfull. We have not seen a bit of Flesh here since Christmas, always Corn & Corn. 2 Americans arrived here & brought 10 wolves & 1 kitt, which they traded for Tobacco, at the Rate of 3 skins a fathom. Gave them a Couple of feet for nothing. They went back Immediately.

Wednesday 23th. About 26 Lodges of the Assiniboines arrived here, among whom was the Petit Vieux & family. The Sioux La-grue & other XY and HB Indians; mostly all R. la Souris Indians. Gave a bit of Tob. to all the grown men in [the] doing of which I expended 2 fm. Tob. One of them (the Maringouin) brought me, 2 wolves & 4 kitts, paid him with amunition. Not one of them had any Tobacco & they were exceeding troublesome for the getting of more. They say they have plenty of skins at their Camp, which is 4 days march up this River & made me promise that I would go & trade with them, as soon as the people would arrive from the Fort, which I told them would be very shortly. They do not Intend to go to the Forts, but in March & say that almost all the Assbn. are upon this River, but higher up, where they have a park, for Catching of Buffalo.

Thursday 24th. The Assiniboins all went down to the Mandans to purchase Corn for dried meat, which they brought for that purpose, as there is no Buffalo here.

Friday 25th. Charbonneau & two men of the Americans, arrived & slept here. Fine weather.

Saturday 26th. Charb. & the two men went off in the morning. Sent by them the 3 horses of the Co/ down to Fort Mandan, where Capt. Clarke [p. 22] told me, he would have them taken Care of, as there is so many Assiniboines. The Assiniboines arrived here from the Mandan villages. The women passed without stopping, But the men Came in to some of whom, I gave a bit of Tobacco, & a few Rounds of amunition. They all went off. I promised them that I would go to them as soon as the people would arrive from the Fort. There is a great many HB & XY Indians there & further on, & If a trade Could be Effected with them here, it would prevent the oppositions from getting their share of those skins for they are Ignorant of the Indian Camps & are unable to find them.

Sunday 27th. Some of these Indians went up, to the Assiniboines Camp. Wind south, & very mild weather. My Landlord went out a hunting, with his family & Band. Gave him 20 Rounds amunition.

Monday 28th. Two young men arrived from the plains, where the Indians are hunting, & say that the Buffalo is all gone, & the hunters doing nothing. 10 more Indians left this village today to go a hunting.

Tuesday 29th. The two young men went off in the morning, wrote a note to Budge the HB trader & sent it by them. More Indians sett off a hunting. Very mild weather, wind S. East.

Wednesday 30th. Went down to the American Fort to get my Compass put in order, the glass being broke, & the needle not pointing due north; & to see how the horses were. Arrived there at 2 P.M. Fine weather.[25]

The Captains were busy, making Charts of the Country through which they had passed, & delineating the heads of the Missouri, according to the Information they had from the Indians, who describe a River as being 4 days march west of the last navigable part of the Missouri, which River say they is very large, & the natives (whom they Call Snake Indians & Flat heads) who inhabit thereabouts, go at a Certain season of the year to that River & there live Entirely upon Fish. The Course of that River they say is nearly south & has a very placid Current. The Captains make no doubt, but that it is a south branch of the Columbia or Ouragan River. I think it is the Rout they will take.

[p. 23] Having nothing to do at the Lodge, I Remain'd here a Couple of days, being pressed so to by the Captains. They took observations for the Longitude & Latitude of the place while, I was with them, & often since their arrival here. They differ much from Mr. [David] Thompson, in the Longitude of this place, & say that

---

[25] Larocque apparently went to Fort Mandan to obtain an answer to a query he had put to the captains at an earlier visit: Could he accompany them on their expedition? Their answer was no. In his entry for February 2, 1805, Clark says that Larocque was "verry anxious to accompany us" (ibid., p. 252). Patrick Gass says that the object of these visits by North West Company employees was "to ascertain our motives for visiting that country, and to gain information with respect to the change of government" (Gass, *Journal*, p. 76).

Mr. Thompson has placed these villages, & this part of the River, a great deal too westerly, which they think is the Case, with all his observations for the Longitude; they observed some time ago an Eclipse of the moon which they say is an Infallible Rule for finding the Exact Longitude of a place. But they do not differ from him in the Latitude.

They Include in their territory as far North as River qui'Appelle, for as it was Impossible for a Line, drawn west, from the west End of Lake des Bois[26] to strike the Missisipi, they make it Run, till it strikes its tributary waters that is the northern Branches of the Missouri, & from thence to the Pacific, which Could not have been done while Louisiana belonged to the French or Spanish, as those powers would not have suffered England to give a Country which did not belong to it & of Course the Line drawn west, would have stopp'd, when it struck, the Spanish or French territory. Cap't. Lewis fix'd my Compass, very well, in doing of which he Employed the whole day, Cleaning it &c.

[February 1805]

Saturday 2nd. Returned to my Lodge. The White Wolf (my landlord) & his band arrived from hunting at the same time, he has been 2 days march up the River, but found no Buffalo, except a few straggling Bulls, which they kill'd, & with the flesh of which, they Returned.

Monday 4th. Morrison arrived at 9 oClock at night, brought all the property he had in the plains with him & his trade which Consisted of 8 kitts & 1 wolf. The HB trade there is 5 kitts & 2 wolves. The Indians have always been flitting, since their departure & have not hunted.

Tuesday 5th. Took an a/ct. of the goods brought back per Morrison. Traded 1 Fox & 3 kitts for amunition & vermillion.

Wednesday 6th. Preparing myself in snow shoes &c, for going to the Fort despairing of the peoples Coming this winter, & being in absolute want of goods, not for these Indians (for the Rascals do nothing), [p. 24] but for the Assiniboines, who are upon this River, & to all appearances loaded with Furrs & who are not to go to the Fort but in the spring.

Thursday 7th. Took an Inventory of my Remaining goods, Amt. of 45½ plues & delivered them to Mr. McKenzie. Bought a dog to

---

[26] Modern Lake of the Woods.

Carry our provisions on the voyage & paid [for] him 20 Rds. amunition, 1 knife, 1 awl, 13 China Beads & a little vermillion. Sett off with Morrison, at sun sett, walked 5 hours & Encamped in the plains,* [no explanation for this asterisk is given in the text] North, by East 2 hours (to get Rid of the Coules) North 3 do.

Friday 8th. Sett off at 6 oClock, Course north 10½ hours, E. of N. ¾ of an hour, W. of north half an hour, & Encamp'd, in a Crick. We had fine weather all day.

Saturday 9th. Sett off at half after six. Course North 2½ hours when we stopp'd on a hill, from whence we could see 2 large Range of Hills, between which we had passed, one bearing S.E. & the other S.W. River la Souris, Right before us, North, a large hill call'd the Blk. Hill lying W. of N. of us. Cross'd River la Souris at half after 9 & proceeded due north, leaving the Blk. Hill to our Right. 'Camp'd at 5 oClock in the plains, without wood. We made some water with snow in a tin kettle, on a fire of Buffalo Dung, which we had trouble Enough in gathering the ground being covered with 9 inches snow. Slept till 10 oClock, but the wind & Cold would not allow us to Remain any longer so we sett off & walked, till half past two in the morning, when we laid down in a Hollow, to Wait for day Break the moon being sett, & the weather Cloudy.

Sunday 10th. Rose at daybreak & found ourselves buried in snow, it snowing very hard & blowing from the N. West, most violently — so that we Could not see 10 steps before us for the drifting snow. I froze the End of my Finger in Belting my Blanket round me in the morning. Luckily we had not untackled our Dogs over night, so that we were soon Ready. Walked as hard as we Could all day but the Strength of the wind greatly Impeded our progress & made us go about 6 miles East of the Line of our Course, which was north. Cross'd the Deep River at 10 A.M. its Course S.E. At sun sett despairing of finding the woods, before dark on the Course we were going, & the bad weather Continuing, struck for R. la Souris, N. by E. at which River we arrived at half past seven. There being no woods upon that part of the River, we again slept without fire, but a great quantity of Reeds & Bull [p. 25] Rushes, in which we Buried ourselves & passed the night, the Bad weather Continuing.

Monday 11th. Sett off at 6 oClock following the River upon the south side, but at some distance, our Course north, arrived at the woods at 10 oClock A.M. being the Elk Head, where we stopp'd to dry our shoes & Refresh ourselves with a few Ears of Roasted Corn, which was all the provisions we had. The weather Clearing up, we

Sett off at 3 P.M. Course N. the river Running nearly the same Course, Cross'd the River & Encamped in some Indian 'Campments.

Tuesday 12th. Sett off at 3 in the morning following an Indian Road which led to the Fort, Course W of North all day, River la Souris running paralell with us, for about 1½ Miles, when it gradually turned to the East. Cross'd the River aux Prunes at 4 P.M. passed by my wintering house of last year at 6, & arrived at Fort Assiniboine at 8 oClock PM. Mr. Chaboillez was absent being gone to River Pain Binat.[27] Heard the news of the Death of Simon McTavish Esq. & the joining of the two Companies [the North West and the XY companies].

Wednesday 13th. The goods destined for the Missouri have been Ready some time, but various Circumstances have prevent'd their being sent, some of the men & horses that are to go are now absent. Morrison, who Came with me from the Missouri is Lame with a pain in his Leg, which is quite swelled.

Thursday 14th. Mr. Heney got 3 dress's skins smoked for the purpose of making shoes for the people that are to Come with me.

Friday 15th. Commis[28] & two men arrived from River la Souris fort, they Report that John McKay of the HB had entirely lost his senses.

Saturday 16th. Sent for the people that are to Come with me & that are absent viz, Turenne, Hool, & Votchagons. The two last arrived at night.

Wednes[day] 20th. Sett of[f] 3 hours before daylight, with 7 men and 5 horses of the Co/ loaded. Slept at the Sandy hills on R. la Souris.

Friday 22nd. Saw a Band of Assiniboines, one of whom Came to us at our Campment. Gave him a pipe of Tobacco, he told me that [p. 26] he was going to the Fort & that all the Assiniboines I had left on the Missouri were Coming behind, & going to the Forts. In Consequence of this Information, I put the High Wines I had for them En Cache, to be taken up by the people on their Return. Kept 1 small Keg Containing 4 quarts & 3 half pts. to give a dram to the men, as they had to walk in water up to their knees all day long. The weather very mild & snow thawing.

Tuesday 26th. Sett off a head, with Fr. Hool, & Votchagons,

---

[27] Modern Pembina River, in eastern North Dakota.

[28] A *commis* was a clerk; although he was an employee, he "differed from the *engagé* in that he was a prospective partner or director of a trading post (McDermott, *Glossary*, p. 54). This sentence, then, should read, "A clerk and two men . . . ."

Intending to get to the Missouri villages, that day, leaving the Horses to be brought up by the Remainder of the people. Arrived at half past 6 oClock, in the village I had left, & found only two Lodges, being my own & Mr. McKenzies, the people of which Lodges had been waiting for me, all the other Indians being gone across the River, The Ice being bad & the water overflowing. On my arrival I sent 5 pieces dried meat to the men who were to Encamp at the Elbow, of the River about 6 Miles off.

Wednesday 27th. The people arrived at 10 oClock A.M. Gave a pipe of Tob. to 14 Indians who were Come from the other side [of] the River on the news of my arrival. Bought some provisions for 50 Rounds amunition, 1 knife, ½ fm. Tobacco.

Thursday 28th.[29] Sent all the goods over the Missouri & Turenne to take Care of them. Made the following outfit for Mr. McKenzie

1 fm. Com. Red Strouds	1 doz' Knives
1 " HB Blue do	4 " Rings
1 doz awls	
1 do wormers	
2 Capots 1 Ell	
1 do — 1½	
3 Battle axes	

---

[29] There is a gap in Larocque's journals from this entry to the one of June 2, 1805, when his "Yellowstone Journal" commences. Some time before that he returned to the Assiniboine River to prepare for his third and final trip to the Missouri River and Bighorn Mountains.

François-Antoine Larocque's "Yellowstone Journal"

IN mid-1805, François-Antoine Larocque, with two companions, traveled with a group of Crow Indians from the Big Hidatsa village to the Bighorn Mountains and returned down the valley of the Yellowstone and Missouri rivers. Larocque left a detailed and accurate account of this expedition, which preceded William Clark's 1806 exploration of the Yellowstone River by more than a year. This journal is a significant one not only for the Mandan and Hidatsa trade, but also for the ethnography of the Crow Indians as well.

Larocque's party was possibly the third such party to explore as far west of the Missouri River as the Bighorn Mountains. He may well have been preceded by François and Louis-Joseph La Vérendrye in 1743, but their account is not precise enough to determine whether they in fact reached the Bighorn Mountains or whether they simply went as far west as the Black Hills of western South Dakota.[1] In any event, a

study of their journal raises many questions. Such is not the case with the straightforward account left us by Larocque. A second visit to the Bighorn Mountains appears to have been made about 1800 by one Ménard, a French-Canadian trader who frequented the Mandan and Hidatsa villages at the turn of the eighteenth century. His visit, however, left us nothing in the way of a journal, Ménard returning with scarcely more than his life.[2]

Larocque's expedition, which began at Fort Montagne à la Bosse, on the Assiniboine River, to the Bighorn Mountains occupied nearly four and one-half months: from June 2 to October 18, 1805. He left the Assiniboine River with Charles McKenzie, William Morrison, Baptiste Lafrance, and two men whose first names are not recorded: Lassana and Souci. McKenzie, Lassana, and Lafrance remained at the Knife River

[1] G. Hubert Smith, *The Explorations of the La Vérendryes in the Northern Plains, 1738-43*, ed. W. Raymond Wood, pp. 2, 127. Charles Chaboillez had assigned Daniel Harmon to travel to the Mandans and on to

the Rocky Mountains in search of beaver in the summer of 1805. Illness, however, prevented Harmon from going and the expedition was instead led by Larocque (Daniel Williams Harmon, *Sixteen Years in the Indian Country: The Journal of Daniel Williams Harmon*, ed. W. Kaye Lamb, p. 88).

[2] See chap. 2, "History of the Fur Trade," n. 88.

villages, and Souci and Morrison accompanied Larocque to the Big-horn Mountains and the Yellowstone River.

Larocque produced a day-by-day journal of his expedition from the time he left Fort Montagne à la Bosse until his return. The original manuscript of this document has been lost. What appears to be a careful copy of it is now in the Baby Collection of the Archives Department, University of Montreal. It was bequeathed to that institution by Judge Louis François Georges Baby of Montreal just before his death on May 13, 1906. There is no information just how or where Judge Baby obtained the manuscript. "It may have formed part of the material collected by Roderick McKenzie, but if so was not acquired by Masson, and in fact does not seem to have been known to him."[3]

The document consists of fifty-one handwritten pages, bound in five signatures of handmade paper measuring 19.5 cm by 31.8 cm. The entire document is written in brown ink, apparently in a single hand. No later editorial emendations are obvious. Internal evidence intimates that the source copied was in English. This, of course, is consistent with Larocque's authorship, since he had learned English in the United States as a child and preferred to express himself in that language for the rest of his life.[4]

The journal is obviously a copy of another manuscript. There are many places where words or phrases were duplicated and then scratched out, suggesting a clerical error and a correction in the transcript. In the present version, interlineations have been brought down to the line, since all of them appear to be words inadvertently missed when the copy was made. There are also numerous blanks where words or phrases were omitted by the copyist—elements which suggest difficulty was encountered in transcribing a rough field journal. There is, in fact, good reason to believe that the original document was not written in an especially distinct hand. Scattered through the journal, along the left hand margin, are the notations "NB," "NB inquire," and "NB what is that?" accompanied by words or phrases which appear in the text opposite. In many cases such "NB" notations appear opposite blanks in the manuscript, a clue that the copyist may have hoped to check with another person (perhaps Larocque himself) about what word or phrase was intended in the original. All words which were underscored in the text appear to have been added in underscored blanks left for the purpose; these terms are italicized here. The entire journal also carries, along its left margin, a set of key words—for example, the names of rivers and of other landmarks—which were apparently added as finding devices.

For the most part, the manuscript is in a clear hand that is not especially difficult to read. There are of course idiosyncrasies which posed problems in transcription. Word

[3] François-Antoine Larocque, *Journal of Larocque from the Assiniboine to the Yellowstone, 1805*, ed. Lawrence J. Burpee, Publications of the Canadian Archives, no. 3.

[4] *Dictionary of Canadian Biography*, vol. 9, s.v. "François Antoine Larocque," p. 455.

157

separation is often ambiguous; some single words are broken in two, and sometimes two separate words are run together. In these cases, modern usage has been used in transcribing them. Other conventions followed are noted in the Editorial Procedures.

This journal has had an unusual publication history. Lawrence J. Burpee first edited and annotated this copy of the journal, which was published as No. 3 of the Publications of the Canadian Archives in 1910. Because of the bilingual publication policy of the Canadian government, this edition was translated into French and published again the following year in Publications des Archives Canadiennes, No. 3.[5] The French edition carried no statement that it was in fact a translation from the English original, except that in it the journal's name is given in its original English form. Both editions of the journal came to be widely used, but in somewhat different circles.

Burpee's transcription, which one is led to believe is a literal one — he called it a "verbatim transcript" — is not a very accurate one. In fact, there are so many careless slips in his edition that it is impossible to believe they are all typographical errors; Burpee must have been working from a very poor copy of the Montreal text. Many words are mistranscribed, and on occasion that error renders the meaning unclear. For example, scholars must have

wondered what was meant by the fact that, after their merger, the differences between the North West and the XY companies were "carried in obligation," when the journal says quite simply that these differences were to be "burried in oblivion."

Burpee also deleted or accidentally eliminated words or phrases — in two cases, entire lines — some of them crucial to the meaning of the text. He also added occasional words, without using brackets, that he felt were obviously omitted: for example, we "saddled [our horses]." Still other changes included the arbitrary changing of ampersands to "and" and vice versa. He also added commas and periods when there were none and deleted many of them that did exist. This repunctuation in general did not improve the text; the journal is in fact in much better English than Burpee's transcription would lead one to believe. Burpee also deleted a paragraph in the "Observations on the Rocky Mountain Indians" which contemporary literary taste deemed too prurient to publish. Such changes, in addition to probably uncorrected typographical errors, seriously flaw Burpee's edition and justify the new transcription offered here.

Ruth Hazlitt, a Montana historian, became familiar with the French edition of the journal published in 1911. Believing that the 1910 English edition was a translation — mistakenly assuming that the journal had originally been written in French because of the obviously French extraction of the author — she translated the French edition back into English. Her version was published in *The Frontier and Midland: A Magazine of*

---

[5] Larocque, *Journal of Larocque*, and François-Antoine Larocque, *Journal de Larocque de la Rivière Assiniboine Jusqu'a le Rivière 'Aux Roches Jaunes,' 1805*, ed. Lawrence J. Burpee, Publications des Archives Canadiennes, no. 3.

the *Northwest* in 1934. It was reprinted in this form several times: by Paul C. Phillips in *Sources of Northwest History*, No. 20; in John W. Hakola's *Frontier Omnibus* in 1962; and elsewhere.[6] This version has been widely used by historians and others in the Northwestern Plains ever since.

Needless to say, a twice-translated document leaves a great deal to be desired. Nearly every sentence, and certainly every paragraph, contains nuances different from those of the original, sometimes distorting the meaning. Many passages that are not downright awkward are frequently misleading. There are also numerous erroneous identifications and implications. Among others, "Cabris" is improbably translated as "caribou" in the entry for June 4, and the text for June 11 implies that

"Serpent Lodge" was a Hidatsa winter village, not a physiographic feature near that village. Hazlitt also translates "Ererokas" as Arikaras instead of the Crows they are meant to be. Typographical errors are not usually important, but some of them are. For example, in the entry for June 15 she says that the Frenchman Ménard had lived at the Mandan and Hidatsa villages for four years instead of forty years—an appreciable difference. Finally, Hazlitt's edition contains only that part of the document covering Larocque's explorations from the Assiniboine River to the Bighorn Mountains and his return: his extensive "Observations" on the Crow Indians are omitted in her edition, as are the supplementary notes on his journal which Burpee published.

JOURNAL OF AN EXCURSION OF
DISCOVERY
TO THE
ROCKY MOUNTAINS
BY
MR. LAROCQUE
IN THE
YEAR 1805
FROM THE 2D OF JUNE TO THE
18TH OF OCTOBER.

[p. 1] Journal of a voyage to the Rocky Mountains from my leaving the Assinibois River on the 2d June 1805.

[6] François-Antoine Larocque, "The Journal of François-Antoine Larocque from the Assiniboine River to the Yellowstone—1805," trans. and ed. Ruth Hazlitt, *Frontier and the Midlands* 14 (1934): 241–47, 332–39; 15 (1934): 67–75, 88.

[June 1805]

At my arrival at *Rivière* fort de la Bosse[7] I prepared for going on a voyage of discovery to the Rocky Mountains and set of[f] on the 2d June with two men having each of us two horses one of which was laden with goods to facilitate an intercourse with the Indians we might happen to see on our road. Mr. Charles McKenzie, and Mr. Lassana[8] sat out with me to go [to] & pass the summer at the Missouri, and having to pursue the same road we kept Company as far as the B. B. village.[9]

Mr. McKenzie with the other men set of about at two in the afternoon, but I having [been] so very busy that I had not as yet been able to write any letters to my friends, remained and wrote Letters and settled some little business of my own. After sunset we supped & bidding farewell to Mr. Chabillaz & Henry[10] & to all the people, departed, every on[e] being affected at our departure thinking it more than probable that I should not return with my men, and I confess I left the fort with a heavy heart, but riding at a good rate I soon got chearful again, and thought of nothin[g], but the mea[n]s of ensuring success to my undertaking. At 10 at night I arrived at the River aux Prunes[11] where I found the people encamped and asleep.

[7] Fort Montagne à la Bosse, or Mount à la Bosse, was on the south or right bank of the Assiniboine River about two miles from the modern town of Routledge, Manitoba. It appears on Arrowsmith's 1857 map of North America showing territories claimed by Hudson's Bay Company (Ernest Voorhis, *Historic Forts and Trading Posts of the French Régime and of the English Fur Trading Companies,* pp. 119, 185).

[8] See McKenzie's account of this trip in Charles McKenzie's Narratives. Lassanna cannot be further identified.

[9] The term "Big Bellies" or Gros Ventres was applied to two distinctly different tribes. Those living on the Missouri River alluded to here have come to be known as the Hidatsas; those living further west were also sometimes called Fall Indians, or Gros Ventres (Big Bellies) of the Prairies; they are now known as the Atsina. Only when the term "Big Belly" refers to the latter tribe is it identified in later passages.

[10] Charles Jean-Baptiste Chaboillez and Alexander Henry the Younger (Larocque, *Journal of Larocque,* p. 12 nn. 1-2).

[11] Modern Plum Creek. Burpee identifies this stream as Pipestone Creek. It flows into Oak Lake and the Plum Lakes, but the stream draining these lakes and entering the Souris River is shown on modern maps as Plum Creek. This creek enters the Souris River from the west near the modern town of Souris. Larocque may have crossed over the Souris River near his camp on this creek, since the first time he notes crossing the Souris in his journal he is doing so from east to west, entering the great meander of the Souris. When he next crosses the Souris, he is leaving the great meander and entering the "Mandan plain" between the Souris and Missouri rivers.

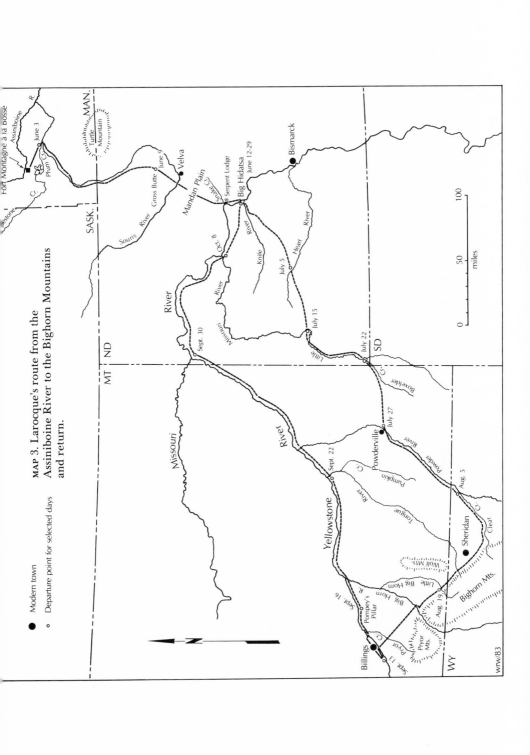

MAP 3. Larocque's route from the Assiniboine River to the Bighorn Mountains and return.

- ● Modern town
- ○ Departure point for selected days

MAN.

SASK.

Fort Montagne à la Bosse

Assiniboine R.

June 3

Plum Cr.

stone

Cr.

Turtle Mountain

Velva

June 9

Cross Butte

Souris River

Mandan Plain

Snake Cr.

Serpent Lodge

Big Hidatsa

June 12-29

Bismarck

Oct. 8

River

Knife River

July 5

Heart River

River

MT ND

Sept. 30

Missouri River

July 15

Little

July 22

SD

Boxelder Cr.

July 27

Powderville

Sept. 22

Pumpkin Cr.

Powder River

Aug. 5

Missouri

River

Yellowstone

River

Tongue River

Sheridan

Clear Cr.

Wolf Mts.

Little Big Horn

Big Horn R.

Aug. 19

Bighorn Mts.

Sept. 16

Pompey's Pillar

Pryor Mts.

WY

Billings

Sept. 13

Pryor Cr.

N

0   50   100

miles

wrw/83

Monday 3d. I sat of early in the morning and stopped at 12 to refresh our horses, and encamped at night at River la Sorie,[12] where we had not been 2 hours encamped, when three, and soon after many other Assiniboins rushed in upon us, a few endeavouring to take our horses, but seizing our guns and running to them we made them dep[a]rt. They came afterwards to our fire and se[e]ing us well armed, and by our looks that we would well defend ourselves and our property they remained quiet. There were 40 Tent of them not 10 acres from us without that we had perceived them.[13] I gave 1 fm. Tobacco[14] to their Chief to make his young men smoke & engage them to remain peaceable. Some of them offered to accompany us to the Missouri; but upon being told that we would like it well they spoke no more of it.

Thinking it how[ev]er not prudent to pass the night so close to them we saddled our horses and departed, although they did all in their power of engaging us to sleep at their tents. One of them conducted us to a good fording place of River la Sourie which we crossed striking in the plain we walked all night to come out of their reach for they are the most cunning horse thieves that ever I saw or heard of. A little before daylight we stopped and took a Nap.

Tuesday 4th. We proceeded on our journey early in the morning having very fine weather all day, and at night encamped on the banks of the River la Sourie at a place called Green River for its having no [blank in MS] wood on its side for about 30 miles.[15] We saw no other animals but four Cabris[16] of which we killed two.

Wednesday 5th. We followed the Green River till eleven oClock when we arrived at the woods, where, [there] being an appearance of rainy weather we encamped. There was Buffaloe in sight. At 12 it began to [p. 2] rain, and continued hard and uninterruptedly until next morning. Here we saw plenty of wild fowls, Duck, Bustards,[17] Geese, Swans &c, and killed a number of them.

Thursday 6th. There being an appearance of fine weather, we sat

---

[12] Modern Souris (or Mouse) River.

[13] That is, that they had not seen before.

[14] A fathom (the equivalent of *une brasse*) was a linear measure equal to 5.328 English feet or to 1.624 meters (John Francis McDermott, *A Glossary of Mississippi Valley French, 1673-1850,* p. 34; L. R. Masson, ed, *Les Bourgeois de la Compagnie du Nord-Ouest: Recits de voyages, lettres et rapports inedits relatifs au Nord-Ouest Canadien,* vol. 1, p. 308 n. 1).

[15] Burpee (in Larocque, *Journal of Larocque,* p. 13 n. 1) identifies this stream as Cut Bank River and notes that Alexander Henry called it Rivière Plé.

[16] Antelope or pronghorn, *Antilocapra americana.*

off and walked about 3 miles, when the Weather being cloudy we stopped to encamp, but before we could make a hut for our goods the rain began again, and fell amazingly hard, so that in a few hours every hollow or valley in the plains were full of water, and every brook or Creek was swellen to rivers. There were plenty of Buffaloes, and the rain ceasing in the evening we killed a very fat young bull & a fat Elk deer. At night the rain began again and continued without intermission until morning.

Friday 7th. The weather continued cloudy, but the sun appearing now and then, we hoped for fair weather and sat of, but as yesterday it began to rain at 12, at two we found some wood on some sandy hills in the plains where we stopped to cover our goods, being completely trenched [drenched]. There being no water on the sand hills, we raised a Bark of Elm trees, and putting one end in a kettle, the other end a little higher all the water that fell on the Bark ran into the kettle and we had presently a sufficient quantity; we also made a tent with Bark and passed the night comfortably enough.

Saturday 8th. We sat of to go to a hill called Grosse Butte[18] to dry our things, and water our horses, but there being none here arrived there in two hours and a half where we stopped for the remainder of the day and night. The Grosse But[t]e is a high hill, which is seen at 20 miles off on either side. At its foot on the North side is a Lake of about 8 Mile in Circumference in which there are middle sized pikes. Between the Lake and the hill there is some wood chiefly Elm. All around are many lakes which by the late rain communicated with each other. From the top of the Hill the *turtle* Mountain[19] was seen being due Nort[h]. River la Sourie likewise was of in N:N:E: [and the] South and South west, being seen on all sides of the hill excepted West.

Sunday 9th. We sat of early in the morning, in a course S.S.W. and at 1 oClock in the afternoon we arrived on the Banks of the River la Sourie. The water being amazing hig[h] we made a Raft to cross our things over the River, and the horses swam over. We

---

[17] Bustards were Canada geese, *Branta canadensis* (Monseigneur [Alexander Antonin] Taché, *Sketch of the North-West of America*, trans. D. R. Cameron, p. 201).

[18] The name "Grosse Butte" is not preserved on modern maps, but a large unnamed hill on the south shore of Buffalo Lodge Lake, in McHenry County, North Dakota, fits all of the particulars mentioned for this hill by Larocque.

[19] Turtle Mountain is a large, timbered, dome-shaped upland area today bisected by the Canadian-American boundary.

saddled immediately and encamped in a Coulé about three miles from the River.[20]

Monday 10th. Leaving this we went and slept in the Mandan plain, saw plenty of Buffaloes all along, but did not dare to fire at them being on the enemies land — is Sioux. It rained a little in the night.

Tuesday 11th. At 8 in the morning I saw the banks of the Missoury, at 12 arrived at the River Bourbeuse,[21] when we unsad[dl]ed our horses [p. 3] where we u[n]loaded our horses and crossed the property on our shoulders there being not more than 2 feet [of] water, but we sunk up to our middle in mud, the horses bemired themselves in crossing and it was with difficulty we got them over the banks being bogs as also the bed of the river. We intended to get [to] the villages today, but being overtaken by a Shower of rain we encamped in a Coulé at the Serpent lodge,[22] being a winter village of the B. Bellys at the Elbow of the River, where I passed part of last winter, being unwilling to untie my things before the Indians at the village. As I must necessarily be put to some expence I took out here a small equipment of different article[s] for present expense, as the sight of my goods would perhaps cause the B: B. to refuse our passage to the Rocky Mountains.

Wednesday 12th. I arrived at 9 oClock in the morning on the banks of the Missury fired a few shots to inform the Indians of our being there and in a few hours many came over with Canoes[23] to cross us and our things. Lafrance proceeded to the Mandans but I and my men with Mr. McKenzie crossed here at the B. Belly's.[24] I entered into dift [dirt, or different?] lodges, gave my men each a small Equipment of knives Tobacco & ammunition to give the[ir] landlords.

---

[20] The point where they rafted across the Souris River was probably near or a little west of the modern town of Velva, North Dakota. The "Mandan plain" mentioned in the next day's entry was the treeless plain between the Souris and Missouri rivers, the major topographic feature of which is the Coteau du Missouri, a prominent escarpment about ten miles southwest of the Souris River which forms the divide between those two rivers.

[21] Known as Miry Creek by Lewis and Clark, it is now called Snake Creek.

[22] Serpent Lodge, or Snake House, was a prominent bluff on the left or east bank of the Missouri River just south of modern Snake Creek; it is now three miles north of Garrison Dam.

[23] These water craft were actually bull boats, the tub-shaped boats of the Plains Indians, made of a willow frame and covered with buffalo hide.

[24] That is, at the Big Hidatsa village site.

Thursday 13. Three Assiniboins arrived here. In the evening 4 Canadians from the Illinois,[25] who are hunting Beaver in these parts came to see me, I gave each of them 6 Inches of [blank in MS] Tobacco which pleased them very much, as they had for several Months not smoked any but Indian Tobacco.

Fryday 14. The Indians here are exceedingly trublesome to sell their horses to us, the prise that we usually pay them for a horse can purchas two from the Rocky Mountain [Crow] Indians who are expected dayly & they would wish us to have no more goods when those Indians arrive, so as to have the whole trade themselves. I told them that the purpose of our coming was not to purchase horses either from them or the Rocky Mountains, that we came for skins and Robes, and that for that purpose one of us was to pass the summer with them and one at the Mandans; that I and two men were sent by the white peoples Chief [Chaboillez], to smoke a pipe of peace & amity with the Rocky Mountain Indians[26] and to accompany them to their lands to examine them and see if there were Beavers as is reported & to engage them to hunt it, that we would not purchase a horse from no one, therefore that their best plan would be to dress Buffalo Robes, so as to have Ammunition to trade with the Rocky Mountain Indians.

They pretend to be in fear of the surrounding Nations, that is Assiniboines, Sioux Chayenne, & Ricaras, so as to have an excuse for not trading their guns with the Rocky Mountain Indians, and likewise to prevent us. Some of those Rocky Mountain Indians have been here already and are gone back, but more are expected, with whom I intend to go.

Saturday 15. I was sent for by one of the Chiefs who asked me what I intended to do, with the pipe Stem I had brought, upon my telling him that it was for the Rocky Mountain Indians, he made a long harangue to dissuade me from going there, saying [p. 4] that I would be obliged to winter there on account of the length of the way, that the C[h]ayennes & Ricaras were enemies and constantly on the Road [warpath], and that it was probable we should be killed by them. He gave the worst character possible to the Rocky Moun-

---

[25] An apparent reference to French-Canadians from the lower Missouri River.

[26] "No important undertaking was entered upon without deliberation and discussion in a solemn council at which the pipe was smoked by all present" (Frederick Webb Hodge, *Handbook of American Indians North of Mexico*, Bureau of American Ethnology Bulletin 30, p. 603).

tain Indians, saying they were thieves and liars of which he gave an example that is of a Canadian of the name of Ménard,[27] who had lived here about 40 years and a few Years ago [ca. 1800] sett of to go to the Rocky Mountains to trade horses and Beavers, these Indians did all in their power to prevent him, but seeing him absolutely bent upon going they let him go. He arrived at the Rocky Mountain Indians tents, where he was well treated, & got 9 horses and 2 female slaves, besides a quantity of Beaver, he left the lodge very well pleased, but were followed by some young men who in the night stole 7 horses, a few nights after his 2 slaves deserted with the other horses & other young men coming took from him every thing he had even to his knife, he came crying to the B. B. Village almost dead, having but his Robe to make shoes (with flintstones) which he tied about his feet with Cords, which so pained the B. B. that they killed some of the Roche Mountain [Indians] for Revenge &c &c. he told me many other stories, to all which I answered that my Chief had sent me to go, and that I would or die.

There is seven nights [have passed] that 5 young men are gone to meet the Rocky Mountain Indians, they are expected dayly & the Rocky Mountains with them.

Sunday 16th. This evening the Indian women danced the scalp of a Blackfeet Indian, which they killed last spring. The Canadians from below said they had killed some white men at the same time, that they had seen Cloths such as Corduroy Jackets and trowsers, Collars Shirts, part of Linnen Tents, Casimer waistCoats, and many other things belonging to the whites. The Borgne[28] the Great Chief of this Village [Big Hidatsa] told me that [that] war party had fired upon and killed people who were going down a very large River, in skin Canoes, but that they could not tell wethere they were Crees or Sauteux [Chippewa] or whites. I spoke to old *Cerina Grape*[29] the

[27] This is the same Ménard that Alexander Henry the Younger erroneously mentions as having been killed by Assiniboins in 1803 on his way to the Missouri River (Alexander Henry [the Younger], *New Light on the Early History of the Greater Northwest*, vol. 1, pp. 311–12).

[28] Le Borgne, or "One Eye," is mentioned by Lewis and Clark and other contemporary accounts. Henry's journal (*New Light*, vol. 1, pp. 345–46) explicitly identifies him as living at Big Hidatsa village on the north bank of the Knife River. Burpee (in Larocque, *Journal of Larocque*, p. 22 n. 2) believed, however, that he lived in a village on the south bank of the Knife.

[29] The father of Wolf Chief. He was also called "the Grape," or "Cal-tar-co ta—cherry (grows [growing] on a bush) old Chief" by Lewis and Clark (Meriwether Lewis and William Clark, *Original Journals of the Lewis and Clark Expedition, 1804-06*,

166

father of the Chief of that party, and to the Chief himself, they swore by the fire, Earth and Heaven, that they were not whites. They made a plan of the Country through which they passed, & in my opinion it is somewhere upon the Sas Ratchavini [Saskatchewan River] or its branches. They showed me part of what they plundered but I saw nothing that could prove them to have killed whites except the quantity of Gunpowder he had, for it was no less than half a keg and at least 200 balls. Their plunder was parted among all the various [men] and their [p. 5] relations. Among the articles that the Cerina Grappe showed me, there was a Coat made of the skin of a young horse wrought with porcupine quills & human hair 2 skunk skins, guarnished with red stroud and blue beads which those Indians generally wear round their Ancles one Musket by Ketland on[e] gun by Barnett,[30] and lastly one scalp which was evidently that of an Indian. But I rally believe they have killed some white people about fort des prairies[31] for they brought more goods than ever I saw in the possession of Indians at one time.

Monday 17. I went down to the Mandan Village [Deapolis] on horseback and purchased a saddle there, for which I paid 30 lb. amunition, desired Lafrance to get some provision made for my voyage as there is no Corn where I live.[32] I returned home to my Lodge. In the evening having settled some business with a man of the name of [René] Jusseaume[33] who was indebted to the company.

Tuesday 18th. The son of the White Wolf fell from his horse & bruised his leg terribly, the flesh was taken clean of the bone from the ancle, round the leg to the Calf. The Indian doctor was sent for who began his cure by blowing and singing &c while the child suffered quietly. Thunder and storm.

Wednesday 19. There being another sik person in my lodge and then [there] being rather too much *fuss* about Medicines, conjuring

---

vol. 1, p. 213; William Clark, *The Field Notes of Captain William Clark, 1803-1805*, p. 172 n. 2) and as "old Choke-cherry" by Henry (*New Light*, vol. 1, p. 367). McKenzie in his Narratives refers to Wolf Chief as "the Chief of the Wolves."

[30] Ketland and Barnett were European gun manufacturers who supplied weapons for the Indian trade (Charles E. Hanson, Jr., *The Northwest Gun*, Nebraska State Historical Society Publication in Anthropology, no. 2).

[31] Burpee (in Larocque, *Journal of Larocque*, p. 19 n. 2) believes that the fort in question was on the South Saskatchewan River.

[32] In other words, on the Assiniboine River.

[33] René Jusseaume was a long-time resident and visitor to the Knife River villages and a guide for David Thompson on his visit to those villages in 1797 (see David Thompson's Journal).

and singing I went & lived in another lodge where I had placed one of my men before. Went to see the Borgne our Chief and being desirous that he should stand by me in case of need I made him a present of ¾ lb. Tobacco, one knife and 50 Rounds of amunition at which he was well pleased he is the greatest Chief in this place, but does not talk against our going to the Rocky Mountains as the other Chiefs do. Thunder and Rain at night.

Thursday 20th. I was again teased by some of the Chiefs to purchase horses and was told the Big Bellys had two hearts,[34] & that they did not know whether they would allow me to go to the Rocky Mountains, and in the Course of a long harangue they made use of all their art to induce me not to go representing the journey as dangerous to the last degree and that the Rocky Mountains [Indians] would not come, for that they were afraid of the Bicaras [Arikaras] & Assiniboines—to all which I could make no answer but by signs, as there was no one present that could speak to them properly, one of my men of the name of Souci[35] spoke the Sioux language, but there was no one there that understood that language. About sunset two of the young B. B. that had been sent to meet the Rocky Mountain [Indians] arrived, they left the Rocky Mountain Indians in the morning and they will be here in 3 or 4 days. Upon the receipt of those news the Chief pretended to have received information that the Crils [Crees] & Assiniboines were assembled to come and war upon them (which is false) and Harangues wer made to the people to keep their guns and ammunition and not to trade them [p. 6] with the Rocky Mountain Indians &c. All this I believe a Scheme to prevent me from going, for as yet they do not like to tell us so exactly, but are forever saying that they have two hearts which means that they are undetermined in what manner to act.

Fryday 21st. I went to see the Borgne enquired of him, what he & the Big Bellys thought of our going to the Rocky Mountains and whether they have a mind to prevent us. He answered to my wish, that the Rocky Mountains were good people, that they had plenty of Beavers on their hands, and that his adopted son, one of the Chiefs of the Rocky Mountains & the greatest would take care of us, for that he would strongly recommend to him to put the white people in his heart and watch over them. I told him that the B B

[34] That is, they were undecided.

[35] Burpee (in Larocque, *Journal of Larocque,* p. 20 n. 1) notes that a Pierre Saucie was listed in the department of Haut de la Rivière Rouge in the Liste des Bourgeois (Masson, *Les Bourgeois,* vol. 1, p. 402). This may be the same man.

had no reason to be displeased for that one of us remains with them, who has plenty of amunition, knives, Tobacco, Hatchets & other articles, wherewith to supply their wants, whenever they would be disposed to trade. He said it was true that no one would molest us[36] —he is the only Chief that speaks so, but as he has the most authority of any I hope by his means we will pass. A certain method to get the road clear would be to assemble the Chiefs, make them a present of Tobacco and amunition, make them smoke & speak to them what occasion I may have for them in [the] future. I like not to do it only when I see that I cannot otherwise for assembling a council, and haranging without a present is no better than speaking to a heap of stones. Besides I am apprehensive that paying as it were for our first going to those nations will give a footing to the B. Bellys which they will endeavore to improve every time we should go there; if a trading Interest takes place, so that if we pass this time without making them any present at all, I believe it will be done away forever. If the Borgne retains that authority he formerly had, he alone will be able to clear the Road for us & he appears to be sincerely our friend.

Saturday 22d. In the beginning [morning] I went to an Indians tent whose two sons had been in that party that defeated the white [men] on the Saskatchion he gave me a full account and more lik[e] truth than any other. He says there were four Linnen tents and four leather do [tents] on the side of the River where there were Skin Canoes, they fired upon the largest Leather tent and killed three men, two of whom were Indians the other they believe to be a white man but are not certain. They brought one scalp & if it is that which they showed me it is an Indian. There was plenty of *tents* of all kinds besides goods, what they would not take with them, they broke and threw in the River.

Sunday 23rd. Three men and one Woman arrived from the Rocky Mountains about noon, the other ar near [at] hand, and would have arrived today but for rain which fell in the evening.

In the evening I went to see the Brother of the Borgne, where I found two Rocky Mountain Indians, one of whom was the [p. 7] Chief[37] of whom the Borgne had spoken with me. I smoked with them for some time when the Borgne told them that I was going with

---

[36] McKenzie's account (see Charles McKenzie's Narratives) contains another version of this speech.

[37] Red Calf, or *Nake sinia*, according to McKenzie's Narratives.

them and spoke very much in our favour. They appeared to be very well pleased.

Monday 24th. Lafrance, with the other white people from below, who reside at the Mandans cam[e] to see the people which were arrived from the Rocky Mountains, who were prevented from coming by appearance of bad weather. It thundered the whole day but it did not rain. I gave a small knive to my Landlady.

Tuesday 25th. About one in the afternoon the Rocky Mountain Indians arrived, they encamped at a little distance from the village with the wariors, to the number of 645 passed through the village on horseback, with their shields & other warlike implements, they proceeded to the little village, *Souliers* and then to the Mandans and returned.[38] There did not remain 20 persons in the village, men women and children all went to the newly arrived camp, carrying a quantity of Corn raw and cooked which they traded for Leggins, Robes & dried meat. There are 20 lodges of the Snake [Shoshoni] Indians[39] & about 40 men. The other bands are more numerous.

This morning the Borgne sent for me, he showed me the Rocky Mountain Chief viz. of the Ererokas [Crow], and told him before me that I was going with him & to take good care of us & he spoke very much in our favour telling me that the B. Bellys were undetermined whether they would allow us to go or not, but that we would go if we liked it for that he would clear the road before us if necessary. I gave to two of the Ererokas each 6 Inch [of] Tobacco and 20 Rounds of amunition.

Wednesday 26th. The Mandans, Souliers, little village people & the people of the village went on horseback and arived to perform the same ceremonys round the Rocky Mountain Camp, as the Rocky

[38] We differ here with Burpee in identifying these villages. As we have seen (n. 28 above), the Borgne was chief of the Big Hidatsa village. The little village, thus, was Sakakawea; the Souliers lived at Amahami; and the right-bank Mandans lived at Deapolis (map 2).

[39] In 1805 the Crows were a much larger and more dominant group than the Plains Shoshonis. As Lawrence L. Loendorf has reminded us, the two groups had what might be labeled a symbiotic relationship, in that both had some reason or reasons for dependence upon the other. The Shoshonis, recently reduced by smallpox, were probably living with the Crows for protection. The Crows, in turn, may have used the Shoshonis as a contact with other Uto-Aztecan speakers along the intermontane trail south into the Spanish settlements. Larocque's statement on September 1, 1805, tends to support the latter idea that the Crows tolerated the Shoshonis for southern trading contacts.

Mountains did yesterday here—they were about 500, but a great many wariors are absent being gone to war.

Thursday 27th. Assembled the Chiefs of the different Bands of the Rocky mountains, and made them a present of

2	Large Axes	16	large knives
2	Small do	12	Small do
8	Ivory Combs	2	lb Vermillion
10	Wampoon Shells	8	Doz Rings
8	fire steels and flint	4	papers Cor'd Glasses
4	Cassetête	4	Doz awls
6	Masses B.C. Beads	1½	D Blue Beads
4	fm Tobacco	2	Doz [do]
8	Cock feathers	1000	Balls & powder

Made them smoke in a stem[40] which I told them was that of the Chief of the White people who was desirous of making them his Children & Brethren that he knew they were pitiful, and had no arms to defend themselves from their enemies, but that they should cease to be pityful as soon as they would make themselves brave hunters. That I and two men were going with them to see their lands and that we took with us some articles to supply their present wants that our Chief sent them those goods that lay before them, to make them listen to what we were now telling them, that he expected, they would treat all white people as their Blethern for that we were in peace and friendship with the Red skined people [p. 8] and did not go about to get a scalp that probably they would see white people on the land from another quarter but that they were our brethren, and of course we expected they would not hurt them, that a few years ago they pillaged and ill treated a white man [Ménard] who went to trade with them, that we would see how they would treat us and if they have behaved well towards us and kill Beavers, Otters & Bears, they would have white people on the lands in a few year, who would winter with them and supply them with all their wants &c &c. I told them many other things which I thought was necessary & closed the Harangue by making them smoke in the *medecin* pipe. They thanked [me] and made a present of 6 Robes, one Tyger [mountain lion] skin, 4 shirts, 2 women Cotillons,[41] 2 dressed Elk skins, 3 saddles and 13 pair leggins. I clothed the Chief of the Ererokas at the same time and gave him a flag and a wampoon

[40] That is, in a pipe.
[41] Shifts or petticoats.

171

Belt & told them that our Chief did not expect, that we would pass many different nations and therefore had sent but one Chiefs Clothing but that in the course of the summer we would fix upon a spot most convenient for them all where we would build and trade with them, if we saw that they wished to encourage the white people to go on their lands by being good hunters and that then all their Chiefs who would behave well would get a Coat.

The ceremony of adopting children was going on at the same time, but I was so very bussy that I could not attend but about the middle of the Ceremony, and therefore can give but an imperfect account of it from my own observation, but as the two people were present I will give an account of it in another pla[ce].[42]

Fryday 28th. I preferred to go of in the evening to the lodge of the Erreroka Chief in order to be ready with them in the morning. But he and the other Chiefs were called to a farewell Council in the Borgnes Lodge, so that I did not stir.

Saturday 29th. Saddled our horses and left the B: Belly village, we remained about half an hour in the Rocky Mountain Camp, when they threw down their tents and all sat of.[43] We marched along the Knife River for about 8 Miles when we stopped and Encamped. The Borgne & many other B. Belly's Came & slept with us.

Sunday 30th. We followe[d] a south course for about 4 Miles and stopped to dine and resumed a S.S.W. course and encamped for the night. Knife River in sight where no hills intervened, about 8 miles on our right, a Thunder storm in the evening.[44]

[July 1805]

Monday lst. We sat of at 8 oClock in the morning and encamped at 12 having followed a South West course; we crossed 3 small Creeks running North and N:East into the Knife River. It began to rain as soon as the lodges were pitched and continued so all day. The

[42] Larocque, however, failed to do so.

[43] Larocque left Le Borgne's village, Big Hidatsa, and marched west. Since he does not specify crossing the Knife River when the group turned south the next day, he may have made the crossing early in the journey, just as they left the village. In any case, on our map of his route (map 3) the crossing is shown near the Borgne's village. Burpee (in Larocque, *Journal of Larocque,* p. 25 n. 1) errs in believing that Larocque left from the south bank of the river.

[44] From this point until the party reaches the Powder River the course and distances in the journal seem to be confused. A literal interpretation of them would take the expedition much too far south; consequently, the route depicted on our map is an interpretation for this part of the journey.

Indians hunted and killed a few Bulls. I gave the people of my lodge a few articles [such] as beeds [and] knives.

[p. 9] Tuesday 2d. We sat out at 9 oClock followed a South course and encamped at 2 after noon. It thundered very much the whole of the afternoon & at sunset there fell such a shower of hail as I never saw before, some of the hail stones being as large as Hen Eggs and the rest as a Yolk; they fell with amazing violence and broke down several tents. The wind during the storm was West, it breesed to the North and continued during the whole night.

Wednesday 3d. We continued our journey for about 4 hours, through a very hilly country and encamped at the foot of a very high hill on the top of which I ascended, but could see at no considerable distance, another range of hills surrounding this on all sides. I lost my spy glass in coming down the hill and could not find it again. Our course was South.

Thursday 4th. We stopped after a south Course for the night on the side of a small hill at a Creek which empties in the Missuri above the Panis village about 5 leagues distant from our last Encampment having crossed another a little before emptying in the Missury about one Mile below the Mandans.[45] The Scouts reported that Buffaloes were at hand.

Fryday 5th. We discovered a thief last night in the act of stealing a gun from under our head thinking we were asleep. The Chief sent two young men to sleep behind the lodge and guard our property. After three hours and a half march in a southerly direction we espied Buffaloes, and stopped all. The Chief harangued and the young men set out to hunt after which we marched on for about a league and a half and encamped. There was no Creek or River here, for water, only a few ponds of stagnant water which by reason of so many dogs and horses bathing in them was not trinkeable being as thick as mud.

Saturday 6th. A Big belly found my spy glass and returned it to me, we set of at 8. At 11 the scouts reported that they had seen enemies. We all stopped, the men armed themselves & mounting their fleetest horses went in pursuite; the[y] returned in a few hours, as what the scouts had taken for Enemies were a party of their own

[45] This entry is clearly confused. The group appears, however, to be on the upper Heart River, which flows east into the Missouri River near the old Mandan villages near present-day Mandan. The Arikara ("Panis") villages were down the Missouri River, not far north of the mouth of the Grand River near the modern town of Mobridge, South Dakota.

people who were gone hunting & not been seen. We proceeded and encamped at one on the side of a small River running West & emptying in the lesser [Little] Missouri. It blew a hurricane in the Evening. Course south about four Leagues.

Sunday 7th. At ten oClock we rose the Camp, and at 3 we saw Buffaloes, harangues were made to the young men to go and hunt While a party of these latter who are a guard of soldiers paraded before the body of the people preventing any one from setting of till all the huntsmen were gone; after which we sat of again & encamped at the foot of a hill, which we had in sight since the day before yesterday.

Course S. West about 18 miles.

[p. 10] Monday 8th. Before we rose the Camp a general muster of all the guns in the Camp was taken and the number found to be 204 exclusive of ours. Our huntsmen had brought in a plenty of Buffaloes. We marche[d] this day by a south course about 7 miles.

Tuesday 9th. From the Big Belly village to the place where I lost my spy glass the country was very hilly; from that to this place it was much more upon a level though not entirely so. The plains produce plenty of fine grass. In the Course of this days journey we passed between two big hills on the top of which as far as the Eye could discern Buffaloe were seen in amazing Number. We encamped on the side of a small Creek running West, into the lesser Missouri. The Indian[s] hunted & killed many Buffaloes. Cours south S. West & S.W. 9 Miles. It blew a huricane at night without Rain many Lodges were thrown down although well tied and Picketted.

Wednesday 10th. We remained the greatest part of the day at this place to dry the meat and bury a woman that died here, and sat of at 4 in the afternoon and pitched the tents by a small Creek running West after having pursued our road S:W: by West for 5 miles. The country was hilly but producing plenty of Grass and numberless flowers of different kinds.

Thursday 11th. We passed through a range of hills of about 3 Miles broad on the top of every one was a heap of stones appearing as if burnt, part of the Rocks had fallen down the hills. Leaving those hills we had a pretty level plain till we reache[d] a small brook running N:West where we encamped, the lesser Missoury in sight at about 4 Miles on our right, by a course southwest we had advanced about 12 miles. On our way we saw a few Rattle Snakes but none of them very large; they are the first I saw in the Indian Countries and none ar to be found more northwards.

Fryday 12th. This day we passed through a pleasant plain and pitched the tents by a small brook 5 miles S:W: of our last encampment.

Saturday 13th. We sat of at 9 through a very hilly and barren country in crossing two small Creeks and arrived at 12 on the banks of the lesser Missouri we crossed it and encamped on its border about 2 miles higher. The river is here about ¾ of an acre in breadth from bank to bank but there is very little water running, the bed appearing dry in many places and is of sand and gravel. A few Liards[46] scattered thinly along its Banks. The rugged and barren aspect of the hills which are composed of whitish Clay looking lik[e] rocks at a distance. The ground on which you stood [was covered] with a prickly heap of [blank in MS] so very thick that one does not know where to set ones feet, no grass at all.[47] The whole forms a prospect far from pleasing. Our Course was for 12 miles S:S:W: A few days ago [p. 11] a child being sik I gave him a few Drops of Tarlington balsam[48] which eased him immediately of his Cholic. This cure gave me such a reputation of being a great phisician that I am plagered to cure every distemper in the Camp. A man came today to me desiring me to act the man midwife to his wife.

Sunday 14th. We remained the whole day here the Indians being bussy with drying meat. I went a little distance up the river and saw a little Beaver work.

Monday 15th. We crossed the river at three different times in the course of this days jurney when it happened to intersect the line of our course which was S:S:W: and encamped on its borders about 14 miles highter up. It has the same appearance in every respect as when we arrived at it. The indians killed a few Beavers, of whom I got two dressed by my men to show them how to do it.

Tuesday 16th. We remained here the whole day. The Indians tried to dance the Bull dance in imitation of the B. Belly's but did it very ill.[49]

46 The cottonwood tree, *Populus deltoides,* var. *occidentalis.*

47 Probably prickly pear, *Opuntia polycantha.*

48 Turlington's Balsam of Life was a popular remedy of the day.

49 A dance performed by members of the Bull Society among the Hidatsas and the Bull club among the Crows is described by Alfred W. Bowers (*Hidatsa Social and Ceremonial Organization,* Bureau of American Ethnology Bulletin 194, pp. 198–99) and Robert H. Lowie (*The Crow Indians,* pp. 204–206). The dance was painted by Karl Bodmer (Reuben Gold Thwaites, ed., *Early Western Travels, 1748-1846,*vol. 25, pl. 51) and George Catlin (*Letters and Notes on the Manners, Customs, and Condition of the North American Indians,* vol. 1, pl. 56), both of whom personally witnessed the

Wednesday 17th. I[t] rained in the morning; at 11 before noon the weather clearing up, we sat of following the river in a course S:S: West about 9 miles. The bed and Banks in many places were solid rock; there is very little water running. There is a few Fir trees on the declivity of the hill here.[50]

Thursday 18th. I went hunting with the Chief while the camp flitted we killed one cow and returned to the river at 3 in the afternoon where we found the people encamped 15 miles S:W: of our last encampment. The banks & bed of the river ar rocks; the plains ar a continual series of high rocky hills, whose sides and tops are partly covered with the red pine, & other wood such as poplar, Elm, Ash and a kind of Maple.[51]

Fryday 19th. We [set out] at an hour before Sunset & encamped 5 miles higher up the River.

Saturday 20th. Some one being sik we did not stir. Here the points of the River are pretty large and well stocked with wood, viz — Liard, Ash & a kind of shrub resembling the prickly Ash which bears a fruit the size of a small Pea, red & of a sourish taste but not disagreeable.[52]

Sunday 21st. The camp rose at 8 in the morning and proceeded along the River for about 15 miles in a S.S. Westerly direction; the Banks & bed of the river ar of soil but muddy. I saw a Beaver lying dead on the banks, here the river is fordable, without wetting ones feet, in stepping over upon loose large stones. As we trotted almost the whole of this days Journey the unusual jolting of the Packages on the horses back occasioned the breaking of my Thermometre.

Monday 22d. From this place we left the lesser Missouri on our left, its course above this appears to be South to North, & stopping in the plains we encamped at one in the afternoon on the side [p. 12] of a little river running into the lesser Missoury our course S.W.[53]

---

ceremony at different times among the Mandan, where it was associated with the Okipa ritual (Alfred W. Bowers, *Mandan Social and Ceremonial Organization*, pp. 88, 117–19).

[50] Douglas fir, *Pseudotsuga menziesii*, is present, albeit rare, along the Little Missouri River.

[51] The Red pine is ponderosa pine, *Pinus ponderosa*, common in this locality. The poplar is probably quaking aspen, *Populus tremuloides;* the elm is *Ulmus americana*, the American elm; the ash is green ash, *Fraxinus pennsylvanica;* and the "kind of maple" is *Acer glabrum*, Rocky Mountain maple.

[52] Buffaloberry, *Shepherdia argentea.*

[53] This is probably modern Boxelder Creek, which enters the Little Missouri about fifteen miles south of the town of Marmarth, North Dakota.

The Banks of L.M. [Little Missouri] in sight. We crossed two small Creeks in which there was no running water but many deep ponds in which there are Beavers. We saw this day plenty of Buffaloes.

We remained at this place 2 days. I have been very sik since some time, and so weak that it was difficult I could keep my saddle, the Indians on that occasion did not flit. I traded a few Beavers.

Thursday 25th. We sat of this morning at 10 following the little Creek on which we were encamped for 4 Miles by a S:W: Course & encamped. Wind S:E.

Fryday 26th. We passed through a Range of hills whose tops and sides are covered with pine, and at the foot are many small Creeks well wooded with Ash & maple there are a plenty of different kinds of Mint here which emit a very odoriferant smell.[54] We crossed 3 small Creeks running North & N:W. into the Powder River whose banks we had in sight from the top of those hills. The wind was N:W: & very strong a hurricane blew at night. The course we have pursued on a very barren soil for 22 miles was West.

Saturday 27th. We arrived at noon at the Powder River after 6 hours ride by course West by South for about 20 miles. The Powder River is here about ¾ of an acre in breadth, its water middling deep, but it appears to have risen lately as a quantity of Leaves & wood was drifting on it. The points of the river are large with plenty of full grown trees, but no underwood, so that on our arrival we perceived diverse herds of Elk Deers through the wood. There are Beaver Dams all along the river. Three of these animals have been felled by our Indians.

When we arrived here the plains on the western side of the River were covered with Buffaloes, and the bottoms full of Elk and jumping Deers & Bears, which last are mostly yellow & very fierce.[55]

[54] Burpee (in Larocque, *Journal of Larocque,* p. 30 n. 1) calls these hills the Powder River Mountains; Hazlitt (in Larocque, "Journal of François-Antoine Larocque," p. 335 n. 21) calls them the Blue Mud Hills. The mint family is a very large and diverse one, but distributions and habitat preferences suggest that Larocque noted some of the following species: *Agastache anethiodora,* or fragrant giant hyssop; *Monarda fistulosa,* or wild bergamot; *Hedeoma hispida,* or rough pennyroyal; *H. drummondii;* and *Mentha arvensis,* or wild mint (Orin Alva Stevens, *Handbook of North Dakota Plants,* pp. 239–46). Wild mint was used by many Plains tribes as a medicine and as a seasoning, and fragrant giant hyssop (first discovered in North Dakota in the Knife River mouth area) is also said to have been used by the Indians as a fragrant herb (ibid., p. 241; and Melvin R. Gilmore, *Uses of Plants by the Indians of the Missouri River Region,* pp. 60–61).

[55] American elk or wapiti, *Cervus canadensis;* antelope or pronghorn, *Antilocapra americana;* and grizzly bear, *Ursus horribilis.* Larocque at no time mentions crossing

It is amazing how very barren the ground is between this and the lessor Missouri. Nothing can hardly be seen but those *Cornin de Raquettes* [prickly pears].[56] Our horses were nearly starved. Here there is grass in the woods but none in the plains, which by the by might with more propriety be called hills, for though there is very little wood it is impossible to find a level spot of one or two mile in extent except close to the River. The current in that river is very strong and the water so muddy as to be hardly drinkable. The Indians sai it is always so, and that is the reason they call it Powder River, from the great quantity of drifting fine sand set in motion by the Const[ant] wind which blinds people and dirtys the water.[57] There are very large sand shoals along the river for several acres breadth and length. The bed [p. 13] of the River is likewise sand, and its course North East.

Sunday 28th. We remained here the whole day to let the horses feed. The women were busily employed in dressing and drying the skins of those animals that were killed yesterday. I traded one 3 Beavers and one Bear skin.

Monday 29th. We rose the camp late in the evening and pitched the Tents about 4 miles higher up the River having followed for that short space a course S:W:

Tuesday 30th. Early this morning we sat out; the body of the people followed the River for about 17 miles S.W. while I with the Chief and a few others went hunting. We wounde[d] Cabris [antelope], Buffaloes and the large horned animal,[58] but did not kill any, which made the Chief say that some one had thrown bad medecin on our guns & that if he could know him he would surely die.

The country is very hilly about the river, but it does not appear to be so much so towards the North. About two miles above the Encampment a range of high hills begins on the West side of the River & continues North for about 20 miles, when it appears to finish. The Tongu River is close on the other side of it. There is a parting ridge between the two Rivers.[59]

---

the Powder River, although he was obviously on its west bank for several days before leaving it. For this reason, our map showing his exploration (map 3) depicts his route as passing along the west bank of the stream from about the modern town of Powderville, Montana, to the mouth of Clear Creek, in northern Wyoming.

[56] Burpee felt that this plant was probably the dogwood, but it seems more likely that this is another reference to prickly pear. See n. 47, above.

[57] This locale is near present Powderville, Montana.

[58] Bighorn sheep, *Ovis canadensis.*

I ascended some very hig[h] hills on the side of which I found plenty of shells of the Cornu Amonys species by some called Snake shell, likewise a kind of shining stone lying bare on the surface of the Ground having to all appearance been left there by the rain water washing away the surrounding earth; they are of different size and form, of a clear water colour, and reflect with as much force as a looking glass of its size. It is certainly those stones that have given the name of Shining to that Mountain. The hills are high, rugged and barren mostly Rocks, with beds of loose red gravel, on their tops or near it, which being washed down by the rain water give the hills a redish appearance. On many hills [are] a heape of calomid stones among which some time I find pumice stone.[60]

When we left the encampment this morning we were stopped by a party of their soldiers who would not allow us to proceed,[61] as they intended to have a general hunt, for fear that we should rise the Buffaloes; but upon promise being made by the Chief whom I accompanied that he would not hunt in the way of the camp, and partly on my account we were suffered to go on. We were however under the necessity of gliding away unperceived to prevent jealousy.

[p. 14] Wednesday 31st. We sat out at 7 in the morning & proceeded up the River in a southern course for about 15 [or 13?] miles, and encamped about mid day; the weather being very warm and the wind from the south. I traded a few Beaver skins.

[59] The Tongue River itself is nearly thirty miles west at about this point (a few miles southwest of the modern town of Broadus, Montana), but Pumpkin Creek, one of its major tributaries, is less than fifteen miles distant.

[60] The early Tertiary (Paleocene) Fort Union formation is the only geological unit exposed in this locality, and its fossils were deposited in a freshwater environment. Burpee's identification of the "Snake shell" (in Larocque, *Journal of Larocque*, p. 31 n. 5) as *Cornu ammonis*, or as ammonites, is in error, for such fossil cephalopod shells are marine in origin and date to a much earlier geologic era. There are, however, several coiled Tertiary gastropods in the Fort Union formation. One of these, *Biomphalaria pseudoammonius*, may well be the "Snake shell"(Gary Glass, Wyoming State Geologist, letter of 14 July 1983). The "shining stones" on the hills nearby were almost certainly of selenite gypsum, common in the Fort Union formation. This formation also contains many seams of coal, some of which have been ignited in the geologic past and are still burning beneath the surface. The burned coal leaves clinkers (erroneously called "pumice" by both Larocque and popularly today). The heat of the subterrenean fires baked the overlying clays, producing a red natural brick which erodes into the "loose red gravel" Larocque mentions. This material is popularly known as "scoria" in the region.

[61] See also his comments on these police on ms. p. 48.

[August 1805]

Thursday 1st August. Rain and thunder storm prevented our stirring this day. The water rose about 6 inches & in the River, and is as thick as mud. The Current very swift.

Fryday 2nd. Last night some children playing at some distance from the Camp on the river, were fired at. The Camp was allarmed & watches were set for the night but nothing appeared. It rained hard during most part of the night. We rose the camp at one in the afternoon following the river for about 9 miles in a south course. The hills of the River are at a less distance from one another than they were heretofore. The bottoms or points of the river are not so large nor so well wooded, and the grass entirely eat up by the Buffaloes and Elk.

Saturday 3d. We sett out at sunrise and encamped at one in the Afternoon having pursued a south course with fare weather and a South East wind. We followed the River as usually; its bends ar very short not exceeding two miles and many not one. The face of the country indicates our approach to the large Mountains and to the heads of the River. A few jumping [deer] or Chevreuils [antelope] were killed today. It has been very cold these few nights.

Sunday 4th. We did not rise the Camp till late in the evening. In the morning we assended the hills of the River and saw the Rocky [Bighorn] Mountains not at a very great distance with [a] spy Glass,[62] its Cliffs and hollows could be easily observed with the wood interspersed among the Rocks. We removed our Camp about 4 miles higher up the River having pursued a S.E. [S.W.] Course.

Monday 5th. We had a thick fog in the morning, the night was so cold that one Blanket could not keep us warm enough to sleep, so that I purchased two Buffaloe Robes. About midday however it is generally very warm. We sat of at 7 and continued our way for about 12 miles by a south course along the River, and with a Nort[h] West wind. We arrived at the forks of the Pine River, which are assunder for about one Mile, and encamped.[63] The water in this

[62] Larocque's group was the third Euro-American party to see these mountains. The La Vérendrye brothers had probably glimpsed them from a distance in early January, 1743 (Smith, *Explorations of the La Vérendryes,* pp. 110, 121, 123); and Ménard, the Frenchman mentioned earlier in this journal, apparently went to or near them about 1800 (see ms. p. 4).

[63] The allusion to the forks of the Pine River is probably to the junction of Clear Creek with the Powder River, about thirteen miles north of the town of Arvada, Wyoming. The two rivers parallel one another for about a mile above their confluence.

River is clear and good, issuing from the mountains at a short distance from this, and is very cold. While that of the Powder River was so muddy [p. 15] that the Indians were under the necessity of making [holes] in the beach and drink the water that gathered in them. We left this last mentioned River on our left, whe[re] we went up the Pine River [Clear Creek], which is between 20 & 30 yards in breadth and runs over rocks. There is a rapid at every point and very little wood along its banks.

Tuesday 6th. We rose the Camp at 7, and proceeded upwards along the Pine River in a S: Western direction for 12 miles, having the Rocky Mountains ahead and in sight all day. The weather was foggy with a N:W: wind. An Indian shot another mans wife in the breast and wounded her dangerously. Jealousy was the occasion thereof. The Indian[s] often inquire when I intend to depart. They appear to wish me to be off. I have 23 Beaver skins which they think a great deal, and more than we have occasion for. They thought that upon seeing the Rocky Mountains we would immediately depart, as the[y] cannot immagine what I intend to see in them. It is hard to make them understand by signs only, especially in this Case for they do not want to understand.

Wednesday 7th. We sat of at 6 & pitched the tents at 9 miles higher up the river having followed a south Course. The Indians hunted & killed many Buffaloes & One Cow came and took refuge among the horses, where she were killed. At 5 in the evening we again flitted, & encamped 5 miles higher up having pursued the same course as in the morning, with a head wind.

Thursday 8th. We marched 24 Miles in a sout[h] West course along the Pine River. Many small Branches fall in it at a little distance from one another. A man and horse were wounded by a Bear but not dangerously. There is much fruit here about & many Bears. Wind S:E: We ar here encamped at the foot of the Mountain.

Fryday 9th. The people went out hunting & returned with many skins to be dressed for tents. The weather is cloudy and the wind south. Rapids succeed each other in the River here very fast & the current between is very swift running on a bed of Rocks.

Saturday 10th. Some Indians arrived from hunting & brought 9 Beavers which I traded for Beads. Weather the same as yesterday.

Sunday 11th. They are undetermined in what course to proceed from this place they have sent a party of young men along the Mountain westerly and are to wait here until they return. They often enquire with anxious expectation of our departure when I intend to leave them, and today they were more trublesome than usual. What I have seen of their lands hitherto has not given me the satisfaction I look for [in] Beavers. I told them that I would remain with them 20 or 30 days more. That I wished very much to see the River aux Roches Jaunes [Yellowstone] and the [p. 16] place they usually inhabit, otherwise that I would be unable to return to them and bring them their wants. They saw it was true, but to remove the objection of my not knowing their lands a few of them assembled and draughted on a dressed skin, I believe a very good map of their Country, and the[y] showed me the place where at different seasons they were to be found. The only reason I think they have in wishing my departure, is their haste to get what goods I still have. Besides we not a little embarrass the people in whose tent we live. They pretend to be fond of us treat us well and say they will shed tears when we leave them.

Monday 12th. In the evening the young men that had been sent to reconnoitre returned & reported that there was plenty of Buffaloes & fruit on the Tongue and Small horn [Little Big Horn] River, that they had seen a lately left encampment of their people who had not been at the Missouri (about 9 lodges) that they were gone across the mountain that they had seen no appearance of their being enemies on that side. A council ensued, and Harangues were made to rise the Camp in the morning and proceed along the Mountain to the River aux Roches Jaunes.

Tuesday 13th. We sat of at half after 8 in the morning following a West Course along the Mountain through Creeks and hills such as I never saw before it being impossible to Climb these hills with loaded horses we were obliged to go round them about the middle of their hight, from whence we were in imminent danger of rolling down, they being so steep that one side of the horses load rubbed against the side of the hill. One false step of the horse would certainly have been fatal to himself and rider. The wind was S.E. in the morning and North W: in the evening and the weather sultry. We encamped at 12 on the banks of a small branch of the Tongue River,[64] whose water was very clear & cold as Ice. The people killed t[w]o Bears today. I traded a few Beavers. I saw a few Crows today which are the only birds I have seen since I left the Missouri except a few wood Peckers.

[64] Perhaps Little Goose Creek, which flows north through the modern town of Sheridan, thence into the Tongue River.

Wednesday 14th. It rained part of the morning, as soon as the rain ceased we sat off when it began again and continued raining until we reached another branch of the Tongue River, where we encamped. We went close along the Mountain all the way for about 10 Miles by a West course crossing many small Creeks all running into the Tongue River; most of them were dry but thickly wooded with the Saule blanc [white willow]: there was no Beaver work. I saw a few Cranes.[65]

Thursday 15th. Fine clear weather. I traded 8 Beavers and purchased a horse for which I paid a gun 200 balls, one flanel Robe, on[e] shirt, one half ax, on[e] battle do, one [p. 17] bow Iron, one Comb, one But knife, one small do, 2 wampoon hair pipes, one [blank in MS], 2 awls, one wampoon shell, 40 B. blue Beads, 2 Mass Barley corn do, and one fm WS Red Stroud.[66] We left this place at 11 before noon & proceeded 9 miles in a north West Course and encamped on another branch of the Tongue River. Wind N:W, fine warm weather.

The Indians killed Buffaloes and a few Bears, the latter they hunt for pleasure only as they do not eat the flesh but in case of absolute necessity. Perhaps the whole nation is employed about a bear, whom they have caused to take refuge in a thicket, there they plague him a long while and then kill him, he is seldom stript of his Skin.

Fryday 16th. I purchased a saddle and [blank in MS] for the horse I purchased yesterday, for which I paid 40 shots Powder. Being short of balls I gave 20 rounds Powder only for a Beaver, 1 knife I sell 2 Beavers, t[w]o [or 10] strings Blue Beads, 1 Beaver & so on. We proceeded along the mountain as usual by a N:W. Course about 15 miles, crossed 3 small Creeks emptying in the Tongue River where we arrived at one in the afternoon, we forded it & encamped on the North side N: & N:E. is a small mountain lying between this River and the large Horn River, they call it the Wolf teeth (Sela is in the Rocky Mountains language and Seja in the Big Belly's).[67] Fine weather wind N:W.

Saturday 17th. The Indian having hunted yesterday we did not rise the Camp but remained here all day. There are many Bears

[65] Probably Sandhill cranes, *Grus canadensis.*
[66] Strouds were coarse flannel blankets.
[67] Larocque's "Wolf teeth" are the Wolf Mountains, which lay northeast of their camp on the Tongue River.

hereabouts, who are attracted by the quantity of Choak Cherries[68] and other fruit, there is here the wood along the Rivers are as thickly covered with Bears Dung as a barn door is of that of the Cattle, large Cherry trees are broken down by them in great number. The Indians kill one or two almost every day. The Tongue River here is small being only about 20 feet broad with two feet water in the deepest part of the rapids. It receives many additional small streams in its way to the River Roches Jaunes. The points of the river are pretty large & well stocked with wood, viz: [blank in MS] & Maple.

Sunday 18th. At 7 oClock we left our encampment and proceeded Northward; at noon we stopped on a branch of the Small Horn River & the greatest part of the Indians went on to the Small Hair [Horn] River to hunt. At half past two in the afternoon we sat off again and crossing the River we encamped on its Borders where we found the hunting party with their horses loaded with fresh meat. We travelled about 15 Miles this day and are farther from the Mountain than yesterday though still Close to it.

Monday 19th. Since we are close to the mountain many women have deserted with their lovers to their fine tents that are across the Mountains, there are no Cattle in the mountain nor on the other side; so that they [p. 18] are loth to go that way, while the desertion of their wives strongly call them there. Harangues were twice made to rise the Camp, and counter order[s] were given before the tents were thrown down. The reason of this is that the wife of the Spotted Crow who regulates our mo[ve]ments has deserted, he is for going one way while the Chiefs of the other bands are for following our old course. Horses have been killed and women wounded since I am with them on the score of Jealousy. Today a Snake Indian shot his wife dead, but it seems not without reason, for it is said it was the third time he found her and the Gallant together. The Small Horn River runs East from the Mountain to this place, here it make[s] a bend N by East and passing round of [*the North end of*] the Wolf teeth it falls into the large Horn River. The bed of the River here is Rocks a continual rapid, the water clear & cold as Ice, the ground barren and the banks of the river thinly wooded, with the same kind of wood as heretofore. I traded 6 Beavers.

Tuesday 20th. We flitted and encamped 3 miles higher up the

---

68 Choke cherries, *Prunus virginiana.*

River on a beautiful spot where there was plenty of fine Grass for the horses—our Course West. I traded 3 Beavers.

Wednesday 21st. I made a present of a few articles to the chief and a few other considered Persons. We remained here all day. There is plenty of Ash here. There were very few persons in the camp that were not employed in making themselves horse whip handles &c with that wood; it was with that design they came here, as that wood is seldom found elsewhere. I saw some Beavers work on that River.

Thursday 22d. Water frose the thickness of Paper last night in horsetracks. I was called to a Council in the Chiefs Brothers Tent Lodge, where the Spotted Crow resigned his employment of regulating our marches, another old man took the office upon himself & told me that he intended to pursue their old Course to the River aux Roches Jaune. I traded 8 Beavers with the Snake Indians in whose possession I saw a kettle or Pot hewn out of a solid stone, it was about 1½ inch thick & contained about 6 or 8 quarts; it had been made with no other instrument but a piece of Iron.

Fryday 23. We rose the Camp at 11 in the forenoon and followed a N:E course for one mile N:W: 6 do & encamped on a branch of the [blank in MS, but the Little Big Horn] River, where there is a Beaver Dam & other work occasionally found. I traded 4 Beaver. Wind S:E. the only roads practicable to cross the [p. 19] Mountain are at the heads of this and the Tongue River.

Saturday 24th. This morning we were allarmed by the report that three Indians had been seen on the first hill of the Mountain and that three Buffaloes were in motion and that two shots had been heard towards the large Horn River. Thirty men saddled their horses and immediately went off to see what was the matter, while all the other[s] kept in readiness to follow if necessary. In a few hours some came back and told us that they had seen 35 on foot walking on the banks of one of the branches of the large Horn River. In less time than the courier could well tell his news no one remained in the Camp but a few old men and women, all the rest scampered off in pursuite. I went along with them. We did not all set off together nor could we all keep together as some horses were slower than others, but the foremost stopped galloping on a hill, an[d] continued on with a small trot as people came up. They did the same when a Chief arrived, he and his band or part of it galopped twice before the main body of the people wh[o] still continued their trot, intersecting the line of their course while one of his friends I

185

suppose his Aide de Camp harangued: they were all dressed in their best Cloths. Many of them wer[e] followed by their wives who carried their arms, and who were to deliver them at the time of Battle. There were likewise many Children, but [only those] who could keep their Saddles. Ahead of us were some young men on different hills making signs with their Robes which way we were to go. As soon as all the Chiefs were come up and had made their harangues everyone set off the way he liked best, and pursued according to his own judgement. The Country is very hilly and full of large deep Creeks whose Banks are Rocks so that the pursued had the advantage of being able to get into places where it was impossible to go with horses & hide themselves. All escaped but two of the foremost who being the Scouts of the party had advanced nearer to us than the others and had not discovered us. They were surrounded after a long race but killed and scalped in a twinkling, when I arrived at the dead bodies they had taken but his scalp and the fingers of his right hand with which the outor was off.[69] [p. 20] The[y] borrowed my hanger [knife] with which the[y] cut off his left hand and returned it [the knife] to me bloody as a mark of honour & desired me to [blank in MS] at him. Men women and Children were thronging to se[e] the dead Bodies, and taste the Blood. Everyone was desirous of stabbing the bodies to show what he would have done had he met them alive and insulted & scoffed at them in the worst Language they could give. In a short time the remains of a human body was hardly distinguishable, every young man had a piece of flesh tied to his gun or Lance with which he rode off to the camp Singing and exultingly shewing it to every Young women in his way, some women had whole limbs dangling from their saddles. The sight mad[e] me shudder with horror at such cruelties and I returned home in quiet [quite a] different frame from that in which I left it.

Sunday 25th. The Scalp dance was danced all night, and the scalp carried in procession throughout the day.

Monday 26th. I[t] rained in the morning as it did yesterday, at Noon the Weather clearing we sat off Cours S:W. [N.W.] wind S:E. fine weather. We encamped in the mountain 9 miles distant from our last encampment by a small Creek in which there was little running water, but an amazing number of Beaver Dams. I cou[n]ted 6

[69] Does this allude to the "outer" or little finger? The two slain Indians are later identified as Assiniboins (see ms. p. 40).

in about 2 Points of the River. But most of them appear to be old Dams. The young men paraded all day with the scalps tied to their horses bridles sing[ing] and keeping time with the Drum and Shiskequais or Rattle.

Tuesday 27th. We remained here all day, 10 young men were sent to observe the motions of those who were routed lately, they are afraid of being attaked having seen the road of a numerous body of people on the larg Horn River. In the evening news came that the Buffaloes were in motion on the Large Horn River, and harangues were made to guard the Camp.

Wednesday 28th. Two hours before daylight, all the Indians horses were saddled at their doors they put all their young children on horseback & tied to the saddles, then they slept the remainder of the night. They likewise loaded some horses with the most valuable part of their property while they in the expectation of being attacked sat in the tents their arms ready & their horses saddled at the door. At broad daylight nothin appearing they took in their children and unloaded their horses. At 9 in the morning 4 young men arrived and reported that they had seen nothing of the enemy, that there were plenty [of] Buffaloes between the Large Horn and the River aux Roches Jaunes.

Thursday 29th. We rose the camp this morning and marched a Course [p. 21] West by North. The Indians hunted and saw strange Indians. There was a continual harangue by different Chiefs the whole night which with the singing and Dancing of the scalps prevented any sleep being had. We pitched the tents on a small Creek running into the Large Horn River distant about 20 miles from our last Encampment.

Fryday 30th. We left the place and encamped on the Large Horn River close to the foot of the mountain & of very high Rocks. Course west about 5 Miles.

Saturday 31st. We remained at this place the whole day. Some young me[n] who had been en decouverte [on reconnaissance] returned from a deserted Camp of about 30 Lodges where they found Chief Coats NB [HB] stroud wampoon shells & other articles, which it seems had been left by the people inhabiting those tents upon some Panic. This is what these Indians say but it is my opinion that those goods are rather an offering to the supreme being which those Indians often make and leave in tree[s] well wrapt up and which our young men found. This River is broad deep and clear water, strong courrent, bed stone and gravel about ½ mile above this encampment, the River runs between 2 big Rocks & loses ⅔ of its breadth but gains proportionally in depth. There is no beach at the feet of the Rocks they are but perpendicular down to the water. It is aweful to behold and makes one giddy to look down upon the River from the top of those Rocks. The River appears quite narrow and runs with great rapidity immediately under our feet, so that I did not dare to look down but when I could find a stone behind which I could keep & looking over it to see the foaming water without danger of falling in.[70] This river does not take its rise in this mountain, it passes through the mountains an[d] takes its waters in the next range. There is a fall in this River 30 or 40 miles above this where presides a Manitoin or Devil. These Indians say it is a man Woolf who lives in the fall and rises out of it to devour any person or beast that go[es] to[o] near. They say it is impossible to kill him for he is ball proof. I measured a Ram's horn which I found when walking along the River, it was 5 spans in length and was very weighty it seemed to me that the animal who carried it died of old age for the small end of the horn was much worn and broke into small splinters, which was not the case in any of the animals I saw killed, nor were their horns of that size neither.

The Mountain is here a solid Rock in most places bare and naked, in other places cloathed with a few [blank in MS] Red Pine. The sides of some Coulé are as smooth and perpendicular as any wall, and of an amazing hight; and in other [p. 22] places there are holes in those perpendicular Rocks resembling much those niches in which statues ar placed; others like Church doors & vaults; the tout ensemble [general effect] is grand and striking. Beautiful prospects are to be had from some parts of those Rocks, but the higher places are inaccessible. The Large Horn River is seen winding through a level plain of about 3 miles breadth for a great distance almost to its Conflux with the River aux Roches Jaunes.

[September 1805]

September 1st Sunday. We left this place and pitched our Tents

---

[70] Larocque's description of this area is graphic and accurate. The course of the Bighorn River through the Bighorn Mountains is through an exceptionally deep and precipitous canyon with very sparse vegetation. Its exit from the mountain is marked precisely as he notes: between two huge rocks with no beach at their bases. Today, the Yellowtail Dam has impounded the river less than one mile upstream. His camp near this point is today a picnic area administered by the National Park Service (see map 3).

FIG. 10. The mouth of Bighorn Canyon, Montana, April, 1952. The arrow (lower right) marks the location of the two large rocks which Larocque said had "no beach" below them. The Yellowtail Dam is today just a few hundred yards upstream from them. The view is southwest. Bureau of Reclamation, U.S. Department of the Interior.

about 3 miles lower down where we remained two days. While we were here a Snake Indian arrived, he had been absent since the spring and had seen part of his nation who trade with the Spaniards; he brought a Spanish B[r]idle and Battle ax, a large thick blanket, striped white and black and a few other articles, such as Beads &c. A Missuri Big Belly fished here and caught 14 moyens [middle-sized] Catfish in a very short time.

We had much dancing at this place still for the scalps. There are Islands in the River here but most of them are heaps of sand. The wooded points of the River do not join, the open plain is seen between them but there is plenty of wood in some places. The leaves beg[in] to fall.

Wednesday 4th. We left the encampment & proceeded N:W. by

North about 15 Miles and pitched the tents on a small Creek running into the Large Horn River. Where we left the River we had a level plain for about 4 or 5 miles when the Country became hilly and barren.[71]

Thursday 5th. We kept the same course as yesterday and encamped on a most small Creek running as the former about the same nature.

Fryday 6th. We rose the Camp early and at 11 before noon arrived at Mampoa or Shot Stone River,[72] from whence the Indians went out to hunt, there being plenty of Buffaloes. On the road to this place the mountains were as follows. The Mountain along which we travelled from the Pine River lay S:E: another called Amanchabé Clïje south. The Boa [or Bod?] Mountain S:W: but appeared faintly on account of a thick fog that covered it.[73]

Saturday 7th. We remained all day here, the Indian women being very bussy to dry tongues and the best part of the meat and dressing skins for a great fea[s]t they ar preparing while their war exploits are recapitulated.

Sunday 8th. I sat off early this morning with two Indians to visit the River au Roches Jaunes and the adjacent part. I in[p. 23]tended to return from this place as the Indians will take a very round about Road to go there. We were not halfways, when we fell in with Buffaloes, my guides were so bent upon hunting that they did not guide me where I wanted, and we returned at night to the tents with meat, but with rain, as it rained from noon till night. The Indians showed me a mountain lying North West which they told me was in a direct line to the Missouri falls and not far from it.[74] We passed throug two new raised Camps of strange Indians, at the

[71] This is probably modern Beauvais Creek, an affluent of the Bighorn River.

[72] This river is today called Pryor Creek. As Larocque later points out (in his entry for September 15), its headwaters are in the Pryor Mountains. Stuart W. Conner (personal communication, April, 1981) informs us that Pryor Creek was called "Stone they Shot" by the Crow Indians. The stream was named by the Lewis and Clark expedition after one of its members, Nathaniel Pryor (Lewis and Clark, *Original Journals,* vol. 5, p. 290).

[73] The mountains along which they had traveled were of course the Bighorn Mountains. Amanchabe Clije would be the Pryor Mountains, and Boa Mountain would probably be the Beartooth Mountains.

[74] The Great Falls of the Missouri River, near the town of Great Falls, Montana, were about two hundred miles northwest of Larocque's position. Big Snowy Mountain best fits this description, but it would be visible only from a very high point as far south as modern day Billings.

door of the largest tent were 7 heaps of small sticks, each heap containing 10 sticks denoting the number of Lodges in the Camp, to have been 70.

Monday 9th. I purchased a horse we had information that four strangers had been seen, who likewise saw our people & hid themselves. At night a young man arrived who saw and conversed (I cannot say he spoke for the whole conversation was carried on by signs they not understanding one anothers language) with a fort de prairie Big Belly [Atsina] they wanted to bring each other to their respective Camps but both were afraid and neither of them dared to go to the other Camp. The B.B. are encamped on the large Horn River behind the mountain and are come on peaceable terms, they are 275 or 300 Lodges.

Tuesday 10th. We rose the camp at 9 and to[ok] a N: West Course to the River aux Roches Jeaunes where we arrived at two in the afternoon distant 16 Miles—we forded into a larg Island in which we encamped.[75] This is a fine larg[e] River in which there is a strong current, but the Indians say there are no falls. Fordable places ar not easily found although I believe the water to be at its lowest. The bottoms are large and well wooded.

Wednesday 11th. 5 Big Bellys arrived and came into our lodge, being the Chiefs Lodge. They brought words of peace from their nation and say they came to trade horses. They were well received by the Indians, and presents of different articles were made them, they told me they had traded last winter with Mr. Donald whom they made known to me a[s] crooked arm.[76]

I went round the Island in which we are encamped, it is about 5 Miles in circumference and thickly wooded in some places—all along the North side of the Island. The Beaver has cut down about 50 feet of the wood. 9 lodges of the people that were left in the spring was joined as they are 15 tents at present, they encamped on the opposite side of the River.

Tuesday 12th. I traded six large Beavers from the Snake Indians. We crossed from the Island to the West side of the River & pro-

---

[75] This island was probably a little west of the modern town of Billings, where the channel is even today quite braided.

[76] Burpee (in Larocque, *Journal of Larocque*, p. 44 n. 3) notes that John McDonald had a deformed arm. These Indians had apparently traded with him on the South Saskatchewan River about Christmas of 1804.

ceeded upward for about 9 miles S:W: and encamped in a point where they usually mak[e] their fall medicines.[77]

[p. 24] Fryday 13th. I bought a Horn Bow & a few Arrows a Saddle & a pichimom, part of a tent, and a few of those blue Glass Beads they have from the Spaniard[s], and on which they set such value that a horse is given for 100 grains.

Saturday 14th. Having now fullfilled the instructions I received from Mr. Chaboillez, which were to examine the lands of the Crow Indians, and see if there is Beaver as was reported, and to incite them to hunt it, I now prepared to depart. I assembled the Chiefs in Council, and after having smoked a few pipes I informed them that I was setting off, that I was well pleased with them and their behaviour towards me, and that I would return to them next fall. I desired them to kill Beavers and Bears all winter for that I would come and trade with them and bring them their wants. I added many reasons to show them that it was their interest to hunt Beavers, and then proceeded to settle the manners of knowing one another next fall, and how I am to find them which is as follows. Upon my arrival at the Island if I do not find them I am to go to the mountain called Amanchabé Chije [Pryor Mountains] & then light 4 dif[feren]t fire[s] on 4 successive days, and they will come to us (for it is very high and the fire can be seen at a great distance) in number 4 & not more, if more than 4 come to us we are to act upon the defensive for it will be other Indians if we light less than 3 fires they will not come to us but think it is enemies. They told me that in winter they were alway to be found at a Park by the foot of the mountain a few miles from this or thereabouts. In the spring & Fall they are upon this River and in summer upon the Tongue and Horses River.[78]

I have 122 Beavers 4 Bears & 2 Otters which I traded not so much

[77]Their camp for this evening was probably just east of the modern town of Laurel. The "fall medecine" may have been the Sun Dance, an important ceremony held about this time of the year by the Plains Indians. William Clark, on July 24, 1806, found a large, conical "council lodge" on an island in the Yellowstone River near the mouth of Canyon Creek, about seven miles above Billings (Lewis and Clark, *Original Journals*, vol. 5, pp. 288–89), reinforcing Larocque's observations relating to the ceremonial significance of this locality.

[78]"This River" is of course the Yellowstone. John C. Ewers (in Edwin Thompson Denig, *Five Indian Tribes of the Upper Missouri*, p. 139 n. 5) identified "Horses Creek" as Pryor Creek—an identification inconsistent with the identification here of Larocque's "Shot Stone" river as Pryor Creek.

for their value (for they are all summer skins) as to show them that I set some value on the Beavers & on our property. The presents I made them I thought were sufficient to gain their good will in which I think I succeeded. I never gave them anything without finding means to let them know it was not for nothing. Had more been given they would have thought that good[s] were so common among us that we set no value upon them, for Indians that have seen few things white men will be more thankful for a few Articles given them than for [a] great many, as they think that little or no value is attached to what is so liberally given. It was therefore I purchased their Bears & likewise as a proof that there is Beaver in those parts, besides it served to distribute the good[s] I had, into the most deserving hands, that is the less lazy.

We departed about noon 2 Chiefs accompanied us about 8 Miles, we stopped and smoked a parting pipe the[y] embrased us, we shook hands & parted they followed us about one mile more at a [p. 25] distance gradually lessening their steps till we were almost out of sight and crying or pretending to cry—they then turned their backs and went home. At parting they promised that none of their young men would follow us to steal our horses or otherwise molest us, they took heaven & Earth to witness to attest their sincerity in what they had told us, and that they had opened their ears to my words and would do as I desired them, they made me swear by the same that I would return & that I told them no false words (and certainly I had no intention of breaking my oath—nor have I still, If I do not keep them my word it certainly is not my fault:).

Our course was N:E: 20 miles, a little before sunset we were overtaken by a storm which forced us into a point of the River where we encamped & passed the night during which our horses were f[r]ightened & it was with difficulty we could get them together again. We kept watch by night.

Sunday 15th. We followed a N:E: Course and crossed the R. Rocher Jeaune at 9, and proceeded along the south side. At 10 we crossed Manpsa River [Pryor Creek] at its entrance into Riv. Roches Jeaunes. Manpoa or the Shot Storm River is about 10 feet in breadth and with very little water it take[s] its waters in Amana-bechief at a short distance there is wood along its Banks, especially close to the mountain and Beaver. On the East side of this river close to its discharge in the Riv: Rocher Jaune is a whitish perpendicular Rock on which is painted with Red earth a battle between three persons on horseback and 3 on foot.[79] At 2 in the afternoon we arrived at a high hill on the side of the river called by the natives Erpian Macolié where we stopped to refresh our horses & killed on[e] Cow.[80] An hour before sunset we sat of again and encamped after dark making no fire for fear of being discovered by horse thieves or Enemies. From Monpoa to this p[l]ace our course was East. Buffaloes and Elk we found in great plenty. Wind S.W.

Sunday 16th. It froze hard last night North, Weather Cloudy N:E. 9 miles and stopped to Cook victuals for the day as we make no fire at night—Elk and Buffaloes in the greates[t] plenty. It rained till 3 in the afternoon, when the weather clearing we sett off and encamped at the Rocks of the large Horn River where we arrived at 8 in the evening.

[p. 26] Tuesday 17th. We crossed the river early in the morning, its points here are large & beautiful, well stocked with wood, we passed through a most abominable country and often despaired of being able to get clear of this place—meeting with Rocks which it was impossible to ascend or go round, so that we were obliged often to go back and take another road which presented us with the same difficulties, at last we ascended the hill but being on the top did not offer a more pleasing prospect, we were often obliged to unload the horses and carry the baggage ourselves and the horses being light we made them chump [jump] over chasms in the Rock and climb precipices, but were near losing them at last at 3 in the afternoon we had passed the whole of that bad road and arrived at the border of the Rock, whence we could see a fine level country before us, but the sun was set before we could find a practicable road to come down to it, which we effected not without unloading the horses, and carrying down their loads part of the way, while the horses slided down upon their Rumps about 25 Yards. We broke some of our saddles, and arrived in the plain just as the day was setting and encamped further on by the side of the River. It is probable that had we had a guide with us we would have avoided

[79] This pictograph has never been found and was probably destroyed long ago (Stuart W. Conner, personal communication, April, 1981).

[80] This "high hill" is probably the eminence which William Clark named "Pompey's Tower," and which he described on his voyage down the Yellowstone River on July 25, 1806, ten months after Larocque's visit to the same area (Lewis and Clark, *Original Journals*, vol. 5, pp. 292-93). This feature, now known as Pompey's Pillar, was named for Sacagawea's son Jean Baptiste, nicknamed Pompey but called Pomp for short by Lewis and Clark.

those Rocks, which our ignorance of the Road made us enter into, & once engaged among the]m] the difficulty was as great to return as to proceed. We kept no regular course, but went on as we could to all points of the Compass in order to extricate ourselves—We killed one Elk.

Wednesday 18th. This morning we saw the points of wood where we encamped last night 9 miles south of us from which we were parted by the River on one side & the Rocks on the other. I heard the noise of the fall or great Rapid Yesterday, but now at too great a distance from the River and too busily engaged to go and see it.[81] It froze hard [*last night*] we lef[t] our encampment late as our horses were tired, but after having set out did not stop till after sunset having followed for 22 miles a North East course. Wind south West, fine weather. Plenty Elk and Buffaloes.

Thursday 19th. Cold and Cloudy and followed the same course as last day for 22 miles stopped at 2 in the afternoon & killed a stag which was very poor being its Rutting Season. We resumed our course to the N: East for 8 miles [p. 27] and encamped for the night.

Friday 20th. We sat this day early out, ascended the hills which are rugged and barren proceeding N:E: for 36 miles. Killed one large [blank in MS] fine weather with a N:E. wind.

Saturday 21st. We had a very bad road, came down to the River to see if we could find a better passage, but it was impossible, the River striking the Rock at every bend, and ascended the hill again, and with difficulty made our way over Rocks. After sunset we encamped on the River a la Langue [Tongue River]. Killed 2 Elks which were very fast [fat]. Course East for 18 miles Wind N:E.

Sunday 22d. We crossed the River a la Langue, and passed ove[r] a plain of about 9 miles in breadth where we came again to Rocks & precipices without number over which we jogged on without stopping till 2 hours before sunset when we encamped on the side of the River close to a Rapid. There is little or no wood here along the River except a few Liards scattered here and there and no grass at all. Course N:E. for about 18 miles Wind S:W:

Monday 23d. We had a pretty level plain the whole of the day 12 miles West [East], and 24 miles N:E: at 10 we Crossed the Powder River, it has no wood on its banks here and is much shallower than when we crossed it going, its water is the same being still muddy.

---

[81] There are no major rapids on the Yellowstone River near this area.

We encamped at night by a small Creek, having been unable to find grass for our horses throughout the day. We were obliged to cut down three Liar[d]s, and let the horses feed on the bark.

Tuesday 24th. Set off early, at 9 in the morning we found a place where there was grass where we stopped and let our horses eat. At three in the afternoon we saddled and went on until we encamped after sunset having followed an Eastern Course for 13 miles. Wind S:W: fine weather. It is 4 nights since it froze.

Wednesday 25th. We passed through a very uneven country, but there being no Rocks we had no very great difficulties, and encamped at night in a very large point of wood in which there was plenty of Deer. Watched all night having seen something like a man creeping on the beach. We had made this day 37 miles by a North course. The fire is in the plains from which the wind brought columns of thick smoke in abundance so that we could barely see. We shoed our horses with raw deer hide as their hoofs are worn out to the flesh, with continual walking since last spring setting their feet on loose stones lames them & sometimes makes them bleed.

[p. 28] Thursday 26th. Was [What] we saw las night and mistook for a man was a Bear whose traks we found this morning. We sat out at 8, and the plain being even we went on at a great rate; at 2 in the afternoon we stopped to kill a Cow, our provision being out. At three we sat off again and met on our road a femal[e] bear eating [blank in MS]. We killed her and took the skin it being good. At 5 we stopped for the night.

Here the river is divided into many channels, forming so many Islands, the bank and Islands ar thickly covered with woods, chiefly Liard, Ash [or Oak?] and Maple. Our cours was North which [we] followed for 39 miles havin the wind ahead, which brought us thick smoke in abundance. We saw this Day plenty Elk and Buffaloes.

Friday 27th. We crossed a plain of about 6 miles & arrived at a bend of the River, where it was impossible to continue on the hill, so that we wer fain to descend to the River and follow the beach. We bemired 3 of our horses & got them out but with great difficulty. At one we stopped to let the horses eat. The wind was south and we had no appearance of smoke but the weather threatened rain. We encamped at sunset after having followed a North course for 24 miles and found plenty of Grass.

Saturday 28th. This whole day we travelled through a level country having fine weather. We made 30 miles in a Northerly direction and passed 3 Indian encampment[s] of this summer, whom I suppose must have been occupied by wariors for the[y] had no tents.

Sunday 29th. We passed through a most beautiful and pleasant country, the river being well wooded. We found here more fine grass than in any place since I left the Missourie, and of course the greatest number of Buffaloes. The wind was N:W: and the weather cloudy and cold. Having made 30 miles by a N:N:E course we encamped on a small Creek round which the river passed.

Monday 30th. We ascended the hill which produces plenty of fine grass; about 6 miles further we saw the forks of the River aux Roches Jaunes and the Missouri. Course N:E: 27 miles and descended to the River (the Missouri) having but a bend. We had followed the River for 7 miles when we heard the report of a Gun twice, and the voice of a woman as Crying. We stopped and sent [William] Morrison en decouverte & I and *Souci* remained to watch the horses & property.[82] Morrison returned in about 2 hours and reported that [p. 29] what we had taken for a womans voice was that of a Young *Cub,* and as to the gun we supposed it proceeded from trees thrown down by the wind, as it blew very hard, and the Buffaloes, Bears & Elk were very quiet in the wood and plains, so that there was no appearance of being any human creature thereabouts. We went on & ascended the hills to cut a large bend of the River following an East cours for 11 miles and encamped in a large point of Elm trees for the night. The weather was Cloudy all day & cold. The wind was North West and very strong tearing down trees by their Roots every moment.

[October 1805]

October Tuesday 1st. Weather Cloudy Raining now and then, wind N:W. very cold—Course North 12 miles. Passing through a Coulé yesterday I found a lodge made in the form of those of the Mandans & Big Belly's (I suppose made by them) surrounded by a small Fort. The Lodge appears to have been made 3 or 4 years ago but was inhabitted last winter. Outside of the fort was a kind of stable in which the[y] kept their horses. There was plenty of Buffaloes heads in the fort, some of them painted Red.

Wednesday 2d. Strong N:W: wind cold and cloudy. Course N:E: 26 miles—killed a Cow—Country even, plenty [of] grass.

Thursday 3d. Set off at 7 through a very hilly & bad country N:E: 20 miles East 15, and encamped on the River. It rained part of the day Wind North West very cold.

---

[82] This is the same man spoken of so highly in McKenzie's Narratives.

Friday 4th. It rained and was bad weather all night, at break of day it began to snow and continued snowing very hard till 2 in the afternoon. Strong N:W wind. We sought our horses all day, without being able to find them till after sunset; the bad weather having drawn them in the woods.

Saturday 5th. Sat off early, fine weather course S:E. by E: 26 miles plenty of Buffaloes on both sides of the river, killed [a] Cow.

Sunday 6th. All the small Creeks & Ponds wer frozen over this morning. Course S:E: by S: 20 miles [blank in MS] Sout[h] passed throug a thick wood of about 4 miles.

Monday 7th. East 2 miles South 11 do arrived at the lesser Missory which we crossed S:E. 3 miles saw many Bears & Skunks.

Tuesday 8th. Ascended the hills, Plains Even 39 miles S:S:E: fine warm weather wind S:W:[83]

Wednesday 9th. Proceeded on the hills through a fine country course E: by S: 12 miles. South 2 miles and arrived at the Big Bellys w[h]o were encamped about 3 miles above their village. I found here a letter of Mr. Charles McKenzie to me.[84]

[p. 30] Thursday 10th. I remained here all day to refresh the horses before I proceed to the Assinibois River. Among other news the Indians tell me that there are 14 American Crafts below the [blank in MS] [villages?] who are ascending to this place.[85]

The Sioux have killed 8 white men last spring upon St. Peters [Minnesota] River & 3 Big Bellys here.

Friday 11th. I intended crossing over [the Missouri River] today but was prevented by the strength of the wind which blew all day with amazing violence from the North West. I got a few pair of shoes made and corn pounded for provision, news came that the Scious were seen encamped at a short distance below. Expecting to be attacked they were under arms all night.

Saturday 12th. About noon the weather being calm and warm we crossed the River; the horses swam the whole bredth of the River & were nearly spent. We met with 3 Assiniboines and their wives on the north sid[e] of the River who wer going to the Big Bellys to

---

[83] This entry was copied twice. The second one (deleted here) was labeled as "Wednesday 9th."

[84] McKenzie's account indicates that he left the villages on August 15, accompanied by Lafrance.

[85] Who these Americans were is unknown; Lewis and Clark had already left the villages for the Rocky Mountains, and no other group of comparable size is known to have ascended the Missouri River at that time.

trade. We went [and] jogged slowly on till sunset when we encamped on the side of a small lake in the Plains which are burning to the West—Course North.[86]

Sunday 13. Fine weather, Wind N:W: plenty of [blank in MS] Buffaloes just arriving in the plains. Few *being on all sides.* The Buffaloes were in motion so that we could not get near enough to get a shot at them, & our horses so tired & fatigued that I did not chuse to run them. We crossed the fire at sunset & encamped by the side of a small lake whose borders had escaped the General conflagration.

Monday 14th. We watched our horses all that night for fear of Assiniboines, of whom we had seen the tracks in the evening; sat off before sunrise and arrived at 10 in the forenoon at the River la Sourie where we stopped for the remainder of the day. The grass on either side of the rive[r] here is not burnt but the fire appears on both sides at a distance West and North. Soon in the evening the Buffaloes wer in motion on the North side of the River which *made us fear for our horses.*

Tuesday 15th. After dark last night we left our Encampment and mar[ched] two and a half hours by star light, when Clouds gathering so as to obscure our sight of the stars and of course being unable to regulate our course we stopped in a Creek & there passed the night being free of anxiety. In the morning we proceeded, weather cold and cloudy Wind N:W. We stopped for the night on the deep River, which does not draw the name of a River, being a hollow *Garl* [?] in the plain in which there are small deep ponds communicating with each other in the spring and rainy seasons only, nor is there a single twig to be found about it. At sunset it began to rain and continued so all night. We covered the property with part of a tent we had & we passed the whole night shivering by a small fire made of Cowdung (which we had taken care to gether before the Rain began) with the assistance of our saddles on our backs by [the] way of Cloaks.

Wednesday 16th. It snowed rained and hailed the whole day, Wind N:W. and amazing strong. We arrived after dark at the woods of one of the Elk Head Rivers,[87] wet to the skin and quite benumbed with cold.

---

[86] Larocque's journal entries for his return trip are too general to determine his route. Consequently, our map showing his return (map 3) makes no effort to chart his voyage from the Missouri River back to the Assiniboine.

[87] Burpee (in Larocque, *Journal of Larocque*, p. 53 n. 5) identifies this as either North or South Antler Creek.

[p. 31] Thursday 17th. Weather cloudy and wind N:W: and very cold so that we were fain to stop, make a fire and warm ourselves, especially as we are not over and above well dressed to keep off the Cold. We wrapt ourselves in Buffaloe Robes, and proceeded to the Grand Coulé and encamped on the very same spot where we had the quarrel last spring with the Assiniboines.

Friday 18th. In the morning we met with a few *Assiniboines* coming from the fort; we stopped and smoked a pipe with them. They told us that *Mount* a la Bosse[88] had been evacuated and that Mr. [Pierre] Falcon was building a house to winter in, about half ways between that and *R. qu'il appelle Fort.*[89] We arrived at Mount a la Bosse fort, where I found Mr. Charles McKenzie and 3 men taking care of the remaining property.

I remained here one day & then went to see Mr. Falcon at the Grand Bois about 15 miles above this, returned the next day & then satt out for River la Sourie fort[90] where I arrived the 22d October. So ends my Journal of my Journey to the Rocky Mountains.

[p. 46] October 1805 [Continued][91]

Upon my arrival at the River la Sourie I found Mr. Pierre Rocheblave who was proprietor and Bourgeois of the Department in Mr. Chabillez stead, who was tran[s]ferred to fort Dauphin department.[92] I passed a very pleasant winter with this gentlemen and F. N: Lamoth nothing remarkable occurring during the whole winter. I made a couple of trips to the Indian tents in the course of the winter and the remainder of the time I passed chiefly in reading as there were plenty of book[s] at the place. In the spring Mr. Lamoth went to take charge [of] Appell Fort in the place of [André] Poitras who was going out. On the 28th Mr. Rocheblave left this place (very sik) for Kaministiquia.[93] Mr. Falcon likewise went out this year [1806] and

[88] From which they had departed on June 2, four and a half months earlier.

[89] This fort was at the mouth of the Qu'Appelle River (Voorhis, *Historic Forts and Trading Posts,* p. 143).

[90] Ibid., p. 165. This fort was on the Souris River near its confluence with the Assiniboine River.

[91] In the original manuscript, and in Burpee's transcription, this section follows "A Few Observations on the Rocky Mountain Indians." It has been placed here to enhance the continuity of Larocque's account.

[92] This department was in the vicinity of Lake Dauphin, in present-day western Manitoba.

[93] This was a major post on the north shore of Lake Superior about twenty-five miles northeast of Grand Portage.

no Clerk remained inland but those that had or was serving an apprentiship viz. 2 at R: Q A [Qu' Appelle River] and Rivière la Sourie where I was myself with tw[o] others.

I passed the summer of 1804[94] at this place and though Buffaloes were at a great distance we lived pretty well and I had greatly the advantage over my neighbours the [blank in MS] in point of trade. This is the only place in the *Assiniboine* River where the [blank in MS] have a summer establishment, so that Mr. Lamoth at R Q A is without an opposition. Having very little to do I kept a sett of books according to the Italian method of duble entry so as not to forget it; in this and in reading I employed my leasure hours. Messrs. Chaboillez, Chr. Henry, Hess & Allan McDonell paid me a visit in the course of the summer and went to the Missouri they returned with Mess: N N: who had passed the summer ther[e] on a trading jaunt.[95]

On the last day of Aug: a man [arrived] from Kamt. [Kamanistiqua] belonging to lower Red River Department he gave me no news of the Brigade of this Department which was not ready to leave Kam: when they sat off. At the latter end of Sept. the brigade for this department arrived under the command of Big Joh[n] McDonell the bourgeois of my first year in this country who [p. 47] was then coming from Montreal. Mr. Rocheblave having heard at Caministiquia of the death of his Brother Noel, went down. Mr. Macdonell continued me [in] the command of the fort being that in which I summered and gave me as companion Mr. Lamothe. This young man had done very well at R. [blank in MS]. It seems that notwithstanding the junction of the two companies[96] and the resolution they had taken of burrying in oblivion all the differences, quarrels &c which the animosity of rivalship in trade had caused that the N:W: Comp: could not forget the Death of the villain [James] King which this Mr. Lamothe killed in his own defense on the Sassratchioin [Saskatchewan] or fort des Prairies department, or rather Mr. A.N: McL[e]od being of those kind of men who can never think themselves forgiven by a person they have grossly injured, because they are themselves incapable of forgiving, and who will

[94] Unless Larocque is reminiscing, he means 1806, not 1804 (*Journal of Larocque*, p. 75 n. 1).

[95] This is a reference to Alexander Henry's Mandan tour, which left Fort Assiniboin on July 14, 1806, and returned on August 9, 1806 (Henry, *New Light*, vol. 1, pp. 304, 415).

[96] That is, of the North West and XY companies in 1804.

continue their hate, ill will and offences to a person because they deserve such from him themselves, this Mr. MacLeod with some others having influence enough on Mr. McDonell made him promise that he would render Mr. Lamothes situation as irksome and as disagreable as possible in order to make him leave the country, they being hurt at the sight of a person who called to their minds the baseness of their proceedings towards him. Mr. McDonell then in order to effect this their design & his promise gave no command or employment whatever to the young man, would neither see nor speak to him and sent him to pass the winter with me hoping that such treatment would effectually rid them of him. Mr. McDonell at different times expressed his sorrow at being obliged he said to use Mr. Lamothe in that manner whom he knew did not deserve it but urged in excuse the necessity he was under of following the Directions of his fellow partners & the acquittance of his promise. Mr. Lamothe bore this treatment with indignation but concentrated within himself, however not to a degree as to influence his usual good humour. He dispised too much the author of it (whom he thought to be Mr. McLeod) to suffer the thoughts to intrude long upon his mind. I found him an excellent companion and in the course of time a friend. He rendered me all the services in his power, and volunteered them every time that the interest of the Company required it, which was very often in dangerous as well as disagreable trips to the Indian tents &c and often did the duty of a common Engagé to promote the Interest of those who ill treated him. I was absent 22 days at one time from my fort, during which time I gave him the charge of it, although I thought it would displease the Bourgois. I found everything on return in the best order possible [p. 48] in short I had numberless obligations to him & we passed an agreable winter together. I had under me one Clerk and an Interpreter one guid[e] who served as Cooper & Interpreter and 9 men. There was a Hudsons Bay establishment on the opposite side of the River [Brandon House], in trading opposition, the master of which was named Thomas Vincent he had 23 men with him, and a great quantity of goods. We entered into some agreements in the fall with regard to the Indians and the trade with them, which we inviolably kept; and which we found to be of mutual advantage. My returns were Superior to those of last year at the same place & superior to my neighbours, but the utmost exertions were used by me and Clerks, we were few men in comparison to our opponents [who] had 22 women and their families to feed. The Buffaloes our almost only resource were at a great distance, the men being hardly able to bring provision in fast enough for such a number of mouths, and with that our Indians & debt to watch and bring in, so that we were unremittingly and constantly on the go: but we succeeded in surpassing the expectation of our Bourgeois who thought that 50 Packs would be the utmost of our return and we had 55. I wrote an exact journal of every days transaction kept regular accounts, and knowing that I would not be there the ensuing winter, I left the whole with a Character of the Indians for the use of my successor.

In May I had the houses and hangards [storehouses] which were not of absolute and immediate necessity thrown down, and had them rafted to a place called Pine Fort[97] (from an old fort that had been there in Mr. Robert Grants time) about 13 miles lower down the River, in pursuance of directions from Mr. J. McDonell who had plan[n]ed the erection of a fort at that place, and the demolition of the one where I had wintered, kept all the men that I could spare at work in rebuilding those hangards and before I left the place all the property was removed to the new fort, and under cover. In consequence of Letters I had received last fall from the family I had determined upon going out to Kaministicoia at least, and perhaps thence to Canada according to the contents of the Letters I would there receive, would influence my mind. Mr. McDonell wished me very much to remain as the Young men that remained inland did not possess his entire confidence, and the time prognosticated a hard and disagreable summer to them, few men could be left with them and there was much work to be done.

On the 3d June I left Pine fort and Mr. Charles McKenzies care and embarked with Mr. McDonell for Kami[p. 49]ministicoia. The brigade with us, Mr. Lamothe had been sent of with a single canoe 3 days before with directions to wait for us at the bottom of the River Ouinipeque. We joined Mr. Henry at [the] fork of the Red River[98] and Mr. Lamothe at Lake Ouinipieque—We all remained at Mr. Wm. McKay's[99] fort a[t] the Bottom of the River Ouinipisque

[97] This fort stood on the north bank of the Assiniboine, west of Pine Creek, between 1785 and 1794. It was also known as Fort des Epinettes (Larocque, *Journal of Larocque*, p. 78 n. 4). The former site of Pine Fort was reoccupied in 1807, as Larocque here describes, and used for a few years thereafter (see A. E. Brown, "The Fur-Trade Posts of the Souris-Mouth Area," *Transactions of the Manitoba Historical Society*, 3d, ser., nos. 17–18 [1960–62]: 85–86).

[98] Where the Assiniboine River and the Red River join in the modern city of Winnipeg.

[99] This name, over which Burpee speculated so diligently, is clearly McKay in the manuscript, not McBay.

3 days in settling the mens accounts unloading the boats and Canoes, giving the canoes their proper loads for Kaministicoia &c. Different brigades from English River[100] and Fort des prairies overtook us here.

I embarked in the same Canoe with Mr. Lamothe. Mr. McDonell gave us a profusion of the best kind of provision the country could afford for our voyage, he and other Burgois in half loaded canoes well manned satt off ahead and got much before us at Kaministicoia, at Lake la Pluie fort[101] I found some letters for me from Mr. McDonell in which he empowered me to take everything I wanted at the fort to make our voyage pleasant and comfortable, that fort being well stored with every Kind of provision.

I left my companion Lamothe at the Mountain being the last portage on the way to Kaministicoia there was a temporary establishment here, and Lamothe was directed to remain there until a Brigade for Montreal was ready to leave Kaministicoia when he would be sent for. This was the last mortification the poor young man had to endure from his employers. We slept but one night on our way down and the next morning we all arrived at the Grand Portage Kaministicoia which fort had been built to supersed the establishment of the Grand Portage which being within the American Territory was liable to subject its proprietors to taxes & Imports from the American Government which to avoid, the N:W: Comp: abandoned their Establishments at that place and erected new buildings upon a greater and more convenient site at the entrance of the River called by the Indians Kaministicoia, [blank in MS] which name means the River whose entrance is full of Islands and Inlets. The bay of Lake Superior in which this River empties [Thunder Bay] is indeed full of large and beautiful Islands, and [p. 50] so is the whole of the North coast of that Lake. The vessels that sail on that Lake can come at the very gates of the Fort, the River being deep, and there Load and unload. Before the conquest the French [blank in MS] had a fort and trading establishment at this very spot.

[Left Lachine] on the 26th of April 1801, and arrived at the Grand portage at the latter end of June.[102] From thence I was sent to fort

---

[100] English River is a tributary of the Winnipeg River.
[101] Rainy Lake House (Larocque, *Journal of Larocque*, p. 80 n. 1).
[102] This segment of his diary consists of various episodes in Larocque's life from

Charlotte[103] and returned back. Some time afterwards I was sent to English River for wintering there. from this place I was sent to fort des prairie—and Red River, passin[g] Lake la pluie fort. Assinibois River. River la Sourie fort. Rapid River. River aux Bois fort.[104]

1802.XY Comp:

1803.

1804

1805. februar. fort of *Mt. a la Bosse.* When I arrived at the Missoury in the fall 1804, I found a party of 40 Americans under two Captains Clarke and Lewis who were sent by their Government to explore the upper part of the Missouri & N.W Countrys to the pacific Ocean, they wintered at this place and on the 28th March 1805[105] proceeded on their voyage of discovery with 7 prirogues having sent the boats in which they came as far as this place, down loaded with all kind of minerals, Roots, plants, carcasses & skins of different animals, and many other things which they deemed worth the attention of the litterary world. I offered to accompany them on their voyage, but for certain Governmental reasons they declined my proposal.[106]

[p. 51] The Mandan village is on the Missouri 1009 miles above the confluence with the Mississipi taking in the windings of the River and

 in North Latitude 47.21.40[107]

  Longitude

 West of Grenwich 99.24.45

From observations of Captain Lewis and Clark

his departure from Montreal in 1801 to notes on his visits with Lewis and Clark in the winter of 1805.

[103] This post was on the Pigeon River end of the Grand Portage trail nine miles from the Grand Portage establishment on the shore of Lake Superior.

[104] Rapid River, according to Burpee (in Larocque, *Journal of Larocque,* p. 82 n. 1) is a tributary of the Assiniboine River now known as the Little Saskatchewan. The River aux Bois fort he believed to have been a slip of the pen for "Rivière Fort de la Bosse," or Fort Montagne à la Bosse.

[105] Actually, they left on April 7, 1805 (Lewis and Clark, *Original Journals,* vol. 1, p. 287).

[106] See ibid., vol. 1, p. 252, for the entries for Jan. 30, 1804, and Feb. 2, 1805, for Clark's comments on Larocque's offer.

[107] Clark gives the latitude of Fort Mandan as 47°21'47" (Lewis and Clark, *Original Journals,* vol. 6, p. 59) and notes that it was sixteen hundred miles from the Mississippi.

[p. 31]
A FEW OBSERVATIONS ON THE ROCKY MOUNTAIN
INDIANS
WITH WHOM I PASSED THE SUMMER
[OF 1805]

This nation known among the Sioux by the name of Crow Indians inhabit the Eastern part of the Rocky Mountains at the head of the River aux Roches Jaunes (which is known by the Kinistinaux [Crees] and Assiniboines by the name of River a la Biche, from the great number of Elks with which the country along it abounds) and its Branches and close to the head of the Missouri.

There are three principal tribes of them whose names in their own language are *Apsarechas*, *Kee the resas*, and *Ashcabeaber*, & these tribes are again divided into many other small ones which at present consist but of a numerous people who were reduced to their present number by the ravage of the small Pox, which raged among them for many years successively & as late as three years ago [1802].[108] They told me they counted 2000 Lodges or tents in their Camp when all together before the small Pox had infected them. At present their whole number consists of about 2400 persons dwelling in 300 Tents and are able to raise 600 Wariors like the Siouxs and Assiniboines. They wander about in Leather tents and remain [p. 32] where there are Buffaloes and Elks. After having remained a few days in one place so that game is not more so plentiful as it was they flit to another place where there are Buffaloes or Deers and so on al[l] the Year around. Since the great decrease of their numbers they generally dwell all together, and flit at the same time and as long as it is possible for them to live when together, they seldom part. The fear of some of their neighbours with whom they ar at war compels them to that, as collectively they can repulse a greater party of their enemies, than when divided into small bands; though at such se[a]sons as they are not liable to be attacked, they part for a short time. In general they are middle sized men, but many of them ar tall & [s]tout and some inclined to corpulency which is seldom the case with American Indians.

Such of them as do not make practice of exposing themselves

---

[108] "The Crow name for themselves is 'Apsāruke,' which early interpreters mistranslated as 'gens de corbeaux,' 'Crow (or Kite) Indians,'" but they referred to themselves as *bī' ruke*, "we." The two grand divisions of the group were the River and the Mountain Crows. The former were called *minésepēre;* the latter, consisting of two subgroups, were the *acarahō'* and *ērarapī' o* (Lowie, *Crow Indians*, pp. 3–4).

naked to the sun have a skin nearly as white as that of white people. Those parts which the women keep concealed ar likewise white, but their face, breast, arms and shoulders are burnt to the common copper Colour of the Indians, by the scorching rays of the sun. Most of those Indians, as they do not so often go naked, are generally of a fairer skin than most of the other tribes with which I am acquainted. It is my opinion that the N:W Americans in general, were they to be brought up in the same manner that we are, and their bodies kept from the burning heat of the sun, would in a few generations be as white as Europeans. Some of them have the hair of the head entirely Gray although young; and though I inquired I could not find that sikness had been the cause the[re]of. They make a practice like the other Americans of eradicating the hair from every part of the body except the head, as fast as it groes, and deem it unseemly in a young man especially to have [a] beard. The old men when they [have] grown careless about their person let the beard grow, and in other parts of the body. The hair it seems grows faster than they could pull it out.

They practice so little walking & running, using horses on all occasions, that they are not so swift in running as their neighbours the Big Bellys and Mandans. I saw more cripples and decrepid old men among them than among any other nation except the Big Bellys and the Mandans. It is said that Sauteurs [Chippewa] and Kinistinaux [Cree] tribes send their enfirms & Old to kingdome come to ease themselves of the truble of attending the care of them. These [p. 33] Nations, however, do it not, their old and infirm are of very little truble to them. The Mandanes and Big Bellys are sedentary and the Rocky Mountain Indians have so many horses, that they can transport their sik without truble. Whethere they did it or not before they had horses I do not know; besides their country abounds so much in Buffaloes and Deer that they find no difficulty in finding provision for a noumerous family, which is likewise the cause of their having a plurality of wives, some of them have 8 or 10 and 12, but in such cases they do not all live with him some are Young girls that are only betustted [betrothed]. But by far the greatest part have only 2 o[r] 3 wives; some have only one, and those reason upon the folly of those that take many wives, and say that it is impossible for them to live happy and quiet as their wives ar jealous & forever wrangling. They are not so stupid as Indians are generally thought to be, they reason justly enough upon such objects as they have had occasion to see and be acquainted with. They certainly express wonder and admiration, when such things are shown them as they have no conception of such as Spy glasses, watches &c but that it certainly no matter of stupidity. They know very well how to make an advantageous bargain in their sales and purchases, and discover no little share of ingenuity in making their Saddles, fabricating knives & [blank in MS] out of a broken piece of Iron &c.

They have not that taciturnity common to the more Northern Nations; I have never seen them remain any time in their tents alone with their head between their Knees and not uttering a word; they are social are fond of company and are lonesome when alone. In walking in their camp numbers of small parties of old men are seen smoking and chatting together while the younger ar playing at diverse games or exercising themselves at firing at a mark and [blank in MS]. When a Sauteux or Assiniboine enter a strangers tent they keep down their head, or muffle it so in their Robe or Blanket that it can hardly be seen. These Indians never do it, they ar bold & keep up their head in any place, and say that it is a sign of having bad designs when one is ashamed to show his face. A few Fall Indians [Atsina] tha[t] I saw are the same.

The North West Indians have been generally greatly misrepresented by some Authors, they have not that stu[p. 34]pidity [and] listlessness which is attributed to them, and I am persuaded that a Child taken young from among his parents might be thought [taught] the sciences and would learn them as easily as any other. It is not out of bashfulness that the Sauteux &c hide their face when entering in a strange tent, but they esteem it polite when they begin to smoke or after they have smoked a few pipes that they uncover theyr face but the Costume is more general with the young men than with those of a certain age.

Jealousy seems to be their predominant passion; many do not go hunting without taking their favourite wife with them. The consequence of infidelity to the Mariage bed is often dangerous to the Wife who is often killed or wounded, & some times the paramour likewise, but the most common revange taken by the enraged husband is killing or taking the horses of the wifes Gal[l]ant, besides unmercifully beating her. They sometimes presend their wife to a stranger for the night, but that is very seldom & is always for some interested consideration.

Like all other Indian nations the women do most of the work, but as they are not so wretchedly situated as those nations who live in forests the women do work here that is done by man among the *Cree*, Sauteux &c & yet have less work to do and are more at ease while the men are proportionally idle. When hunting they kill the Cattle and their wives who generally follow them skin the Animal, and dress it while they sit looking by; they do not even saddle their own horses when their wives are present, nor do they take off their shoes or Leggins when they come in, to go to bed. In flitting the women ride & have no loads to carry on their backs as is common among other nations though it is certain that had they no horses, they would be in the same predicament as their less fortunate neighbours—for though the men are fond of their wives & use them well, yet it is not to be supposed they would take a greater share of work than other Indians. The women are indebted solely to their having horses for the ease they enjoy more than their neighbours. They are very fond of their children but seldom or never reprimand them.

They ar much more deacent in their talk and behaviour than most other nations not exposing to public view their private parts as the Big Bellys, Mandans and Assiniboens nor so often talking bawdy as the Crees and Sauteux. A shocking [p. 35] costume they have is when on a long journey without women, they copulate with their mares or young cows, which the[y] catch on purpose. On horseback they pursue bands of Buffaloes, throw a cord around a heifers neck and stop it, fetter its 4 Legs and copulate one after another.[109]

They live upon Buffaloes & Dear, very few of them eat Bears or Beaver flesh, but w[h]en compelled by hunger: they eat no fish. They are most improvident with regard of Provision. It is amazing what number of Buffaloes or other Quadrupeds the[y] destroy—Yet 2 or 3 days after a very successful hunt if [the] beef is gone. When hunting they take but the fattest and cut part of an animal & carve [leave] the remainder; but it is no wonder that in a country abounding so much in Deer of all kind & Buffaloes & where the inhabitants kill it with so much ease to themselves, being always on horseback that their love of good eating should expose them to the danger of a temporary fast. As deer keep generally in the woods it bears but little proportion to the Buffaloes that are killed, excepting Cabri [antelope] a small kind of Deer resembling the Roe which always keeps in the open country.

The hunting matches are regulated by a Band of Young men who have much authority[110] causing them to encamp or flit at their pleasure tell them where there ar Buffaloes & to go hunting, they prevent them from setting one after another and make those that are

---

[109] This entire paragraph was expurgated in the transcription of Burpee's *Journal of Larocque.*

[110] Members of military societies in Plains Indian tribes had police functions for the time the group was on the march.

first ready wait for the others so that they may all go together and have an equal chance. Those that behave refractory to their orders are punished by a beating or their arms are broken or their tents cut to pieces. It is generally an old Chief who conducts their business and he causes his orders to be executed by those young men whom we call soldiers. Every young man enjoys that Dignity in his turn. There are generally 10 or 12 chosen at a time for that purpose, both the conductor and the young men are chosen by the other Chiefs. As long as the conductor is pleased with the post he keeps it, upon his resignation another person is chosen. Their authority does not extend to every thing they only regulate the great hunting matches: [in] the encampments in everything else everyone does as he pleases. They also regulate the medicin feasts. The conductor as he is called never does anything [p. 36] of consequence without consulting the other Chiefs, and it is in consequence of the resolution taken in Council that he harangues and acts. His tent is thrown down the first when the[y] rise the camp, he goes foremost all the way (except a few young men who go far before as scouts) and pitches his tent the first, all the other encamp about him. Previous to their fliting he rides about the Camp, and tells them to throw down their tents, that they are going to such a place & for such and such reason. Some of the soldiers go far ahead and others remain far behind to watch and see if there be no enemies. W[h]en Buffaloes ar seen on the Road and the men a[re] to hunt the[y] cause the people to stop and the old man haranging from one end to the other. W[h]en all are ready the huntsmen set off and the both of the people follow slowly.

When a quarrel happens between two persons they interfer[e] and try to reconcile them by fair mea[n]s (that is when they push their quarrels to[o] far) but I do not know that they ever employed an authoritative one. Generally a present of a horse or gun is made to the offended person, as the means of reconciliation. But there happen few quarrels, and they are generally occasioned by their wives an Jealousy. The young men seldom hunt until they are married, their whole time previous to that epoch being dedicated to dress and parade. A young man rises late in the morning, about midday he begins to dress & has not finished till late in the evening he then mounts on his horse on whom he has spread 2 fais Red and Blue, and in company with his associates he rides about the Camp, with the wing of a Bustard or hawk before his face in lieu of a fan to keep him from the burning sun, at night he dismounts courts the women or goes to the place of rendevory [rendezvous] & at daylight comes in to sleep. The married men dress fine but when the[y] rise the Camp and on certain occasions. To please the females and attract their attention is the motive of the young mens attention to dress. They in their turn [dress] as clear and fine as they can to please the young men. I have seen courtship carried on in much the same manner as we do, whither it is their usual custom of wooing the girls before marriage or not I do not [p. 37] know as I could not get the proper information; but some attention & deference seems to be paid to the young females.

I do not know what they believe as to their origin or their Religious opinions, more than that they believe in Good and bad Spirits, and in a Supreme master of life. A pipe is never smoked without the first whiffs being offered to the rising midday and setting sun, to the earth, to the heavens to these the stem is pointed to the respective place they occupy and a whiff blown to the same quarter, then a few whiffs are blown to diverse spirits which the smoker names and to whom he mutters a few words and then the pipe goes round each person smoking 4 whiffs & no more. The pipe must always [go] to your left hand man, as that is the course that the sun takes. What they call spirits are Quadrupeds or fowls which the[y] think act as guardian Angels to them. They have no notion of spirits in the sense that we it is certain, but the[y] believe that these are invisible beings who have power to do them Ill and Good and to them they make their offerings. One thinks it is the moon that watches over him and another thinks that it is a Bea or Mouse and so on. It is their Dreams that cause them to worship one thin[g] rather than another, but the sun, moon stars, heaven and Earth are of general worship & an Oath on one of them is reckoned inviolable. Ther[e] is not an animal, fowl, reptile, or insect that is not worshiped by some of these Indians who think that the object of his worship can save his life & render him invulnerable, whether it be a [blank in MS] or a mouse. Inanimate things, such as a ball & stone &c are likewise thoug[h]t to be able to do good or hurt.

They have no representation of the thing they worship, as Idols, nor do they pray at any other time but when lighting their pipes. They have great *Medicine* feasts, but this they make only in the fall, and I had no opportunity of seeing them.[111] They are most superstitious with regard to the pipe which is the object of their most sacred regard. Numberless are the ceremonies attended on smoking a pipe of Tobacco. The regulations common to all are these, the pipe and stem must be clean, a coal must be drawn out of the fire to

[111] The Sun Dance is probably being referred to here.

211

light the pipe with care must be taken not to light the pipe in the flames or ashes and none must empty the ashes out of the pipe but he that filled or lighted it. There being but little fire I once lighted the pipe in the Ashes, my Landlord told me a few days after, that his eyes were sore and my lighting the pipe in the Ashes was the occasion therof. Some will not smoke if the pipe has touched grass, another if there ar women in the tent if there are guns. If shoes are seen when smoking, if a part [p. 38] of wearing apparels be thrown over the pipe, if some one blows in the pipe stem to clean it, if the pipe pass over *Assichimous;* some will not allow the stem to pass before the Door, another must empty the ashes on Cow dung brought in on purpose, another again will not smoke unless every smoker be naked and none but smokers are allowed to remain in the tent & to one the pipe must be given the stem foremost, to another the reverse, another will not take it unless You push it to him as hard as you can, to some it must be given quite slowly. In short every man has his particular way of smoking from which it seems he has vowed never to swerve and cause to be attended by those with whom he smokes or he would think himself under the displeasure of that invincible thing (his guardian angel) and incur its resentment, he therefore in such a case does pennance. A pair of Leggins were once thrown over a pipe stem, a person present whose [blank in MS] [vow?] forbade any such doings in his presence had the contents of the stem, which was full of Tobacco juice blown in his mouth & he swallowed it; the potion he took was so disagreable that he was near fainting but he attributed his weakness to the anger of the Deity that had been offended. Some who are to[o] ceremonious in their smoking do not smoke but with their intimates, and those that are well acquainted with their mummery; those that are less so take care to sit next to a man that known in what manner the pipe is to be given to them. The women never smoke. Before the smokers begin, he that has some peculiarity in his way of smoking tells in what manner it is, and every one attends to [it].

Their Doctors perform their care by the application of simples with very few of which they are acquainted and by blowing on the afflicted part, smoking and singing, they likewise burn the leaves of Fir trees or some coals, the physician spreads his hand over the wound as close as possible without touching it. Internally they have purging Roots which the[y] take, and prepare some other, but as no one was sik while I was with them I had no opportunity of seeing them perform any cure of consequence. They appear to be a healthy people.

They have no other tame animals but Dogs and horses, few of the former but many of the latter, whom the[y] use on all occasions, for war and for hunting, they have them in trade from the flathead Indians in great numbers and very cheap. They sell part to the Big Bellys and [p. 39] Mandans at duble the price they purchase them and carry on a continual trade in that manner. They had as yet given no Guns or Amunition to the Flathead Indians in exchange of horses, but this year as they have plenty they intend giving them some.[112] He is reckoned a poor man that has not 10 horses in the spring before the trade at the Missouri takes place, and many have 30 or 40. Everybody rides, Men, Women & Children. The females ride astride as the men do. A Child that is too young to keep his saddle is tied to it, and a small whip is tied to his wrist—he whips away and gallops or trots the whole day if occasion requires. Their saddles are so made as to prevent falling either backwards or forwards, the hind part reaching as high as between the shoulders, and the fore part to the breast. The woman[s] saddles ar more especially so. Those of the men are not quite so high, and many use saddles such as the Canadians make in the N:W Country.

They are excellent riders, being trained to it from their infancy. In war or hunting if they mean to exert their horses to the utmost the[y] ride without a saddle. In their whealings and evolutions they often are not seen, having only a leg on the horse back and clasping the horse with their arms round his neck, on the side opposite to where the ennemy is. Most of their horses can be guided to any place without bridle, only be leaning to one side or the other they turn immediately to the side on which you lean, and will not bear turning until you resume a direct posture. They are very fond of their horses and take good care of them; as soon as a horse has a sore back he is not used until he is healed: no price will induce a man to part with a favourite horse on whom he places confidence for security either in attack or flight.

They say that no equal number of other Indians can beat them on horseback, but that on foot they are not capable to cope with those nations who have no horses. They pass for brave and courageous among their neighbours: they seldom go to war, or to steal horses but defend themselves with courage when attacked. They keep an

---

[112] The Salishan-speaking Flatheads, living in the Rocky Mountain area west of the Crows, traded with the latter in an exchange network described by John C. Ewers ("The Indian Trade of the Upper Missouri before Lewis and Clark: An Interpretation," *Missouri Historical Society Bulletin* 10 [July, 1954]: 429–46).

excellent lookout and have always Young men night and day at 2 or 3 miles from the camp upon the watch, besides they often send parties of young men on a two or three days scout on the road they intend to take. Any person of any nation going to their camp will be well treated and received, but when coming at night or seen skulking about need not expect mercy; they cut and hash to pieces their enemies slain in battle, but do not eat them. The young men and Children such the blood [p. 40] and play with the Carcass, but I have not seen any Chief or respectable person meddle with the dead bodies. On the day they have got a scalp & the two ensuing ones they dance in the evenings. Their scalp dance is as follows, as I saw them dancing it when they killed two Assiniboines. 17 Young men, their faces painted black and dressed as fine as possible stood in a demicircle singing and beating time with Drums & Shrishi-quois or Rattles; before them 30 young women dressed in the war habilements of the men & carrying their weapons, their faces black, danced to the music of the Young men, 2 of them carried the scalps tied to the *Endosa Pole* they danced in a circle & while dancing the[y] advanced slowly towards the Center, making the ring smaller, they then returned to their former station and began again; and shaking their heads always in unison with the Music. There were soldiers standing outside of the Ring to prevent the people from thronging too much on the Dancers. About the middle of the Ceremony one of the Chiefs took hold of the bridle of a horse on which rode a young man plainly dressed & led him in the middle of the Dancers haranguing at the same time, the young man had killed one of the *Assiniboines*. The Chief then led him out, and they danced again, the other person that killed the 2d Assiniboine was led in the Circle in the same manner by another Chief and a little after the dance finished. At night a band of Young men walked about the Camp singing they stopped at the door of every Chief, and sang songs in which were rehersed the exploits of the Chief at whose door the[y] were. These ceremonies continued 3 days. In the day time the Scalps were tied to the bridle of horses on which Young men rode singing & beating the Drums.

Their arms are Bows and arrows, lances & guns. When they go to war they take their medicin bags at least the Chief of the party does, when they have found out their enemies, & and on the point of beginning the attack the bag of medicin is opened they sing a few airs but very shortly smoke and then attack. It is generally at the break of day that they fall upon their enemies when they they are fast locked in the Arms of sleep. One of the Chiefs has part of a magic lanthorn [lantern] on which he reckons as upon his chief support. The figures that are painted on the glass he thinks ar spirits & that they assist him; he never leaves them behind when he goes to war.

They are excellent marksmen with the Bow and arrow, but poor shots with the gun, but they practice dayly as of late years they have more ammunition than usual.

They have never had any traders with them, the[y] get their kettles guns, ammunitions &c from the Mandans & Big Bellys' in exchange for horses, Robes, Leggins & shirts, they likewise purchase Corn Pumpkins & tobacco from the B: Bellys' as they do not cultivate the ground themselves.

[p. 41] Their Dress for men and women

The men weare tight Leggins made of the skin of Cabri or other small deer reaching up to the hips and the end tacked in a belt or girdle, the seam is ornamented with beads, porcupine quills, horse and human hair died with divers colours.

Their shirts are made of the same kind of skin and are composed of 3 skins, 2 making the body and one the sleeves. The skins are joint together on the shou[l]der only & the sleeves also which are left open under the pit of the arm; The neck of one of the skins hangs on the breast and the other behind. They are guarnished on the sleeves with the same materials as the leggins, and their shoes are likewise decorated in the same manner and are made in the manner of mittens having a seam round the outside of the foot only without *pleats.* Over this part of the dress they wear a Buffaloe Robe on which is painted their war exploits, or garnished with beads and porcupine quills ove[r] the seam. *A slip* of Wolf or Skunk skin is generally worn round the ancle and is left to drag behind as they walk, bits of red cloth are sewed to it. The skin of the Bears foot with the claws the[y] w[e]ar on the breasts with as many buttons as they can find sewed to it 12 or 15 Bear Claws threaded and tied round their neck is also very fashionable. Over their forehead suspended from their hair are two skins of coloured Beads, with a few *hawk Bells* or buttons a little horse hair stained yellow which dangles on each side [of] their nose on their head they wear a *killion* feather be[l]ts of brass and Tin. None of them are [blank in MS] those who have long hair gum them into 10 or 12 flat [blank in MS] plaistered over with white earth, except the end which is well combed. Those whose hair is not long enough lengthen them with horsehair, which they gum to their own and divide in the same

215

manner a[s] the other. I saw one that had two large white horsetails gummed to his hair, that was as black as sloe, when he walked the hair dragged 2 feet behind him on the ground; they are fond of long hair.

The womens dress consists in a pair of leggins reaching to the middle of the thigh & tied with a garter below the knee, they wear no hair in their ornaments, but the seams of their leggins are covered with blue beads (which is the kind they are the most fond of) and buttons when they can have them. Their Leggins are round like stockings and have no fringes as the men's their shift or Cottillon reaches midleg and lower and are made of Elk skin, but the finer [p. 42] ones are mad[e] of two large Cabri or Mountain Ram skins, like the man's shirts, the bottom or lower part is cut out into fringes and garnished with Porcupine. The skins are joined below as high as the Ribs where an aperture is left on each side to suckle their Children. The sleeves are joined to the body of the shift on the shoulders only and encircle the arm from the Elbow to the wrist, the upper part of the arm beeing covered only outside, but part of the leather is left to flap down so as to hide the pit of the arm.

Their Robes and shoes are likewise garnished, but the former are never painted, they wear no ornament on their head [but] paint their faces red. The children of both sexes are dressed in the same manner as the Sex they belong to the boys go naked till they are 8 or 10 years of age not for want of Clothes, but to be more at their ease, but the Girls never. Both sexes are very cleanly, washing and bathing every morning in the River, and in the winter in the snow; they keep their clothes always clean, and as white as snow, with a kind of white earth resembling chalk, with which they dayly clean their Cloths. This earth has not only the property of Whitening but also clears leather & cloth of spots of grease and other dirt; it is an article they are never without. A woman never sets the kettle on the fire in the morning without first washing her hands: and the men do not eat without the same precaution.

They seldom wear breech cloths, except when they do not put on their leggins, as their leggins ar so made that if they had a waist band they might be called trowsers. They wear shells and Beads in their ears, but they do not cut them as the Sauteux and Siouxs.

One of them had the tail of a Spanish Cow in his medicin Bag, and when he intended to dress fine or went to war he would put it on his head.

They cut their hair and scarify their limbs at the death of their

216

Relations. They are very fond of small blue glass beads that they get from the Spaniards but by the second and third han[d].

NB. The low waters are Generally in September.

[p. 43] Their language is evidently a corruption of the Sioux's as is the Mandane & Big Belly's to which last it bears much affinity,[113] and resembles it in the same degree as the Kinintinaux does the Algonquin or Chipeway viz.

	Big Belly's	Rocky Mountain
One	Nowaza	Ama té
two	Nomba	Nomba
three	Nomini	Namini
Four	Tobas	Shobas
Five	kichon	Kichons
Six	Akaw was	Akaw
Seven	Shapois	Sápois
Eight	Noobassé	Noobassé
nine	Noobetzapé	Amatapé
Ten	Pirakau	Pirakau
100	Pirakau tié	Piraké sash
20	Noom bau Pirakas	the same
	&c	&c
large	Eties	se
small	Carishta	Casota
head	Auto	Austio
River	Amjé	Amjé
knife	Matsé	Mitsé
Man	Matray	the same
Woman	Meay	Meay
My Child (male)	Matisay Eshié	Matsay sa
Robe or	Ituwjé	I saw jé

They make very expressive signs with their hands to the person that does not understand theyr language, they often told me long stories without hardly opening their lips & I understood very well.

[113] The Crow and Hidatsa languages, or dialects, are closely related. Mandan and the various Dakota Sioux languages are mutually unintelligible and more distantly related to Crow and Hidatsa, although all four languages are classified as Siouan.

They represent a Sioux by passing the edge of their hand across their neck, a Panis [Arikara] by showing large Ears, a Flathead by pressing with both hands on each side [of] their head &c.

All the Animals in their country are the following.

Buffaloes	Fallo Deer or	Kitts
Bears	Chevreuil	a few Foxes
Beavers	of both kinds	a kind of Tiger
a few Otters	viz. White	(which I suppose
Elk Deer	Bektails.	is the Pant[h]er
Cabri	vid: (a) on the	like that of the
Large horned animal	following page	Allegany mountains)

[p. 44] (a) T[h]is is a kind of small animal [prairie dog] who lives in holes in the ground like Badgers, but assemble in very large band[s] and make a kind of village. Upon any disturbance they issue out of their [holes] and bark at what disturbes them with a great deal of virulence. It is hard to get a shot at them as they stand upon the borders of their holes and jump in upon the l[e]ast motion. When killed they fall in their holes from whence it is difficult to get them out. Captain Lewis caught one by filling its hole with water & as it always rose above the water upon its appearance It was caught hold of, and kept all winter in a cage at their fort on the Missuri.[114] It fed on flesh & Roots, they are of the size of a Muskrat and of a Greyish colour. Numbres of their villages are to be seen about the Missuri & some ar 3 or four acres in circumference.

Of fowls along the River Roches Jaunes I saw a flock of birds like the *Grow[s]e*, much larger, having a broad [tail] which is spread when flying.[115] I could not shoot any of them they were lying on the ground amon[g] herbs and I never saw them until they were gone and flying; the whole flock did not rise upon the flight of one, but each went of as it was disturbed In the same manner as the Groners, or as we call them her Phesants.

The Flatheads inhabite the Western side of the Rocky Mountains

---

[114]This event is described by Lewis and Clark (*Original Journals,* vol. 1, pp. 141–42.) One of these animals was dispatched to President Jefferson from Fort Mandan in April, 1805 (Donald Jackson, comp., *Letters of the Lewis and Clark Expedition, with Related Documents, 1783-1854,* p. 236).

[115] Probably the sage grouse, *Centrocercus urophasianus.*

at the heads of Rivers that have a S. Western Course & flow in the Western Ocean. The Ridge of Mountains that parts those waters with the Missouri can be crossed in two days, and no more Mountains ar found to the Ocean. They come every fall to the fort of the Missouri or thereabouts to kill Buffaloes of which there are none across that range of Mountains, dress Robes, dry meat with which the[y] return as soon as the winter sets in. They have deers of different kinds on their lands & beaver with which they make themselves Robes, but they prefer Buffaloes. They have a great number of horses which they sell for a trifle and give many for nothing. They say there is white people who inhabit the lower parts of the River upon whose heads they dwell from whom the[y] get glass beads and a kind of small cylindrical stick like wampoon.[116] Those people they say carry on no fur trade, what Beaver these Indians kill are singed & the skin eat with the flesh. They spear both fish and Beaver with Darts made of Deers horns; they have [live] part of the year upon fish, which by the description they give of it I think is Salmon.

Whenever the[y] get a brass kettle from their neighbours the[y] do not use it for culinary purposes, but cut it into small pieces with which they ornament and decorate their garments [p. 45] and their hair. Elk teeth are likewise very orna[men]tal amongst them and they will give a horse for 70 or 80 of them. They trade chiefly with the Ererokas [Crows], and give horses & horn bows for such articles as the Ererokas get from us, the Mandans and Big Bellys. The arrows they make use of in war are poisenous and as much smaller than those they make use of in hunting. They generally fight on horseback & have 2 Bows & 2 quivers full of arrows, with which they defend themselves and greatly annoy their Enemies even in flying. They are expert horsemen. They represent their country as so very good that what fruit trees grow here as shrubs are there tall trees. They generally speak very low, their language is difficult to be learned, none of the surrounding nations speaking it, it resembles the sound made by a number of small bits of glass shaken together. Their bows are almost all made [of] the horns of different kinds of deers and of one piece. They never saw a Moose dear.

The Snakes [Shoshonis] dwell East of the Flatheads upon the same range of mountains and on the head of Rivers that have like-

---

[116]The shells of *Dentalium,* a tusk-shaped marine shell which reached them through intertribal trade from the Northwest Coast.

wise a southerly course.[117] They say there is much Beaver on their lands and that they partly dress with it they are all on good terms with the Rocky Mountains [Indians] with whom they carry on such a trade as the Flatheads. This nation is very numerous & each tribe has different names. The more southern tribes have dealings with the white[s] of New Mexico from whom they get thick striped *Blankets,* Bridles & Battle axes in exchange for Buffaloe robes and Deer skins, but it is probable that this Trade of the Snakes is carried on at a second or thir[d] hand and that they themselves have no direct trade with the Spaniard[s].

One of their tribes has been destroyed and the remainder being about 12 tents live with the Rocky Mountain Indians, who are at peace with the whole nation & from whom they get in trade a kind [of] sweet intoxicating herb, which they smoke as Tobacco. Their pipes are made of a transparent stone. They have horn bows & horses which they give in exchange of Knives, Tobacco, &c. This nation as well as the Flatheads trade as yet no guns from the Ererokas but this year the Ererokas intend selling them a few as they have many.

From the following few words of their language [it] can easily be observed that they must be of a quite different origins of the Big Bellys and Rocky Mountain Indians. [p. 46]

One — shemits	Far — Mawna low
Two — Wawk	near — Mish tits
Three — Pa its	good — tsanti
Four — Waw tsouts	Bad — tish tsent
Five — waw ni kith	I love you — Makaw makun
Six — waw watch	come — keman
Seven — tawt souts	go — Mean
Eight — Na waw tsouts	Run — kech tan
Nine — sheman doun	they call Sho Shone
Ten — Toshamb	themselves that Tribe
11 — shemits shemandou	that I saw at
12 — wawk o mandou	the Rocki Mountains
13 — Part o mandou	
20 — warok on torhamb	

[117] See n. 39, above.

Charles McKenzie's Narratives

As a young clerk in the employ of the North West Company, Charles McKenzie participated in four trading expeditions to the Hidatsa and Mandan villages on the Missouri River between the years 1804 and 1806. His accounts of these trips provide one of the earliest first-hand descriptions of the life of these village peoples. Accounts of earlier visits to the Mandans and Hidatsas, with the exception of David Thompson's memoir, which was written many years after the fact and based to a large extent on memory, contain little ethnographic information of this kind. Because McKenzie's narrative was in existence decades before Thompson's memoir, although not in published form, McKenzie deserves recognition as one of the earliest ethnographers of the Hidatsas.

McKenzie's accounts provide a valuable cross-reference with other first-hand accounts left by men who either participated in the same trading expeditions or who visited the villages at the same time as McKenzie. McKenzie's first two trips to the Missouri were in parties headed by F.-A. Larocque, whose journals of these expeditions are published earlier in this book. During his fourth and last visit to the villages, in 1806, McKenzie met two North West Company partners, Charles Chaboillez and Alexander Henry (the Younger), who had come to the Missouri River to obtain horses for themselves and generally to see the country. Henry has left a lengthy account of his visit which was edited by Elliott Coues and published in 1897.[1] While at the villages, McKenzie met and interacted with the famous American explorers Meriwether Lewis and William Clark as well as employees of the Hudson's Bay Company sent to the villages for the same reason as McKenzie— to conduct trade with the natives. The information left to us by McKenzie, Henry, Larocque, Lewis and Clark and other members of their exploring party, and the masters of the Hudson's Bay Company's Brandon House provide a large, tightly cross-referenced body of ethnohistorical documentation on the Mandan and Hidatsa. This mass of eyewitness testimony is unrivaled until

[1]Alexander Henry [the Younger], *New Light on the Early History of the Greater Northwest*, ed. Elliott Coues, vol. 1, pp. 285–416.

the 1830s, when men such as Prince Maximilian, George Catlin, and Francis Chardon produced voluminous written descriptions of Mandan and Hidatsa life for the period immediately before and during the devastating smallpox epidemic of 1837–38.

Relatively little is known of McKenzie's life.[2] He was born in Scotland in 1774. It is not known when he emigrated to Canada, but he was first employed by the North West Company in 1803 as a clerk. His early years in the company were spent in the Red River Department, from which he was transferred in 1807 to the region between Rainy Lake and Albany Factory in what is

now central Ontario. He was absorbed into the Hudson's Bay Company as a result of its 1821 merger with the North West Company and remained one of the Honorable Company's servants until his retirement in 1854. McKenzie seems never to have advanced above the position of clerk in either the North West Company or the Hudson's Bay Company. George Simpson, governor of the Hudson's Bay Company's Northern Department, recorded the following unflattering description of McKenzie in his 1832 "Character Book":

No. 53 McKenzie Charles. A Scotchman about 56 years of Age. 29 Years in the Service. A queer prosing long Winded little highland body, who traces his lineage back to Ossian and claims the Laureatship of Albany District now that Chief Factor Kennedy is gone. Never was a bright active or useful man even when there was a greater Dearth of Talent in the country than now, but fancies himself neglected in being still left on the list of Clerks notwithstanding a Servitude of nearly 30 years: his Day is gone by, and I think it would be highly inexpedient to promote such men who have no other claim to advancement than their antiquity. Stationed in Albany District.[3]

McKenzie died on March 3, 1855, at the Red River Settlement, leaving an Indian wife, three daughters, and a son, Hector Aeneas, who also worked in the fur trade for the Hudson's Bay Company.

McKenzie wrote a separate account of each of his four Missouri

[2] Summaries of his life are presented in L. R. Masson, ed., *Les Bourgeois de la Compagnie du Nord-Ouest: Recits de voyages, lettres et rapports inedits relatifs au Nord-Ouest Canadien*, vol. 1, pp. 317–21; W. Stewart Wallace, comp., *The Macmillan Dictionary of Canadian Biography*, p. 466; and Henry, *New Light*, vol. 1, pp. 345–46 n. 59. A few details may also be gleaned from four letters written from Charles McKenzie to Roderick McKenzie which are now in the holdings of the Public Archives of Canada (Manuscript Group 19, C1, vol. 33). Three of these letters, written between 1809 and 1842, specifically concern the narratives of his Missouri River expeditions; transcriptions can be found in Charles McKenzie, "Charles McKenzie's Narratives of the 'Mississouri Indians': A New Transcription," ed. Thomas D. Thiessen, pp. 210–25. Correspondence written by members of Charles McKenzie's family during the period 1828 to 1888 also exists in the Public Archives of Canada (Manuscript Group 19, A44) but has not been found useful for the present study. The letter from Charles to Roderick reproduced in this chapter is not part of either of these collections of correspondence but exists only as part of the Narrative C manuscript; it was published by Masson (*Les Bourgeois*, vol. 1, p. 325).

[3] Glyndwr Williams, *Hudson's Bay Miscellany, 1670–1870*, Hudson's Bay Record Society Publications, vol. 30, p. 218.

River expeditions, plus a supplement to the account of the second expedition. These accounts differ from most other contemporary records of visits to the Mandan-Hidatsa villages in that they were written as a reminiscent memoir several years after the events they describe, although it is likely that McKenzie relied on his personal journals, now lost, when he wrote the narratives. Most of the other accounts, in contrast, are in the form of daily journals written by their authors as events unfolded. A notable exception to this is David Thompson's memoir, which was written many years after his 1797–98 visit to the villages, in Thompson's old age.[4] Thompson's memoir, drawn largely from memory with the aid of his journals, contains considerable ethnographic information on the Mandans and Hidatsas that is not recorded in Thompson's journal.

McKenzie's accounts were apparently written about 1809–10 and transmitted in at least two installments to Roderick McKenzie,[5] as attested by surviving correspondence from Charles to Roderick. Roderick had planned to publish a number of first-hand accounts of the North West Company's fur trade and the native peoples with whom the company traded but failed to do so before his death in 1844. Subsequently, most of the material he collected, including Charles McKenzie's narratives, was edited by L. R. Masson and published in 1889 and 1890.[6]

The original documents on which Masson's published version is based consist of four separate handwritten manuscripts in the Department of Rare Books and Special Collections, McLennan Library, McGill University, Montreal. These documents are written in four different hands, and they differ considerably from each other in content and coverage of the various expeditions. Three of these manuscripts, transcribed in their entirety by Thiessen,[7] have been designated Narratives A, B, and C for convenience of reference. Table 6 in the Appendix shows the extent to which these four documents relate to each of McKenzie's expedition accounts and the supplement to the second expedition as well as to several other contemporary sources.

One of these four documents, bearing catalog number CH 19.S55, is virtually identical to the published version and may be a copy produced for the use of the printer. Because it closely resembles the published version in spelling, organization, omissions, and footnotes and bears editorial notations in Masson's

---

[4] David Thompson, *David Thompson's Narrative of His Explorations in Western America, 1784-1812,* Publications of the Champlain Society, vol. 12, ed. J. B. Tyrrell. Thompson's journal entries relating to his 1797–98 visit to the Mandan-Hidatsa villages are to be found *verbatim* in David Thompson's Journal in this volume.

[5] Roderick McKenzie, a cousin of the famous trader-explorer Sir Alexander Mackenzie, joined the North West Company in 1785 and eventually became one of the company's partners. He retired from the trade in 1801. Neither Roderick nor Alexander is known to be related to Charles (Wallace, *Canadian Biography,* p. 468).

[6] Masson, *Les Bourgeois,* vol. 1, pp. 315–93.

[7] McKenzie, "Charles McKenzie's Narratives."

hand such as "Ready for Print," it will not be further considered in this chapter.

Narrative A (catalog number CH 20.S56) is written in an unknown hand in brown ink on wove paper measuring 20.2 cm by 24.6 cm.[8] It consists of twenty-four unbound folded leaves of four pages each. The leaves have been numbered by hand in brown ink in the upper-left corner of the first page in several series as follows: second expedition, 1 to 7; the supplement to the second expedition, 1 to 5; the third expedition, 1 to 5; and the fourth expedition, 1 to 7. The account of the first expedition is missing or perhaps was never included as part of this manuscript. The upper-left corner of the second and fourth pages of each leaf bears a four-digit number stamped in blue ink in the series 2056 to 2100, inclusive. Text appears only on the first and third pages of each folded leaf, and is written in a very indistinct hand which is difficult to read. The narrative has been heavily emended in the same hand and contains numerous "false starts," deletions, and interlineations.

Narrative B (catalog number CH 24.S60), an account of only the fourth expedition, is written in brown ink on laid paper measuring 20.2 cm by 32.0 cm.[9] There are 35 pages of text, which are paginated sequentially in black pencil; this pagination has been retained in the transcription that follows in this chapter. Pages 2–32 are folded and bound with thread as one signature, while pages 33–35 comprise a separate folded leaf of four pages. The last page of this leaf (which would be page 36 if numbered) bears the following notation in brown ink in a hand different from that in which the text is written: "Chs McKenzie — original 4 Expedt — Missouri." Also written here in black pencil, possibly in Masson's hand, are the notations "Letter d Chs McKenzie" and "Printed." The paper in the large signature bears a watermark consisting of a crown surmounting an oval, double-lined cartouche enclosing a seated Britannia figure.[10] The countermark is the date 1809. The smaller signature bears a similar but not identical watermark and a countermark consisting of a cypher above the date 1808. The handwriting is clearer than that of Narrative A but is not as easy to read as that of Narrative C. It is a distinctive handwriting, easily distinguishable as that of Charles McKenzie by comparison with letters known to be in his hand.[11] The lowercase *e* is formed in a particularly distinctive way in the original manuscript, and often occurs as an extraneous terminal letter on words. In *ei* or *ie* combinations, the letter *i* is frequently undotted and the *e* closed, making it difficult to distinguish between the two forms. In such cases the transcribed spelling

---

[8] John Carter, *ABC for Book Collectors*, p. 210.

[9] Ibid., pp. 125–26.

[10] The watermark is generally similar to watermarks 203–24 illustrated in Edward Heawood, *Watermarks Mainly of the 17th and 18th Centuries*, Monuments Chartae Papyraceae Historia Illustrantia 1.

[11] Comparison was made with four letters written between the years 1809 and 1842 (Public Archives of Canada, Manuscript Group 19, C1, vol. 33).

has been rendered in accordance with proper modern spelling.

Narrative C, cataloged as CH 21.S57, comprises accounts of all four trading expeditions as well as the supplement to the second expedition. The document is written in an unknown hand on wove paper measuring 18.8 cm by 23.3 cm. It consists of forty-eight folded leaves of four pages each plus one sheet of two pages (181 and 182) torn from a leaf and one fragmentary sheet (pages 185 and 186) of the same width as the leaves but of indeterminable length. The upper corner of each sheet bears an embossed heraldic device and the legend "London Superfine." Sixteen horizontal alignment guide lines have been lightly penciled on each page. There is continuous pagination penciled in black on each page beginning with the first page of the second leaf, except for pages 183 and 184, which are missing. Several pages of the original manuscript were paginated but otherwise blank. Each leaf except the first is also numbered in the upper left corner of the first page in brown or blue ink, as follows: the letter to Roderick McKenzie through the end of the first expedition, 1 to 11; the second expedition, 1 to 10; the supplement to the second expedition, 1 to 7; the third expedition, 1 to 7; and the fourth expedition, 1 to 10. In addition, the upper left corner of pages two and four of each leaf bears a four-digit number stamped in blue ink in the series 1969 to 2054, inclusive. Numbers of this series are not found on the first two leaves (the first page of the first leaf bears the number 2355). The narra-

tive was formerly bound through two holes near the left edge, about 3.5 cm apart. The narrative is written in both brown and blue ink in a very clear, but unidentified, hand. It has been emended in both of these colors of ink as well as in black pencil; these emendations appear to be in the writer's hand. There are marginal notations in French on pages 78 and 89 which are probably in Masson's hand; they are clearly of an editorial nature and concern changes in the organization of the narrative. Pages 183 and 184 are missing and appear to have been replaced by pages 185 and 186 (the last page, 186, is blank). The text on page 182 is written in blue ink, but the last line ("At this conclusion the Parties whirled") has been deleted in brown ink and the word "end" has been added to the bottom of the page and lined out, both in brown ink. Page 185 is written entirely in brown ink; it appears to be a hastily written copy, possibly in another hand.

Transcriptions of Narratives A, B, and C were made from 35-mm positive-image, roll microfilm copies obtained from McGill University and subsequently verified by comparison with the original documents during a visit to Montreal in June, 1979. These three documents are written in different hands, and they differ from one another and the published version both in the expeditions that they relate and the information that they provide about common incidents and observations. Nevertheless, Narratives A, B, and C together comprise a collection of lengthy documents containing much redundant information. Consequently, it was necessary to select only a portion of the available material for republication in this volume in order to avoid repetition and thereby reduce the volume of the material. Narrative C, written in an unknown hand, is the most complete of the three documents and describes all four expeditions and the supplement to the second. In contrast, Narrative B contains only the fourth expedition account, while Narrative A lacks the first expedition account. Because of its completeness, and because it differs primarily in minor ways from Narrative A, which is less complete, Narrative C was selected for this chapter, except for its description of the fourth expedition. We have chosen to replace the fourth expedition account of Narrative C with the Narrative B account of the same expedition for three reasons. First, Narrative B is the only one of the three manuscripts that is actually written in Charles McKenzie's hand, as determined by comparison with correspondence written by McKenzie. Second, it is also substantially different in content from the published version and from the fourth expedition accounts in Narratives A and C. In editing for publication, Masson omitted a great deal of information—found only in this narrative—concerning horse trading at the villages and McKenzie's critical view of Henry's behavior at the villages. Third, the literary quality of Narrative B is better than that of the other two manuscript narratives or the published version.

The transcriptions that follow in this chapter are as faithful to the original handwritten documents as possible in spelling, punctuation, and paragraph separation. However, many of these matters are ambiguously rendered in the original documents, and it probably has not been possible to follow the author's original intention in all instances. Information contained in Narrative A and the portion of Narrative C relating the fourth expedition account which significantly complements the information reproduced in the transcriptions in this chapter has been inserted in brackets or as indented paragraphs where appropriate. Minor differences between the narratives, such as alternative wording or sentence structure, have been ignored for the sake of the continuity of the narrative unless they contribute information useful to the reader's understanding. When information is inserted from the unpublished Narrative A and the fourth expedition account of Narrative C, the intrusions are identified, along with page references for the original document in which the information appears.

The original pagination used in Narrative C is explained above, but an arbitrary system of pagination has been adopted by the editors for Narrative A and requires further explanation. As mentioned above, each expedition account in Narrative A comprises from five to seven four-page folded leaves. There are two pages of text to each leaf; herein they are designated with the number of the leaf (as written by hand on the original documents) followed by "a" or "b" to designate the first or second text pages of the leaf, respectively. For example, a reference to "Narrative A, p. 4b" in a bracketed insertion in the third expedition account of Narrative C means that the intruded information is taken from the second page of text in the fourth leaf comprising the series of leaves describing the third expedition account in Narrative A.

The facts that only an account of the fourth expedition is in Charles McKenzie's handwriting and that neither of the narratives describing the other expeditions or the supplement to the second is actually in his hand suggest that not all of the installments originally prepared by Charles for submission to Roderick McKenzie have survived. Consequently, it is not possible to determine the precise nature or extent of editorial changes that Masson may have made to McKenzie's original manuscripts. Comparison of the published version with the only surviving manuscript in McKenzie's hand, the fourth expedition account in Narrative B, suggests that such editorial changes were considerable.

Who, then, wrote the other documents labeled as Narratives A and C? These narratives are written in different hands, both presently unidentified. Neither is in Masson's hand. One of them may possibly be in the handwriting of Roderick McKenzie, but we have not been successful in locating known examples of Roderick's handwriting for comparison. Perhaps one of the hands is that of the "Mr Haldane" (probably John Haldane)[12] mentioned in

Charles McKenzie's 1809 and 1810 letters who conceivably could have written one of the narratives at Charles' dictation. This possibility is remote, however, in view of the fact that both Narratives A and C contain an account of the fourth expedition, which is also described in Narrative B, known to be in McKenzie's hand. It is unlikely that Charles would have composed two different versions of the same expedition and submitted both to Roderick. The most likely possibility, in our opinion, is that both hands are those of later copyists and that the original documents have been lost except for Narrative B, which must have comprised at least part of one of the installments originally sent to Roderick McKenzie.

In conclusion, the remainder of this chapter consists of Charles McKenzie's accounts of his first, second, third, and fourth expeditions to the Missouri River as well as the supplement to the second expedition. The first, second, and third expedition accounts and the supplement to the second are taken from Narrative C, which is in an unknown hand and probably does not represent Charles' original composition on these subjects, which is now lost. Narrative B, a manuscript written in McKenzie's hand, is reproduced in its entirety

---

[12] John Haldane was a partner of the North West Company from 1804 to 1821. After 1821 he became Chief Factor for the Hudson's Bay Company's Columbia District, and he retired from the fur trade in 1827. He died in 1857 (Wallace, *Canadian Biography*, p. 291). It is clear from McKenzie's 1809 and 1810 letters in the Public Archives of Canada (Manuscript Group 19, C1, vol. 33), as well as from the letter prefacing this narrative, that Haldane encouraged McKenzie to set down his Missouri River experiences on paper.

as the fourth expedition account. In view of the importance of McKenzie's eyewitness testimony about the Mandan and Hidatsa Indians, and in light of the uncertain circum- stances surrounding most of the McKenzie narratives and who wrote or edited them, it is most unfortu- nate that Charles McKenzie's original journals are not known to exist.

[p. 1]

Some account
of the Mississouri Indians
in the years 1804, 5, 6, & 7

By Charles Mackenzie

[p. 5]

Nipigon, Spring 1809

Roderic Mackenzie Esqr.
    Sir,
        I promised at *Camanistiquia*[13] to send you an account of the *Missouri Indians*. This I delayed from time to time until my friend Mr. Haldane[14] induced me to select from my Journal the *Extracts* which will be handed to you by him with this letter. I wish these Extracts were better and more deserving of your acceptance. I am sensible that their greatest merit consists in their veracity; for I was an Eye witness to most of the scenes which they expose. If the present specimen will please, [p. 6] I shall take delight in transcribing more passages for your perusal. Two motives encourage this desire. One is, that I almost despair of ever having it in my power to testify sufficiently that grateful sense which I shall always entertain of your uniform kindness towards me: the other is—that by reading these simple observations, you will be more able to judge

---

[13] The field headquarters of the North West Company on Lake Superior near modern Thunder Bay, Ontario; also known historically as Fort William. Rendez-vous were held there each summer and were attended by clerks and wintering partners from the interior.

[14] See n. 12, above.

whether my Services comparing them to those of others, in my line, Should not have recommended me to more attention in the Scale of promotion than I have hitherto experienced.

I have, Sir, the honor to be,
Your very humble Servant
(Signed) Charles Mackenzie

[p. 7]

First Expedition to the Mississouri

In the fall of 1804 Mr. Charles Chaboillez,[15] one of the Partners of the North West Company, then acting in the Department of the *Assiniboine River*, having agreed with his opponents in Trade that neither party should make any Outpost exceeding those already established found himself with more men and goods than were necessary in that Quarter. He therefore thought it expedient to send the overplus to the Mandane [p. 8] Country, which was beyond the limits of his agreement;— he hired for that purpose a Free man of the name of *La France*— being the only Frenchman who was acquainted with the *route*— and having been a Mississouri Trader for several years, procured to him on the present occasion the treble appointments of Guide, Clerk, and Interpreter; though I must own that he was very unequal to the discharge of either of these duties— Matters being thus settled, we watched an opportunity to steal ourselves away from our opponents on account of the trade— and from the Assiniboines on account of their enmity to the Indians of the Mississouri— At length [p. 9] finding a fair opening we took our departure.

Our party consisted of Mr. La Roque, Mr. La France, four Voyageurs and myself.[16] Four horses carried our assortment for trade,

---

[15] Two men named Chaboillez, father and son, were active in the fur trade along the Red and Assiniboine rivers at this time. Coues (in Henry, *New Light*, vol. 1, pp. 60–61 n. 61) states that the father, Charles Jean Baptiste Chaboillez, had charge of the Assiniboine River department from Montagne à la Bosse during the winter of 1804–1805, when Charles McKenzie made the journey that is about to be described. The son, Charles junior, became a partner of the North West Company in 1799 and was active in the Red River and Assiniboine River area before 1807. It was the younger Chaboillez who in 1806 visited the Mandan-Hidatsa villages, in company with Alexander Henry, where the two partners found Charles McKenzie during the fourth trading expedition described in this chapter (Henry, *New Light*, vol. 1, pp. 60–61 n. 61; Wallace, *Canadian Biography*, pp. 126–27).

[16] Larocque's journal for this trip ("Missouri Journal") identifies, in addition to the guide, J. Baptiste Lafrance, the four voyageurs as William Morrison, Joseph

and twice as many were assigned to carry ourselves— the whole in charge of Mr. La Roque, a deserving young Gentleman. As for myself, happening to be newly arrived in the Indian Country, I was placed as an assistant to Mr. La France, for he did not know how to write. We proceeded, but to avoid the natives we were obliged to lengthen our journey by taking a circuitous *route*, which conducted us through many extensive plains; most of which were in flames, as is generally the case at this season of the year.

In the course of a few days we [p. 10] observed whole herds of Buffaloes with their hair singed— some were blind; and half roasted carcasses strewed our way. We suffered great inconvenience through the scarcity of wood and water; and our horses were as badly off for water and food as we were— In this manner we smoothly jogged on until we came to the *Dog Lodge*,[17] a remarkable place which the Sioux warriors often frequent in their hostile excursions— after crossing this chain of Mountains, all of a sudden we heard the signal cry of Indians in a valley below us; and I must acknowledge that we were not a little alarmed— but we continued our *route* determined to fight our way— On our approach we discovered the Indians to be Assiniboines from River a la *Souris*, one of the North West Company's Establishments. —[18]

Azure, Baptiste Turenne, and Alexis McKay. Little is known of these individuals. A "JBte. Lafrance" is listed among the men that John Macdonell sent to the Mandans on December 10, 1793, and February 17, 1794 (W. Raymond Wood, ed., "Journal of John Macdonell, 1793-1795," pp. 90, 98). The master at Brandon House recorded in his journal on May 3, 1808, that Lafrance had "died last Winter of a Consumption" at the Mandans (H.B.C.A., B.22/a/15, fo. 12d).

[17] See David Thompson's Journal, n. 17.

[18] See François-Antoine Larocque's "Yellowstone Journal," n. 85. Authorities disagree on how long this North West Company post was in existence. David A. Stewart, *Early Assiniboine Trading Posts of the Souiris-Mouth Group, 1785-1832*, Transactions of the Historical and Scientific Society of Manitoba, no. 5, p. 19, states that it was established in 1804 or 1805 and possibly remained in use until 1821. Ernest Voorhis, however, believes it to be identical with McDonnell's House or Fort Assiniboine, built in 1794 on the south side of the Assiniboine River at the mouth of the Souris River (*Historic Forts and Trading Posts of the French Régime and of the English Fur Trading Companies*, p. 33). In the most recent assessment of the problem, A. E. Brown ("The Fur Trade Posts of the Souris-Mouth Area," *Transactions of the Manitoba Historical Society*, 3rd ser., nos. 17–18 [1960–62]: 78–91) suggests that this was a post erected by the XY Company about 1800 but taken over by the North West Company at the merger of the two companies in 1804 and used until 1807 when it was relocated across the Assiniboine River. According to her, there

[p. 11] After smoking the pipe and hearing the news, an Assiniboine who had not taken any share in either, boldly laid hold on one of our horses— Mr. La Roque without hesitation snatched the bridle out of the Indian's hand— then the Indian bent his bow to shoot the horse— at this moment one of our men levelled his piece, and would have dispatched the Indian had not Mr. La Roque compelled him to desist. Soon after this disagreeable interruption, a strong gust of wind accompanied with sand, and burnt dust, obscured the sky, and obliged us to seek shelter in a deep *Ravelin* for the rest of the day:— Our horses were left to graze close by. Next morning three of them were missing for which we looked in vain during two days.— their tracks could be distinguished [p. 12] here and there, but could not always be followed in the burnt plains— we therefore were obliged to abandon the pursuit and gave them up as lost.

We proceeded on our journey— arriving within sight of the Mississouri, the natives flew in crowds to meet us, wishing us joy and congratulating themselves upon our appearance as traders amongst them— these were of the *gros Ventres* nation.[19] Here we found four of the Hudson's Bay Company's Servants like ourselves on a trading expedition.[20] They had arrived six days before— and informed us that having lost their way they had fallen in with a party of Assiniboines, who detained them prisoners for seven days, and compelled them to pay handsomely for their liberty [p. 13] Which incident greatly diminished their stock for trade— but expecting no opposition they raised the value of the remainder and thereby entertained hopes of making ample amends for the loss sustained by the hostile Indians. However the Mandanes had not

---

were three North West Company posts named Fort la Souris or Rivière la Souris operating in different locations near the mouth of the Souris River at various times between 1793 and about 1820 or 1821.

[19] That is, Hidatsa Indians.

[20] This is probably the party of three men—George Budge, George Henderson, and Tom Anderson—that set out from Brandon House on the Assiniboine River on October 19, 1804. Henderson returned to Brandon House with furs on January 3, 1805, and was followed by Budge and Anderson on March 15, 1805 (H.B.C.A., B. 22/a/12, fos. 6d, 8d, and 10d). John McKay, the master at Brandon House for that season, complained in the journal that the North West Company agents obtained the greater part of the Mandan-Hidatsa trade that year (H.B.C.A., B.22/a/12, fos. 9d–10). If Budge's party was delayed and possibly plundered enroute to the villages, as McKenzie states, McKay failed to record it in his journal.

entered into their views; and finding our prices more moderate we soon obtained the command of the whole of their furs.—

Here we also found a party of forty Americans under the command of Captains Lewis and Clark exploring a passage by the Misssissouri to the Pacific Ocean— they came up the River in a Boat of twenty oars accompanied by two *Peroques*. Their fortifications for winter Quarters were already complete— they had [p. 14] held a council with the Mandanes, and distributed many presents; but most of the Chiefs did not accept any thing from them. Some time after Captain Lewis with three Interpreters paid a visit to the *Gros Ventres* Village, and went directly to the Serpents Lodge where he passed the night;[21] next morning he came to the village where I was—[22] and observed to me that he was not very graciously received at the upper Village. "I sent a word, said he, to inform *Le Blet qui porte les cornes* ["The large one who wears horns"] that I intended to take up my Quarters at his Lodge— he returned for answer that he was not a[t] home; this conduct surprised me, it being common only among your English Lords not to be at [p. 15] home, when they did not wish to see strangers. But as I had felt no inclination of entering any house after being told the Landlord would not be at home, I looked out for another lodging which I readily found."

After haranguing the Indians and explaining to them the purport of his expedition to the Westward, several of them accepted clothing— but notwithstanding they could not be reconciled to *like* these strangers as they called them:— "Had these Whites come amongst us, Said the Chiefs, with charitable views they would have loaded their Great Boat with necessaries. It is true they have ammunition but they prefer throwing it away idly than sparing a shot of it [p. 16] to a poor Mandane." The Indians admired the air Gun as it could discharge forty shots out of one load— but they dreaded the magic of the owners. "Had I these White warriors in the upper plains, said the *Gros Ventres* Chief, my young men on horseback would soon do for them, as they would do for so many

[21] This is evidently a reference to a Hidatsa winter village near the elbow of the Missouri (see Larocque's "Yellowstone Journal," n. 22). For the location of Fort Mandan, see map 2.

[22] Evidently McKenzie had taken up residence in another Hidatsa winter village, different from the one mentioned in the preceding footnote, on the left bank of the Missouri River.

FIG. 11. Big Hidatsa village, on the north bank of the Knife River. The view is east-northeast. North Dakota State Highway Department.

wolves— for, continued he, there are only two sensible men among them— the worker of Iron, and the mender of Guns."

The American Gentlemen gave flags and medals to the Chiefs on condition that they should not go to war unless the enemy attacked them in their Villages. Yet the Chief of the wolves, whose brother had been killed in the [p. 17] fall previous to our arrival, went soon after with a party of fifty men to revenge his death— but not finding the Blackfeet Indians who were the agressors, or rather having found them too numerous, the party wisely retraced their steps with out making an attempt. But on their return having found some Canadians they killed four of them, and raised their scalps, which were disposed, in the course of their traffic, to the Rocky Mountain Indians.

About Christmas the Buffaloes drew near the Villages, and we lived on the fat of the land. Hunting and eating became the order of the day. Large parties, who went in pursuit of the buffaloes, often killed whole [p. 18] herds, but returned only with the tongues— the wolves feasted upon the carcasses— and the wolves thereby becoming too heavy to make their escape were easily overcome by the hunters of the ensuing day.

The Indians in this quarter seldom use Guns for Buffaloes, Wolves &c. for these they make use of arrows. Beavers are plentiful but the Indians will not take the trouble of attending to them. They often remarked to me that they would think it a pleasure to supply us with beavers if they could be secured the same as Buffaloes by a chace on horseback— but they consider the operation of searching for [p. 19] them in the bowels of the earth to satisfy the avarice of the *Whites* not only troublesome, but very degrading.—

"White people, said they, do not know how to live— they leave their homes in small parties; they risk their lives on the great waters, and among strange nations, who will take them for enemies:— What is the use of Beaver? Do they preserve them from sickness? Do they serve them beyond the grave?" I remarked that the Northern Nations were very industrious and great friends to the white people: "We are no slaves, rejoined the Chief— our fathers were not Slaves— in my young days there were no white men— and we [p. 20] knew no wants— we were successful in war; our arrows were pointed with flint, our lances with stone; and their wounds were mortal— Our Villages rejoiced when the men returned from war; of the scalps of our enemies they brought many. The white people came, they brought with them some goods: but they brought the small pox, they brought evil liquors— the Indians Since are diminished, and they are no longer happy."

In February our Trading goods were nearly finished, and the few goods that still remained were laid aside for a hunting party, who were absent [p. 21] Since the fall— apprehensive that the Hudson Bay Traders had an eye upon this party, Mr. La Roque sent for one Charbonneau who was with the American party as Interpreter,[23] in order to accompany us, and to have the Start of our troublesome neighbours. Every thing being ready for our departure, the difficulty now was how to set out unperceived by our opponents. Mr. La Roque and I agreed in opinion that the best plan would be to drive their horses out of the way— with this view we cautiously

[23] Toussaint Charbonneau. See François-Antoine Larocque's "Missouri Journal," n. 9.

234

watched until the people of the Village were asleep:— then the horses were detached from their confinement and quietly conducted to a considerable distance in the Plains— then thinking all safe, [p. 22] We saddled our horses— but our guide who slept apart could not be found— This incident threw us into grievous perplexity— I set out without him accompanied by the Interpreter and another Canadian who also was attached to the American expedition. When we got to a certain distance we waited for day light— in the mean time we sent Charbonneau back for the guide, but he returned without him:— he, however, learned that the Hudson Bay Traders missed their horses— were alarmed and employed Indians who soon found them, and brought them back to the owners, who having found out our views went a different route. Mortified at my [p. 23] disappointment I resolved upon continuing my Journey by means of the track of the other party.

But a Storm of drift and snow having obscured our horizon we lost our way, and we were obliged to seek shelter under the banks of a small Creek; where the badness of the weather detained us for three days. Here we found plenty of Buffaloes. The Buffaloes did not mind our presence; and we Killed four of them for the sake of their hides, which we required for shelter. A party of Indians who were upon a hunting excursion fell in with our encampment. I agreed with one of them; and he conducted us to our [p. 24] destination— where we learned that our opponents had been there, and had taken their departure the day before our arrival— but the Indians having had intelligence of our approach, they reserved for us our share of the Trade. When we returned to the village we found our friends greatly alarmed for our safety, fearing that we had lost our way, or that we were misled by the Natives.

We were now short of Goods— a band of Indians, who were loaded with furs, were on the eve of arriving; and from circumstances our opponents might have a decided advantage over us— and the idea cast a gloom upon our party— My Landlord observing [p. 25] this change felt uneasy and inquired whether he or any of his family had given us offence— I said no— but that his Tribe having apparently decided in favour of our opponents, we of course would withdraw ourselves never to return. This declaration distressed the old man— He took me by the hand, "Do not go, do not abandon me, my Son, Said he, the Indians who are coming to morrow will be kind to you— I will go with you to their Village— Your mother and your Sister will join us, and we shall talk of you. The Indians love my family, and you shall have all their furs— take courage, my Son, quiet your mind and go to rest."

[p. 26] We followed this good man's advice— next morning the old man was as good as his word. We paid a family visit to the Indians upon their arrival. His Son presented them with the pipe— he himself went upon the top of a house and harangued in our favour— while his kind females were busily employed from place to place collecting the skins until the whole hunt was thus secured.

Two bands of Assiniboines of a hundred Lodges each, who passed the winter at the Forks of the little Mississouri,[24] Sent daily to the Villages to barter for corn, Beans &c. They were troublesome to us, but they advised Mr. La Roque [p. 27] to send for an assortment in order to trade their hunt. But this measure required consideration:— the snow was too deep for horses, and for the same reason men would require snow shoes— the frames of which could easily be provided, but no one knew how to knit them.— We were informed of an old man who used to talk of Snow Shoes— but this man was blind with age and therefore could not afford us any assistance. The Old man remarked that in the days of his youth, he in common with many others made use of the like for walking, and could run with them in those days as fast as the horses run at present.

[p. 28] Having been disappointed in our expectations of the old man, we went to work ourselves, and made *Raquettes*[25] by passing thongs at right angles one across another, something like a riddle. In the evening Mr. La Roque with the only man we then had remaining took their departure accompanied by a Dog to carry their provisions— The journey to the Fort and back again we supposed might require at least twenty days to perform— I was left in charge of all. The horses caused me much uneasiness— I was afraid the Indians might take a fancy to them, and carry them off.

Being now on the eve of Spring [p. 29] the snow began to thaw, the River to run, and the natives to cross their effects to their summer residence on the opposite Banks of the Mississouri— of this change I was not aware at the departure of Mr. La Roque, therefore no provision was made for it. To remove all the property was inconvenient— to remain with it after the departure of the Indians

---

[24] This is probably a reference to the Little Missouri River, which flows into the Missouri River approximately fifty miles upstream from the mouth of the Knife River where the Mandan-Hidatsa villages were located at this time.

[25] That is, snowshoes.

was dangerous; however circumstances would only admit of the last alternative; and at length I found myself reduced to the company and protection of my old worthy Landlord. He remained behind his friends merely to oblige me. He notwithstanding thought our situation very insecure, and was [p. 30] consequently perpetually on his guard, being greatly in dread of the enemy. In the day time he repaired to the top of the highest hill in our neighbourhood; at night he could not sleep in peace; and when he did slumber it was always under arms. Seeing my hospitable friend in this continual state of alarm and anxiety, I began to feel uneasy and proposed to give communication of our apprehension to the American Gentlemen who were stationed about nine miles from us. The old man was highly pleased at my design, and he consented to remain alone the following day during my absence on this flattering message.

[p. 31] But the same evening Mr. La Roque made his appearance, and the old man was happy— he fired away all his powder in demonstration of his joy. Mr. La Roque had been very expeditious, almost incredibly so.[26] But he was disappointed, I may say doubly disappointed. The Indians who had engaged him in the journey made the greatest part of their hunt over to others in Mr. La Roque's absence— Nor did he find Mr. Chaboillez at home— he was on a visit to Mr. Henry in Lower Red River.[27] Report was in circulation that the Company of Sir Alexander Mackenzie had coalesced with the North West Company, both forming but one concern. [p. 32] This was good news— for opposition of interests creates dreadful disturbance, both in means and morals throughout these Savage Countries.[28]

---

[26] Larocque left the villages with Morrison on February 7, 1805, and returned on February 26, having made the round trip in twenty days. See Larocque's "Missouri Journal."

[27] This is a reference to Alexander Henry the Younger, who figures prominently in McKenzie's fourth expedition account in this chapter.

[28] McKenzie is here referring to the merger of the North West Company and the New North West Company, also known as the XY Company and as Sir Alexander Mackenzie and Company. This company was formed in 1800 through an amalgamation of several interests opposed to the North West Company and a defecting partner of the latter concern, Sir Alexander Mackenzie. The two companies competed fiercely for several years but merged on November 5, 1804, upon the death of Simon McTavish, a leading personality in the North West Company (W. Stewart Wallace, ed., *Documents Relating to the North West Company*, Publications of the Champlain Society, no. 22, pp. 17–20).

237

Notwithstanding the difficulty of procuring horses and other necessaries our people with those from Hudson Bay as well as our returns were on the way home in less than four days after Mr. La Roque's arrival— the Returns formed loads for seven horses.

Mr. La Roque and I having nothing very particular claiming attention, we lived contentedly and became intimate with the Gentlemen of the American expedition; who on all occasions seemed happy to see us, and [p. 33] always treated us with civility and kindness. It is true Captain Lewis could not make himself agreeable to us— he could speak fluently and learnedly on all subjects, but his inveterate disposition against the British stained, at least in our eyes, all his eloquence. Captain Clark was equally well informed, but his conversation was always pleasant, for he seemed to dislike giving offence unnecessarily.—

The Missouri was free of ice the Second of April. Then the American Gentlemen sent off their twenty oar Boat with ten men for the United States; and on the 8th. following the [p. 34] Expedition proceeded up the River towards the Rocky Mountains. It consisted of one large peroque; and seven small wooden Canoes— containing the commanding officers, thirty men, and a woman— the woman who answered the purpose of wife to Charbonneau was of the Serpent Nation, and lately taken prisoner by a war party:— She understood a little Gros Ventre, in which she had to converse with her husband, who was a Canadian, and who did not understand English— A Mulatto who spoke bad French and worse English served as Interpreter to the Captains— [29] So that a single word to [p. 35] be understood by the party required to pass from the Natives to the woman, from the woman to the husband, from the husband to the Mulatto, from the Mulatto to the Captain. I was once present when vocabularies were making of the languages of the Mandane Villages. The two Frenchmen who happened to be the medium of information had warm disputes upon the meaning of every word that was taken down by the expedition— as the Indians could not well comprehend the intention of recording

[29] This was Charbonneau's wife Sacagawea, who achieved fame through her participation in the Lewis and Clark expedition and about whom much has been written. According to Gary E. Moulton (personal communication, July 26, 1983), who is currently preparing a comprehensive edition of the Lewis and Clark journals, the identity of the "Mulatto" has not been established, although it has sometimes been erroneously assumed in the past that this individual was York, Lewis's black servant.

their words, they concluded that the Americans had a wicked design upon their Country.—

[p. 36] Buffaloes and other animals are in immense numbers destroyed every winter by the Missouri Indians. In stormy weather whole droves run from the Mountains and plains to seek shelter in the woods which form the margin of the Mississouri— many of them attempting to cross when the ice is weak sink and are drowned— and in the Spring both sides of the River are in several places covered with rotten carcasses and Skeletons of Buffaloes, Elks &c.— these dead animals, which often float down the current among the ice for hundred[s] of miles, are preferred by the natives to any other kind of food:— When the skin is raised you will see the flesh of a greenish [p. 37] hue, and ready to become alive at the least exposure to the sun; and is so ripe, so tender, that very little boiling is required— the stench is absolutely intolerable— yet the soup made from it which is bottle green is reckoned delicious:— So fond are the Mandanes of putrid meat that they bury animals whole in the winter for the consumption of the Spring.

The water of the Mississouri this Spring was uncommonly low, and in consequence drowned animals were not so very abundant as usual at the breaking up of the Navigation. However there were still plenty, and I had the opportunity of observing the courage and dexterity of the young Mandanes among the [p. 38] floating ice, hauling ashore some Scores of these nauseous carcasses, while the women, as active as they, were Securing for fire all the drift wood within their capacity.

The Mandanes are excellent swimmers— I was no less alarmed than astonished to see the men in the drift ice leap from piece to piece, often falling between, plunging under, darting up elsewhere and securing themselves upon very Slippery flakes:— yet no serious accident happened. The women performed their part equally well with the men. You would see them slip out of their leather Smocks, despising danger, plunge [p. 39] into the troubled deep to secure their objects; nor did they seem to feel the smallest inconvenience from the presence of crowds who lined the beach. The men and women of this place do not think it necessary "To sew Fig leaves together to make themselves aprons— and when they appear in public naked they are not ashamed."

Drift wood supplies the villages with fuel— which as well as the timber for their houses are dragged home always by the women— horses are never employed on these occasions. Wood is scarce here; which is the cause that Villages are often removed. A great quantity of dry and green wood is [p. 40] required every winter— the dry for fuel and the green for provender— a certain portion of poplar branches is provided for each horse:— the bark which the horse clears off is reckoned little inferior to oats.—

In the Spring so soon as the weather and the state of the ground will permit, the women repair to the field, cut the stalks of the Indian corn of the preceeding year, and drop new seed into the socket of the remaining roots. A small kind of pumpkins which are very productive they plant with a dibble and raise the ground into hillocks the same as those about Indian corn. Their Kidney Beans [p. 41] they plant in the same manner— they cultivate a tall kind of Sun flower, the Seed of which is esteemed good eating; dry and pounded with fat and made into balls of three or four ounces is found excellent for long journeys— One of these balls with the addition of a few roots gathered occasionally in their way is considered sufficient food for a man [for a] whole day. Warriors who generally travel to a great distance in quest of an enemy, and who dare not raise a Smoke, or fire a shot for fear of discovery, find these balls useful, light and convenient.

The only implement used among the Mandanes for the purpose of [p. 42] agriculture is a hoe made from the blade of the Shoulder of the Buffaloe and which is ingrafted upon a Short crooked handle— With this crooked instrument they work very expeditiously and soon do all that is required for their supplies.—

The men never trouble their heads about the labours of the field, unless to reprimand the women for some noted neglect, and to sow a few squares of tobacco— with which, being a sacred plant, the women who are considered unclean must not interfere, except in preparing the ground for its reception. The tobacco Squares are carefully Kept clear of weeds— the blossoms [p. 43] of this plant are cautiously collected which dried in the Sun is reckoned the very best of tobacco:— the plants do not exceed a foot in height— they resemble spinage, and are dried the same as the flowers— then pounded and mixed with grease for use. This kind of tobacco is weak, tastes differently from ours, and the smell which the Smoke emits is very disagreeable to strangers. I could not discover whence the Indians had that plant originally; but we must suppose from below, and that it found its way the same as the horses from the Spaniards.[30]

In due season some men and horses arrived from the Assiniboine [p. 44] or Red River.[31] We crossed to meet them at the Mandane Village— where we found the Indians in great alarm; having that morning discovered at the entrance of the Village some strange arrows and an old shoe:— insolent Signals:— and the position of the enemy was anxiously looked for all day in the vicinity, but without success. In course of the ensuing night several Shots were heard;— this created an uproar: singing, dancing, drums beating and war whoops occupied all hands to the dawn of day, when the whole village moved forward to brave the enemy. But all the vestiges they found consisted only of a dead horse [p. 45] with five arrows through his body. From this incident it was inferred that the number of the enemy did not exceed the number of arrows found in the horse— that these five were horse stealers, and that finding only one horse they could not make a division, and therefore settled the business as is customary on such occasions in this summary manner.—

Mr. La Roque having made the necessary preparations for our journey we left the Mississouri on the 22d. April and arrived at Assiniboine Fort on the 2d. May— where Mr. Chaboillez received us kindly, thanked us for our winter toil, and as a token of his approbation made each of us a present of a horse.—

So ended my first trip to the [p. 46] Mississouri— my next task will be to relate the observations made in my Second expedition.—

[p. 49]

Second Expedition to the Mississouri.

1805.

In the course of our first Expedition to the Mississouri, having seen several Rocky Mountain Indians,[32] we made enquiries regarding the

[30] Gilbert L. Wilson's *Agriculture of the Hidatsa Indians: An Indian Interpretation,* University of Minnesota Studies in Social Science, vol. 9, provides an excellent description of Hidatsa horticulture. See also George F. Will and George E. Hyde, *Corn among the Indians of the Upper Missouri.* The "squares" to which McKenzie refers are the garden plots of the Indians.

[31] This probably refers to the arrival of Hugh Heney in the villages, on December 14, 1804, according to Larocque's "Missouri Journal." Heney apparently remained in the villages until December 20, when he departed to return to the North West Company post near the mouth of the Souris River. See Meriwether Lewis and William Clark, *Original Journals of the Lewis and Clark Expedition, 1804-06,* ed. Reuben Gold Thwaites, vol. 1, pp. 237–38, 266.

[32] That is, the Siouan-speaking Crow Indians. McKenzie refers to them as Rocky Mountain Indians or Corbeau ("Corbeaux").

state of their Country, the Trade &c. We learnt that Beavers were as numerous in their Rivers as Buffaloes and other large animals in their plains or meadows— which account was confirmed by an old Voyageur lately from that quarter.— [Narrative A, p. 1a: . . . by Ménard an old Canadian who had lately been rambling Among the Rocky Mountains.][33]

In consequence of this information Mr. Chaboillez formed the plan of establishing a trade with the Natives, and Mr. La Roque was apointed to carry that plan into execution. I was ordered to accompany the Expedition as far as the Mandanes.

[p. 50] On the 3d. of June all was ready, & we took our departure. The party consisted of Mr. La Roque, Mr. Lafrance, two Voyageurs and myself—[34] provided with thirteen horses. Soon after falling in with a large band of Assiniboines we experienced some difficulty to get clear of them with our property in safety. It was the same band that pillaged the Hudson Bay party the preceeding Fall. The Chief, who was a rogue, we Satisfied underhand, [Narrative A, p. 1a: . . . he was bribed . . .] and we escaped unhurt— we had Scarcely arrived on the banks of the Missouri when the *Gros Ventres* sent Canoes to ferry us over to their vil[p. 51]lages. Here we were surprised to find the whole of the Inhabitants with blackened faces— and the young men Singing and dancing round the place with a Scalp [Narrative A, p. 1a: . . . with an Indian scalp]. We observed a great change in their dress; which in many instances consisted of Articles foreign to these distant Tribes— viz. Russia Sheeting [?] trowsers, swans down Vests, Corduroy Jackets, Calico shirts, &c. all resembling Canadian Voyageurs clothing:— from which we had reason to suspect that these people had successfully attacked some of the North West Company's Establishments. We enquired repeatedly how they came by these fineries— but no one Seemed inclined to inform us— all [p. 52] gave evasive answers— however we at length discovered that a party had been to war upon the Blackfeet Indians, and Killed those who had been in possession of these articles— this in a manner confirmed our doubts. By & by the truth came out— the Indians who

[33] Ménard was a long-time resident at the Mandan and Hidatsa villages. See Part One.

[34] In his Yellowstone journal, Larocque recorded that McKenzie and two men named Lassana and Soucie accompanied him (see Larocque's "Yellowstone Journal," nn. 8 and 35). It is clear from Larocque's September 30, 1805, journal entry that Morrison was also part of this party.

had reaped no benefit from the spoil, through jealousy, divulged the Secret. They reported that the chief of the *Wolves* with his Young men had recently returned from a war Expedition in the Blackfeet Country, where they killed several of the white people, and carried away their Effects; which were the same that we now observed worn in the Village. [p. 53] We immediately spoke to the Chief of the *Wolves,* and he acknowledged the whole as follows:—

"The evening before the attack observing some people at a considerable distance near the banks of the great North River, I thought we discovered the enemy and my heart was glad— we became impatient but we waited for night to make our approach; coming within a certain distance and hearing the drum beating, we delayed until all was silence— and it was at the dawn of the morn when our Young men fired on the Fort [Narrative A, p. 1b:... tent...], whence we heard the drum. At the first discharge the persons who were within rushed out. It was then I discovered our error, that our attack was on white men.— [p. 54] I was sorry, but I could not prevail on the Young men to cease firing and be wise. The white men fled to their Canoes— and the Young men carried away the things which were left in the camp:— I did not kill any of the white men— but I did believe they were Serpent Indians our enemies— I am sorry they were your friends."

By this discourse we concluded that these Indians had killed some of our people on the South branch of the Saskatchewin River.[35] The Indians of the Village perceiving by our looks that we were acquainted with the outrage committed upon our friends discontinued their rejoicing and the exhibition of their plunder.— [p. 55] My business being confined to the Villages and their vicinity I lost no time in adopting the necessary measures for securing the trade in that Quarter.

Mr. La Roque, who was to ascend the Mississouri on discovery, was opposed in his views by the Indians who insisted upon his return

---

[35] Burpee and Davidson have suggested that the Hidatsa had killed several North West Company men, under the command of John McDonald of Garth, along the Saskatchewan River in reprisal for McDonald's refusal to aid the Hidatsas' battle with the Blackfeet (Lawrence J. Burpee, *The Search for the Western Sea: The Story of the Explorations of North-Western America,* pp. 367–69; Gordon Charles Davidson, The *North West Company,* University of California Publications in History, vol. 7, p. 82 n. 59). Both authors refer readers to McDonald's account of this ambush in Masson, *Les Bourgeois,* vol. 2, pp. 33–34. See Larocque's "Yellowstone Journal," entry for June 16, 1805, for additional remarks in this matter.

to Red River without going any further on his Expedition. They asserted that if the white people would extend their dealings to the Rocky Mountains, the Mandanes would thereby become great sufferers— as they not only would lose all the benefit which they had hitherto derived from their intercourse with these distant Tribes;— but in measure as these tribes obtained arms they would become independent and insolent in the [p. 56] extreme. This remonstrance was made in a tone which could not fail to give uneasiness to Mr. La Roque— and he was at a loss how to steer his course. He therefore applied to the Head Chief called the *Borgne* (who was then confined to bed) for advice. This Chief is reckoned a very Superior Character [Narrative A, p. 2a: . . . is reckoned a great rogue]. Mr. La Roque exposed his difficulties, he listened with attention, then made the following reply.—

"My Son, Said the Chief, were I in health when you arrived, you would have been quartered in my Tent— and the Indians would have been more civil to you— but the Indians have no Sense— the Chief of the White people wishes you to visit the [p. 57] Rocky Mountains and you shall visit them, when I shall be well, no one dare hinder you. The Indians call for Goods— but they have already too many Goods;— I am angry at the Chief of the *Wolves*— he ought to be ashamed— he has abused the goodness of the white people. He offered me part of his plunder, but I declined his offers. Have patience, my Son, lend a deaf ear to bad talk— I adopted a Son among the Tribes of the Mountain— he is a good man— and he is a great Chief:— he will soon be here, and you shall accompany him and be Safe. But hearken to my words, My Son— When the Mountain Indians arrive, be kind to them— they know not white men— You will hand to them your pipe of ceremony [Narrative A, p. 2b: . . . pipe of medicines]— You will [p. 58] clothe the Chief— you will give him a flag and a Stem— and you will make him a present— for he is a great man. But I shall be well then, and I will assist you. Take courage, My Son, but do not throw evil medicines among the Indians."

Mr. La Roque deriving confidence from these favourable professions of the great Chief was much relieved from his anxiety— and he assured the Chief, that he would attend to his words and think of him hereafter as of a Father; and would be happy to see him at our great Fort on the Assiniboine River. We then returned to our Quarters: Still the Indians persisted in plaguing us— but as we were successful in our application at [p. 59] Head Quarters we had reason to think less of their importunities.

About the middle of June the Rocky Mountain Indians made their appearance. They consisted of more than three hundred Tents, and presented the handsomest sight that one could imagine— all on horseback. Children of small size were lashed to the Saddles, and those above the age of six could manage a horse— the women had wooden Saddles— most of the men had none. There were a great many horses for the baggage, and the whole exceeding two thousand covered a large space of ground and had the appearance of an army; they halted on a rising ground behind the Village; formed into a circle— when the Chief addressed them, [p. 60] they then descended full speed— rode through the Village, exhibiting their dexterity in horsemanship in a thousand shapes— I was astonished to see their agility and address:— and I could believe they were the best riders in the world. They were dressed in leather, looked clean and neat— Some wore beads and rings as ornaments. Their arms were Bows and arrows, Lances, and round stones enclosed in leather and slung to a shank in the form of a whip. They make use of shields, and they have a few Guns.—

On the following day the Mississouri Indians dressed in their best fineries returned the compliment by a similar exhibition. [p. 61] These having the advantage of residing in the vicinity of trading Establishments were better provided with necessaries and consequently had a more warlike appearance; but they were inferior in the management of their horses.—

In the mean time *Le Borgne* sent for us in order to introduce Mr. La Roque to the Rocky Mountain Chief, whose name is *Nakesinia* or Red Calf. When we offered to shake hands with this great man, he did not understand the intention, and stood motionless until he was informed that shaking hands was the sign of friendship among white men:— then he stretched forth both his hands to receive ours. *Le Borgne* said a great deal in favour of the North West [p. 62] Company, but he did not praise the Americans.

Mr. La Roque's great pipe was handed round as a precious offering and each took a few whiffs— then Mr. La Roque presented to the Red Calf a Flag; a Stem,[36] with some mercantile articles; and the Chief to testify his Sense of the obligation adopted Mr. La Roque as Father, and promised to respect and consider him as such for ever after.

Les Gros Ventres made the Corbeaux [Crows] (for so the Rocky Mountain tribe was called) Smoke the pipe of friendship, and at the

---

[36] This is a reference to a ceremonial pipe used in trading ceremonies by many Plains Indians.

same time laid before them a present consist[p. 63]ing of two hundred guns, with one hundred rounds of ammunition for each, a hundred bushels of Indian Corn, a certain quantity of mercantile articles, such as Kettles, axes, Cloths &c. The Corbeaux in return brought two hundred and fifty horses, large parcels of Buffalo Robes, Leather Leggins, Shirts [Narrative A, p. 3b: . . . and Smocks &c. in great abundance.] &c. &c.

This exchange of trading civilities took place dancing— when the dancing was over, the presents were distributed among the Individuals in proportion to the value of the articles respectively furnished— this dance therefore is a rule of traffic [Narrative A, p. 3b: This dance therefore is meant as a fair for traffic]. The Mandane Villages exchanged similar civilities with the Same Tribe. It is incredible the great [p. 64] quantity of merchandize which the Missouri Indians have accumulated by intercourse with Indians that visit them from the vicinity of Commercial Establishments.—

I traded a few things with the *Corbeaux*. Their beaver Skins were badly dressed and split upon the back in place of the belly— a sign that they were not much acquainted with the importance of that favourite article of commerce— Afraid to ask too small a price they seemed averse from dealing with me— for they would have a white man pay four times the value of a thing, [p. 65] or often let him go without. When the Corbeau Indians were on the eve of departure— the Borgne Chief sent word to Mr. La Roque to make ready and join them— He immediately began to arrange his matters for the journey. The *Gros Ventres* perceiving the intention of the preparations crowded into our quarters, and threatened Mr. La Roque with their displeasure should he persist in his design— At this moment the Great Chief entered with a Battle Axe in his hand— Staring around him with an imperious air, he asked in a thundering tone why so many Indians were assembled there? "They answered that they came to take their last farewell of the white men, whom they [p. 66] expected never to see again." "Why, said the Chief with a sneer, should you feel so much concern, if the white men are inclined to risk their lives in a [*large*] strange land, that is no business of yours— you have warned them sufficiently of the danger— yet they will go on." By this time the Indians went one by one sneaking out of the way. Then we accompanied the Chief— Mr. La Roque leading his horse by the bridle.

When we entered the Camp of the Corbeaux— we could perceive many of that tribe disapproved Mr. La Roque's intention, for some of them exclaimed "Where are you going, white men? [p. 67] Return, go home— we do not wish for your company— Some of our Young men have no discretion— we are afraid. These insinuations had no effect on Mr. La Roque's resolution— he was determined. But one of our party, a *Voyageur,* thought himself indisposed, and applied for leave to remain with me; I see plainly the cause of your indisposition, Said Mr. La Roque, your courage fails you like an old woman; you may remain:— this severe reprimand threw the fellow into a violent passion, and he became extremely abusive. However Mr. La Roque took no particular notice of his conduct, for he could not punish so much insolence before so many Strange Indians without risking the loss of their good opinion [p. 68] of him, and thereby the success of his Expedition.[37] This unpleasant disagreement caused a bustle in the Camp, and most of the Indians collected around us— finding this a favourable opportunity, the Great Chief, our friend *Le Borgne,* addressed the Strange Indians and his adopted Son the Red Calf as follows:—

"My Son and my friends, rejoice— White men are to visit your Land and you will feel easy in their company— but we shall regret their absence. White men are curious— they came from far— they know much and wish to learn more. Three only form their party; [p. 69] Your party consist of a thousand and more— you see their skin, it is white— their hearts are as white as their skin— they are good and will do you no harm. Give them plenty to eat; let them have the best, and be the first served— let your women be kind to them— never ask any thing from them: they are generous, and they will pay you for your kindness— White men love Beaver and they are continually in search of Beaver for its Skin— What use they make of the Skin I know not:— but they give us good things in return— they exchange it for Guns, Ammunition &c. Our Fathers were not acquainted with White men— We live better than our Fathers lived. Do your Neighbours the Serpent nation[38] enjoy [p. 70] the Security and happiness we enjoy? If the white men could furnish the Serpents as they furnish us with arms, we should not carry away so many of the Serpents' Scalps— the white men are powerful— they are like magic— I, therefore, once more entreat you to protect with indulgence those I recommend— You, my Son, must

---

[37] Since Morrison and Souci are known to have accompanied Larocque on his trip to the Yellowstone River country, this reluctant *voyageur* may have been Lassana. See Larocque's "Yellowstone Journal," entry for September 30, 1805.

[38] That is, the Snake Indians, or Shoshonis. Larocque's "Yellowstone Journal" contains ethnographic notes on them.

never let the Young white Chief out of your Sight— go with him wherever he goes— should any misfortune happen to him we shall be ashamed to meet white men. This Summer I intend to visit the Great White Chief at his Fort— I shall tell him that his Young friends are safe in charge of [p. 71] my Son who is a Great man— and the Great Chief of the white people will be Kind to you:— but I have heard some of the Women, as I was passing through the camp, call out "Return, white men, go home, we are afraid;" Say, my friends, what means this?

After a pause of some minutes, an elderly man raising his voice Said, "We were suspicious of these white men— we were afraid they might throw evil medicines among us and Soil our Lands; but you have removed our fears, and you can depend upon our goodness. The *Corbeaux* are in two Tribes— they have two Chiefs: the *Red Calf* who receives favours from the white men; and the *Red Fish* who receives none; It [p. 72] was the *Red Fish* that told us to be angry."

No sooner had the old man ceased Speaking than the *Red Calf* addressed Mr. La Roque:— "Father, said he, if you are willing to go with us, we are willing to receive you— but should an enemy stand in our way, or attack us in our Journey— You and Your Young men must assist us in beating him off."

Mr. La Roque said he would assist his friends on all occasions. [Narrative A, p. 5a: Then the Red Calf told his new Father how he was to conduct himself in order to keep friends with all and assure a Safe Journey.] Then *Le Borgne* made a harangue of great length [Narrative A, p. 5a: . . . made a harangue which lasted two hours . . .], and concluded by observing, "that his heart was full, and that he would be in a state of anxiety until the return of the white men.—

[p. 73] My affairs requiring my presence in the Villages, I shook hands with my friend Mr. La Roque, and withdrew— Le Borgne has been of great Service to us; if his influence will accompany Mr. La Roque in his journey the Indians will be very careful not to give him any offence.

The men of the *Corbeaux* nation are generally of the middle size, inclining to corpulency with fair complexion and a pleasant countenance— the women are handsome, but their beauty fades early— even children have gray hairs. The Nation is in two Tribes *Kegh-chy-Sa* and *Hey-re-ro-ka*— Governed by two Chiefs, the *Red Calf* and the *Red Fish;* and may muster about six hundred warriors [Narrative A, p. 5b: The nation is in two tribes . . . and may produce about 600

warriors each—]. They speak a dialect [p. 74] of the *Gros Ventres*.[39]
The origin of the *Corbeaux* is accounted in the following manner.—

Two Brothers of the *Gros Ventres* named *Regh-Chy-Sa* [Narrative
A, p. 5b: ... Kegh chysa...] and *Hey-re-ro-ka* were wicked men—
They murdered numbers of their own relations, and were in consequence obliged to fly for safety to distant recesses of the Rocky
Mountains:— there falling in with the *Flat Heads* they provided
themselves with wives from that nation— who speaking a different
language, the offspring of that connec[t]ion became a new tribe—
speaking a new dialect which being a mixture of the other two is
understood by the three Tribes. [p. 75] Les *Gros Ventres* call themselves *Ena-sa.* the *Corbeaux Kech-chy-sa* and *Hey-re-ro-ka*— [Narrative
A, p. 5b: ... Kegh-chy-sa and Hey-ro-ro-ka...] while the Corbeaux
call the *Gros Ventres É-na-ta,* and themselves *Keigh-chy-ta* and *Hen-ne-
no-ta* [Narrative A, p. 5b: ... Kegh chy ta and Hen ne no ka—].
Most of the words in both Languages begin the same but end differently, as follows—

Gros Ventres	*Corbeaux*
Arrach bugja wrach baga	Annach bogu minnach baga
Elangé bugji wrach baga	Etangé bugich minnach Baga
Ma-pork-cha wrach Baga	Ma-porkta minnach Baga
Aitché shilbisha wrach baga	Aitche jibbla minnach Baga

[Narrative A, p. 5b, lists the meanings of these phrases:

Meaning

Mandans nation
Spotted Robes nation
Serpent nation
Blackfeet nation]

The Corbeaux Tribes cannot pronounce the letter V. [Narrative
A, p. 5b: ... cannot pronounce the letter r] but the *Gros Ventres* speak
Corbeau fluently. All these Tribes dress in the same manner. The
men have [p. 76] long hair which trail[s] on the ground— but to
make it appear long, they add horse hair by a cement of gum.—

---

[39] McKenzie is correct in attributing a linguistic relationship between the Crows
and Hidatsas. Both groups had been united several hundred years before, and did
indeed speak different dialects of the same language. The Hidatsas are sometimes
called the River Crows to distinguish them from the Mountain Crows, or Crows
proper. See W. Raymond Wood and Alan S. Downer, "Notes on the Crow-Hidatsa
Schism," *Plains Anthropologist,* Memoir 13 (1977): 83–100.

They comb only the forehead, and for combs they substitute porcupine Tails— The women are careless about their hair, which scarcely reaches the Shoulders. To make it look fine they sometimes throw a little water over it. The Corbeaux do not cut off joints of their fingers, nor slash their own flesh as the *Gros Ventres* do. But they are much addicted to an abominable crime— the crime of *Sodomy;* this I could not credit. To convince me the Chief called in a Young man of that tribe— After exchanging the usual civilities he inquired of the Young [p. 77] man why he did not come oftener to see him. Then putting on a Serious air, "he asked whether the Corbeau Tribes did not sometimes make use of extraordinary means to satisfy certain appetites"? "Why do you put that question to me since you know the answer already"? [Narrative A, p. 6a: You have lived with our nation.] "I do know the answer— I told it to the white man— but he doubts my words— say how many species you have known personally"?

After a little silence the Young man held out the fingers of one hand; then gave the explanation— but some of these he observed were inanimate or nearly so. After the Young man retired the Chief remarked "that his people were seldom guilty of such excesses— the few instances which came to his knowledge occurred among war parties at a great [p. 78] distance from home."[40]

About the beginning of August the three men [Narrative A, p. 6a: . . . the free man . . .], whom we had dispatched on our arrival to our Establishment on the Red River, returned and informed me that Alexander Henry had arrived from Fort William— concluding from circumstances that a change had taken place in our Department, I became anxious for my departure.

After the Rocky Mountain Indians were gone I had scarcely any occupation, and saw little or nothing worthy of notice— several bands of *Assiniboines, Crees,* and *Sauteux,*[41] visited the Villages, but nothing strange occurred. I must not forget to mention [p. 79] that there was a fine harvest at the Mississouri this season— I never

---

[40] McKenzie's discussion of sodomaical practices among the Crows was omitted from the version published by Masson. Larocque included a brief discussion of this subject in the section of his "Yellowstone Journal" entitled "A few Observations on the Rocky Mountain Indians with whom I passed this Summer" (ms. pp. 34–35). Prince Maximilian (Reuben Gold Thwaites, ed., *Early Western Travels, 1748–1846,* vol. 22, p. 354) also commented that the Crows "exceed all the other tribes in unnatural practices."

[41] That is, Algonquian-speaking Chippewa Indians.

witnessed any thing equal in richness [to] the appearance of the fields— The Stalks of the Indian corn were generally eight feet high [Narrative A, p. 6b: . . . were from Six to eight feet high . . .];— the leaves of the Kidney beans were entirely covered with blossoms, promising abundance. The pumpkins were already gathered, cut into Slices, dried in the Sun, and ready for use.—

On the 15th. August I crossed the Missisouri with Seven horses. Here I lost half a day waiting for my fellow traveller Mr. La France—[42] he had three horses—but he gave me a very poor account of the property intrusted to his care; which did not realize half the value. In the evening we left the Banks of the Missisouri. Eight horses [p. 80] carried our returns— two for ourselves— La France led the Van— I in the rear drove the horses after him. In this manner we jogged on and no one can judge of the difficulties we had to encounter, but such as had travelled in the same route with a like incumbrance— travelling from the break of day to the dusk of the evening— Still our daily progress was small.

Our *route* was through plains or meadows so thickly covered with Buffaloes that we were often under the necessity of frightening them out of our way by means of Gunpowder;— and we were in constant dread of being overrun and crushed by them at night in [p. 81] our Encampments. The flies were extremely troublesome and tormenting— and we had no means for fire but dry dung which burnt like spunk— provisions were supplied daily as required from the chace.

After leaving the Buffaloe Meadows a dreadful scarcity of water ensued— we had to alter our course and Steer to a distant lake where we intended to encamp, but when we got there we found the lake dry. However we dug a pit that produced a kind of stinking water of which we all drank— it was Salt and bitter and caused an inflamation of the mouth, and left a disagreeable roughness in the throat, and it seemed to increase [p. 82] rather than diminish our thirst— our horses also partook of this unsavoury beverage— we passed the night under great uneasiness. Next day we continued our journey— but not a drop of water was to be found any where on our route, and our distress became insupportable— Lafrance lost his patience and swore so much that he could Swear no more. He gave the Country ten thousand times to the Devil, and wished himself any where

---

[42] Lafrance appears to have been a sometime resident of the Mandan-Hidatsa villages. He participated in McKenzie's first expedition to the Missouri. See note 16, above.

else— at length his eyes became dim, and We believed that he was drawing near a Serious Crisis. All at once our horses became so un[p. 83]ruly that we could not manage them— we observed that they manifested an inclination towards a Hill which was close by. It struck me that they might have Scented the air of water from that direction— and I immediately ascended to the top of the hill when to my great joy I discovered a small pool of water at a small distance from me. Forgetting the distress of my fellow traveller through the excess of my own; I flew to the heavenly liquid and Swallowed Several droughts. My horse plunged into it and began to roll himself before I could muster time to prevent him— I then returned to the edge of the hill, and beckoned to La France who [p. 84] was still at too great a distance to hear me— at length he reached me— The poor man seemed more dead than alive;— his countenance was entirely changed into a dark hue— and a thick scuff affected his mouth. [Narrative A, p. 7b: . . . and a thick scurf appeared round his mouth]. He instantly got into the water, of which he partook so plentifully that I was fearful of the consequences. The horses also drank largely; and I was afraid that they might also be injured. After resting for some time in the vicinity of the water— we renewed our course; but we did not proceed far, when our late extrafant [extravagant?] libations began to operate both upon ourselves & upon our horses. [p. 85] Notwithstanding this effect, we thought it prudent to return and pass the night at the same pool; because we might fare worse by continuing and be obliged to encamp without water.—

Next morning at day break we went on and that evening arrived at the Fort: Where we found Mr. Henry in charge. He and his people in a State of Starvation. We were welcome guests, for we had plenty of provisions.—

So ended my Second Expedition to the Mississouri.—

[p. 89]

Supplement to the Second Expedition

July 10th. 1805. To celebrate a great Festival all the old men of the Enasis Village assembled at the Lodge of the first Chief to appoint proper officers in order to keep the peace during its duration.—[43]

---

[43] Here follows the first recorded description of the Hidatsa Naxpike, or Hidebeating Ceremony. This ceremony is more fully described by Alfred W. Bowers, *Hidatsa Social and Ceremonial Organization,* Bureau of American Ethnology Bulletin

11th. This morning at the break of day, an old man harangued through the Village. Soon after appeared twelve robust young fellows with their heads in bladders, bodies bare; painted half way with vermillion and half with white earth— the emblems of punishment and pardon united in the same person. These Guardians of the Public Welfare entered into every lodge giving instructions for good order. The women were directed to go into the woods for branches to cover the Medicine Lodge; while the men were occupied in dressing *themselves.* [p. 90] When all were ready, the men walked into the lodge with their pipes and drums; the women went with kettles and dishes full of the best of things to prepare for the feast. At the door of the lodge the Vessels were aired over a blazing fire, made of certain Hay or weeds selected for the occasion— and ample offerings were variously made to the Sun.— When the eating part was over, the remainder of the day was joyfully passed in innocent recreations, such as smoking, dancing &c.

[The Narrative A version, on p. 1a, is considerably different and contains much deleted information and several illegible words, as follows:

These gaurdians of the Noble Order entered every lodge giving directions [*and directed the women to go into the woods for branches to cover the Medicine Lodge. When this lodge whose frame is always Standing in the field at Some distance from the village— and Supported upon a pillar, which rises in the Center, twenty five feet high. When the Lodge was ready*] When the Medicine Lodge was prepared The Men with their pipes and Drums [*walked into it*]— entered The women followed [*them*] with an assortment of the best of [one word illegible] [*things that could be found for the feast*]— The dishes were aired over a fire at the Door [*of the lodge made for the purpose*]— and an offering out of each was made to the Sun [*which — — was left for — — Days* —the blanks indicate single illegible words]— When dinner was over — all [*hands*] Smoked and danced for the rest of the [*day*] Evening—]

12th. This forenoon Several young men placed themselves in a row on their bellies: An old man, holding an arrow approached them— with the barb of it [p. 91] he pierced a hole at the shoulder blades of each,

194, pp. 308–323. The self-torture aspects of the ritual are reminiscent of the better-known Mandan Okipa ceremony. McKenzie has earlier related that Ena-sa is a Hidatsa name for themselves. The village in question is probably the Big Hidatsa site (map 2).

through which he passed a pin of hard wood about four inches long and half an inch in thickness. To this pin he fastened a cord of eight yards in length. At the end of these cords were tied seven Bulls' Heads or more according to the quality of the Warrior— Such as had killed some of the Enemy and taken Scalps; had a man's Scull attached to each breast [Narrative A, p. 1b: . . . had a mans Scull tied on each side of his breast . . .] and a Scalp fastened a little below the Eyes, holding a cane in the right hand, to which also was fastened a Scalp. But such as were less successful in war were not distinguished by so many ornaments— they had not the honour of dragging So many Bulls' heads after them— and their canes in lieu of human [p. 92] Scalps were ornamented only with Eagle Tails. These young warriors were entirely naked, but painted white;— when the old man had finished this first part, the Young Warriors started up and moved forward. But the baggage of Bulls' Heads which they trained, having all their horns, became often entangled, and rendered their progress Slow and painful. One, however, who was more loaded than any of the rest rushed through the crowd unmindful of all obstacles that stood in his way, soon gained his destination in the great Lodge, where he was received by a multitude of Spectators with Shouts of applause. The others would [p. 93] fain have followed the example— but their hearts failed them— they often leaned upon their canes. In measure as the warriors arrived at the Lodge all the heads were thrown over a high beam, and their weight served as a counterpoise raised the *Bearers* from the ground. In this position they remained suspended like so many criminals upon a Gibbet.—

In the mean time spectators of all Sexes and sizes united in singing, dancing, and beating their drums &c. while the old man approached the principal Hero [Narrative A, p. 2a: . . . first hero . . .] and asked him what he was disposed to offer to the Sun; So that the Sun might continue to shine upon him with kindness? [Narrative A, p. 2a: . . . that the Sun might continue to shine upon high with kindness—]? [p. 94] "I shall give to the Sun, said he, in order to shine upon me with kindness, two stripes of flesh from each of my arms, beginning at my shoulder blades and finishing at my wrists— I shall also give to the Sun one of my fingers, and Shall allow you, moreover, to imprint with a Red hot Iron an emblem of the Sun upon my breast."

The same question was put to each of the others who were fifteen in number— but they were much more moderate in their devotional Donations— they contented themselves by giving only a fin-

FIG. 12. Maker of Roads, Addíh-Hiddísch, a Hidatsa chief, painted by Karl Bodmer at Fort Clark, North Dakota, in the spring of 1834. InterNorth Art Foundation, Joslyn Art Museum, Omaha, Nebraska.

ger or a Slice of flesh respectively.— The old man who was [p. 95] provided with the necessary instruments for the execution of his duty [Narrative A, p. 2a: The old man who had the execution of this affair in charge was provided with a Knife an awl and the bitt of a Spanish bridle.], began his operations upon the boldest of the heroes— He began by cutting on each Shoulder two circles from which he raised two stripes in parallel lines down to the wrists; [Narrative A, p. 2a: during this operation which was performed upon both arms the Spectators renewed their noise so that the groans of the Sufferer if he uttered any could not be heard—] then the little finger of the right hand was cut off at the second joint— [Narrative A, p. 2a: That of his left hand Seemed to have experienced the Same ceremony on a former occasion—] and then the bit of a Bridle was introduced red hot and applied to the breast until the flesh in a large circle rose into a hard crust.

All this time the sufferer as well as his companions on trial were hanging suspended from the beam of the lodge by the cords through the incision in their Shoulders— their feet at some distance [p. 96] from the ground; unable to stir during the operation. The noise of the spectators was very great— if the sufferers complained, they could not be heard. As soon as each had undergone the pains which he had imposed upon himself, he was released from his elevated station at the Beam, and allowed to return from whence he came, still dragging his original Equipage of Heads after him, until he placed the whole where he found them; and where fit persons were stationed on purpose to untie and receive them. When the wooden pins were [p. 97] taken out of the Shoulders, an old woman sucked the blood from the wounds, which she stuffed with a preparation made by her teeth from a certain root for the purpose. Then the suffering Hero, or whatever we may choose to call him, took his stripes of flesh and his finger joint, placed them into a neat little bag with which he hastened to the outside of the village (Singing a lamentable dirge as he went) to deposit as an offering to his God.—

Tired of so dreadful a scene after passing some time I withdrew and returned to my quarters; where I found the Guards of police indulging their amorous propensities to their full extent with the Girls during the absence [p. 98] of their parents— As to the Warriors the Sun was high the following morning before the last of them left his conspicuous stand at the Beam to take his painful turn before the old Priest.—

The old priest was handsomely rewarded for his trouble and attendance— The Young warriors on whom he operated so signally

[Narrative A, p. 2b:... The Young warriors upon Whom he conferred so many Signal obligations...] loaded him with presents, that the next morning [Narrative A, p. 2b:... the next evening...] he was one of the richest men in the village.

The Indians, as it is well known, are extremely attached to their Children, and become inconsolable when [p. 99] they have the misfortune of losing any of them— such is their distress that they throw away all their property, cut off joints of their fingers, and commit a thousand extragances [extravagances?]. On the other hand they are cruel enemies, and will go any lengths for revenge:— Still there are surprising instances of generosity [Narrative A, p. 3a:... even to an enemy discovered among them.] experienced among them— the following in particular deserves to be mentioned:—

"In the fall of 1804, a Party of *Enasas* being in need went towards the Rocky Mountains in Search of horses, which they determined to take and make their own, right or wrong wherever found. After travelling several days through extensive [p. 100] plains in rain, they came to the foot of the Rocky Mountains and resolved upon crossing them. In a valley beyond the first range they discovered a small camp of the *Flat Heads* or Snake Indians consisting of four or five Tents— which in the following night they approached at day break;— [44] next morning the men of the Camp mounted their horses, and rode off for the chace.— The Warriors taking advantage of the absence of the men, flew upon the camp and destroyed all the women and Children within their reach, and carried away the property.— Looking out for horses among the [p. 101] Rocks in the vicinity, they perceived in a small grove [Narrative A, p. 3a:... in a small cave...] a woman making her escape with her two children, whom they pursued; but upon coming near, the Chief was seized with compassion. The woman was beautiful; he spared her life, and the lives of her two Children; made them his captives, and carried them off prisoners to the Missouri.

The hunters on their return to the camp finding the cruel ravages of an enemy in their absence were distracted. The owner of the Captive [Narrative A, p. 3a: The husband of the Captive...] prisoners not finding a vestige of them among the slain, searched for them among the Rocks— he called on his wife by the name; but alas! She was out of his reach— Some of the other women, [p. 102] who had the good fortune to escape the massacre, recognized

---

[44] McKenzie's own uncertainty about whether these Indians are Flatheads or Shoshonis makes the identification of this group impractical.

his voice; they flew from their hiding places and mingling their cries and tears with his, informed him that the enemy was scarcely out of sight, and of what had happened, and what became of his family. He immediately formed the bold and desperate resolution of pursuing the enemy in hopes of an opportunity for retrieving his loss. His friends endeavoured to persuade him to the contrary, but he would not hearken to reason— he was unhappy and instantly took his departure. He soon came in sight of his enemies— watched unperceived in their rear, and hovered [p. 103] about their Camps without finding an opportunity for more than a month— when at length the Party reached their village.

The War Chief having by this time determined upon making his beautiful Captive one of his wives, applied to his Father in Law to adopt her as a daughter; by which means the Children would be naturalized, and considered as of the *Enasas* Nation [Narrative A, p. 3b: by Which means her children became his own and would no longer be considered in the light of Slaves but as forming part of the Enasas nation—].

The unfortunate Husband now having lost all hopes of ever Seeing or of recovering his family by stealth, mustered the courage to sacrifice himself. He ascended to the top of a high hill which was in the vicinity of the Village; when he boldly made his appearance, singing his [p. 104] Death Song. The Enasas Seeing the boldness of this Stranger, took the alarm, thought he was a spy and that the enemy was at hand. The Village assembled, consulted; the men armed and in a body ascended the hill— when within a small distance the Stranger in a firm and loud voice hailed them as follows:—

"Enasa Nation, you who are the Authors of my wretchedness, be not alarmed where there is no danger. You see me naked and alone— I have no arms— I am a *Flat Head*— My friends are beyond the Great Mountains— they are in mourning. But I am not here to revenge for their loss.— [p. 105] I came for my wife and my Children whom your young men have carried away captives— If they are your Slaves, make me also your Slave;— if they are not among you, and are no more, let me go with them to the land of Spirits. Here, Enasas, dispatch me! I cannot live! I am your enemy".

Moved with compassion the Enasas received the unfortunate stranger with open arms— conducted him to the Village and treated him with kindness. Returned to him his wife and Children— presented him with horses and other presents [Narrative A, p. 4a: . . . gave him four fine horses loaded with presents . . .]— and invited him to remain in the village as long as he pleased. He declined staying for any time— but he assured his Benefactors that the desire of his [p. 106] Speedy return arose entirely from a Sincere wish of testifying to his friends the happiness he enjoyed— and to make them as sensible as himself of the high value that ought to be placed upon the friendship of the *Enasas*; whose generosity on the present occasion would certainly be the means of paving the way to an amicable and lasting intercourse between the two Nations [Narrative A, p. 4a: to a [one word illegible] of past injuries by encouraging in them a mutual exchange of good offices.].—

After these protestations of everlasting friendship, the Snake or Flat Head Indian with his wife and two Children took their departure; promising that he and some of his friends would pay the Village a visit the ensuing [p. 107] Summer. He Kept his word— for I was present, as already mentioned, when three hundred Tents of the Rocky Mountain Indians made their appearance. It was then that I was made acquainted with the preceeding circumstances.— [Narrative A, p. 4b: He kept his word— the following Spring he and several of his tribe appeared in the company of 300 lodges of Rocky Mountain Indians when he and his friends made a present of six famous horses with a great quantity of dressed leather to the Enasas— Who returned the Compliment in Christian goods— I was an Eye witness to this last part— by which I came to learn the first part of the Story—]

The Enasas make it a rule to protect all strangers from insult or injury while they remain within the limits of their villages— even the natural enemy of their own tribe are safe there. For which reason the Enasa Villages have become a Sanctuary for fugitives from all the surrounding Tribes; who go about fearlessly speaking their respective languages. These strangers, however, [p. 108] cannot be accommodated with the use of wives from among the Natives— but must confine themselves in that kind of happy liberty to the use of Slaves, or to women taken in war— Even the Mandanes who are neighbours are treated as Strangers in this respect.

But some of these strangers often make an ungrateful return. They often destroy their Benefactors and fly with the Scalps to their own nation, and thereby obtain forgiveness for the offence which caused their banishment. Though the Enasas are sensible of this treachery from dire experience, they still encourage the perpetual presence of Strangers. [p. 109] For they sometimes find it convenient to make use of them as Interpreters to traffic with the many Indians that resort to that quarter in the Summer Season; and Sometimes as ambassadors to distant Nations for the arrangement of differences.

[Narrative A, pp. 4b-5a: The Enasas are from dire experience sensible of this treachery Still they continue to encourage the presence of Strangers among them— for they Serve as Interpreters to the many nations who Send in the Summer to trade for the Commodities of the Mississouri— Some of these Interpreters Speak four or five different languages and some times are Sent as Ambassadors to distant nations to make up differences.]

I happened to be acquainted with one of the Strangers, who was of the *arrigira* Tribe,[45] and had lived with the Mandanes for several years— He was a handsome, bold fellow, but of very incorrect principles: and was the cause of much bloodshed to his protectors— who had employed him occasionally as an ambassador, but had been in the habit of betraying his trust, (*by giving information to the enemy*) [Narrative A, p. 5a: And he was in the habit of betraying them & of giving information *against them* to the enemy.]:— his treachery was [p. 110] at length discovered. In consequence a consultation of the wise men took place and his death was determined. But none of the Tribe was bold enough to put the Sentence in Execution— being thus embarrassed, they sent a deputation to the famous War Chief of the Enasa Tribe, to inform him of the treachery of the *Arrigira* Indian, of the Sentence of the Chiefs, and of the inability of the Mandane Indians to do it justice— at the same time insinuating a wish that he should favour them with his Services on the occasion. He understood their drift and replied:— "Is it true that the Mandanes [p. 111] have not so much courage as will manage a *Bad Dog*— and must my hands be ever Stained with the blood of their enemies? but since the safety of my friends the Mandanes depends upon the strength of my arm and the boldness of my heart, this Bad Dog shall not see another day.

At this he started from his seat, laid hold of his Battle ax and desired two of his young men to accompany him. Arrived at the Mandane Village, he immediately entered the Tent of the *Arrigira* Indian. They talked as usual familiarly together— until the accused, perceiving the evening approach, got up and said that it was time for him to look out [p. 112] for his horses. The Enasa got up also and accompanied the other attended by his two young men to the outside of the Village where there was a remarkable large stone.

---

[45] This refers to the Arikara Indians, Caddoan-speaking neighbors of the Siouan-speaking Mandans and Hidatsas, who resided at this time near the mouth of the Grand River in north-central South Dakota. The Arikaras are linguistically related

"Look here, *Camarade,* Said the Chief, I dreamed last night that this Stone was Stained with your blood, and my dream must be fulfilled this evening— Go, however, go for your horses, and pass here on your return— do not disappoint me— you know I can always find you even in the centre of your own nation [Narrative A, p. 5b: . . . even in the village of your own nation—]."

"If I should not pass here this evening with my horses, Said the [p. 113] Arrigira Indian, it will not be through the apprehension of danger from you, my Friend;" and went his way. The Chief instructed his young men, and each took his Station— When the *Arrigira* Indian on his return came to the fatal Stone, the Chief gave the Signal of death; and the young men shot the guilty Indian through the heart. The body was left to the wolves; and the Great Chief returned home in his glory, loaded with presents and with praise.—

End.

[p. 117]

Third Expedition to the Mississourie

Fall 1805. Mr. De Rocheblave[46] who succeeded Mr. Chaboillez in the Red River Department as Manager of the Company's Concerns did not approve of the Mississourie trade; but from the measures already taken he was under the necessity of continuing that business for another Season— and I was appointed to conduct it. [Narrative A, p. 1a: *after I had assisted in the full arrangement of the other outfits*—] On the 18th. Nov.[47] to our great joy our worthy friend Mr. La Roque and his party made their appearance from their visit to the Rocky Mountains.

It is not necessary that I should give the particulars of his journey as Mr. La Roque himself had kept an account of it. [p. 118] I shall therefore, merely observe that he was disappointed in his Expedition— Suffered great hardships during his absence, and had taken

to the Pawnees of eastern and central Nebraska and are sometimes called Pawnees or Panies in early accounts.

[46] Pierre Rastel de Rochblave was another partner in the North West Company. He was in charge of the Assiniboine district from 1804 to 1806. After 1821 he retired from the fur trade and pursued a career in politics. He died in 1840 (Wallace, *Canadian Biography,* pp. 641-42).

[47] McKenzie errs in the date, which was actually October 18. See Larocque's "Yellowstone Journal," ms. p. 31.

no less than thirty six days on his return to our Establishment. Mr. La Roque, after remaining a short time at my Post, I accompanied to Head Quarters— [Narrative A, p. 1a: He remained a short time with me at Montague a la Bosse the post I had in charge then I accompanied him to Head Quarters—] where Mr. De Rocheblave was relieved from much anxiety and received us with great kindness.

The arrival of Mr. La Roque in the Department having rendered my presence less necessary, all matters being arranged, I took my departure on [p. 119] the 24th. Nov. for my third Expedition to the Mississourie Country.[48] Three men and six horses accompanied me with assortment for the Trade [Narrative A, p. 1a: . . . with an assortment of proper goods for the trade—].— But no less than five other Traders forming as many different Interests had taken the lead of us for the same quarter.[49]

When I arrived at the Mississourie my friend the Borgne received me with open arms and conducted me to his tent. But finding the Hudson Bay Traders there before me,[50] I observed to the Chief that they and I having contrary objects in view could not agree together— he offered to send the others away— but knowing that his tent was not the most suitable to my purposes I [p. 120] thought it most advisable to thank him for his good intentions; then went directly to my old Landlord's Tent where I was cheerfully received and presented with a horse in testimony of his continued friendship and countenance. Indeed all the Indians seemed happy to see me again among them, which promised in my favour a decided advantage over my opponents [Narrative A, p. 1b: . . . and I enjoyed the preference in trade—].

About this time the Mississourie Indians to the number of three hundred and fifty warriors, under the influence of the *false horn* Chief, went to war towards the Sioux Country. [p. 121] After an absence of four days the party returned— they met the enemy, gave them battle, which lasted for a whole day. They Killed and wounded many, and brought with them Seven Scalps. But our party suffered also for it— had one Killed and seven wounded. On this occasion

[48] McKenzie is evidently again mistaken about the date. The master at Brandon House recorded in his journal that McKenzie departed for the Mandan villages with three men on October 27, 1805 (H.B.C.A., B.22/a/13, fos. 10d-11).

[49] The identity of these "interests" is not known. See Part One.

[50] This would be the Hudson's Bay Company party comprising George Budge, John Corrigal, and John Learth (H.B.C.A., B.22/a/13, fo. 10).

the Indians went through the usual ceremony of Singing and dancing round the Village with the new trophies: but the relatives of the unfortunate warriors, who suffered in battle, turned all their effects out of doors and did not join in the rejoicings. [Narrative A, p. 1b: The Immediate relations of the unfortunate warrior did not join this rejoicing they turned (*The father and mother threw all*) their effects out of doors. (*Where they were abandoned to the wind for they are* [?] *of those that chose to carry them away—*)]

Next day the people of our village went to the Mandane Village to a Dance. This dance was entirely confined to the Young Women [p. 122] of the different Villages, dressed in their best smocks and finest ornaments. These females went round the village dancing as they went, and Singing in praise of the Young victorious warriors. They received presents; which they did not carry away, but left them on the Spot [Narrative A, pp. 1b-2a: . . . which however were left to to Such as thought proper to take them away]. A Servant of the Hudson Bay Company, who happened to be present among the Spectators, carried off in presence of his Master, a fine horse and two Buffaloe Robes elegantly painted. I could not admire this conduct— as the white people were not of the war party and had not furnished any thing towards the [p. 123] Dance they certainly had no claim on the property which I conceived was given and abandoned by the natives from religious principles and as a sacrifice.

The preceeding night the noise was so great that I could not sleep a wink— the next day all the villages having had their turn I had reason to hope that the affair was ended— but I was greatly mistaken; they continued their merriment for a whole fortnight, when it was succeeded by another which was derived from an incident of a more cruel nature.

A Young man, brother to the great Chief, Sent for me to his Lodge or Tent; I went— after [p. 124] exchanging the usual civilities, he observed that during my absence in the Summer he had been at war: "and I killed, said he, a Serpent Chief, two young men, with Several women and children— I saved a young Slave, brought her here— I used her kindly, because I intended her for you. But at the end of three days she deserted in the night and carried off a fine horse from my tent. "Where did she go, I said: "She went, answered he, to her relations where she is arrived before now. This is the third time she was taken prisoner, and the third time she effected her escape. The former times She [p. 125] carried nothing but her own Simple robe away; but this time she is well dressed and has two knives— she is very pretty— none of our women equal

263

her— She is the greatest beauty of all the Indian Tribes— We know the white men would love her [Narrative A, pp. 2a-2b: . . . and would give a generous price to us for her.], and I saved her life on account of the white men."

I wish you had not been so merciful, my son, exclaimed an old blind woman, "I wish you had killed the B——h [*sic*], for She has stolen my knife which I had for three winters— it was a good knife— only the handle of it was broken." "Yes, Said a young Girl from the opposite corner of the tent; the bad Slave has stolen my knife also— [p. 126] I wish she was dead"! These wishes were not lost— In a short time after while the Village was still in an uproar, rejoicing for their late success in war; four young men who had been employed in the pursuit of the flying beauty appeared with her head at the end of a pole, which they planted at the door of the tent whence she had made her escape; and the horse she had stolen was delivered to the owner. They then retired in Silence to their respective tents— nor did the men of the village heed their arrival— for they considered the head or Scalp of a [p. 127] woman beneath their notice. Not so the women; overjoyed at the Spectacle, they collected around it in great numbers, dancing and turning it into ridicule. They pulled it by the hair from the pole— tossed it with their feet from tent to tent, throughout the Village, the one exclaiming to the other:— There is the Enemy! take care! be kind to her! At length the Head was consigned over to the boys, as a mark to exercise their arrows. [Narrative A, p. 2b: Not So the women overjoyed at the Spectacle they collected in numbers and danced for hours together round this object of their hatred— turning it into ridicule— they pulled it down from the pole by the hair and took delight in tossing it with their feet from one Lodge to the other— each as she kicked it to the rest called out— take care! be kind to the enemy who is going to See you! Yes! Yes! exclaimed the other rising her foot and repeating this appelation as she passed the joke on to the next. In this manner the severed head was bounced Several times round the village— & at length it was consigned over to the boys as a mark to exercise their arrows.]

The young men who went to look out for this unfortunate woman, it seems, followed her track by means of the marks left when she digged up roots for her sustenance. [p. 128] When she reached the Mountain thinking herself beyond research and safe, she took her time; killed a Buffaloe with her Bow and arrows— built a cabin of green branches, and began to dry and prepare a stock of provisions for her Journey across the Mountains to her own Country. The young men having lost her track wandered several days in the Mountains, and it was on their return home that they accidentally fell in with her hut and dispatched her by plunging their lances into her bosom.— [Narrative A, p. 3a: The winter being far advanced and considerable Snow upon the ground thousands of Buffaloes resorted to the vicinity of of the villages. We had great pleasure in Seeing the Indians go into the fields Surround and Kill whole droves of them— & so many to fall— one upon the other. The best parts only of the meat were taken home— and we lived like Kings At Other times the Indians would Contrive to conduct large bands to the Mississsouri and multitudes of people flying from every direction would form a lines which would confine them by gradual approaches into a narrow Space Where the ice was weakest until by the weight and pressure large squares perhaps of fifty Yards would give way covered with animals which in an instant the force of the current would carry under the other ice to a marr [that is, mare, the French word for pond or pool] a little distance below where they again emerge, float and were watched by men women and children Who being provided with the proper means haul them out of the water— until the ice was completely Strewed With dead Carcasses. Here they were left for some time to Season into a flavour then carried home and at feasts are reckoned a great delicacy—]

All the Traders who were in oppo[p. 129]sition to me, despairing of any success, returned to the Red River and left me in the Sole possession of the Mississourie Trade. I now divided my assortment into small parcels and made several outfits which I placed under the charge of my men for the purpose of carrying on the business with the natives to the best advantage, and my success generally speaking did not fall short of my expectations.

On the eve of my departure home, the *Black Cat*, a Chief with whom some of my men had Lodged in the Mandane Village sent me word by an Indian to call at his tent as soon as possible;— this I did [p. 130] immediately and asked him the cause of so pressing an invitation. "Your white men, Said he, do not mean to return with you—they have disposed of their own private property in favour of the Indians and would have done the same with yours, but I knew they were bad white men. They were dealing with bad women, and I have secured your property."

I thanked the Chief, then expressed a wish to cross in order to adopt steps for the punishment of these bad white men [Narrative A, p. 3b: . . . to take them prisoners and have them punished—]. "No, Said the Chief, that will cause difficulties— [Narrative A, p. 3b: . . . that will bring on a quarrel between me and the Indians in whose lodges they are—] for the Indians are bound to [p. 131] protect all Strangers." Seeing I could not do justice to my feelings without creating disturbance, I had all my property, assisted by Indians, transported to the Upper Villages. Two days after I returned [Narrative A, p. 3b ... with Morison[51] to my deserted residence—], Saw my men, tried to persuade them from their design; but they would not yield— I was, therefore, obliged to leave them and to hire a freeman in their place. This was in the month of February; and the first fair weather we took our leave of the Mississourie—

We had ten horses loaded with returns, including provisions. The first day we travelled until dark in hopes of falling in with a good spot of grass for our horses— but the Plains having been burnt in the fall and [p. 132] covered with Buffaloes all winter, the whole Country was as bare as the palm of the hand— Scarcely a Sprig of grass was to be Seen in any direction. We encamped in a swamp of dry Rushes; cleared a small space from snow, kindled a fire with small bits of dry wood provided for the purpose; and after satisfying our appetites by way of Supper with cakes [Narrative A, p. 4a: ... Corn Cakes ...] and Snow water, we laid ourselves down to rest: it snowed in the night; the air was raw— still we had a comfortable rest under the new fallen snow which completely covered our beds. In the morning we discovered [p. 133] that Seven of our horses were missing and could not be found in the vicinity of the Camp. We, therefore, secured our baggage under the snow— mounted the three horses that remained and returned to the Village. Here we learned that the horses which were missing were in the possession of an Indian; who on application readily surrendered them: he gave us lodgings for the night, and treated us with great kindness. The ensuing morning we set out early for our camp, found our baggage safe, loaded our horses, and continued our course until night came on without Seeing any appearance of wood for fire, nor of grass for our horses. We, therefore, found [p. 134] it necessary to continue, guiding our course by the North Pole [Narrative A, p. 4a: I desired Morison Who led the way to go on and guide his Course by the North Pole];— one of our men did not seem at ease— he however did not complain, but soon after began

---

[51] Throughout the Narrative A manuscript, Morrison's name is spelled with two r's, but one of the r's is lined out. The name is spelled with two r's, however, in Larocque's "Missouri Journal."

to lag behind. In measure as we advanced on our journey the snow became deeper and deeper; to pass over some heaps we were at times obliged to unload. This made travelling, particularly at night, very unpleasant. About midnight the Sky darkened;— the Stars disappeared, and a dreadful Storm ensued from the North— Now having no Star to guide, I desired the man leading the horses [identified as Morrison in Narrative A, p. 4b] to continue keeping [p. 135] the wind directly in his face and that I would endeavour to drive the horses after him. We had not advanced far in this manner when we heard the other man's voice [the other man is identified as "Roi" in Narrative A, p. 4b[52]] from a distance in the rear. We of course waited his arrival; he complained of fatigue and indisposition, then threw himself down upon the *à corps perdu* exclaiming *je ne partirai jamaiy dici ni mort ni en vie* ["In the manner of a lost body, I am not going to go from here dead or alive."]. We represented to him the critical situation we were in, and the very great danger we should run by stopping in the open plains exposed without any shelter to the violence of the Storm. The poor man would not or could not hearken to reason [Narrative A, p. 4b: . . . and would not Stir an Inch]. Seeing him in danger of losing his life if [p. 136] abandoned, I ordered the horses to be unloaded; and with the Baggage we formed a Rampart or Screen as Shelter against the Storm. We then made a bed of Buffaloe Robes upon which we placed the Sick man, who appeared motionless; we believed that he was gone or the next thing to it— we rubbed his face, his hands, his feet, wrapped him in Several Blankets. In a short time we could perceive some symptoms of life— he began to breathe, to shiver, and to move; he was restored— but we suffered severely from our attentions to him by the cold. To secure the horses we tied them to the [p. 137] baggage— then secured ourselves under the Buffaloe Robes. [Narrative A, p. 4b: Had it not been for that hardy excellent man Morison neither I nor Roi would have passed the night. We all three got into the robes;] My face and hands pained me greatly; which added to the whistling of the tempest through the manes of the horses deprived me of rest. In the morning the snow was on a level with the top of our fortification, and so heavy above our Buffaloe Robes that we had some difficulty to move under the load. Two of the horses broke their halters in course

---

[52]Coues (in Henry, *New Light,* vol. 1, pp. 186–87 n. 3) lists several fur traders named Roi, Roy, or a variant thereof but does not identify any of them with the Roi of this account.

of the night, but did not go far out of the way [Narrative A, p. 5a: They were already at Some distance but Morison soon brought them back]— the others were standing with their feet as it were united under them up to their bellies in snow and trembling— with their bridles frozen in their mouths. However we loaded our horses and having inclosed [p. 138] ourselves in our Robes, in hopes of setting the weather at defiance, we set out, but the drift and snow were so heavy that we could not see to the distance of fifty yards— with no marks to guide our steps, we kept on all day at random [Narrative A, p. 5a: . . . we Kept on all day without Knowing Whether we were right or wrong—]; but by observing the direction of the wind we endeavoured to keep the same direction. Towards the evening the drift flying in columns before the wind, gave us an opportunity of descrying at a distance the resemblance of trees; to which we immediately repaired, and came to a small creek where we found plenty of wood and water. I cannot [p. 139] describe my feelings on this occasion— my heart leaped with joy— nothing upon the face of the earth could have given me more pleasure than I experienced at that moment. We were provided to our satisfaction— but our horses, the poor animals were almost starved through cold, fatigue, and hunger— four days without eating a morsel they could scarcely muster strength to stand upon their legs. We procured for them the tops of trees, of which they seemed to partake with a good appetite. The following day we still had bad weather; but we remained in our Camp until the afternoon, when the Sky cleared: and we then discovered [p. 140] that we had gone out of our course considerably. After this we proceeded regularly, but the bad weather continuing, our progress was small— our horses were fatigued— we made trains which did not avail us much— found small Lakes, but they were frozen to the bottom. To make amends for this misfortune, we collected ice into heaps, wood being near, we lighted a fire in the top of the heaps, which in measure as the heap melted the horses licked the liquid for drink— Now perceiving that we were near our journey's end, I dispatched a man to the Fort for [p. 141] assistance who within a short time returned with plenty of men and Dogs who took charge of our baggage. I and one of the men took the horses in charge— but the horses unfortunately gave up and I was under the disagreeable necessity of abandoning them— nor had I scarcely a decent shirt to my back, nor a whole blanket to sleep in at the time. Next day we got to the Fort; which was the twenty third day from the Mississourie. [Narrative A, pp. 5a–5b: that we had gone out of our Course Considerably— We now went on Straight and got to Riviere a La Souris where bad Weather detained us Several days without making much progress. The Snow was now very deep and fatiguing for the Horses— Morison made trains Which however did not avail us much— passing again Through the plains we Threw them away. The Horses began to fail and I dispatched Morison a head to the Fort for assistance— Having come to a lake we pierced The ice for water— but there was none The Water being shallow it was all frozen to the very bottom— To make amens for this What was to us an additional misfortune— we collected ice into heaps wood being near we lighted fire in the top which as the ice melted the horses licked of the liquid— and Served them as drink— At length plenty of Men and Dogs Came to Meet us and took Charge of our baggage. Roi and I Kept the horses in Charge— but unfortunately they gave up and I was under the disagreeable necessity of leaving them in the middle of a large plain without Shelter and without Provender— excepting what they could scrape from under the Snow— My two horses were of the numbers— They were my only property nor had I scarcely a Shirt to my back nor a blanket to Sleep on at the time— Next day we got to the Fort— which was the twenty third day from the Mississouri]

The desertion of my men at the Mandanes and the failure of the horses in the way home injured my reception [Narrative A, p. 5b: . . . with Mr. Rochblave]. However when my returns were examined and the horses had recovered, my Expedition was thought more of and in the end I had no reason to complain.—

[p. 1]

[Fourth Expedition to the Missouri]

June, year 1806 — —

Mr. Rocheblave being on the eve of taking this departure for Fort William, it was incumbent on him by terms agreerd upon, to send people to the Missurie to draw Debts he hade made the preceding winter to a free-man [Narrative C, p. 149, identifies this man as a Canadian], who was to trade the indebted goods to or with the Pawnees,[53] & who promised to bring their value in furs from thence to the Gros Ventre Village, & there to be delivered to the person

[53] This is a reference to the Arikaras, who are linguistically related to the Pawnees and are often called by the latter group's name.

acting for NW. Co. who hade the first right to the surplus of the furs (after the debt being paide) at the Missurie Price— At the time Mr Rocheblave had made this debt he was little aware of the danger of sending men to the Missurie who when there thought themselves at liberty to act according to their fancy— Especially those who had very little to loose by dersertion but their Character. After experiencing the desertion of those who accompaniede me last winter & knowing how ready others were to follow their Example, Mrr. Rocheblave was loath to hazarde any more of them— After informing me of his embarrassments he asked me if I could possibly undertake the voyage with only Mr Caldwell—[54] I did not hesitate to tell him that there was some danger to travel at that season with horses & property & with so few people to accompany them; but notwithstanding that I woulde make a trial of it & avoid all danger if possible— Therefore every thing being got ready we departed on the 4th. of June— Myself & Mr. Caldwell had Six of the Company's horses to bring back the intended furs, & some articles for trade, & to purchase horses in Case of want A free man who had taken Debts at the H.B. had joined us [Narrative C, p. 149: . . . accompanied by a Canadian Freeman.], & we all three continued our march by long & crooked roads to avoid falling on some Indians whether friends or enemies, for in fact all were our enemies for carrying goods to the Missurie— & tho' we had seen some vestiges we had good luck to arrive on the bank of the Missurie [with]out seeing an Indian— Although the face of [portion of manuscript torn and missing from text] [p. 2] was in its full verdure, & every thing had the most sprightly appearance, the villages did not appear to be so gay as they use to have been— The reasons of these changes were that some of their young men had been Killed by the Serpents, among whom there was the son of one of the Chiefs, & all those who were able to Carry Arms had been gone to revenge the stroak (excepting a few that were taking care of the Villages) & those who remainede had abandoned themselves in sickness & mortality—

There was at this time a violent Cough, or a Chincough among the Missurie Indians which carried away, by their own calculation, 130 souls old & young in less than a months time— [Narrative A, p. 1a, and Narrative C, p. 146, refer to this as "Hooping Cough] The old men & women whose constitution was worn out, fell an easy

---

[54] James Caldwell, a clerk with the North West Company (Henry, *New Light*, vol. 1, p. 259 n. 10). Little is known of this man.

prey unregrated to this disease & the Children had not strength enough to resist its violence

Indeed many a person of a middle age were carried away in the carnage— It was not a strange thing to see two or three dead in the same Lodge at once; & I was apprehensive that myself & Mr. Caldwell might caught it which luckily we did not— It was no less than a touching scene to see the poor old women groaning away their *last*, in some corner without the least notice being taken of them— If they recovered they got to ate when they prepared it, & if they died they were removed when their survivors were at leisure— But their *simple* attention to their Children was great— their lamentation, drumming singing & jugglay [?] were insupportable to hear—[55]

However I believe that all their juggleries & roaring were of no more service to the sufferers than they were to me, which I must own was of some consolation to me because I could hear none of their groans among their rattling of the drum, & to such noise, mine ear was well accustomed— The disease began to slaken & death [became] less frequent soon after our arrival— The warriors arrivede at last, which seemed to put a fin [p. 3] end to their suffering— It is no less than surprising that about 600 horse-men would be out upwards of two months & would not be ashamed to come back in such triumph with only 3 Scalps: The fact was that they revenged themselves on the first [Indians] they met with & I believe that it is a common maxim with every Indian nation to turn back when they shed blood or after the first attack— thinking that they gain laurels enough if they attack at all; tho their passion for revenge is not quenchede— These warriors entered the Village triumphantly with the Scalps held up on long poles, & those who were lingering in sickness got there feet & joined the process— Without enquiring after thier relations, which the hand of death had prevented from a reciprocal rejoicing; the procession continued to the other Villages; & the bewailling for their Children, their nearest relations, as well as the death of those young men who were Killed at war turned to rejoicing— if singing dancing & riotting can be so called— Notwithstanding, a mother could be heard to burst out a crying in

[55] North American Indians had no immunity from diseases introduced from Europe and acquired by contact with advancing frontiers of European culture. Small-pox and other diseases swept through the upper Missouri River tribes several times with drastic consequences for the native cultures.

the heat of joy for the loss of images more dear to her than the Scalp of an enemy—

If I may hazard an opinion of my own, I believe that whosoever will look into the Indian passions will find them to be transitory, & all their life, a life of extremes— No being can bear with more manly fortitude a wound if attained at war, than they do; but should they cut their feet with an Ax, or fell ill with natural sickness they are on the other extreme— They are indolent, capricious, contemptuous & revengeful to the last degree; & yet their passions do not seem to disturb the quiet of their mind, which almost always appears regular & Calm— Indians in general bear Femine with great fortitude; & when they have it in abundance they devour their vitals [p. 4] like wolves & swell themselves like young pups for their jaws are never at rest, only while they are smoking or when they are at the Chace—

It is when they return from that exercise that their predominant passion for domineering has its sway— It is then that the stranger can see how an Indian is respected in his own Hut:—

No sooner the Children descry his approach than every one begin to clear the way, lest his feet should be entangled on his entering— their work is abandoned & their mirth recoils back on itself— On his entering none dare to salute him or even look in his face— he will put his weapons by him; & set himself on his hams, with great composure & air of dignity before a blaring fire, then each know what part is to be acted— The most Slavish of his women (as Indians in general have more than one woman) will approach him & take off his Shoes & Leggins, while another gaves him water to drink, & a third prepares his eatibles, which he begins to devour without speaking a single word since his entering into the hut, only that he will respire at intervals with great vehemence— as it were to breathe with more ease after his toil. During this time, every body is curious to know his good or bade success, but no one is bold enough to make an enquiry— The women & Children are looking about him with Keen eyes to see if they can discover a drop of blood or a hair about his Knife or clothes— If they do discover the sign of slaughter, they will keep the secret, lest they should offend their Sire, or the women their Lord

My lorde being now satiatede, & his first pipe smoked nearly to the bottom; he'll in a low tone begin to relate the adventure of the day— The same Silence since his arrival is now Kept with double restraint lest they should loose a part of his narrative— If successful he'll tell the women where they may find the animals

with every [p. 5] other [detail] relative to the Chace & his belief—
to throw a certain part away, & to hang another on a tree &c—
But if not successful he'll often blame the women for not paying
particular attention to his Commands— that he is sure they had
given certain bones to the dogs, or that they did not put the inviolable parts of the last animal he had Killed, as they ought to
have been put— or he'll begin by telling the many bad dreams he
had had the last night, & the encounters he had in the morning
with Certain birds & insects— not as an excuse for himself but to
convince his auditers that he could not hope for success after so
many bad omens— but at the same time these omens take all the
blame of his lucke—

But to return to the Missurie, on my arrival I founde some free
men to whom I had made some advances the preceding winter—
& who made a reasonable spring hunt on the Upper part of of the
Missurie in Beaver & Bears— They payed me, & I traded the remainder of their furs— I had likewise a better trade with the Indians
than I expected so that my goods were getting short— but the time
appointede by the man who had taken Debts at the Fort (& went
to trade them with the Pawnees) was not yet arrived, & I could not
leave the Missurie till the time was expired— About this time a band
of the Shawyens or Chaw-yens[56] came to offer terms of Peace to the
Gros Ventres & Mondans— They were received with great seeming
friendship & entertained for several days— A Chaw yen boy being
taken prisoner some years before by the G. Ventres they told them
at their departure, should his father come for him that he would get
him, to prove that the peace which they had accepted & offered was
sincere— In some time after the father came for his son, accompanied
by several of the Chawyens who brought a message from their [p.
6] great Chief to a young man of the Gros Ventres who opposed
him in the last Battle that was fought between the two nations; enticing him in the warmest terms to go & see them & holding up every
alurements to make him consent— The young man who was a great
Chief among the G. Ventres for his exploits at war did not appear
unwilling to go himself but the most of the G. Ventres opposed his
design for fear of treachery— Many were the Councils held on this
event but the young man (whose name was the Rattle Snake) was
afraid that his popular character should be attacked by those who
envyed him, & his courrage suspected by his enemies; he therefore

---

[56] That is, the Algonquian-speaking Cheyenne Indians.

resolved to carry all opposition before him, & reason brought them all to his side— During these controversies, I being in the Borgne's Lodge where all councils were held & every stranger hade the first access, I had an opportunity of seeing all strangers, whom I use to question regarding trade, & their mode of living & hunting— All strangers treated me with the greatest kindness & those who never had seen a White before they saw me looked upon me with great admiration. Some of them were afraid to come near me, but the most of them were too troublesome, feeling my skin, & would wish to put their hands w[h]ere they [had] nothing to do— but curious to Know if I were made like themselves:— But the Shawyens had seen & traded with several white people, tho' they had no traders on their lands— They were very intimate with me for I could understand & be understood by the Common signs of the Plain's Indians—[57]

The Shawyens who were here making Peace were enticing me to go with them to trade— telling me that they would load two horses for me with Beaver & those who Came for the Rattle Snake seconded those in their invitations— [p. 7] The remaining part of my goods was not with [worth] 5 £ [pounds sterling] & that same of a very indifferent quality— but I know that my goods would bring a far better price at the Shawyens, than they woulde [have] done at the Missurie— I therefore resolved to accompany the Rattle Snake & his following to the Shawyens but I had other opposition of whom I was not much aware of— & this was the Gros Ventres who would not hear of my going their with goods but putting a shadow over their real motive, by wishing to discourage me with personal danger, to which I was deaf— They Kept many private counsels & tryed every means to thwart my designs— I showed them the goods I intended to take with me. after dividing them in two— & told them that I would leave Mr. Caldwell the one half to trade with them in my absence— "It is not the goods we want," said they, "but if you should be Killed the Chief of the white people will never sent another here" I told them if they would not let me go that I would never come to them again— The council broak up— & several of them came back with Buffalo Robes which I would not trade— The Borgne with [which] is the greatest Chief & who was my landlord asked me many questions concerning what we did with Beaver & was much surprised that people who had every good thing that the

---

[57] McKenzie is here referring to the use of sign language, a system of hand signals used for intertribal communication throughout the Plains.

mind could imagine or whatever was of value would come so far from their native country for Beaver— 'Tis true said I, we have many good things but we have no Beaver— After a hearty laugh from the Borgne & his smokers— I told them with what contempt the Chief of the white people will look upon me if I will not go to the Shawyens who will tell him said they that the Shawyens have Beaver? he is a man said I that knows every thing & he'll be very angry with my Father (for so I called the Borgne) [p. 8] if he'll prevent me from going— If that be the case my son said the Borgni, you shall have full liberty to go to morrow morning, but should you be Killed tell your Chief not to blame me— He then got up with great composure & got his *sacred* Pipe & Stem, which he lighted, & after making the 4 Elements smoke, he pointed the stem towards the Fort, began a harranguing the Chief of the white people not to be irritated, telling him how often he had served him & his white people since he come to the world & how many Beaver skin of his own Killing he got—

The Borgne mentioned many services he rendered the white people to which I was quite a stranger till then— some of them were in themselves meritorious tho they were not all to the interest of the NW—

When done, he said since you say that my Comrade & equal (for so he call'd Mr Chaboillez) knows every thing he must have heard me & must know that my heart is good— I told him to the affirmative, & then they began to make conjectures concerning the the the Chief of the whites, what Kind of being he must be that Knows every thing at such a distance of his manly strength, of his might & power, of his stature & Bulk, & above all of his dress & offensive arms— Said they aman who has so much scarlet cloth to give for Beaver, cannot fail of being dress[ed] in Scarlet himself— In short they dressed the Chief in their minds to their own fancy & formed a high idea of his outward appearance, which I soon had every reason to regrate & which I will relate here after— The Borgne got me a young man to assist on the way, & I left the Village with the dawn to joine the Rattle Snake & his party in the other vilages I had taken 3 of the Cos. horses— one for myself one to carry the goods, & one for the young man that was to assist—

[p. 9] Going through the villages every one called me a fool, & the poor women were afraid I should never come back— At last the Rattle Snake & 12 young Scamps like himself, came out of the Village & having joined 10 Shawyens we began our march

Soon after this a party of the Mandans overtook us so that we

were about 40 in all, & we were to have the one common enemy—
Among the Mandans there [was] one Mr. Gissom of whom I had
occasion to mention in the first part of this journal—[58] Mr Gissom
informed me that he was going to the Shawyens *En Pipe*— that he
was sure of being better received & would gain more than to trade
the few articles he had; that he hoped by that means to pay me the
Debts he owned the NW. beside that it was the custom of these
Indians, that they new nothing about trade— I suppose said he
that you intend to push them a Pipe? I know nothing concerning
pipes said I, but if they are not accustom to trade, I can get a
better bargain, On the Contrary said Mr. G. they'll laught at you—
Then I'll Keep my goods said I & you will have the whole for
yourself— Gissom would have me to throw away my goods upon
Chance till he found all his arguments in vain— I asked him how
much goods he intended to put upon the pipe— I intend said G. to
put his horse, this Gun, a Fathom Cloth, 100 Balls & powder, & a
Large ax— Altho' I have more articles than you have said I, Yours
are of more value— which was a not [?] fact— At night the Rattle
Snake & his young men were much disheartened & they began to
question me what I would do were [we] to me[e]t with some enemies
or were the Shawyens to put us to death on our arrival— As to
enemies said I if we will meet them, I will follow your example
& as for the Shawyens there is no danger— But said the Chief we
have no Ammunition, will you give us [p. 10] some in case we
should see enemies? By all means said I, when I see danger— You
will better give each of us some now said this Chief— No I'll give
you some when there is necessity for it— Well said he you shall
turn back to morrow with some of the others who are to go back

I told him I would not, even were the whole of them to turn
back, that I would follow the Shawyens— They all said in one voice
that the white man was a fool, & that I did not see to what danger
I was exposed— The young men were very troublesome asking me
[for] vermillion & Tobacco— At last I told the Chief that he promised my father (the Borgne) to take care of me, & that I did not
expect such treatment of him—

This had the desire[d] effect for they never troublede me afterwards The second day several of the Gros Ventres began to drop
behind, so that at night there were only six & the Chief who did

[58] This refers to René Jusseaume, a long-time resident among the Mandans and
Hidatsas. See Part One.

not turn back— In this manner we Continued our rout[e] for four days through an extensive Plain, without meeting with any obstacle excepting some false alarms from the sudden movements of the Cattle— It would be in vain for me to attempt a description of the Landscape through we passed— It is there that the uncultivated mind could pass its days agreeably, & the Philospher could spend his life & find new objects to Keep his busy mind employed!— We crossed three Large Rivers that is navigable Rivers, with very strong current— Viz. Clearwater River, Heart River, & La *Rivier ou Bullet* [Narratives A, p. 3a, and C, p. 158, refer to the last as "Ball River"]:—[59] There was no wood to be seen excepting a few clusters of Poplar here & there along the banks of these Rivers— as it were to Shelter the inhabitants of these vast plains from the bitting jaws of winter!— If small things can be compared with great, the herds of Cattle coming to quanch their thirst at these Rivers could be compared to an *only* Ale-house in a market Place, where the busy crowd go to moisten their palates in the heat of the day— So were the Cattle in the heat of the day Kno[c]king down one another in the [p. 11] passes of the rivers— some going at their leisure, some coming with more hast & others taking their repose on the banks— The Beaver (which was here in great plenty) reign'd here undisturbed, for nothing seemed to make war upon him— nor were the Banks of the Rivers confined to the Buffalo alone; but there were numerous flocks of Red & Fallow Deer to be seen; the most of which in the h[e]ight of the day were lying on the face of the hills excepting those who were on the watch Sniffing the fresh gale, while their Companions past their time in watchful slumber— In short, on either side of us where we passed the face of nature appeared in full motion from the number of cattle which we put to flight—

There were likewise several muddy Creeks, that our horses had enough to cross them— In these creeks there was no water excepting a little here & there which the Beaver had conserved by stopping the course of the rivilets—

The fifth night being within twelve miles of the Shawyen's Camp there were many preparations to be made— more indeed than I think worth while to explain

---

[59] The first of these refers to modern Square Butte Creek. Heart River is still known by that name, and *La Rivier ou Bullet* is the Cannonball River. These are all eastward-flowing tributaries of the Missouri between the Knife River and the present-day boundary between North and South Dakota.

However the Rattle Snake & Mr. Gissom each took his intended
Pipe & filled it with all the ceremonies that superstition could
invent— then Cutting a green branch of Chock-Cherry & passing it
through a piece of fat dried meat the same which they planted in
the ground along side of each Pipe— this being done, a deep
silence reignede for some minut[e]s, when the Rattle Snake burst
out in a Kind of a lamentation or a lamentable Song, which lasted
for a quarter of an hour— Thus sung, a heavy murmur was heard
at every fire as a Thanksgiving— Then the Rt. Snake gave his pipe
to a lad who sat along side of him— & who after seeming to make
the four elements Smoke without lighting the pipe made a very
hearty harrangue in which he mentioned all the fates [fetes] the
Rattle Snake had ever accomplished, & implored the pity & the
assistance of all the living [p. 12] animals, fowls & insects— All these
ceremonies being over & the pipe & green branch carefully put by—
Mr. Gissom was desired to go through the same ceremony— but
Monsieur declined making a lamentation— saying that he would act
like the Father of all the white people (meaning the King) when he
made peace with his Children)— After making a grim face he hung
down his head in deep meditation— & here I was obliged to leave
the fire side for shame & laughter, & I did not come back till I
heard the hoarse murmer of all the *listeners*— When I came backe
the pipe was in the hands of a Mondan who was questioning Monsieur Gissom concerning his belief

Monsieur told him to make the Raising Sun smoke & to implore
the Pity of a certain Being who can dispose of life according to
his will & pleasure & who was wont to assist every White man in
distress!— that he (Monsieur) never Killed a man, that his main
aim was to do good that he lived in fraternal love with Every being
whether White people or Indians— The Mandan having had, as it
were collected the general heads of Monsieur's belief & actions commenced a very long harrangue almost in the following words—
Hoo-ho-hou! Smoke thou, bright Son of the East! & thou great
Being who disposeth of the white people's life at thy pleasure; do
thou not dispose me, tho I Know thee not, I implore not thy assistance for myself but for the aid of one of your own white people,
whom thou didst assist on former occasions— But should this Being's
power be deficient I implore all the animals of the Mondans to
assist.—

It is not to aid the warrior I call ye! no! it is to pity & to do
charity to a good sort of a man who lives like a Mandan, to whom
he brings Tobacco to Smoke Powder, Ball, Guns, Kettles, Axes,

FIG. 13. Flying War Eagle, Máhchsi-Karéhde, a Mandan, painted by Karl Bodmer at Fort Clark, North Dakota, in the winter of 1833–34. InterNorth Art Foundation, Joslyn Art Museum, Omaha, Nebraska.

Blankets, Cloth, & Knives to cut our vitals, Awls to make our Shoes, with Every thing else that is good— Hooee!— great Bull of the medow, be thou there with thy white Cow! sagacious [p. 13] wolf be thou there! Ye Bears & cats be ye there! Ye Eagles & Ravens be ye there! Ye Monsters of the hill, be ye there with your claps of thunder & fire! Thou great Serpent of the bitter sting be thou there & do not come alone but bring all thy Slaves & lesser Slaves to thy aid. . . .

Thus he continued for a great length of time greeting every thing the that his wild imagination made more frightful than they were by nature, to aid Monsieur Gissom in his bold undertaking in pushing the Pipe to the Shawyens— If I have erred in this harrangue or from the beginning of these ceremonies, it is by omitting a thousand absurdities which they commited in words & deeds— Nor would I have mentionede any of these absurdities which I was so much accustomed to hear every day, even by the Children; were it not to show how soon a Civilized being reconciles himself to the Savage life, & falls into the absurdity of their belief!— The ceremony being ended Monsr. gave a bit [of] Tobacco to the Mondan who pleaded in his behalf then addressed himself to me, saying that he was glad the Shawyens had seen how much attention the Indians payed to his Pipe— I told him, that it was ashame any man who professede Christianity to put the least faith in the most barbarous errors, which nothing but his credulity could point out as objects of Faith!— As we could not agree on this subject I gave up the point—

The nixt morning, & the sixth of our march two young Shawyens started very early to inform the Camp of our approach— & we began our slow pace with the Rattle Snake & Monsr. Gissom, each with his pipe in one hand & the Branch of Chock-cherry with the fat meat on, in the other,— walking before us, & singing a lamentable song The Branch & meat an emblem of Peace & Plenty: & the Pipe that of Social union— Many were the ceremonies which we were all obliged to observe— At lenght we spyed several horse men coming full drive before us [p. 14] who when they came to the Pipe bearers stopt short— when the Rattle Snake, succeeded by Monsr. Gissom, with a humble step & downcast eyes went up to them & held them the pipe which each Chawyen seemed to have drawn three whiffs— then claping their hand on their breast, which was as much as to say it did my heart goode— In this manner they served every one we meet with, till the Chief arrivede with about 200 horse-men in his suite— The Chief was mounted on a milk-white horse, & dressed in his war dress, harranging the Shaw-yens as he was coming along— his followers passed on our right hand & came up behind us— when the Chief cryed out to us to make a general hault— then came down from his horse & embraced the Rattle Snake, then striping himself as naked as his was the day he came to the world he clothed the Rl. Snake with his flashy war dress & with the assistance of others mounted him on his white horse— This being done the Chief lead the horse by the Tether barefooted & barebodyed to the Camp* (*Some nations have the custom of carrying the Ambassadour of a neighbouring nation into their Camps on their Shoulders but most frequent[ly] on a Blanket or a fathom of Cloth; but if none, on a Buffalo Robe between four Men.—) which was 3 good miles off [the published version, p. 380, gives this distance as six miles; Narratives A and C do not give any distance estimate], & the pipe which he received in his right hand the end of the stem pointed to the Camp & himself sang or lamenting all the way, in a language which none of us could under-stand, if there were any thing in it to be understood— But Monsr. Gissom followed him without the least notice being taken of him— All the others as well as myself followed behind— I drew the at-tention of the curious, & was surrounded by many, both olde & young who treated me with great seeming Kindness— At last we got sight of the camp which was pitched on an elevated spot on the L. bank of a beautiful River [the published version, p. 380, indicates the north bank; Narratives A and C do not specify a par-ticular bank of the river]— The Leather Tents were pitched in a circle which circumferenced the space of six acres— The exact number of Tents [p. 15] was 220. On entering the Camp I was con-ducted by one of their eminent Chiefs to his Tent, to whom I hade been recommended by the Borgne through the medium of the other Shawyens

I was actually lookede upon as the Borgne's Son, though they knew I was a White man— My new Host after giving me to eat of the best Which this lodge & the Camp could afford made a long har-rangue, commanding those that had furs to come & trade them with [the] Son of the Gros Ventre Chief— which they readily obeyed so that before sun set I had not a Single article for remaining nor had they any thing to trade excepting Buffalo Robes which being well Garnished they Kept or asked a higher price for than they were worth— However I sold the few art. [articles] I had to advantage having got about a hundred weight of Beaver, 4 of the finest Bear Skins that ever I had seen together with some fine B. Robes— My furs being tied up I went to see Monsieur Gissom, who I found very pensive sitting in a lodge smoking his pipe— After enquiring what was his success, he tolde me that it was less than he had a right to expect, but that I was the cause of it— for said he, they were bringing me furs very fast when you sent a man through the Camp harranguing that you would pay high prices for their Beaver, & those who had some in their hands to throw on my pipe turned on their heels & went to you with them, & since that time I got only few Robes— So continued he, for my Gun, cloth, Ax, ammunition, & horse, I got an inferior horse to the one I had given: 3 Beaverskins & 6 B. Robes—

Had I put myself in their Powder [power] as you wished me to have done I should not have a fourth of what I have at present, said I, & Monsr. I told you all along that you would be a looser— But he saide— *Il faut faire comme celu pour etre considrés par les Sauvages* ["One must do as he is considered by the Savages"]— The Gros Ventres were much caressed by the Shawyens & we all agreed to remain six days with them on condition that they should [p. 16] come & Camp half way to the Missurie, that a free intercourse should be between them & the Missurie Indians for the remainder of the season.— These six days I past with the greatest pleasure that the savage life could afford among variety of new objects & changes— I here witnessed greater slaughter upon Buffalo than I hade been accustom to see at the Missurie— I have been with the Shawyens a hunting, or surround the cattle, with[in] 20 acres of their Camp, when they Killed (without saying too much) 250 fat Cows which they left on the field as they fell; excepting the Tongues which they dried for a general feast they were to make for the Missurie Indians, whom they expected all in a Band when we should get home— At length we took our departure accompanied by some of the Shawyens, who were to invite the Gros Ventres, & the Mandans, & especially the Borgne, for whom they had the Skin of a White Buffalo, which to a Gros Ventre is too tempting an article to refuse, for when a man has a white Buffalo hide his fortune is made— On the third day we got to the village, where I found Mr. Caldwell very lonesome for my return— The time being expired in which we were to be back, they thought that we were all destroyed

After many councils [were] held, the Borgne consented to go to the Shawyens with some of his young men & if he found that they were not fond of their horses (to use their o[w]n expression) that he would send for the Gros Ventres to trade horses for European goods—

I gave a few articles to the Borgne to trade a horse for me, having the loading of the six horses I brought from the Fort already, beside my expectation that the free man who was trading at the Pawnees would come & pay his debts, which if he did I would be obliged to leave behind for want of horses— The Borgne then went to the Shawyens & I began to make preparations [p. 17] for my voyage to the Fort— Myself & Mr. Caldwell were thus occupied on a fine day, when of a sudden I heard my name repeated at the door of the lodge enquiring if I was within by a voice which seemed familiar to my ears— Dressed as I was in the Indian dress, I made haste to the door when my senses were surprised to view Mr Charles Chaboillez, Mr Alexr Henry & Mr Allen McDonell,[60] accompanied with 3 men standing at the door:— Their first salutation was to reprive me for being in an Indian dress, which at all times I found most convenient in an Indian Lodge & very light & cool in the warm seasons— Let any man who lives with the Indians take the *Idea* of Savage from it, & he shall find their dress much to his interest, he can pass through the crowd day & night without inciting curiosity or draw the throng of Children &, the barking of Dogs upon, which generally follows a white man in a Gros Ventre Village— It was for these reasons I had worn the Indian dress while in their Village, & not for my desire of adopting their manners which my two years residence might have attracted— Having announced the eminence of these strangers it runed [ran] through the Village like Shot— Many incited by *Indian* hospitality came with a part of the best their humble Huts could afford, for the visitants such as fresh & dried fruit, sweet corn pre-paired in different manners, green pumpkins & beens, meats green & dried; while others thronged in from mere curiosity to see the North Chiefs of whom they had hearde so much since they were accustom to see the white People & of whom they had formed such romantic ideas while at a distance, which could not fail of falling below their expectations when before their eyes— For the sake of Mr Chaboillez & Henry's characters, I gave a bit of Tobacco to those who brought them to ate, & though it was less than they expected on that occasion they said nothing

[p. 18] The Chiefs who were more bold began to question me

---

[60] The last-named individual is Allan McDonell, who was a clerk of the North West Company from 1804 to 1816, when he became a partner in the company. He was deeply involved in the North West Company–Hudson's Bay Company conflict over Lord Selkirk's Red River Colony from 1816 to 1819. He served the Hudson's Bay Company in responsible positions from 1821 to 1843. The date of his death is not recorded (Wallace, *Canadian Biography*, p. 444).

concerning the dignity & influence of these strangers & what were their motives for coming to the Missurie— I tolde the Indians that they came to see them to purchase fine horses, & were curious to know the country & its situation— I endeavoured to force from them that respect due to such personages, by launching out in their praise & eminence, but in vain— The Indians saw nothing in their mien or dress that would command respect, & much less by their liberality— They were accustomed to see white people who brought them their necessaries, but they were accustomed to look upon every white man as an inferior being to themselves Therefore those traders whom they had seen formerly (myself included) used to extort respect from them by threats to which they submitted in case of offending the Chief of the whites:

The Gros Ventres had heard by tradition of some Indians who had been at the Spainish settlements in former times, & who had been admited to the presence of the governor, he being in a shining dress, surrounded by his domesticks & guards had made an impression upon their minds accompanied with liberal presents that those who heard the tradition related form[e]d the same idea of our Chiefs or proprietors in the North

The Indians, indeed, could scarcely believe me that Messrs. Chaboillez & Henry were those whom we called our Chiefs— for said they, were these the Chiefs of whom all the North Indians speak, they would have at least a *pipe* of Tobacco to give to an Indian

The Indians began to ask me, who made them Chiefs, were they warriors or what made them superior to other white men?— I told them that they were Chiefs by the multiplicity of their riches, & superior to others, by the many Charities they made to the Indians— But the more I said in their praise, the more contempt they shewed me & if ever I regrated any thing in my life, it was for having said too much, tho, consistent with truth I could not support, from the meanness of their appearance [p. 19] On the other hand Messrs. Chaboillez & Henry were much disappointed from the ideas they formed of the Indians before they left their homes— They promised themselves a pleasant voyage— they had a long & disagreeable one— They were accustomed with Indians who praised them due respect— The name of a Proprietor goes a great ways among the northern tribes; but that name was not known at the Missurie— Therefore men of dignity must deck their persons with better apparels than the common dress of a voyager before they can assume the character which they ought to assume at this time, as the Indians

have no idea of mental abilities there must be something in the outward appearance to attract notice & command respect— Having said
so much I must explain what figur they made at the Missurie— Mr.
Chaboillez hade on a Capot,[61] which had been once white, a good
leather *Brix*, & a weather-betten Hat, with a stout black Beard of
nine day's growth— Mr. Henry differed only in the Capot for he
had on a corduroy Jacket— But as they were made sensible of the
same weather during their voyage, their dress were euqually weather-
damaged now see them thus arrayed entering the village sitting on
their snorty steeds. Each with a bundle of merchanddise tied behind
his saddle— As the purport of their vayage was to purchase horses—
it was on the goods contained in the bundles that depended their
future satisfaction— Being accustomed to hear so many extrave-
gance related of the Missurie horses, to which they gave so much
credit that they thought them superior to those of Arabia— The
horses being taken into the village at night they had an opportunity
of seeing them all, but to their great surprise they found them Four-
footed like every other animal of their species & not made to fly as
they had been informed!— I went from Lodge to Lodge with them,
pointing out every horse that had the name of being a famous Runner: but could point out none among 1500 horses to their taste—
either the colour or their make were [p. 20] against them all, & when
they fell by chance upon the colour they wanted (that is Iron-gray
with a white tail & mane) the horse was either too old or ill shaped
& had all the qualities but the quality sought— In their search, they
met indeed with many a noble beast which they could not but admire, but then the colour & then their Ears were split & at a nearer
view they were not so well proportioned as one would take them to
be with an oblique glance of the eye, they hung down their heads
their eyes were too much sunk, their breast too narrow their rump
rather high their back too short, & their hoofs badly made, with
many other defective qualities— Thus we past the evening in search
of a horse without *a fault* which I assured them that there was not
such a horse in any of the Gros Ventre Villages— Mr Henry avowed
his disappointment, & showed his destestation of the Indians & of
those who hade former dealing with them— In short he was displeased with himself, dissatisfied with his equal, & disgusted with

---

[61] A capote is a three-quarter or full-length coat made from trade blankets and
was a common item of apparel among Canadian traders.

his inferiors — I was kept busy in procuring provisions for them while they honored me with their Company, but after procuring the best food in the Village, at a high price & some trouble (with the goods I had in charge) the meat was condemned as unwholesome food, the fruit sour, the corn raw, & myself insulted (if a person in my situation could take an insult)— Mr. Chaboillez on the contrary was as much at his ease as if he were in his own house — Every thing pleased him & therefore [he] felt no disappointment, he set himself in the throng & smoked the pipe when it came to his turn with as much facility as if he were bred a Gros Ventre — but Mr Henry kept at a distance from the crowd & smoked his pipe alone — When the heat of passion was a little abated & seeing that the truth could be heard without offending I told them if they wished to purchase horses, that they had came very opportunity because the Indians [p. 21] were expecting an invitation from the Chawyens to trade horses & therefore that the Gros Ventres would part with theirs & with less reluctance than they would have done at any other time — but that they had very little time left to make critical remarks & finding faults to every horse — that many of those in whom they found so many faults would not be purchased for their weight in gold — I told Mr. Chabz. if he would wait for the Borgne's arrival, that I would assure him of the best horse in the whole Villg. on conditions that he should be satisfied with horse & start no objections to his colour — Mr C. being so far satisfied I had next morning to go to every Indian who had a famous horse & use all my endeavours to make them part with one but in vain, after naming the articles they were to get in return they all sent me off with a direct refusal or a smile — some of them indeed came to see the goods & w[oul]d have accepted them had not Mr. Henry adapted an opinion that their horses were inferior to the horse of those that would not sell theirs' & would wish them to run them before him but the Indians were not inclined to give him that satisfaction — About midday the Borgne's brother & some more of the Gros Ventres came back from the Shawyens to tell the Missurie Indians that the Borgne was wanting them all to go to the Shawyens to trade & that he would wait their arrival at the Shawyens — This news soon got sent throught the different Villages, & all the men & women began to make preparative to repair thither next morning The Borgne's brother had that famous horse of the Borgne's, which when that noble beast was examined by Messrs C. & H. they declared him to be without a fault excepting his colour, which was of a nut Brown — Having [told] this young man that Mr. Chaboillez was the Chief who sent the Chiefs Clothing to his brother two years ago & that he came in purpose to get a good horse— but that the Gros (Ventres treated) him with contempt & would not sell him a good horse—

[p. 22] "You know" said the young man to me, "how foolish the Gros Ventres are, & how fond they are of their horses? but it is a pity that my brother is not here, for he would give him his own famous horse immediately"—

Having told Mr C. what the young man had said, his heart throbed within him between fear & hope; & [he] consented to wait for the Borgne's arrival— Mr H. began to shew some envy & spleen to us all for the easy way we got a famous horse for Mr C.— Many of the Indians solicited Mr H. to purchase their horses merely to get goods to go to the Shawyens; but as I was obliged to do justice to the horse which [he] was to get & to tell the truth, he having solicited my opinion I told him that these horses were inferior to that of the Borgnes'— Mr Henry declared as he had came so far for a horse, that he would not accept of an inferior one for nothing, nor woulde he purchase his Equal— I told him then that he would have to carry his good[s] back to the Fort for a superior horse to the Borgnes' was not at the Missurie, & if any of the Indians had his Equal that I was sure they would not part with him— Nothing could have vext Mr. H. more & he said with a stern look— "I do not Know from whence it proceeds, but every d——ned [sic] rascal that comes to the Missurie goes back to the Red River with a famous horse, & I who am here with plenty goods of the best quality cannot get a horse, even to carry me back?" I told him that there had been rascals & honest men at the Missurie, & if they got horses that they were more easy to please, & that the NW books could testify their honesty: but that he might do as they did look out for himself— that for my part I would not open my mouth to an Indian for the future— When Mr Henry recovered a little from anger, he proposede to us to go to the Shawyens along with the Gros Ventres & Mandans to buy a horse [p. 23] to his taste & fancy— After some reluctance I consented to accompany them thither, & then Messrs. C. & H. went back to the Mandans where they fixt their abode during their stay at the Missurie— Next morning I went to find them & left Mr Caldwell once more alone taking care of the property. So many Indians cannot be expected to be ready all at the same time, we were obliged to wait for them on the hills— At length being all collected on the same hill, we were about 900 persons including men women & Children &

287

as many horses, some of which were loaded with Corn & other produces of the Missurie, with European articles of traffick— Our March
was beat with Ind. songs & flying Colours & the Indians being dressed
in their best there was something in the appearance of the procession
that would attract the eye of a traveller, & that would give him a
higher idea of the Indian taste than is generally given to the world
by those who travel among them—

Notwithstanding Mr Henry's prejudice against the Missurie Indians he could not help saying that there was nothing more grand to
be seen in this Country & had he not seen it himself that he could
never be pursuaded that the Indians had any notion of a regular
march or of putting themselves into files & figures—

The Young noble men selected themselves from among the
women & Children, & put themselves into Fil[e]s of eight every
way— that is eight men in breast & eight in depth— Being in eleven
files of right squares the number of able men that went with us to
the Shawyens must have been about 700 warriors— So that 300 of
them were Absent, for the Americans found their number to be a
little better than 1000 men able to carry arms— (Gros Ventres &
Mandans included)

We continued our march all day in the above manner, the regular
men at the head with a slow trot while the women & Baggage jog[g]ed
on behind so considering their form, their weapons which [p. 24]
consisted of Bows & arrows, Lances & Battle Axes, & Chields (not
but they had guns) they appeared like a small forest & would unwillingly bring to mind what is related of ancient times when our fore-
fathers made War— At night we camped all on a level plain where
there was hardly a drop of water to be founde— Many were the
offers that Mr. Henry got of horses which he would not accept, &
even Mr Allen McDonell would not buy any of them notwithstanding the many truths I told them both— & Mr C. himself was even
afraid that they would get better horses at the Shawyens than the
one he was to get from the Borgne— Next morning we continuede
our march in the same regular form, but more gaudy with Paints
& Feathers &c. & as we were approaching our destination the Shawyens were me[e]tting us. band succeedede band, till the whole of
that nation joined our procession— & such a sight was not a small
allurement to the curious eye, or to the mind fond of novelty.— But
Mr Henry's mind was too much allured by horses, to cast his eye at
large & catch the beauty of a splendid throng— tho he confessed
that such two War-like nations he had never seen & that the sight

was worthy of coming so far to see it— So many horses being gathered together & being trained to the *Chase* & *war,* were so much animated that they might be said not to walke but danced & pranced all the way Their Riders, to shew their agility in managing a horse, pranked & kissed & capered so much that their horses in a manner became unmanageable— What a field of temptation thus was to Mr Henry & who could blame him for not being decisive in his choice?

To choose the very best out of upwards of 2000 horses was not an easy matter— & not to choose the very best was a disgrace— Every horse then that attracted his fancy, I was dispatched to enquire of the owner if [p. 25] he would sell him— some of those gave me to understand by signs that they would not sell their horses & others shooke their Head, & Mr Henry had been often bargaining with the Gros Ventres, in my absence for the very horses he had refused that very morning but the bargain was immediately at an end when I assured him of his error— We arrived at the Shawyens Camp some short while before sun set— Where we were all received with Cordial amity— & having accompanied the Borgne's brother to where the former resided— & being informed of the dignity of the strangers the Borgne received them with tokens of more respect than the rest of the Gros Ventres paid them—

The Borgne asked our liberty to go & recommend good amity between the nations that they should not steal nor quarrel with one another but be as firm in their friendship as one nation— having got upon his famous horse he passed like lightening through the middle of the camp, which was as throng[ed] with people & horses as a market-place, haranging them in friendly terms— to have good understanding among them, & when he Came down from his horse at the Door of the Lodge, he put the bridle of his horse into Mr Chaboillez's hand— Mr C. being sensible of the Borgne's generosity he gave him his bundle of goods untied— The Borgne appeared much satisfied [with] the goods tho' I knew that at another time double the quantity would allure him to part with his horse, but to show his consequence to the Shawyens, he launched out on the many tokens of respect confered in him by the White people & that these Chiefs came from the Red River purpos[e]ly to see him & that he was sorry that he had not a good horse to give to Each

Mr Henry began to despair of getting a horse to his taste— & I myself enquired of the Borgne if he had [p. 26] got me a horse for the articles I had given him on his departure "My Son, said he "tomorrow I am to Adopt one of the Shawyens for my Son, & to offer them a pipe, on which the Gros Ventres will put all their goods & the Shawyens their horses— [62] according to our manner of trade we ought to expect at least 200 horses as we have that number of guns besid[es] other articles to put on the Pipe,— out of that number you can choose out a horse for yourself for you shall have the first choice"— If Mr C. was happy I was glorious to think that I was to choose a horse out of so many! I had been bargaining with a Shawyen for a fine Gray horse for Mr Henry— but he told me that the horse was to be put on the pipe of the G Ventres I consoled myself with the hopes that I would have for the Compy. the horse that was refused to one of its *members*— Mr. Henry said that if I was to get the horse for the Company that he would take him for himself & pay the Compy. the goods I had given for the horse, or return me some goods to buy an inferior horse for the Compy, as the Compy did not want famous horses— I told him that he might take the horse provided he would pay 300 Livers for him the price I could sell him for the Compy at the Red River— that I was bound to turn the goods given me in Charge to the best advantage, & thus it was indifferent to me to whom I sold them, whether to a Proprietor [or] an engaged,[63] or an Indian provided they were equally good pay: Mr. Henry said that he would take the horse in spite of me, being bought with the Company's property Having said that I would put him or any other in defiance to take from me the least article of the Compy, property while I did with it what was most necessary to be done, & that I acted there independant of him

Mr Henry told [me] that I was very Pert. [impertinent] but Mr C. showed us the folly of quarreling for a thing that was [p. 27] yet in the possession of Chance. & I was of too much utility at that time & place, to Mr Henry to Keep his anger any lenght— A short while after sun set, a horrid uproar arose through out the whole Camp, & every one with utmost speed were run[n]ing up a hill where more than the half of the two nations were already gathered, who by their motion & Cry seemed in an open quarrel— As every body went we

---

[62] In other words, the calumet ceremony would be performed on the next day to facilitate trade between the two groups. Ritual adoption and establishment of fictive kinship ties, as well as ceremonial pipe smoking, played major roles in this ceremony, which was practiced by virtually all Plains Indians. See Donald J. Blakeslee, "The Plains Interband Trade System: An Ethnohistorical and Archeological Investigation," for a generalized description of this ceremony.

[63] That is, an *engagé*, or laborer in the employ of the company.

followd their Example— This was occasioned by three Assiniboines who having arrived at the Missurie after our departure had followed our tracks hither— The Assiniboines & the Shawyens not being on peaceable terms, the latter were wishing to put the former to death— but the Gros Ventres & Mondans, whose protection the Assiniboines relied on & implored, would not allow the Shawyens to destroy them unless they wished to violate the breach of faith between the two Nations— The many threats on both sides nearly brought them to immediate hostility but the G. Ventrs. & Mandans having fortified the Assiniboines on either side they brought them Safe to the centre of the Camp— The Shawyens were enraged to see themselves deprived of their prey by those whom they considered in their heart as their bitter Enemies— Many were the attempts they made to break through the G. Ventrs. ranks with naked weapons to kill the Assiniboines who walked in the middle Singing their death Song— waiting, as it were, with patience their death Blow— but the Borgne who walked round & round the poor trembling Assiniboines, brandishing his Battle Ax in the air & threatening immediate revenge on the first who would do the least harm to the Assiniboines but at the same time used all his eloquence to peusiphy [pacify] both nations who were on the eve of engaging in hostility—

The weighty sound of the Borgne's voice was a [one word illegible] to his own nation, & was of terror to the Shawyens (& Mr Henry himself owned that he had a heroical aspect) which put an end to their mutual contest for a time in appearance but not in their heart—

[p. 28] The Assiniboines being in the middle of the Camp it is a rule with some Indians not to shed an enemy's blood within the limits of their huts or Camp, which perhaps saved the lives of these Assinbs. at this time— A party of the Scieux being with the Shawyens at the time had taken the Assbs. under their protection for that night, & every body turned home, but with a different countenance from what he had before Confidence was gone on both sides, & suspicion, anxiety & hatred took its place— Solitude & Coldness were seen in every bodys face instead of the mutual amity which reigned over all on our arrival— Some of them indeed made many efforts to raise the cloud from off their Countenance by various topicks, but the Bane of revenge being planted once in the Savage breast was not to be removed by forced smiles & superficial gestures— We went to rest, but could not sleep with the noise in the Camp— the Gros Ventres suspecting the Shawyen's perfidy did not go to rest but kept a watch over their actions all night— Mr Henry & I went in the morning went to look for the owner of a beautiful Speckled horse

291

which we were bargaining the night before— but that noble animal attracted the notice, if not the envy of all the G. Ventres but nevertheless, we got the owner to come to see the goods & when he saw them he was dazzl'd with the quantity & their quality but gave us to understand that he would see the result of the day & the decision of the nations about the pipe— Harang succeeded harang to get a long *shade* made by the women of Leather lodges for the reception of the Pipe & Dancers [in Narrative A, p. 6b, and Narrative C, p. 178, this ritual in preparation is called "the ceremony of adoption"], but none seemed in a hurry to execute their orders, till it was late of the day—

A certain number of respectable men being selected on both sides to execute every formal motion of the Pipe & adopted Son— Those on the intended Son's side sent him naked & crying to the Borgne, who received him with the tenderness of a real father & he & his Selected party Clothed him with every thing that was gaudy— [p. 29] then lead him with great many ceremonies to the Shade, which was strewed with flowers & weeds, Bulls heads, human sculls, bones, Scalps, & with many other absurdities— The young men began to Dance *le Grand Calmnete,* & some of the G. Ventrs. came with small articles of trade & lay them down,— the Shawyens brought a few lean & old horses— but the former misunderstanding between the nations made every thing come slow— & the old leven was fermenting afresh— The Selected made themselves hoarse haranging their respective nation those of the Shawyens animating them to bring their horses & these of the Gros Ventres to bring their Guns Ammunition & other European commodities, but in vain— nothing come

The Gros Ventres represented to the Borgne, that if they were to give their Guns & ammunition away to the Shawyens & render themselves defenceless, that the Shawyens would immediately fall upon them & destroy the whole of them with their arms & ammunition— & said they "Shalt these horses that we are to get in exchange defend us or carry us home in safety? & if they did, must we abandon our women & Children who are here exposed to the treachery of a perfidious nation?— Did not the Shawyens destroy 12 of the Rocky Mountain Indians who went to treat for Peace with them, no longer ago than last Spring? & do they not wish to do the same with us, if we are foolish enough to disarm ourselves & put ourselves in their power?— have we not horses as well as they have? We have, & ammunition & Guns more than they have "Then let us Keep that superiority to ourselves, & if the Shawyens wish for our friendship let them Keep their horses and be friends"— "But if on the contrary let us show once more that we are men, & that none but women are able to be terrified with threats"—

Thus, & more than this, said the representative of the Gros Ventres in the full hearing of the Shawyens [p. 30] but while he was yet speaking the Cry of *War* was heard in every quarter of the Camp— The Shade in an instant was pulled down about the Ears of those that were yet under it, & the adopted *Son* threw his fine Clothing to the Borgne & ran to his lodge to arm himself & to use them against he that was to be his father— Nothing could be more horrible to hear, than the Cries of these Savage *Animals* ready to devour each other! & the hurry among men woman & Children— Every body running to the fields for their horses, Shawyens, as well as G. Ventres & Monds & *we* white men among the rest— We soon got on horse back & in passing through the Camp, we met with the owner of the Speckled Horse, & having asked him if he would Sell his horse now? he shook his head several times with rage in his Countenance, & made signs to us to be off with the back of his hand— as it were to say *be off in time or worse may befal you*— Now every Petty Chieftian bent his *Bow,* & invited the companions of his former prowess to follow him— to animate them the more the Chieftians put them in mind of their valour in former battles where they had been successful—

The G. Ventres & Mandans being all got on an eminence or a raising ground above the Camp, we all made a halt—& while every body was fixing himself for the attack the Borgne who was on foot came to Mr Chaboillez, saying my *equal* lend me your horse that [I] may go & speak to these Dogs to know whether prefer Peace to War"— Mr. C. did not relish the idea of parting with a famous run[n]er at the time but the Borgne pressed him in a commanding voice to obey— while Mr C. was taken the Saddle off the horse I took the opportunity of asking the Borgne if they were to fight— My son, said he we have too many women & Children here to commence hostility ourselves— but if we [p. 31] are attacked we must not flinch— When the Borgne had been seated on his horse he soon passed through the crowd inviting all those who wore Breech-clouts to follow him— The other Chiefs huranged the throng with menacing voice to turn to the Charge— being now gathered on the brow of a hill in the sight of the Shawyen Camp which was now no more for when the Cry of war broke out, the women pulled down the lodges & huddled their Alls [?] on their horses & dogs & went off with speed— The Shawyens were all under Arms at the distance of a Parley froms us— The Borgne then spoke to them— I thought said he, Shawyens that I made myself known to you several times before &

yet you treat me with contempt— You invited me to come to see you in peace— I obeyed you with an open heart & brought peace along with me, but you allow me to go home on foot, with an heart full of anger— But I speak to you now not to reproach you, or to praise myself; but to get your decisive answer whether you prefer war to peace— Speak— When the Borgne ceased speaking, the Shawyens said to him— We know you very well & we did not invite you to our lands to make war upon you— The most of the present discord had begun among ourselves— & when that discord is adjusted you will hear our decisive answer

For the present there are too many women & Children on both sides to declare war— Therefore go home in peace— take your time & fear not— The two nations turned their back, or whilred about— Each taking the course that pleased himself, & thus ended the memorable *Fright* we gained by following the Gros Ventres to the Shawyens, & thus ended a discord which at first seemed serious but the nations being afraid of each other, the question was which of the two would run off first, & with honour— [p. 32] Having advanced towards home about 2 leagues we all encamped on a small rivulet— & the Borgne not being pleased with the answer he received from the Shawyens determined not to go further till he got a more satisfactory one— Therefore he sent three Young men to them in the night who returned before day— with a promise that the Shawyens should come to trade to the Gros Ventres Village when the Corn would be ripe— We started early from this campment as we intended to get to the Missurie that night

Mr Henry & Mr A. McDonell each with his bundle of goods behind him on the Saddle— Those horses which they despised going to the Shawyens— they asked to purchase them now, but their offers were rejected in turn— Some of the Indians indeed were malicious enough to enter into bargain with them & to work them further woe; broke off in the middle & went away laughing at their Credulity— others again came merely that they might hear from me what quantity of goods they would get for a famous [horse], tho' they had none to sell

By this time I had the name of every article [in] the bundles of good[s] contained at the butt end of my tongue & could rattle them off like *A.B.C.* Therefore it was not a hard task for me to satisfy the Curious, but whatever went wrong I was reproached, & if a Gros Ventre would not consent to part with his horse [he] was a great rascal, by Mr Henry's way of thinking, & if another offered his horse he concluded him as the greater rascal of the two, for he would wish

294

to Cheat— after a disagreeable voyage of four days we arrived at the Missurie— Where I found a Free man who Came up from the Pawnees, & who assured me that the free-man who had taken Debts from the NWCo— had been taken prisoner by the Sieux &c &c The Debts of course were lost— I did not wish to leave the Missurie so soon but Messrs Chaboillez & Henry prest me so hard [p. 33] that I was obliged to consent— Mr Henry accompanied me to the Gros Ventre Village where I procured him a horse at last & he returned to the Mandans that day— but the Gros Ventre regatting his horse went with the Goods to Mr Henry & brought back his horse in the night—

The Borgne got me a stock horse from some Rocky Mountain Indians who arrived during our absence & from whom I got some Beaver for the remainder of my Goods— Next morning I crossed the Missurie with 6 horses well loaded with one thing or other— & 2 light to carry myself & Mr Caldwell— I was not a little proud when I considered that I had been the first North trader who crossed the Missurie with 4 Packs of Beaver— I waited for some time on the Bank of the Missurie for Messrs C. & H. who joined me at last accompanied by Mr McDonell, an Indian boy, & 4 Canadians, which made us 10 in number, & having 24 horses amongst us, we were a good band, & in high Spirits— Mr Henry bought a horse from the Mandans that would better fill his station in a Cart & plough than under a saddle— but Mr. A. McDonell was not so lucky— he could not get a horse & his goods went for nothing— that is Messrs. C. & H. had taken them to buy sweet-Corn for their Children—

I bade a final adieu to the Missurie— & we had for a time a pleasent voyage, till the histories of the places through which we past, & we had to pass made such deep impression upon the mind of those who were not accustomed to those places that they were alarmed at every object they spied at a distance— Some of these objects were imaginary & some real, such as, Bulls, Deer, & wolves &c, which at times prevented the necessary portion of Sleep— The truth is that Mr Henry was eager to get home, where he could be more at his ease than in an open plain Exposed to all danger— & when we assured him that the danger was not so great as he thought, & that 10 resolute men armed as we were, were able to defend ourselves against any party of enemy we might Expect to meet with in these places— But Mr H. looked upon us with contempt, & told us that our defense was in flight— He hurried us on that we could not enjoy the Calm that reigned through the face of nature nor the plenty of its produce— so much so that my [p. 34] loaded horses were nearly jaded by Keeping up with light horses I often told Mr Henry to go on according to his fancy but to leave me & my horses alone— & as he had a guide of his own that he might do in one day more than I could do in two— & if he wished to hurry me on, why did he not Cause some of his men to assist me in unloading & reloading the horses— seeing that myself & Mr Caldwell did the duty of four men— Mr H. asked me why did I do it? I do it said I, to save the Company the wages of so many men— If that be your motive said he, you are a d——n [sic] fool, for the NWCo. will never give you more than your due— I said that I never expected more & that it was enough to the Company to [be] just & not to be generous— My horses being fatigued I gave them a day of rest, to the displeasure of Mr Henry— Having departed from thence, we made a good days journey & Camped in an open plain where the musquitoes tormented us much & our horses more— Having tied mine I was not apprehensive that they would go off, & I told the others to do the same but they only tied some of them & left the rest at liberty— Not being able to sleep with the flies Some of us got up, & lo! Eight of the horses were missing— We all got [to] our feet at the mention of the loss, & luckily for me none of mine were gone— Mr Chaboillez's famous horse, & 2 more of his were among the number astrayed— one of Mr. Henry's one belonging to the Compy. which had been lent to the man who guided the Monseiurs to the Missurie, & 3 others belonged to the men Having secured mine the most of us went look for them, but found none— In short we sought them during the space of 3 days but we sought them in vain— Having arranged matters in the best manner in our power we began to move Slowly towards the Fort & with great difficulty got there on the 3rd. day to the no Small satisfaction of Mr Henry & Chaboillez—

Well might they say, with he that said "Let no man say hereafter, this shall be a *Voyage* of happiness."— Indeed they had rather too high an idea of the Missurie before they started,— but by falling far short of their expectations they Could not enjoy the natural pleasing objects which appeared before them— The Indians in the same [p. 35] way, respected them while at distance: but no sooner saw them than all that respect vanished— To say the truth, their appearance was not to their Credit nor to the interest of the Company— It is was no less galling to me who understood some of the Indian language, to hear them despised, & the American Captains praised whom the Indians hated till then—[64]

---

[64] Henry recorded a quite different view of the events of the several days before, and of his own behaviour, in his journal (*New Light*, vol. 1, pp. 322–416).

TABLES

TABLE 1. Documented Round Trips by Canadian Traders Between the Mandan-Hidatsa Villages and the Assiniboine River, 1738–1818

Departure Date	Return Date	Party Composition	Product	Notes and Sources
18 Oct. 1738	10 Feb. 1739	Elder La Vérendrye, François La Vérendrye and one other brother; La Marque and his brother; plus a servant, a slave, and twenty-five Assiniboins	Exploration	The expedition left from Fort La Reine. Two unnamed men were left at the Mandan villages to learn their language; they did not return for eight months. La Vérendrye, 1927 Smith, 1980
Apr. 1741	—	Pierre La Vérendrye and one of his brothers	Exploration	The party left from Fort La Reine and visited the Missouri River; little is known of the visit. La Vérendrye, 1927 Smith, 1980
29 Apr. 1742	2 Jul. 1743	François and Louis-Joseph La Vérendrye and two *engagés*	Exploration	The expedition left from Fort La Reine and explored as far west as the Big Horn Mountains or the Black Hills. La Vérendrye, 1927 Smith, 1980
Winter 1773		— Mackintosh; no companions named	Exploration?	Arrived at the Mandans on Christmas Day; no primary source survives. Schoolcraft, 1853, vol. 3:253 Jackson, 1982:14
Mar. or Apr. 1781		North West Company: Donald MacKay and four voyageurs		

Early 1787		North West Company(?): James Mackay; no companions named	Not specified	Carried with him "some few Merchandizes." The trip to the Missouri took 17 days; he remained there 10 days. Nasatir, 1952, vol. 2:492
1793		Free traders: David Monin / — Morgan / — Jussomme / — Cardin	None	Leaving from Pine Fort, Monin wanted to obtain a "capital horse" on the Missouri. Monin and Morgan were slain by Assiniboins on their return. Gates, 1965:112
—	22 Dec. 1793	Free traders?: Two Canadians	A "great Quantity of Beaffaloe Robes"	"Two Canadians from the Misisurrie River arrived at the Canadian houses." H.B.C.A., B.22/a/1, fo. 13d
10 Dec. 1793	4 Feb. 1794	North West Company: Raphael Faignau / Antoine Bouriur *dit* Lavigne / Joseph Dube / JBte. Lafrance / Joseph Tranquille / JBte. Bertrand / Chrisostome Joncquard / Louis Houle / François La Grave	Not specified	Leaving from Fort Espérance, the party took goods worth 272 skins, "Chiefly ammunition." Only seven men returned, two having deserted: Jonquard and La Grave. The former, as well as Juan Fotman (Tremont; see below), was in Saint Louis by 1795. Nasatir, 1952, vol.1:333–34 Wood, 1984:89-90, 96-97
17 Feb. 1794	13 Apr. 1794	North West Company: JBte. Lafrance / Jos. Dube	2 bales wolves; 2 bales robes; ½ bale	The expedition, which left from Fort Espérance, took goods worth 282 plues, "chiefly

TABLE 1. *Continued*

Departure Date	Return Date	Party Composition	Product	Notes and Sources
		Jos. Tranquille Hugh McCrachen Louis Houle JBte. Bertrand Ante. Bourier Lavigne — d'Allard (guide)	peltries	ammunition." Jusseaume and Cardin returned from the villages with this party, but Joncquard and La Grave still did not wish to return. Wood, 1984:98, 104
17 Oct. 1794	19 Dec. 1794	North West Company: Jos. Tranquille Hugh McCrachen Jussome Juan Fotman (Tremont)	Not specified	After leaving Fort Espérance, Tranquille and McCracken met Jusseaume at "River La Sourie." The group apparently left for the Missouri from "River La Sourie" on 17 Oct., arriving on the Missouri on 27 Oct. They built a small fort between the Mandans and Hidatsas; Juan Fotman deserted down the Missouri River. "The Missouri men" returned to Montagne à la Bosse on 19 Dec. without Jusseaume, who returned with a subsequent expedition on 6 May 1795. Nasatir, 1952. vol. 1:331 Wood, 1984:119, 137 H.B.C.A., B.22/a/2, fo. 19d

Jan. 1795	Peter Grant's Company: —— Cardin	Not specified	6 May 1795	Peter Grant sent Cardin to the Missouri from Montagne à la Bosse. Cardin returned with the NWC expedition on 6 May 1795. H.B.C.A., B.22/a/2, fo. 19d Wood, 1984:123-24.
——	North West Company: Dubé and unspecified number of other men	Not specified	6 May 1795	The place and date of departure of this party are not known. It may have comprised the seven men whom Macdonnell equipped for the Missouri in late January "least Cardin and Peter Grants men should have it all their own way." However, this party did not depart on 27 Jan. 1795 for fear of hostilities between the Missouri River Indians and others. Dubé deserted and remained on the Missouri. The party returned to River la Sourie, accompanied by Jusseaume and Cardin. H.B.C.A., B.22/a/2, fo. 19d Wood, 1984:124,137
26 May 1795	Free trader: Jessomme		—	Jusseaume returned without Cardin. H.B.C.A., B.22/a/3, fo. 1

TABLE 1. *Continued*

Departure Date	Return Date	Party Composition	Product	Notes and Sources
12 Nov. 1795	26 Dec. 1795	Hudson's Bay Company: Thos. Millar James Slatter Unspecified no. of hired "Canads."	142 MBr equivalent "in Wolves Kitts & Robes also 2 horses"	H.B.C.A., B.22/a/3, fos. 8d, 10
—	6 Nov. 1795	North West Company: participants not specified by name or number		"Mr. Augees Men arrived from the Mandalls." H.B.C.A., B.22/a/3, fo. 8
2 Jan. 1796	3 Apr. 1796	Hudson's Bay Company: Thomas Millar James Slatter Robt. Robinson	120 MBr and 3 horses	This party had a very difficult time, losing 3 horses and some goods, and incurring considerable expenses. H.B.C.A., B.22/a/3, fos. 10d, 15d
2 Jan. 1796	—	North West Company: "two Canads from Mr. Augees and Mr. Baskey"		They departed in company with an HBC party the same day; after the return of the HBC party, it was reported that "the Canadians that went with Mr Millar he believes most of them are going to the Illinois." H.B.C.A., B.22/a/3, fo. 10d
—	1 July 1796	North West Company: five men	6 horses and 6 bundles of buffalo robes	"Five men arrived from the Mandals belonging to the N.W. Company." H.B.C.A., B.22/a/4, fo. 3

25 Oct. 1796	North West Company(?): Neel McKay	The Brandon House master noted that Neel McKay arrived "from the Mandals" on this date. One of his men, probably "Chayé," deserted from him at the Missouri River villages. Neel McKay brought with him James Mackay's proclamation prohibiting British subjects from trading at the Mandan-Hidatsa villages. According to John Evans, this party arrived at the villages on 8 October. H.B.C.A., B.22/a/4, fos. 16–16d Nasatir, 1952, vol. 2:461–62, 479, 496
24 Nov. 1796 16 Jan. 1797	North West Company: participants not specified by name or number, although one was probably named Desmairais	"A band of Canadians . . . went for the Mandals." They carried James Sutherland's letter to John Evans at the Mandans. The group returned with Evans's reply. They were "obliged to leave all their furs and Indian Corn which they had Traded" because their horses had strayed away. H.B.C.A., B.22/a/4, fos. 20d 28–28d Nasatir, 1952, vol. 2:478–80

TABLE 1. *Continued*

Departure Date	Return Date	Party Composition	Product	Notes and Sources
21 Jan. 1797	25 Feb. 1797	Hudson's Bay Company: James Slettar James Yorston	160 MBr equivalent	These men probably traveled with a party of NWC employees. The HBC men returned with "4 Sleds well loaded with Furs." H.B.C.A., B.22/a/4, fos. 28d, 31, 32d
26 Feb. 1797	12 Apr. 1797	North West Company: five unnamed men		Party returned with news of John Evans's departure from the Mandan villages. Jusseaume and La France were probably members of this party, which may have reached the villages on 13 Mar. 1797, according to John Evans. H.B.C.A., B.22/a/4, fos. 31, 35 Nasatir, 1952, vol. 2:496–97, 502–503
12 Nov. 1797	—	North West Company: a Canadian and a number of Assiniboins		"I understand McDonell has sent one Cadian to the Mandles in company with a number of Assiniboils to learn if the Spaniard is there." H.B.C.A., B.22/a/5, fo. 18

13 Nov. 1797	27 Jan. 1798	Hudson's Bay Company: James Slater Wm. Louttit Jno. Christian	300 MBr	The party left behind "3 packs which they could not take." They probably left the villages on 28 Dec. 1797. H.B.C.A., B.22/a/5, fos. 18, 26d Thompson's journal, ms. p. 41
26 Nov. 1797	3 Feb. 1798	North West Company: David Thompson René Jussomme Joseph Boisseau Hugh McCracken Alexis Vivier Pierre Gilbert Fras. Perrault Tousst. Vaudril Ls. JBte. Houl JBte. Minie		One of the men's equipments was worth "150 skins." Nine men accompanied Thompson, but sixteen people returned with him. On its return the party included two additional Canadians, two "natives of that place, and two slave women." H.B.C.A., B.22/a/5, fo. 27 Thompson's journal
3 Feb. 1798	1 Apr. 1798	Hudson's Bay Company: James Slater Jno. Christian James Carston James Short	200 Br equivalent	H.B.C.A., B.22/a/5, fos. 27, 33
4 Feb. 1798	26 Apr. 1798	North West Company: Hugh McCraghen Minier Murray and two other Canadians		The five Canadians set off for the "Mandles" with eleven sledges. This party evidently returned accompanied by "Menor" (Ménard). This may have been the party that Thompson says was headed by Hugh Mc-

TABLE 1.*Continued*

Departure Date	Return Date	Party Composition	Product	Notes and Sources
				Crachan, which was ambushed by the Sioux. H.B.C.A., B.22/a/5, fos. 27, 34d-35 Thompson, 1916:240 Thompson's journal, ms. p. 48
29 Sep. 1798	11 Nov. 1798	Free traders: Menire (Ménard) Jussomme	Ménard "is going away he havg traded with the Summer Master here upwards of 60 Wolves."	Evidently some Mandans had accompanied Jusseaume to the Souris-mouth posts, as the 17 Nov. 1798 entry records their visit to BH. Ménard appears to have not returned with Jusseaume. H.B.C.A., B.22/a/6, fos. 1, 8, 9d
11 Oct. 1798	23 Dec. 1798	Hudson's Bay Company: James Slater John Christian Magnus Tait John Anderson	400 MBr equivalent	H.B.C.A., B.22/a/6, fos. 5, 16
19 Nov. 1798	7 May 1799	Free trader: Jessomme		"towards Evening Mr. Jessomme an old Residenter at the Mandalls came here." He had traveled back to the Assiniboine River down the Souris

14 May 1799				River in a "Buffalo Canoe." H.B.C.A., B.22/a/6, fos. 9d, 36d
<u>c30 Sep. 1799</u>				H.B.C.A., B.22/a/6, fo. 37d
10 Oct. 1799	19 Dec. 1799	Free traders: Jessomme Minor (Ménard)		H.B.C.A., B.22/a/7, fo. 1
10 Oct. 1799	19 Dec. 1799	Free traders: Jessomme Minor (Ménard)	Jusseaume was "well loaded with Wolves & Kitts"; Ménard sent two horses loaded with "110 Skins & 130 MBr in furrs"	Goodwin found these two men at BH on his arrival for the 1799-1800 trading season. H.B.C.A., B.22/a/7, fos. 4, 10
		Hudson's Bay Company: James Slater, Senr. John Learth William Luttit Andrew Fubbister		This group was accompanied by the free traders Jusseaume and Ménard to the Mandan villages and return. H.B.C.A., B.22/a/7, fos. 4, 10
30 Dec. 1799 (possibly delayed until 6 Jan. 1800)	27 Feb. 1800	Hudson's Bay Company: James Slater, Senr. John Learth (Searth?) Magnus Tait Andrew Fubbister Peiry Sutherland		H.B.C.A., B.22/a/7, fos. 11, 19
—	<u>30 Mar. 1800</u>	Free trader: Jessomme		H.B.C.A., B.22/a/7, fo. 24
27 Sep. 1800	22 Nov. 1800	Hudson's Bay Company: James Slater, Senr.	500+ MBr 2 horses	James Slatter, Senr. stayed behind in the villages to

TABLE 1. *Continued*

Departure Date	Return Date	Party Composition	Product	Notes and Sources
		James Slatter, Junr. Wm. Yorston Wm. Lutitt Andrew Fubbister George Budge		continue trading. He returned with the HBC expedition of 10 Feb. 1801. H.B.C.A., B. 22/a/8, fos. 3d, 6d
1 Dec. 1800	10 Feb. 1801	Hudson's Bay Company: James Slatter, Junr. Wm. Yorstone Wm. Lutitt Andrew Fubbister George Budge	600 MBr 3 horses 5 dogs	James Slater, Senr., returned with this expedition. H.B.C.A., B.22/a/8, fos. 7d, 12d
—	23 Jan. 1801	North West Company: participants not specified by name or number		"Some Canads. came from the Mandalls." H.B.C.A., B.22/a/8, fo. 11
9 Oct. 1801	21 Dec. 1801	Hudson's Bay Company: Jas Slater, Senr. Jas. Slater, Junr. Wm Louttit Jas Moar Wm Yorston	300 Br equivalent 8 horses	James Slater, Senr., remained at the villages to continue trading. After an expedition initiated on 18 Jan. 1802 was aborted because of Indian unrest, James Slater, Senr., was left to find his way to BH with opposition traders. H.B.C.A., B.22/a/9, fos. 9, 12d–13
—	24 Apr. 1802	North West Company(?): three Canadians	"10 horses well loaded"	The Canadians were probably NWC employees, but this is

Date	Traders	Amount	Notes
22 Oct. 1802			not clear from the records. They were accompanied by James Slater, Senr., who returned with 150 Br and three horses. H.B.C.A., B.22/a/9,18d
18 Apr. 1803	Hudson's Bay Company: Jas. Slater Wm. Lutitt Thos. Johnson Wm. Luttit (Henhouse)	780 Br 8 horses	H.B.C.A., B.22/a/10, fos. 5, 8d
10 Dec. 1803	Hudson's Bay Company: Wm. Louttit George Budge Wm. Yorston Tom Tavill	252 Br equivalent 1 horse	Carried with them five horses "well assorted." George Budge remained in the villages to continue trading; he returned on 30 Mar. 1804 with 117 "Br" and three horses. H.B.C.A., B.22/a/11, fos. 3, 5–5d
12 Oct. 1803	North West Company(?): two Canadians		These men traveled with the HBC party that departed on the same date. H.B.C.A., B.22/a/11, fo. 3
—			
30 Mar. 1804	Free trader: Manor (Ménard)	211 Br	"Mr. Manor a Man to whom I gave debt to last Fall brought me 211 Br." Ménard apparently traveled from the Mandan-Hidatsa villages in the company of George Budge, an HBC man. H.B.C.A., B.22/a/11, fo. 11
—			

TABLE 1. *Continued*

Departure Date	Return Date	Party Composition	Product	Notes and Sources
—	14 Sep. 1804	Free traders: Manor (Ménard) Hany	136 Br	"Mr. Manor arrived from the Mandals he Brought me 136 Br. in sorts, a Mr Hany came with him who wants to agree in the service." "Hany" is apparently Hugh Heney, who found employment with the NWC after being turned down by HBC. H.B.C.A., B.22/a/12, fo. 5d
—	13 Nov. 1804	North West Company(?): two Canadians		Hugh McCrachan was probably one of these men, who appear to have arrived at the villages about 15 Oct. 1804. Lewis and Clark, 1904–1905, vol. 1: 206 H.B.C.A., B.22/a/12, fo. 7d
19 Oct. 1804	3 Jan. 1805	Hudson's Bay Company: George Budge George Henderson Tom Anderson	208 Br. "of sorts"	Budge and Anderson remained in the villages, returning on 15 Mar. 1805 with 424 "Br." Lewis and Clark noted the arrival of this party at the villages on 8 Nov. 1804. H.B.C.A., B.22/a/12, fos. 6d, 8d Lewis and Clark, 1904–1905, vol. 1:218

Date	Company/Personnel	Goods	Account
11 Nov. 1804 12 Feb. 1805	North West Company: F.-A. Larocque Charles McKenzie Bte. Lafrance Wm. Morrison Joseph Azure Bte. Turenne Alexis McKay	(See below)	Larocque Journey No. 1 and McKenzie Journey No. 1; they carried a "good supply of Arms and Ammunition" to trade. After leaving Fort Assiniboine, the party arrived at the villages on 27 Nov. 1804. Larocque returned to the Assiniboine R. with Wm. Morrison on 12 Feb., leaving the others at the villages. The entire party returned to Assiniboine Fort on 2 May 1805. Larocque's "Missouri Journal" McKenzie's Narratives, first expedition account Thwaites, 1904–1905, vol. 1:227
Dec. 1804	North West Company: Heney	545 Kitts 57 Wolves 4 Foxes 7 Beaver skins 5 Bags Corn 1 horse	Very little is known of this trip. Larocque recorded Heney's arrival in the villages from Fort Assiniboine on 14 Dec. 1804; he probably left the villages on 20 Dec. 1804, returning with the furs collected by Larocque. Larocque's "Missouri Journal," ms. pp. 13–14 Thwaites, 1904–1905, vol. 1:237–38, 266

TABLE 1. *Continued*

Departure Date	Return Date	Party Composition	Product	Notes and Sources
20 Feb. 1805	2 May 1805	North West Company: F.-A. Larocque Bte. Turenne JBte. Houl Votchagons		Larocque Journey No. 2; he returned to Fort Assiniboine briefly. Larocque's "Missouri Journal," ms. pp. 25–26 McKenzie's Narratives, first expedition account, ms. p. 45
2 June 1805	18 Oct. 1805	North West Company: F.-A. Larocque Charles McKenzie Lassana Wm. Morrison Baptiste Lafrance Souci Lafrance		Larocque Journey No. 3 and McKenzie Journey No. 2; the expedition originated at Fort Montagne à la Bosse. McKenzie, LaFrance, and Lassana remained at the Missouri River to trade; Larocque, with Souci and Morrison, explored as far west as the Bighorn Mountains. Larocque's "Yellowstone Journal" McKenzie's Narratives, second expedition account and the supplement to the second expedition

—	16 Jul. 1805	North West Company(?): five Canadians		These men traded their furs to the NWC and may have been their employees. H.B.C.A., B.22/a/13, fo. 5d
22 Oct. 1805	30 Mar. 1806	Hudson's Bay Company: Ge. Budge J. Corrigal J. Learth	840 "Skins of different Kinds"	Learth returned to BH on 6 Dec. 1805 in the company of Lafrance (see below) but left again for the Missouri ten days later with Lafrance and William Coarsey, another HBC employee; all three men eventually returned to BH on 30 Mar. 1806 with the remainder of Budge's party. H.B.C.A., B.22/a/13, fos. 10d, 15
22 Oct. 1805	6 Dec. 1805	Free trader: Lafrance	403 "beaver assorted furs"	Lafrance accompanied the preceding HBC party to the Missouri but returned to BH in the company of John Learth. It is not clear from the available records whether Lafrance was acting on his own or as an HBC agent during this trip. H.B.C.A., B.22/a/13, fos. 10d, 11d
22 Oct. 1805	10 Jan. 1806	Free trader: Heney	280 "Skins of different Kinds of furs"	Heney accompanied the preceding HBC party to the Missouri but returned to BH alone.

TABLE 1. *Continued*

Departure Date	Return Date	Party Composition	Product	Notes and Sources
				H.B.C.A., B.22/a/13, fos. 10d, 12
27 Oct. 1805 or Nov. 1805	—	North West Company: Charles McKenzie Morison two other unnamed men	"Ten horses loaded with returns"	McKenzie Journey No. 3. He went to the Missouri to collect 200 beaver skins owed the NWC by "five Canadians." He met Budge's HBC party at the villages. While there, two of his men deserted, and he and Morrison hired a free trader named "Roi" to assist them back to BH. There is disagreement between the two sources as to the departure date. McKenzie's Narratives, third expedition account H.B.C.A., B.22/a/13, fos. 10d-11
16 Dec. 1805	30 Mar. 1806	Free trader: Lafrance Hudson's Bay Company: Jn. Learth Wm. Coarsey	(see HBC expedition of 22 Oct. 1805, above)	Lafrance and Learth had accompanied the preceding HBC expedition to the Missouri but had returned to BH on 6 Dec. 1805. On 16 Dec. 1805 they and William Coarsey "went of with good for

Date	Party		Notes
			"Ge. Budge who remained at the Mandan River." They returned to BH with Budge's party. H.B.C.A., B.22/a/13, fos. 12, 15
May 1806	—	Free trader: La France	La France appears to have obtained goods at BH and returned to the villages in May, where Alexander Henry encountered him on 20 Jul. 1806. Henry, 1965, vol. 1:329
4 June 1806	North West Company: Charles McKenzie (James) Caldwell plus an unnamed free trader	"6 horses well loaded" including "4 Packs of Beaver"	McKenzie Journey No. 4. McKenzie returned with the following NWC expedition. McKenzie's Narratives, fourth expedition account Henry, 1897; 1965
14 Jul. 1806	North West Company: Alexander Henry Chaboiller A McDonald T. Viandiear Hugh Maceacan Joseph Dercharme plus Putchauconce, a Chippewa Indian		Henry and Charles Chaboillez visited the Missouri villages to obtain horses for themselves and to explore the country. McKenzie and Caldwell, already at the villages, returned to the Assiniboine River with this party. Larocque notes that a "Mess: N N" returned with them, "who had passed the summer ther on a trading jaunt."

TABLE 1. Continued

Departure Date	Return Date	Party Composition	Product	Notes and Sources
				Henry, 1897; 1965 Larocque's "Yellowstone Journal," ms. p. 46 McKenzie's Narratives, fourth expedition account
18 Oct. 1806	20 Dec. 1806	Hudson's Bay Company: George Budge James Slater George Moad Willm Corsey Thomas Anderson Jacob Corrigal	400 MBr 1 horse	Budge remained in the villages to trade. H.B.C.A., B.22/a/14, fos. 5, 8d
30 Dec. 1806	27 Apr. 1807	Hudson's Bay Company: "the 5 mandal men," presumably Slater, Moad, Corsey, Anderson and Corrigal	390 MBr "and a few Buffalo Robes" 3 horses	Expedition was pillaged by the Assiniboin Indians on its return, with the loss of six horses and part of the furs. George Budge returned with them. H.B.C.A., B.22/a/14, fos. 9, 15-15d
26 Oct. 1807	9 Oct. 1808	Hudson's Bay Company: Hugh McKrachin La France		These two free traders were hired by the master of Brandon House. On 3 May 1808 the master learned that La France had died at the villages during the winter;

Date	Date	Party		Source / Notes
29 Oct. 1808				when McCrachan returned he "bro't nothing." H.B.C.A., B.22/a/15, fos. 5d, 12d
	15 Dec. 1808	Hudson's Bay Company(?): Hugh McCrachan and two Canadians	"5 loaded horses"	McCrachan may have undertaken this trip on his own, or as an agent of the HBC. H.B.C.A., B.22/a/16, fos. 5, 6d
—	30 Sep. 1809	Free traders(?): three Canadians and two Mandans		"To day Arrived 3 Canadians and 2 Mandanes in Company from the Missi Sourie." The Mandans returned with the 9 Oct. 1809 HBC expedition. H.B.C.A., B.22/a/17, fos. 6d, 7; James, 1966:26–27
9 Oct. 1809	6 Dec. 1809	Hudson's Bay Company: Wm. Yorstone Christopher Harvey Humphry Tavill Jas. Searth and two Mandans	"better than 700 Wolves of the worst quality"	Expedition intended to trade with Americans at the villages ("under a Mr. Choteau") but was forced to trade with the natives under threat of being plundered. H.B.C.A., B.22/a/17, fos. 7, 12d
—	23 Dec. 1811	Free traders: an "old Canadian" and an American		"An American with an old Canadian arrived here from the Mandan Villages." The American intended to return

TABLE 1. *Continued*

Departure Date	Return Date	Party Composition	Product	Notes and Sources
				with the joint HBC-NWC party of 8 Jan. 1812, but it is not clear if he did so. H.B.C.A., B.22/a/18b, fo. 6d
8 Jan. 1812	14 Mar. 1812	Hudson's Bay and North West companies: Yorston and three men in company with North West Company employees	"about 60 beaver skins a few buffalo Robes 7 wolves and a bear Skin- & my neighbors people the same number"	This joint expedition was for "our mutual security, and to protect ourselves against the Natives." The men reported that Americans at the villages traded to better advantage than they. H.B.C.A., B.22/a/18b, fos. 8, 12
	Dec. 1812	North West Company: two unnamed employes		"they came under pretext to trade dressd Buffaloe Skins, and made some Presents to the Chiefs, and began to harangue against the american traders. . . . ," Luttig, 1920:122
9 Feb. 1813	8 Mar. 1813	Hudson's Bay Company: Peter Fidler, Kiveny (Kivney) and eight other men	"Indian Corn, Beans, Pumpkins, & Tobacco for seed in the Colony—"	The Brandon House post journal for 1817-18, written by Fidler, mentions that he was personally in the villages at this time, a trip that is corrob-

Date	Party	Returns	Notes
			orated in the 27 Feb. 1813 and 18 Mar. 1813 entries in Miles Macdonell's journal. Seeds were brought back from the villages for planting by Lord Selkirk's colonists on the Red River. H.B.C.A., B.22/a/20, fo. 36d P.A.C., MG19, E1, pp. 16798–99 and 16807–808 Moodie and Kaye, 1969:527
Winter of 1816–17	North West Company		The only reference to this expedition is a passing remark recorded by Peter Fidler in the Brandon House Post Journal for 1817–18. H.B.C.A., B.22/a/20, fo. 21
15 Nov. 1817 15 Dec. 1817	Hudson's Bay and North West companies: "Mr Greille Rough" (apparently two individuals) [Joseph] North three Murons [Dugald] McDonald [Angus] McLennan in company with North West Company employees	131 whole beaver skins 26 scrap Do. 110 Half Beaver 3 large Bears 1 small Do. 13 Red foxes 4 saddles 20 fn. line 3 Horses	The returns from this joint expedition were divided equally between the two companies. The Brandon House master paid the "Canadian Hunter" seven skins and the "NW Interpreter & Trader" eight skins for their services. The value of the returns was £ 232.17.0 and the outfit value was £ 51.15.4, leav-

TABLE 1. *Continued*

Departure Date	Return Date	Party Composition	Product	Notes and Sources
				ing a profit of £181.1.8, but the entry is not clear as to whether this was the HBC share or the entire joint returns. H.B.C.A., B.22/a/20, fos. 21, 24–25
2 Dec. 1818	26 Dec. 1818	Red River colony and Hudson's Bay Company: Archibald McDonald Pisk Kipling, Angus Matheson, and a "Souteu" Indian	10 Horses 166 "Beaver skins of sizes also a few foxes"	This expedition was sent from Lord Selkirk's Red River colony, but most of the settlers —including "Old La Grave the Mandan Interpreter"— returned to Pembina before reaching the villages. The expedition was accompanied by two Brandon House employees, Pisk Kipling and Angus Matheson. The expedition arrived at the villages on 12 Dec. and remained there six days. The horses obtained at the villages cost "above double the price they are got for" in the Assiniboine River area. H.B.C.A., B.22/a/21, fos. 38–38d, 40 Cole, 1979:85–86 P.A.C., MG 19, E1, vol. 53, pp. 20502, 20527

ABBREVIATIONS: BH = Brandon House
                  NWC = North West Company
                  HBC = Hudson's Bay Company
                  H.B.C.A. = Hudson's Bay Company Archives
                  P.A.C. = Public Archives of Canada

NOTE: Underscored dates indicate "reverse" expeditions, that is, journeys made to Brandon House originating in the Knife River villages. Participants' names are spelled as they appear in the documentation for each expedition. Full citations of sources will be found in the references section.

TABLE 2. Summary of Goods Traded South to the Missouri River,
1797–1806

Firearms:
　Trade guns and pistols
　Powder and ball
　Wormers
　Flints
　Powder horns
　Shot bags

Edged and Pointed Tools:
　Knives, large and small
　Butcher knives
　Axes, large and small
　Half-axes
　Battle axes
　Cassetete à calumet (hatchet or tomahawk pipe)
　Hoes
　Lances, some up to three feet long
　Awls
　Hatchets

Personal Vanities:
　"Trinkets"
　Vermillion ("paint")
　Looking glasses (mirrors)
　Combs, some of them ivory
　Cock feathers
　Rings, usually of brass
　Hawk bells
　Soap

Stimulants:
　Tobacco (by the carot, fathom, and pound)

Woven Goods (Clothing and Blankets):
　"Chief's clothing"
　Laced coats
　Capots (coats) of different sizes
　Cotton shirts
　Corduroy trousers
　Flannel robes
　Leggins
　Blankets
　Flags

322

TABLE 2. *Continued*

Hudson's Bay red and blue strouds
Red and blue strouds
Calico

Beads:

Wampum belts
Wampum hair pipes
Wampum shells
Pipe beads (by the string)
China beads
Seed beads (by the pound)
Barley corn beads
Blue beads

Miscellaneous Items:

Brass and copper kettles
Bow irons
Peppermint
Tenae (in bottles)
Firesteels
Flints
"Iron works"
"Killion quills"
Papers of "cor'd glasses"
Sugar
"White powder"

TABLE 3. Inventory of Trade Goods at Fort Espérance,
December 29, 1793*

3 La. Red & green striped Blkts.	2½ Dozn. Clasp knives
14 Blkts 3 pts.	3 Cartouche knives
36 Do 2½ pts.	4 Dozn. La: knives
7 Do 2 pts.	12 Dozn. Small
3 Do 1½ pts.	2½ Dozn. Razors
5 Do 1 pt	12 Land Hats
1½ Piece fine Aurora striped strouds	8 Com. Vt. Rd. Hats
½ Piece Red striped strouds	2 Masses blue Beads
	2½ lbs. Vermillion
4 Ps. HB blue strouds	10 Small worsted Belts
2 Do Com. blue stds	10 Prs. worsted Hose
1 Piece Com. Red strouds	7½ Milld Prs.
11 Chiefs Coats	7 Mill'd Caps
6 La: Land Capots	2 Dozn. Guimblets
1 Capot 4 Ells	8 steel Tobacco Boxes
2 Do 3½ Ells	3 Glass'd Japanned Do Do
5 Do 3 Ells	4 Small pewter Basons
11 Do 2½ Ells	3 Bayonets
12 Do 2 Ells	2 Hand Daggs.
34 Do 1½ Ells	2½ Dozn. P.C. Lookg. Glasses
28 Do 1 Ell	10 Chiefs feathers
9 Prs. Leggings	2 Dozn. Prs. scissors, small
47 Prs. La: Sleeves	4 Prs. Buss shoes
13 Prs. Moyen, a	1 Gray surtout Coat
12 Prs. Sma: Sleeves	4 lbs. Net thread
3 Callico Mautlets [?]	2 Bunches Holld. Twine
7 Callico Do	1 Net & Maitre
21 Chldns. Robes	11 Kegs H wines
1 Callico shirt	4½ Do powder
1 R.S. shirt	1½ Bale Kettles
7 Mens white shirts	3 Cases Guns
11 Boys Do Do	1 1/3 Sack Ball
12 Childns. Do Do	2° Do Shot
1 Pr. RS. Trowsers	2 Bales Carrot Tobacco
3 Prs. Callico Do	1 Roll Spencers Twist
22 Prs. Garting	¾ Roll Brazil
6¾ Gro[ss]: Rings	2 Stock Locks
2 Gro: Hawks Bells	3 Gun Locks
5 Gro: Thimbles	1 Case knives N# 5
	10 Half axes
	6 Moyen axes

TABLE 3. *Continued*

2 Gro: Awls	7 Capetetes
3 Gro: Gunworms	53 Darts
16 Doz. fine Steels	11 Broad Trenches
3 Sacks flints 250 ea.	35 Narrow Trenches
4 Rings Collar Wire	14 Kegs Mixd Rum
10 Rings Ear wire	
1 Do Snare	

*From W. Raymond Wood, ed., "Journal of John Macdonell, 1793–1795; in *Fort Espérance in 1793-1795: A North West Company Provisioning Post,* by Daniel J. Provo, pp. 92–93.

TABLE 4. Inventory of Trade Goods at Brandon House, 1810-14

Item	1810–11	1811–12	1812–13	1813–14
Awl blades	204	60	11 doz	137
Baize, unspecified		25 yds		
blue	30 yds			
red			16 yds	
white			14¼ yds	
Bands, arm	7	2	1	1
wrist	48 pr	9	9	13
Basins, pewter	2			1
Battle axes	1			
Bayonets, unspecified	35	14		
small			12	
large				24
Beads, common	88 #	20 #	42 #	24¼ #
China	28¼#			
fine				1½ #
Bells, hawk	75 pr		36 pr	
horse	20			
Blankets, 1 point	45		4 pr	
1½ point	9			
2 point	32	14	8 pr	3½ pr
2½ point	92	9	6½ pr	9½ pr
3 point	89	20	1½ pr	22 pr
large striped	7	6	9	31
Boxes, egg	6			
tobacco japann'd	6			
tobacco w/burning glass	4			
Brandy, English	797½ gals	52½ gals	249 gals	22 gals
Buttons, pewter waistcoat	8 doz	8 doz		
gilt coat				6 doz
Cards, playing	4 packs			
Chisels, ice	8	3	27	47
Cloth, blue plain		20 yds		30 yds
blue cord	243¾ yds	136 yds	110¼ yds	205 yds
blue fine	18 yds			
red cord	282 yds	13½ yds	82 yds	159¼ yds
red fine	24¼ yds	10 yds	7½ yds	7½ yds
Cloth, green		7½ yds		46½ yds
white	57 yds	36 yds	28½ yds	52½ yds
Combs, horn	17			
horn, large		14	14	1/3 doz
" small			35	2 1/3 doz
ivory		1	4	1 doz

TABLE 4. *Continued*

Item	1810–11	1811–12	1812–13	1813–14
Cotton, printed	33¾ yds			10 yds
Duffle	124 yds	40 yds	34¼ yds	115⅞ yds
Epaulets	3	3		
Feathers, worsted	38	36	4	4
Files, unspecified	39	23	36	
flat bastard				42
Flannel	22½ yds		3 yds	9 yds
Flints	2848	928	1180 #	2207 #
Fringe, worsted	38 yds	29 yds		
Frocks, duck				5
Gartering, common	1200 yds			
quality		206 yds	2 3/120	6¾ gross
Glasses, looking book	48	36	7 9/12 doz	95
Guns of 2½ feet	11	4	8	14
3 "	6	3	8	18
3½ "	30	8	7	8
4 "				1
Handkerchiefs, cotton				1
silk bandanna			2	
silk fancy			5	
silk soosee		2	5	
silk black	6			
silk colored small	7			
Hatchets, unspecified	77			
large			25	54
small			42	56
No. 1		21		
No. 3		30		
Hats, common			1	4
fine	1		1	
bands and buckles				3
Hooks, codfish	90	56	39/100 (pr 100)	1 6/100 (pr 100)
trout			1 (pr 100)	
Horns, pr powder ½ #		4		
Jacket, blue serge lined	1			
Kettles, copper	198¾ #	68½ #	152¼ #	160¼ #
Camp No. 1	2			
Camp No. 2	3			
Camp No. 3	3			
Camp No. 4	5			
Camp No. 6	2			

TABLE 4. *Continued*

Item	1810–11	1811–12	1812–13	1813–14
Camp No. 7	3			
Knives, clasp	73	1		4½ doz
roach handle	574	24	7 doz	56 doz
yew handle	484	203	29 6/12 doz	27½ doz
Lace, orris	70 yds	41 yds	15 yds	14 yds
worsted	574 yds	76 yds	37 yds	24 yds
silk	793 yds			8 yds
bett	191 yds			
Lances		8		
Lines, net	32			
Molton, blue				38 yds
green				55¾ yds
red				7½ yds
white				95 yds
Needles	1191	417	273	4 7/25 (pr 100)
Pans, tin, pudding small	6			
No. 1		4		
No. 2				4
No. 3		1		2
No. 4		1		
Pipes, hunters		7½ doz		1 gross
tobacco long			1/12	
Pistols	4	8	7	16
Pots, japann'd, ¼ pint	2			8
½ pint	7			9
1 pint	7			6
1 quart				4
tin, 1 pint				3
1 quart	1			
Powder, gun	745½ #	575½ #	497 #	866 #
Raven, duck		12 yds		28¼ yds
Razors	24	30		
Ribbon	60 yds			
Rings, pr ear silver	470 pr	18 pr		
finger, do	40 pr			
Rum, unspecified	26 gals	138½ gals		
Jamaica				8½ gals
Leeward Island		170 gals	681⅛ gals	
Sashes	13	3		
Scissors	4 pr		4 pr	2 pr
Serge, embossed	33¼ yds			11¼ yds

328

TABLE 4. *Continued*

Item	1810–11	1811–12	1812–13	1813–14
Settees, serge blue, No. 4				1
No. 5			2	2
No. 6				1
Shirts, checked, linen	2		2	
cotton white	4			
cotton, striped				3
calico, infant				6
calico, youth		1		4
calico, boys				4
calico, adult		2		
Shoes, common			1	
adult common	15			
adult fine	2			
Shot, assorted	681 #			
ball	1126 #			
of numbers		215 #	1 cwt	
BB		184 #	1 cwt	4.28 cwt
Low India		536 #	9.2 cwt	15.0.1 cwt
Spoons, table		6		5
Steels, fire	147	96	35	9
Stockings, worsted				8 pr
Thread, unspecified	5 7/16 #			
colored		¾ #	½ #	2 11/16 #
Tobacco, unspecified			1213¼ #	1774¾ #
Brazil	295½ #			
cut	11 #			
Spencer's Twist	604½ #	736 #		
Traps, steel	13	14		13
Trinkets, silver, No. 1	6			
No. 5	17			
No. 6	3			
No. 10	6			
Trousers, cloth	2 pr			
duck, 17/na			1 pr	10 pr
duck, 18/na	1 pr	2 pr	2 pr	4 pr
Trunks, small	4			
Tumblers, japanned, 1 pint				6
½ pint				6
¼ pint				6
Twine, fine	81½ skeins	8 skeins		
No. 1		9 skeins	84 skeins	
No. 3			1 skein	

TABLE 4. *Continued*

Item	1810–11	1811–12	1812–13	1813–14
No. 6			30 skeins	
No. 9			18 skeins	
No. 10		16 skeins		36 skeins
No. 11			13 skeins	4 skeins
Vermilion	12 #	2½ #	5½ #	7 #
Vittery				50¼ yds
Waistcoats, flannel	10		1	
Worms, gun	120	24	36	10
powder, ¾			3	
powder, ½			3	
Value of total inventory	£ 1821	£ 628	£ 877	£ 1726
Value of inventory remain-ing at end of season	£ 235	£ 196	£ 91	£ 114

Sources: 1810–11: H.B.C.A., B.22/d/1, fos. 2d–7; 1811–12: H.B.C.A., B.22/d/2, fos. 1d–6; 1812–13: H.B.C.A., B.22/d/3, fos. 1d–4; 1813–14: H.B.C.A., B.22/d/4, fos. 2d–7.

TABLE 5. Comparison of the Gross Value of Fur Returns from the Mandan-Hidatsa Villages and the Upper Red River District

Trading Season	Value of Mandan-Hidatsa Returns*	Value of District Returns	Percentage of District Returns Comprising Mandan-Hidatsa Returns
1795–96	262 MB	4100 MB*	6.4%
		4207½ MB‡	6.2%
1796–97	160 MB	1233 1/12 MB‡	13.0%
1797–98	500 MB	6800 MB*	7.4%
		6858 7/120 MB‡	7.3%
1798–99	684 MB	6200 MB*	11.0%
		8023 19/24 MB‡	8.5%
1800–1801	1100 MB	3900 MB*	28.2%
1802–1803	780 MB	5486 MB*	14.2%
1803–1804	580 MB	4215 7/12 MB*	13.8%
1805–1806	1523 MB	6399 5/12 MB‡	23.8%
1806–1807	790 MB	5000 MB*	15.8%
		5103 11/30 MB‡	15.5%

NOTE: MB denotes made-beaver standard of value.

*Denotes estimate recorded in the Brandon House Post Journal for that season.

‡Denotes value recorded in the Albany Factory Account Book for that season.

SOURCES: Brandon House Post Journals: B.22/a/3, fos. 10, 15d, 23; B.22/a/4, fo. 32d; B.22/a/5, fos. 26d, 33, 36d; B.22/a/6, fos. 1, 8, 16; B.22/a/8, fos. 6d, 12d, 19; B.22/a/10, fos. 8d, 10; B.22/a/11, fos. 5–5d, 11, 12d; B.22/a/13, fos. 11d, 12, 15; B.22/a/14, fos. 8d, 15, 15d, 17; Albany Factory Accounts books: B.3/d/106, fo. 61; B.3/d/107, fo. 63; B.3/d/109, fo. 46; B.3/d/110, fo. 45; B.3/d/119, fo. 28.

TABLE 6. Interrelationships Among Charles McKenzie's Narratives and Other Contemporary Sources

First	Second	Supp. to Second	Third	Fourth	Author/Document
	×	×	×	×	McKenzie Narrative A (hand one)
				×*	McKenzie Narrative B (McKenzie's hand)
×*	×*	×*	×*		McKenzie Narrative C (hand two)
×	×	×	×	×	McKenzie's fourth narrative (hand three—published by Masson)
(Trips 1 and 2*)	(Trip 3*)				F.-A. Larocque's journals
				×	Alexander Henry's journal
×					Lewis and Clark Expedition journals
×					Brandon House Post Journals

*Transcriptions reproduced in this volume.

References

ARCHIVAL MATERIAL

Diocese of St. Hyacinthe, Saint Hyacinthe, Quebec, Canada
Burial record of François-Antoine Larocque, leaf 3, Volume 4, *Registre des Baptêmes, Mariages, Sépultures*, Bishop's Residence, Cathedral of St. Hyacinthe.
Hudson's Bay Company, Winnipeg, Manitoba, Canada
Brandon House Post Journals, B.22/a; Brandon House Account Books, B.22/d; and Albany Factory Account Books, B.3/d, Hudson's Bay Company Archives, Provincial Archives of Manitoba.
McGill University, Montreal, Quebec, Canada
John Macdonell, "The Red River," CH 183.S164, Department of Rare Books and Special Collections, McLennan Library.
Charles McKenzie's four narratives, CH 19.S55, CH 20.S56, 24.S60, and CH 21.S57, Department of Rare Books and Special Collections, McLennan Library.
Missouri Historical Society, Saint Louis, Missouri
Letter from Pierre Chouteau to Secretary of War William Eustis, December 14, 1809, Chouteau Collection, Box 7, Pierre Chouteau Letterbook, pp. 146–47.
Montreal University, Montreal, Quebec, Canada
François-Antoine Larocque's "Yellowstone Journal," Baby Collection, Archives Department.
Papers of Thomas Douglas, fifth Earl of Selkirk, Manuscript Group 19, E1, Series 1, Selkirk Collection, 1769–1870.
National Archives and Records Service, Washington, D.C.
Letter from Joshua Pilcher to Lewis Cass, December 1, 1831, Record Group 75 (Records of the Bureau of Indian Affairs), M234 (Correspondence of the Office of Indian Affairs, Central Office, and Related Records, Letters Received, 1824–1881), microfilm roll 749 (Saint Louis Superintendency, 1829–1831). Copy in Western Manuscripts Collection, Missouri State Historical Society, Columbia, Missouri.
Letter from Joshua Pilcher to William Clark, February 27, 1838, Record Group 75 (Records of the Bureau of Indian Affairs), M234 (Correspondence of the Office of Indian Affairs, Central Office, and Related

Records, Letters Received, 1824–1881), microfilm roll 884 (Saint Louis Superintendency, 1836–1851).

Ontario Public Archives, Toronto, Ontario, Canada
Manuscript journals and fair journal copies of David Thompson's travels.

Public Archives of Canada, Ottawa, Ontario, Canada
François-Antoine Larocque's "Missouri Journal," Manuscript Group 19, C1, Volume 33.

PUBLISHED AND OTHER SOURCES

Allen, John Logan. *Passage Through the Garden: Lewis and Clark and the Image of the American Northwest.* Urbana: University of Illinois Press, 1975.

Alwin, John A. "Pelts, Provisions & Perceptions: The Hudson's Bay Company Mandan Indian Trade, 1795–1812." *Montana: The Magazine of Western History* 29 (July, 1979): 16–27.

American State Papers: Indian Affairs. 2 vols. Washington, D.C.: Gales and Seaton, 1832, 1834.

Berkebile, Don H. *Carriage Terminology: An Historical Dictionary.* Washington, D.C.: Smithsonian Institution Press and Liberty Cap Books, 1978.

Berry, James Jesse. "Arikara Middlemen: The Effects of Trade on an Upper Missouri Society." Ph.D. diss., Indiana University, 1978.

Blakeslee, Donald J. "The Plains Interband Trade System: An Ethnohistoric and Archeological Investigation." Ph.D. diss., University of Wisconsin, Milwaukee, 1975.

Bougainville, Louis Antoine de. "1757: Memoir of Bougainville." Trans. and ed. Reuben Gold Thwaites. *Collections of the State Historical Society of Wisconsin* 18 (1908): 167–95.

Bowers, Alfred W. *Hidatsa Social and Ceremonial Organization.* Bureau of American Ethnology Bulletin 194. Washington, D.C.: Government Printing Office, 1965.

———. *Mandan Social and Ceremonial Organization.* Chicago: University of Chicago Press, 1950.

Brown, A. E. "The Fur Trade Posts of the Souris-Mouth Area." *Transactions of the Manitoba Historical Society*, 3d ser., nos. 17–18 (1960–62): 78–91.

Bruner, Edward M. "Mandan." In *Perspectives in American Indian Culture Change*, ed. Edward H. Spicer, pp. 187–277. Chicago: University of Chicago Press, 1961.

Bryce, George. "The Assiniboine River and Its Forts." In *Proceedings and Transactions of the Royal Society of Canada for the Year 1892*, pp. 69–78. Ottawa: John Durie & Son, 1893.

Burpee, Lawrence J. *The Search for the Western Sea: The Story of the Explorations of North-Western America.* Toronto: Musson Book Co., 1908.

Camp, Charles L. "Edgar Allan Poe: 1840." In *Henry R. Wagner's The Plains and the Rockies . . . 1800-1865*, p. 121. 3d ed. Columbus, Ohio: Long's College Book Co., 1953.

Campbell, Marjorie Wilkins. *The North West Company.* Toronto: Macmillan Company of Canada, 1957.

Carter, John. *ABC for Book Collectors.* 5th ed. London: Rupert Hart-Davis, 1972.

Carver, Jonathan. *The Journals of Jonathan Carver and Related Documents, 1766-1770.* Ed. John Parker. Saint Paul: Minnesota Historical Society Press, 1976.

————. *Travels Through the Interior Parts of North America, in the Years 1766, 1767, and 1768.* 3d ed. London: 1781; reprinted, Minneapolis: Ross and Haines, 1956.

Catlin, George. *Letters and Notes on the Manners, Customs, and Condition of the North American Indians.* 2 vols. Minneapolis: Ross & Haines, 1965.

Chardon, Francis A. *Chardon's Journal at Fort Clark, 1834-1839.* Ed. Annie Heloise Abel. Pierre: South Dakota State Department of History, 1932.

Chittenden, Hiram Martin. *The American Fur Trade of the Far West.* 3 vols. New York: Francis P. Harper, 1902; reprinted in 2 vols., Stanford, Calif.: Academic Reprints, 1954.

Chomko, Stephen A. "The Ethnohistorical Setting of the Upper Knife-Heart Region." In *Papers in Northern Plains Prehistory and Ethnohistory.* South Dakota Archaeological Society, Special Publication, no. 10. Ed. W. Raymond Wood.

Clark, William. *The Field Notes of Captain William Clark, 1803-1805.* Ed. Ernest Staples Osgood. New Haven, Conn.: Yale University Press, 1964.

Cole, Jean Murray. *Exile in the Wilderness: The Biography of Chief Factor Archibald McDonald, 1790-1853.* Seattle: University of Washington Press, 1979.

Collot, Victor. *A Journey in North America.* 2 vols., one atlas. Paris: Arthur Bertrand, 1826; reprinted, Florence, Italy: O. Lang, 1924. Also published in microform in *Western Americana: Frontier History of the Trans-Mississippi West, 1550-1900.* New Haven, Conn.: Research Publications, 1975.

Cowie, Isaac. *The Company of Adventurers: A Narrative of Seven Years in the Service of the Hudson's Bay Company During 1867-1874 on the Great Buffalo Plains With Historical and Biographical Notes and Comments.* Toronto: William Briggs, 1913.

Davidson, Gordon Charles. *The North West Company.* University of California Publications in History, vol. 7. Berkeley: University of California Press, 1918; reissued, New York: Russell & Russell, 1967.

Denig, Edwin Thompson. *Five Indian Tribes of the Upper Missouri: Sioux, Arickaras, Assiniboines, Crees, Crows.* Ed. John C. Ewers. Norman: University of Oklahoma Press, 1961.

De Voto, Bernard. *The Course of Empire*. Boston: Houghton Mifflin, 1952.

Dickson, Frank H. "Hard on the Heel of Lewis and Clark." *Montana: The Magazine of Western History* 26 (January, 1976): 14–25.

Dollar, Clyde D. "The Journal of Charles LeRaye: Authentic or Not?" *South Dakota Historical Collections* 41 (1983): 67–191.

Draper, Lyman C. "Traditions and Recollections of Prairie du Chien." *Report and Collections of the State Historical Society of Wisconsin, for the Years 1880, 1881, and 1882*, vol. 9 (1882): 282–302.

Ewers, John C. *The Horse in Blackfoot Indian Culture*. Bureau of American Ethnology Bulletin 159. Washington, D.C.: Government Printing Office, 1955.

———. "The Indian Trade of the Upper Missouri Before Lewis and Clark: An Interpretation." *Missouri Historical Society Bulletin* 10 (July, 1954): 429–46. Reissued in slightly revised form as "The Indian Trade of the Upper Missouri before Lewis and Clark," in John C. Ewers, *Indian Life on the Upper Missouri*, pp. 14–33. Norman: University of Oklahoma Press, 1968.

Foley, William E., and Charles David Rice. "The Return of the Mandan Chief." *Montana: The Magazine of Western History* 29 (July, 1979): 2–15.

Gale, John. *The Missouri Expedition, 1818-1820: The Journal of Surgeon John Gale, with Related Documents*. Ed. Roger L. Nichols. Norman: University of Oklahoma Press, 1969.

Gass, Patrick. *A Journal of the Voyages and Travels . . . to the Pacific Ocean*. Pittsburgh: David M'Keehan, 1807; reprinted, Minneapolis: Ross and Haines, 1958.

Gates, Charles M., ed. *Five Fur Traders of the Northwest*. Saint Paul: Minnesota Historical Society, 1933; reissued, 1965.

Gilmore, Melvin R. *Uses of Plants by the Indians of the Missouri River Region*. Lincoln: University of Nebraska Press, 1977.

Gorrell, James. "Lieut. James Gorrell's Journal." Ed. Lyman C. Draper. *First Annual Report and Collections of the State Historical Society of Wisconsin for the Year 1854*, 1 (1855): 24–28. Reprinted and reissued, State Historical Society of Wisconsin, 1903, under the editorship of Reuben Gold Thwaites.

Grignon, Augustin. "Seventy-two Years' Recollections of Wisconsin." Ed. Lyman C. Draper. *Third Annual Report and Collections of the State Historical Society of Wisconsin for the Year 1856*, 3 (1857): 197–295. Reprinted and reissued, State Historical Society of Wisconsin, 1904, under the editorship of Reuben Gold Thwaites.

Hafen, LeRoy R. "Touissaint Charbonneau." In *The Mountain Men and the Fur Trade of the Far West*, ed. LeRoy R. Hafen, vol. 9, pp. 53–62. Glendale, Calif.: Arthur H. Clark Co., 1972.

Halkett, John, ed. *Narratives of John Pritchard, Pierre Chrysologue Pambrum, and Frederick Damien Heurter, Respecting the Aggressions of the North-West*

Company against the Earl of Selkirk's Settlement upon Red River. London: John Murray, 1819.

Hanson, Charles E., Jr. *The Northwest Gun.* Nebraska State Historical Society, Publications in Anthropology, no. 2. Lincoln, Nebr.: Nebraska State Historical Society, 1955.

Harmon, Daniel Williams. *Sixteen Years in the Indian Country: The Journal of Daniel Williams Harmon.* Ed. W. Kaye Lamb. Toronto: Macmillan Company of Canada, 1957.

Hearne, Samuel. *A Journey from Prince of Wale's Fort in Hudson's Bay to the Northern Ocean in the Years 1769, 1770, 1771, and 1772.* Publications of the Champlain Society, vol. 6. Ed. J. B. Tyrrell. Toronto: Champlain Society, 1911.

Heawood, Edward. *Watermarks Mainly of the 17th and 18th Centuries.* Monuments Chartae Papyraceae Historia Illustrantia 1. Hilversum, Holland: Paper Publication Society, n.d.

Henry, Alexander [the Younger]. *New Light on the Early History of the Greater Northwest: The Manuscript Journals of Alexander Henry and of David Thompson, 1799-1814.* Ed. Elliott Coues. 3 vols. New York: Francis P. Harper, 1897; reprinted in 2 vols., Minneapolis: Ross and Haines, 1965.

———. "A New Transcription of Alexander Henry's Account of a Visit to the Mandan and Hidatsa Indians in 1806" (manuscript). Ed. Thomas D. Thiessen. National Park Service, Midwest Archeological Center, Lincoln, Nebr., 1980.

Hodge, Frederick Webb. *Handbook of North American Indians North of Mexico.* Bureau of American Ethnology Bulletin 30. Washington, D.C.: Government Printing Office, 1907–10.

Hyde, George E. *Red Cloud's Folk: A History of the Ogalala Sioux Indians.* Rev. ed. Norman: University of Oklahoma Press, 1957.

Innis, Harold A. *The Fur Trade in Canada: An Introduction to Canadian Economic History.* Rev. ed. New Haven, Conn.: Yale University Press, 1962.

Jackson, Donald, comp. *Letters of the Lewis and Clark Expedition, with Related Documents, 1783-1854.* Urbana: University of Illinois Press, 1962.

Jackson, John C. "Brandon House and the Mandan Connection." *North Dakota History* 49 (Winter, 1982): 11–19.

James, Edwin. *Account of an Expedition from Pittsburgh to the Rocky Mountains.* 2 vols. with atlas. Philadelphia: H. C. Carey and I. Lea, 1823; reprinted, New York: Readex Microprint Corporation, 1966.

James, Thomas. *Three Years Among the Indians and Mexicans.* Ed. Milo M. Quaife. New York: Citadel Press, 1966.

Kehoe, Alice B. "The Function of Ceremonial Sexual Intercourse among the Northern Plains Indians." *Plains Anthropologist* 15 (May, 1970): 99–103.

Kehoe, Thomas F., and Alice B. Kehoe. "The Identification of the Fall or Rapid Indians." *Plains Anthropologist* 19 (August, 1974): 231–32.

Kelsey, Henry. *The Kelsey Papers.* Ed. Arthur G. Doughty and Chester Martin. Ottawa: Public Archives of Canada, 1929.

Kerr, Robert F. "President's Biennial Address." *South Dakota Historical Collections,* vol. 5, pp. 69–84. Pierre, S. Dak.: State Publishing Company, 1910.

Ketterer, David. *The Rationale of Deception in Poe.* Baton Rouge: Louisiana State University Press, 1979.

Lamalice, André L. J. "François-Antoine Larocque." In *Dictionary of Canadian Biography,* vol. 9 (1861–70), pp. 455–56. Trans. J. S. Wood. Toronto: University of Toronto Press, 1976.

Larocque, François-Antoine. "The Journal of François Antoine Larocque from the Assiniboine River to the Yellowstone—1805." Trans. and ed. Ruth Hazlitt. *The Frontier and Midland: A Magazine of the Northwest* 14 (1934): 241–47, 332–39; and 15 (1934): 67–75, 88. Reprinted in Paul C. Phillips, ed., *Sources of Northwest History,* no. 20, pp. 3–26. Missoula: State University of Montana; and in John W. Hakola, ed., *Frontier Omnibus,* pp. 1–28. Missoula: Montana State University Press and Historical Society of Montana.

———. *Journal of Larocque from the Assiniboine to the Yellowstone, 1805.* Ed. Lawrence J. Burpee. Publications of the Canadian Archives, no. 3, pp. 1–82. Ottawa: Government Printing Bureau, 1910.

———. *Journal de Larocque de la Rivière Assiniboine Jusqu'a la Rivière 'Aux Roches Jaunes,' 1805.* Ed. Lawrence J. Burpee. Publications des Archives Canadiennes, no. 3, pp. 1–82. Ottawa: Imprimerie de L'État, 1911.

Larpenteur, Charles. *Forty Years a Fur Trader on the Upper Missouri: The Personal Narrative of Charles Larpenteur, 1832-1872.* Ed. Elliott Coues. 2 vols. New York: Francis P. Harper, 1898; reprinted in 1 vol., Minneapolis: Ross and Haines, 1962.

Lavender, David. *The Fist in the Wilderness.* Albuquerque: University of New Mexico Press, 1979.

La Vérendrye, Pierre Gaultier de Varennes, Sieur de. *Journals and Letters of Pierre Gaultier de Varennes de la Vérendrye and His Sons.* Publications of the Champlain Society, vol. 16. Ed. Lawrence J. Burpee. Toronto: Champlain Society, 1927.

Lehmer, Donald J. "Epidemics Among the Indians of the Upper Missouri." In *Selected Writings of Donald J. Lehmer,* pp. 105–111. Ed. W. Raymond Wood. Lincoln, Nebr.: J & L Reprint Co., 1977.

———. *Introduction to Middle Missouri Archeology.* National Park Service Anthropological Papers, no. 1. Washington, D.C.: Government Printing Office, 1971.

———. "The Other Side of the Fur Trade." In *Selected Writings of Donald J. Lehmer,* pp. 91–104. Ed. W. Raymond Wood. Lincoln, Nebr.: J & L Reprint Co., 1977.

———, W. Raymond Wood, and C. L. Dill. "The Knife River Phase" (manuscript). National Park Service, Interagency Archeological Services, Denver, 1978.

[LeRaye, Charles.] "The Journal of Charles LeRaye." In *South Dakota Historical Collections*, vol. 4, pp. 150–80. Sioux Falls, S. Dak.: Mark D. Scott, 1908.

Lewis, Meriwether, and William Clark. *Original Journals of the Lewis and Clark Expedition, 1804-06.* Ed. Reuben Gold Thwaites. 8 vols. New York: Dodd, Mead and Co., 1904–1905; reprinted, New York: Arno Press, 1969.

Lowie, Robert H. *The Crow Indians.* New York: Holt, Rinehart and Winston, 1935.

————. *Indians of the Plains.* New York: McGraw-Hill Book Co., 1954.

Luttig, John C. *Journal of a Fur-trading Expedition on the Upper Missouri, 1812-1813.* Ed. Stella M. Drumm. Saint Louis: Missouri Historical Society, 1920; reprinted, New York: Argosy-Antiquarian Ltd., 1964.

McDermott, John Francis. *A Glossary of Mississippi Valley French, 1673-1850.* Washington University Studies, New Series, Language and Literature, no. 12. Saint Louis: Washington University, 1941.

McKenzie, Charles. "Charles McKenzie's Narratives of the 'Mississouri Indians': A New Transcription" (manuscript). Ed. Thomas D. Thiessen. National Park Service, Midwest Archeological Center, Lincoln, Nebr., 1980.

McMorran, G. A. "Souris River Posts in the Hartney District." *Papers Read before the Historical and Scientific Society of Manitoba*, 3d ser., no. 5 (1950): 47–62.

McNeish, R. S. "The Stott Mound and Village Site near Brandon, Manitoba." *Annual Report of the National Museum of Canada for 1952-3, Bulletin* 132 (1954): 20–65.

Masson, L. R., ed. *Les Bourgeois de la Compagnie du Nord-Ouest: Recits de voyages, lettres et rapports inedits relatifs au Nord-Ouest Canadien.* 2 vols. Quebec: de L'Imprimière Générale A. Côte et Cie., 1889–1890; reprinted in 2 vols., New York: Antiquarian Press, 1960.

Mattison, Ray H. "Report of Historic Sites in the Garrison Reservoir Area, Missouri River." *North Dakota History* 22 (January–April, 1955): 4–73.

Moodie, D. W., and Kaye, Barry. "The Northern Limit of Indian Agriculture in North America." *Geographical Review* 59 (October, 1969): 513–29.

Morgan, Dale L., ed. *The West of William H. Ashley.* Denver: Old West Publishing Co., 1964.

Morton, Arthur S. *A History of the Canadian West to 1870-1871*, 2nd ed. Ed. Lewis G. Thomas. Toronto: University of Toronto Press, 1973.

Moulton, Gary E., ed. *The Journals of the Lewis and Clark Expedition.* Atlas volume. Lincoln: University of Nebraska Press, 1983.

Murray, Robert A. "First Tracks in the Big Horns." *Montana: The Magazine of Western History* 26 (January, 1976): 2–13.

Nasatir, Abraham P. "Anglo-Spanish Rivalry on the Upper Missouri." *Mississippi Valley Historical Review* 16 (June, 1929–March, 1930): 359–82, 507–28.

————. *Borderland in Retreat: From Spanish Louisiana to the Far Southwest.* Albuquerque: University of New Mexico Press, 1976.

————. "Jacques D'Église on the Upper Missouri, 1791–1795." *Mississippi Valley Historical Review* 14 (June, 1927–March, 1928): 47–56.

————. "John Evans, Explorer and Surveyor." *Mississippi Valley Historical Review* 25 (January, 1931): 219–39; (April, 1931): 432–60; and (July, 1931): 585–608.

————., ed. *Before Lewis and Clark: Documents Illustrating the History of the Missouri, 1785–1804.* 2 vols. Saint Louis: Saint Louis Historical Documents Foundation, 1952.

————., trans. and ed. "Documents: Spanish Exploration of the Upper Missouri." *Mississippi Valley Historical Review* 14 (June, 1927–March, 1928): 57–71.

Nute, Grace Lee, ed. *Documents Relating to Northwest Missions, 1815–1827.* Saint Paul: Minnesota Historical Society, 1942.

Oglesby, Richard Edward. *Manuel Lisa and the Opening of the Missouri Fur Trade.* Norman: University of Oklahoma Press, 1963.

Ottoson, Dennis R. "Touissaint Charbonneau, a Most Durable Man." *South Dakota History* 6 (Spring, 1976): 152–85.

Parker, Donald D. "Early Explorations and Fur Trading in South Dakota." *South Dakota Historical Collections and Report*, vol. 25, pp. 1–211. Pierre: South Dakota Historical Society, 1950.

Phillips, Paul C. *The Fur Trade.* 2 vols. Norman: University of Oklahoma Press, 1961.

Poe, Edgar Allan. "The Journal of Julius Rodman." *Burton's Gentleman's Magazine* 6 (1840): 44–47, 80–85, 109–13, 179–83, 206–10, 255–59 (published as six separate chapters).

Prud'homme, L. A. *Les Successeurs de la Vérendrye—Sous la Domination Française—1743–1755.* Proceedings and Transactions of the Royal Society of Canada, 2nd ser., vol. 12, 1906.

Quaife, Milo M., ed. "Extracts from Capt. McKay's Journal—and Others." *State Historical Society of Wisconsin, Proceedings for 1915*, pp. 180–210. Madison: Cantwell Printing, 1915.

Ray, Arthur J. . "History and Archaeology of the Northern Fur Trade." *American Antiquity* 43 (January, 1978): 26–34.

————. *Indians in the Fur Trade: Their Role as Hunters, Trappers and Middlemen in the Lands Southwest of Hudson Bay, 1660–1870.* Toronto: University of Toronto Press, 1974.

————., and Freeman, Donald B. *"Give Us Good Measure": An Economic Analysis of Relations Between the Indians and the Hudson's Bay Company Before 1763.* Toronto: University of Toronto Press, 1978.

Reid, Russell, and Gannon, Clell G. "Natural History Notes on the Journals of Alexander Henry." *North Dakota Historical Quarterly* 2 (April, 1928): 168–200.

Rich, E. E. *The Fur Trade and the Northwest to 1857.* Toronto: McClelland and Stewart, 1967.

――――. *Hudson's Bay Company, 1670-1870.* 3 vols. Toronto: McClelland and Stewart, 1960.

Robinson, Doane. "The Putrid Fever of 1812." *South Dakota Historical Collections* 12: 67-70. Pierre, S.Dak.: Hipple Printing Co., 1924.

Ross, Alexander. *The Red River Settlement: Its Rise, Progress, and Present State.* London: Smith, Elder and Co., 1856; reprinted, Minneapolis: Ross and Haines, 1957.

Schoolcraft, Henry R., ed. *Information Respecting the History, Condition and Prospects of the Indian Tribes of the United States.* 6 vols. Philadelphia: Lippincott, Grambo & Co., 1851-57.

Scott, W. B., and E. J. Crossman. *Freshwater Fishes of Canada.* Bulletin 184. Ottawa: Fisheries Resource Board of Canada, 1973.

Simmons, Marc. "New Mexico's Smallpox Epidemic of 1780-1781." *New Mexico Historical Review* 41 (October, 1966): 319-26.

Smith, G. Hubert. *The Explorations of the La Vérendryes in the Northern Plains, 1738-43.* Ed. W. Raymond Wood. Lincoln: University of Nebraska Press, 1980.

――――. *Like-a-Fishhook Village and Fort Berthold, Garrison Reservoir, North Dakota.* National Park Service Anthropological Papers, no. 2. Washington, D.C.: Government Printing Office, 1972.

Stevens, Orin Alva. *Handbook of North Dakota Plants.* Fargo: North Dakota Institute for Regional Studies, 1963.

Stewart, David A. *Early Assiniboine Trading Posts of the Souris-Mouth Group, 1785-1832.* Transactions of the Historical and Scientific Society of Manitoba, no. 5 (n.s., Winnipeg: Historical and Scientific Society of Manitoba, 1930.

Stewart, Frank H. "Mandan and Hidatsa Villages in the Eighteenth and Nineteenth Centuries." *Plains Anthropologist* 19 (November, 1974): 287-302.

――――. "Village Movements of the Northern Horticulturalists (Mandan and Hidatsa), 1675 to 1860" (manuscript). Deposited in the library of the National Park Service, Midwest Archeological Center, Lincoln, Nebr., 1975.

Sunder, John E. *The Fur Trade on the Upper Missouri, 1840-1865.* Norman: University of Oklahoma Press, 1965.

――――. *Joshua Pilcher: Fur Trader and Indian Agent.* Norman: University of Oklahoma Press, 1968.

Tabeau, Pierre-Antoine. *Tabeau's Narrative of Loisel's Expedition to the Upper Missouri.* Ed. Annie Heloise Abel. Norman: University of Oklahoma Press, 1939.

Taché, Monseigneur [Alexander Antonin]. *Sketch of the North-West of America.* Trans. D. R. Cameron. Montreal: J. Lovell, 1870.

Thiessen, Thomas D., comp. "Excerpts from the Brandon House Post Journals Relating to Trade with the Mandan and Hidatsa Indians, 1793-1830" (manuscript in possession of compiler, 1981).

Thompson, David. "David Thompson at the Mandan-Hidatsa Villages,

1797–1798: The Original Journals." Ed. W. Raymond Wood. *Ethnohistory* 24 (Fall, 1977): 329–42.

———. *David Thompson's Narrative, 1784-1812.* Publications of the Champlain Society, vol. 40. Ed. Richard Glover. Toronto: Champlain Society, 1962.

———. *David Thompson's Narrative of His Explorations in Western America, 1784-1812.* Publications of the Champlain Society, vol. 12. Ed. J. B. Tyrrell. Toronto: Champlain Society, 1916; reprinted, New York: Greenwood Press, 1968.

———. *Travels in Western North America, 1784-1812.* Ed. Victor G. Hopwood. Toronto: Macmillan Company of Canada, 1971.

Thwaites, Reuben Gold, ed. *Early Western Travels, 1748-1846.* 32 vols. Cleveland: Arthur P. Clark Co., 1904–1906; reprinted, New York: AMS Press, 1966.

Toom, Dennis L. "The Middle Missouri Villages and the Early Fur Trade: Implications for Archeological Interpretation." M.A. thesis, University of Nebraska, Lincoln, 1979.

Truax, Allen L. "Manuel Lisa and His North Dakota Trading Post." *North Dakota Historical Quarterly* 2 (July, 1928): 239–46.

Truteau, Jean Baptiste. "Trudeau's Journal." Ed. anonymously. *South Dakota Historical Collections*, vol. 7, pp. 403–74. Pierre: State Publishing Co., 1914.

Voorhis, Ernest. *Historic Forts and Trading Posts of the French Régime and of the English Fur Trading Companies.* Ottawa: Natural Resources Intelligence Service, Department of the Interior, 1930.

Wagner, Henry R. *Peter Pond, Fur Trader and Explorer.* Yale University Library Western Historical Series no. 2, 1955.

Wallace, W. Stewart, comp. *The Macmillan Dictionary of Canadian Biography.* 3d ed. Toronto: Macmillan Company of Canada, 1963.

———., ed. *Documents Relating to the North West Company.* Publications of the Champlain Society, vol. 22. Toronto: Champlain Society, 1934.

Weist, Katherine M. "Plains Indian Women: An Assessment." In *Anthropology on the Great Plains*, pp. 255–71. Ed. W. Raymond Wood and Margot Liberty. Lincoln: University of Nebraska Press, 1980.

Wheat, Carl I. *Mapping the Transmississippi West, 1540-1861.* 5 vols. San Francisco: Institute of Historical Cartography, 1957–1963.

Will, George F., and George E. Hyde. *Corn Among the Indians of the Upper Missouri.* Saint Louis: W. H. Miner Co., 1917.

Williams, David. "John Evans' Strange Journey." *American Historical Review* 54 (January, 1949): 277–95; and 54 (April, 1949): 508–29.

Williams, Glyndwr. *Hudson's Bay Miscellany, 1670-1870.* Hudson's Bay Record Society Publications, vol. 30. Winnipeg: Hudson's Bay Record Society, 1975.

Williams, Gwyn A. *Madoc: The Making of a Myth.* London: Eyre Methuen, 1979.

———. *The Search For Beaulah Land.* London: Croom Helm, 1980.

Wilson, Gilbert L. *Agriculture of the Hidatsa Indians: An Indian Interpretation.* University of Minnesota Studies in Social Science, vol. 9. Minneapolis: University of Minnesota, 1917.

———. *The Horse and the Dog in Hidatsa Culture.* American Museum of Natural History Anthropological Papers, vol. 15, part 2. New York: American Museum Press, 1924.

Wishart, David J. *The Fur Trade of the American West, 1807-1840.* Lincoln: University of Nebraska Press, 1979.

Wood, W. Raymond. "The John Evans 1796-97 Map of the Missouri River." *Great Plains Quarterly* 1 (Winter, 1981): 39-53.

———. "Plains Trade in Prehistoric and Protohistoric Intertribal Relations." In *Anthropology on the Great Plains*, pp. 98-109. Ed. W. Raymond Wood and Margot Liberty. Lincoln: University of Nebraska Press, 1980.

———, ed. "Fur Trade Documents Bearing on the Mandan-Hidatsa Trade with Northwest Company Posts in Central Canada, 1793-1805: Four New Transcriptions" (Manuscript). National Park Service, Midwest Archeological Center, Lincoln, Nebr., 1979.

———, ed. "Journal of John Macdonell, 1793-1795." In *Fort Espérance in 1793-1795: A North West Company Provisioning Post*, by Daniel J. Provo, pp. 81-139. Lincoln: J & L Reprint Company, 1984.

———, and Downer, Alan S. "Notes on the Crow-Hidatsa Schism." *Plains Anthropologist*, Memoir 13 (1977): 83-100.

———, and Moulton, Gary E. "Prince Maximilian and New Maps of the Missouri and Yellowstone Rivers by William Clark." *Western Historical Quarterly* 12 (October, 1981): 372-86.

Index

Note: Individuals and voyages in Table 1, pp. 298–321, are not indexed.

Early Fur Trade on the Northern Plains,

designed by Bill Cason, was set in various sizes of Baskerville by the University of Oklahoma Press and printed offset on 55-pound Glatfelter B-31 by Cushing-Malloy, Inc., with case binding by John H. Dekker & Sons.

49,556

DATE			
FEB 18 1992			
FEB 8 1993			
DEC 15 1998			
DEC 04 1998			
DEC 13 1999			
DEC 8 1999			

© THE BAKER & TAYLOR CO.